Cities Perceived

**Urban Society in European
and American Thought, 1820-1940**

For Edward and Laura

Andrew Lees

Cities Perceived

**Urban Society in European
and American thought, 1820-1940**

Manchester University Press

Published by Manchester University Press
Oxford Road, Manchester M13 9PL

British Library cataloguing in publication data
Lees, Andrew
 Cities perceived: urban society in European
 and American thought, 1820-1940.
 1. Cities and towns—History
 I. Title
 307'7'64'09034   HT119

 ISBN 0-7190-1725-4 *cased*

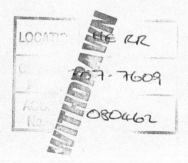

Phototypeset in Great Britain by Saxon, Derby
Printed and bound in Great Britain by
Biddles Ltd, Guildford and King's Lynn

Contents

List of Illustrations

Preface

The rise of the big city in Europe and America during the nineteenth and twentieth centuries had an enormous impact not only on the structure of society but also on patterns of thought and feeling. The consequences of urbanization in the cultural and intellectual realm have, however, not yet received the attention they deserve. I have set about trying to explore these changes by pursuing a number of closely related lines of inquiry. In general, I have sought to understand how articulate men and women perceived and evaluated what was happening to the countries in which they lived as a result of urban growth. More specifically, I have attempted to answer questions such as the following. How did perceptions of urban life vary from decade to decade, from country to country, and from one occupational and social group to another? In what ways did conflicts of opinion about cities reflect larger conflicts in the areas of social and political ideology? And in what ways did thought about urban problems both stem from and stimulate efforts to solve them? These are the questions that lie behind this book.

Unlike most other historians who have considered various aspects of my subject, I have sought to encompass a very large number of writers and as much attitudinal diversity as I could find. My primary sources consist of well over a thousand books and essays, written by close to a thousand individuals during a period of slightly more than a century in four countries. (The criteria I used to accumulate these sources are explained in a bibliographical essay at the end of the book.) They illuminate main currents of opinion among large numbers of social scientists, clergymen, medical doctors, architects, planners, administrators, novelists, publicists, and other writers. Some of these people were and are well known, but most have always been obscure and are likely to remain so. Most of their ideas are not especially interesting for their originality or any intrinsic merit, but they remain essential to an understanding of that elusive phenomenon currently known as *mentalité*. As we shall see, they also evince a great deal in the way of ambivalence and enthusiasm as well as the anti-urban hostility that has bulked so large in most previous scholarship.

I have begun in 1820 because around then men began to reflect more and more widely on the issues raised by urban growth. The reasons for concluding in 1940 are less clear-cut but still persuasive. By that date at the latest the biggest cities had reached their zenith, and the major problems associated with urbanization as a social process had been analyzed and debated to the point where there was little more to be said. At the same time, the start of a war that was to devastate many European cities marked an obvious break in their history. Since then, on both sides of the Atlantic, the study of urban sociology has accelerated, but to continue the story in order to include subsequent developments in this area would necessitate another book. Moreover, the new concerns stemming since 1945 from the greatly increased use of the automobile and the consequent flight to the suburbs point in the same direction.

I have focused on Britain, France, Germany, and the United States because it was there that men and women considered the urban phenomenon most broadly and intensively. They are also countries with whose languages and cultural history I have some familiarity. There were counterparts to the thinkers I treat in Belgium, in Italy, in Russia, and in other European (and non-European) countries, but I leave them to the labors of others. I should add that although I am an American my training is in European history, and I have not attempted to research developments in my own country as thoroughly as developments in the other three. I shall be satisfied if experts in American history regard what I have to say about their territory as a modest contribution that earns its place in this book as part of a larger synthesis.

Two further disclaimers are in order. Although I refer to novels and poetry in several chapters, I make no claim to having done original scholarship in the history of imaginative literature or even to having mentioned all of the major literary documents that bear on city life. For books and articles on these works, readers may consult my bibliography. Nor do I pretend to have written a book that treats the full range of ideas about urban public policy and city planning. I am concerned here with values and beliefs that constituted a large part of the emotional and conceptual climate in which a whole host of pleas for preventive or remedial measures by private groups and by governments germinated — some to reach fruition, many to go nowhere. But the shaping of specific plans and the pursuit of particular policies lie largely outside the boundaries I have drawn. Ideas about such matters make their appearance in my pages from time to time, but they have already figured prominently in works by others. They therefore remain subordinate in this book to the basic perceptions and attitudes that helped to shape men's sense of what was necessary and possible.

Although my subject is consciousness rather than society, many of the men and women with whom I deal conveyed facts as well as judgements, data as well as prejudice, knowledge as well as opinion. The particular sorts of phenomena different groups of writers chose to record varied greatly, for reasons which were only partially related to variations and changes in the nature of urban society itself. Nonetheless, the decidedly empirical thrust of much of the writing with which I am concerned ought to enable the reader to gain a fuller understanding not only of several chapters in the history of thought but also of the complex social entities to whose spectacular growth the writers were responding.

It is a real pleasure to acknowledge some of the many debts I have incurred during the dozen or so years that have elapsed since I began the research on which this book is based. At the outset, I received generous financial support from Amherst College in the form of a Trustee Faculty Fellowship. Since then, I have received a grant from the German Academic Exchange Service, one from the National Endowment for the Humanities, and several from the Rutgers University Research Council, one of which has helped to defray the costs of publication. Just before his untimely death, H. J. Dyos made it possible for me to spend the academic year 1978-79 at the University of Leicester as a fellow in the Department of Economic and Social History. The staff members of several libraries, especially the British Library, the Bayerische Staatsbibliothek, and the Deutsche Staatsbibliothek in West Berlin, have patiently kept me supplied with a steady stream of volumes from their stacks. Closer to home, Norma DiStefano has seen to it that numerous works which I needed found their way to the Interlibrary Loan Department at Rutgers in Camden. Two other staff members at Rutgers in Camden to whom I am much obliged are Ann Orbanus and David Gwalthney, who have enabled me to take advantage of some of the opportunities offered by word processors.

Among those who have supported and helped to shape my work in other ways, I wish to thank the following friends and colleagues, all of whom have read and commented on one or more of my chapters: Rodney Carlisle, Philip Collins, David Glassberg, Kenneth Jackson, Coral Lansbury, James Muldoon, English Showalter, and Anthony Sutcliffe. Robert Fishman, a fellow historian of urban culture, has been especially generous with his time and helpful with his advice, and I owe him a great deal. I also wish to acknowledge the help of our friends, Robert Kaplan and Edna Dick, in the task of proofreading. My greatest debt is to my wife, Lynn, who reads everything I write about urban ideas with the skeptical eye of a historian of urban society. The book is dedicated to our children, in the hope that some day it will help them to understand why their parents chose to raise them in Philadelphia.

1

Introduction

The urbanization of society

Cities started to grow in the nineteenth century on both sides of the Atlantic at an extraordinary pace, and well before the middle of the twentieth century the leading nations of Western and Central Europe and the United States were preponderantly urban. Cities had already been expanding in many areas in the late eighteenth century, but their increase was roughly proportional to the overall growth of the countries in which they were located. It is only after about 1800 that we can detect the explosive increases that were to produce modern urban society.

The statistics of urban expansion (some of which appear in Tables I-III) tell a dramatic story of social change. Old towns grew at rapid rates, and new ones grew even faster. In little more than a century (1800-1910), greater London rose from around 1.1 million to 7.3 million and Manchester from 75,000 to 714,000; Paris from 547,000 to 2.9 million and Marseilles from 111,000 to 551,000; Berlin from 172,000 to over 2 million and Essen from 4,000 to 295,000. New York leapt from 60,000 to 4.8 million, and Chicagoans created a metropolis almost half that size on land that had been almost totally uninhabited until the 1830s. As a result of such changes, statisticians in many countries began to distinguish between the ordinary or medium-sized city and the big city (otherwise known as a large town, a *grande ville*, or a *Grossstadt*), with its population in excess of 100,000. The number of such places in Europe and America increased more than sevenfold. Even more striking was the emergence of cities whose populations surpassed the million mark. In 1800, only London had crossed this divide, and it could not have done so without help from its suburbs. By 1940, fourteen more cities between the Urals and Portugal and another five in America had joined the club.[1] The largest of these cities were now designated metropolises, *métropoles*, or *Weltstädte*. The German term, which means literally 'world cities', best captures the essence of these vast agglomerations. They were highly cosmopolitan, and their influence extended far beyond the confines of a single national society.

What made the process of urban growth profoundly revolutionary was not so much the sum total of changes in the size of individual cities but rather an enormous shift in the way people were distributed in space. Not only did cities and city dwellers become much more numerous; because of the fact that the urban population grew more rapidly than the overall population, society as a whole was increasingly citified. Between 1800 and 1910, the percentage of Europeans who could be considered townsmen tripled, and in America it multiplied sevenfold. Between 1800 and 1950, the share of Europeans residing in big cities multiplied more than sevenfold, and in America it grew between 1800 and 1940 from zero to over one-fifth. These changes of proportion constituted the statistical essence of urbanization as opposed to mere urban growth.

The rise of the city did not stem from an internally generated population surplus. High death rates during the early part of our period and low birth rates during the later part — themes we shall take up in some detail below — meant that many cities would have been unable even to maintain constant populations on their own and that none of the major ones would have increased as fast as the population in general. Urban centers grew more rapidly than the countries in which they were located only because of the demographic boost they received from outsiders who migrated into them from farms, villages, and small towns. Almost half of the total increase between 1821 and 1851 in the size of large towns in England other than London resulted from immigration, and in France virtually all urban growth after 1861 bore witness to the influx of outsiders. In Germany between 1871 and 1910, Barmen would have risen from 75,074 to 115,924 in the absence of migration, whereas it actually rose to 169,214. Gelsenkirchen would have risen from 16,023 to 24,742, whereas it rose in fact to 169,513. In the United States, migration was especially significant. In 1910, at least one-third of the total urban population consisted of American natives of rural origin, and close to another quarter consisted of foreign-born.[2] Wherever cities expanded, they did so largely because men and women moved there from somewhere else, usually a place in which they and their forebears had led a very different sort of life from the one that awaited them in their new surroundings.

Peasants and villagers migrated to towns primarily because it was there that they could find the most remunerative employment. The major stimulus to rural-urban migration was the prospect of economic advancement. The fact that cities could offer this prospect was intimately linked to commercial development and especially to the process of industrialization. In the age of the steam engine and the railroad, industry gravitated increasingly toward the cities, in turn attracting migrants in search of work. But entrepreneurs also helped to create cities almost from scratch, especially in areas that lay close to coalfields and major iron deposits. There, what had been tiny mining villages experienced phenomenal growth as heavy industry began to boom. In the absence of these economic and technological changes, neither Europe nor America would have urbanized to anything like the extent they did in this period. It is particularly noteworthy that the areas of most intense urban concentration in Britain and Germany were Lancashire and the Ruhr Valley, major centers of manufacturing.

Industry also played an important part in the growth of London, Paris, Berlin, and New York, but the great metropolises seemingly acquired a momentum of their own that cannot be fully explained with reference to economic variables. Some of them benefited from their status as national capitals. (The growth of Berlin after 1871 is an obvious case in point.) All of them attracted newcomers at least in part because of the positions they occupied at the center of their nations' cultural, intellectual, and social life. They were the places where people who did not know quite what to do with their lives could discover the widest possible assortment of choices and opportunities.

The peculiar mix of social structure, economic development, and geography produced different sequences and configurations of urban growth in each country. Britain, the first country to industrialize, was also the first to urbanize, and by the early twentieth century it had come pretty close to the end of the road. British urbanites were concentrated disproportionately around London, in coastal ports, in the industrial areas of the north and the Midlands, and in the belt from Glasgow to Edinburgh. French cities grew slowly in the early nineteenth century, more rapidly for several decades thereafter, and then again at a rather leisurely pace. Paris stood out during the whole period, with city dwellers elsewhere clustering in Mediterranean and Atlantic port cities, in the Rhone Valley, and in a few northern industrial towns. The numerous towns that had dotted the Central European landscape since the Middle Ages were largely stagnant until around 1850, but between then and 1910, as German industry thrived, the German people flocked to their cities in droves, and they continued to do so thereafter, though at a somewhat reduced rate. Old commercial towns and regional capitals grew markedly, but the most spectacular increases occurred in the Ruhr Valley and in the industrial areas in Saxony and Silesia. American cities displayed even more dynamism. After growing sluggishly at best between 1800 and 1820, they soon took off, and they never stopped. By the eve of the Second World War, the United States surpassed the other three countries combined in industrial output, and it had three-quarters as many big cities. In 1860, five of the nine big cities stretched along the Atlantic seaboard, from Boston to Washington, D.C. In subsequent decades, the industrial belt from Pittsburgh to Chicago was a major area of development, but big cities sprang up in every section of the nation.[3]

I have touched only briefly on the causes of urban growth and shall say little more about them. My main concern is with consequences. The modern city was both an index of and a motor behind profound social and cultural

Table 1　The urbanization of Europe and America

Europe	Britain	France	Germany	United States
1750: 13.8	1750: –	1750: –	1750: –	1750: –
1800: 14.5	1801: –	1801: 20.5	1816: 26.5	1800: 6.1
1850: 22.3	1851: 50.4	1851: 25.5	1849: 28.3	1850: 15.3
1880: 32.4	1881: 67.1	1891: 37.4	1880: 41.4	1880: 28.2
1910: 43.8	1911: 79.6	1911: 44.2	1910: 60.0	1910: 45.7
1920: 47.6	1931: 80.0	1931: 51.2	1939: 69.9	1940: 56.5

Figures indicate the population of towns at specified dates as a percentage of total population. For Europe as a whole (Russia excluded) towns are defined as municipalities or other administrative units numbering 5,000 or more inhabitants; for Britain, France, and Germany, 2,000 or more; for the United States, 2,500 or more. German figures for the period before 1880 are for Prussia. The source for Europe as a whole is Paul Bairoch, 'Population urbaine et taille des villes en Europe de 1600 à 1970: présentation de séries statistiques', in University of Lyon, *Démographie urbaine, xve-xxe siècle* (Lyon, 1980), 7. Other sources for figures on individual countries in Tables I and II: Adna Ferrin Weber, *The Growth of Cities in the Nineteenth Century* (New York, 1899), 47, 58, 71, 82, 90; Great Britain, Central Statistical Office, *Annual Abstract of Statistics*, 84 (1948), 13; Michel Huber *et al.*, *La population de la France* (Paris, 1937), 30; Wolfgang Köllmann, 'The Process of Urbanization in Germany at the Height of the Industrialization Period', *Journal of Contemporary History*, Vol. 4, No. 3 (1969), 59-76; Dietmar Petzina *et al.*, *Sozialgeschichtliches Arbeitsbuch, Band III: Materialien zur Statistik des Deutschen Reiches 1914-1945* (Munich, 1978), 37; U.S. Department of Commerce, *Historical Statistics of the United States*, I (Washington, D.C., 1975), 11-12.

Table II　The growth of the big cities

Europe	Britain	France	Germany	United States
1800: 2.9 (21)	1801: 8.2 (1)	1801: 2.8 (3)	1816: 1.9 (2)	1800: 0.0 (0)
1850: 4.8 (43)	1851: 21.8 (11)	1851: 4.6 (5)	1849: 3.1 (4)	1850: 6.3 (6)
	1881: 29.5 (24)	1891: 12.0 (12)	1880: 7.2 (14)	1880: 12.4 (20)
1900: 12.3 (143)				
	1911: 40.7 (39)	1911: 14.6 (15)	1910: 21.3 (48)	1910: 22.1 (50)
1950: 21.8 (374)	1931: 44.2 (44)	1936: 16.0 (17)	1939: 31.6 (61)	1940: 28.9 (92)

For each country, the first column indicates the population of cities numbering 100,000 or more inhabitants as a percentage of total population. Figures in parentheses give the total number of such cities. Percentages for Germany before 1880 are for Prussia; absolute numbers are for the area that was to be unified in 1871. The source for Europe as a whole is Charles Tilly, *An Urban World* (Boston and Toronto, 1974). Other sources: works cited under Table I; B. R. Mitchell and Phyllis Deane, *Abstract of British Historical Statistics* (Cambridge, Eng., 1962), 24-26; Charles Rist and Gaetan Pirou, eds., *De la France d'avant guerre à la France d'aujourd'hui* (Paris, 1939), 18-19; *Statistisches Jahrbuch deutscher Städte*, 19 (1913), 846-47, and 34 (1939), 330-31.

Table III The growth of the giant cities

	London	Paris	Berlin	New York	Chicago
1800/01	1,117,000	547,000	172,000	60,000	0
1850/51	2,685,000	1,053,000	419,000	516,000	30,000
1880/81	4,770,000	2,269,000	1,122,000	1,165,000	503,000
1910/11	7,256,000	2,888,000	2,071,000	4,767,000	2,185,000
1940/41	8,700,000	2,830,000	4,332,000	7,455,000	3,397,000

The cities indicated above are all the cities in Europe (excluding Russia) and America that had more than 2 million inhabitants in 1940. Sources: B. R. Mitchell, *European Historical Statistics, 1750-1970* (New York and London, 1975), 76-78; Bayrd Still, *Urban America* (Boston, 1974), 210-11, 356-58; Ira Rosenwaike, *Population History of New York City* (Syracuse, 1972), 16.

transformations, with quantitative and qualitative changes being inseparably intertwined. The effects of the often abrupt transition from a rural social order to an urban one were as problematical as they were diverse. What men sought in the city was one thing, but what they found and experienced was often something else. Especially in the early phases of their growth, cities presented scenes of dreadful overcrowding and disease. For many, life was indeed nasty, brutish, and short. High levels of density produced not only high levels of illness and mortality but also profound changes in the ways men interacted (or failed to interact) with their neighbors and other citizens. Individuals felt a sense of liberation from traditional agencies of social control, such as the Church and the family. Moreover, as residential segregation according to income levels crystallized, there was growing social as well as spatial separation between classes. The members of these groups became increasingly aware that although they shared residency and some of the rights of citizenship in the same municipality they did not belong to a moral or cultural community. This is not to say that the small town had itself constituted such an entity — only that whatever social bonds between the top and the bottom of the social hierarchy may have existed earlier were appreciably loosened in the city and that splits among classes were made much more manifest as a result of sheer increases of numbers.

The city was, however, by no means simply a solvent. It also facilitated the pursuit of common goals and shared objectives, although what was aimed at was not always congenial to members of the upper strata. The city fostered the flowering of mass politics, and it provided a laboratory for progressive reformers. Its residents invented new modes of cultural expression and new life styles. These exerted powerful influences not only on other urbanites but also, especially in the age of mass media, on men and women who remained physically outside the city's reach. At the same time, all of these problems and possibilities powerfully stimulated the anxieties and the hopes, the emotions and the intellects, of thoughtful and articulate observers of the social scene.

The intellectual inheritance

Before we can begin to assess the impact of urbanization in the realms of thought and feeling, we must at least cursorily consider some of the views of cities that had found expression prior to the nineteenth century. Long before the period treated in this study, cities had given rise to reflection and controversy. They had been celebrated and condemned, reprobated and praised, loved and hated by writers who discerned in them the worst and the best that life had to offer. Early expressions of attitudes that were to become much more widespread in more recent times are especially significant in the case of negative sentiments, which sometimes drew almost as much sustenance from literary traditions as from contemporary realities. It is essential, however, to recall as well the examples of delight and pride in the city that are no less a part of European and American culture.

Biblical and other early Christian writers regularly excoriated the city as a symbol of man's estrangement from God and as the theater of man's spiritual degeneration. According to Genesis, the first city builder was Cain, who established Enoch in order to acquire for himself protection from other men, protection he might have received instead from God had he been a man of faith. Also in Genesis, we encounter Nimrod, the founder of Babylon, Akkad, and Calneh, of Nineveh, Rehoboth-Ir, Calah, and Resen, all of which served as headquarters for war and conquest, bloodletting and self-aggrandizement. His cities stood condemned, moreover, as places where the chosen people of Israel suffered in bondage. In the books of Daniel, Isaiah, and Jeremiah, Babylon in particular was singled out as *the* city, incorporating and synthesizing the evils of all cities in the world. As Jacques Ellul puts it,

> She is the head of, and the standard for the other cities.... Babylon (representative of all the others) is the hub of civilization. There everything is for sale, the bodies and souls of men. She is the very home of civilization and when the great city vanishes, there is no more civilization, a world disappears. She is the one

struck in war, and she is the first to be struck in the war between the Lord and the powers of the world.

The Jews, originally a nomadic people held captive in cities constructed by others, rebuilt Jericho after they had conquered it but became accursed as they did so. Their holy city, Jerusalem, occupied a special place in the divine scheme of things, being destined, according to the prophets, for ultimate rebirth, whereas Babylon was destined only for ruin. But as a secular institution embedded in historical time, it too was to be condemned as an expression of man's willful pride and his false sense of self-sufficiency.[4]

The anti-urban impetus carried over strongly into early Christianity. The Gospels portrayed Christ as a countryman, who found his first followers among his own kind and encountered his most formidable opposition in cities and towns. Again and again, he anathematized the city, pronouncing judgement against it as if it were an independent being while still holding out the promise of salvation to its individual inhabitants. It was only fitting that his crucifixion should occur just outside the gates of Jerusalem, a place, like Babylon, in which all true prophets could expect to be persecuted. Using a much larger historical canvas nearly four centuries after Christ's death, Augustine, in *The City of God*, depicted the city of man as the scene of supreme sin and folly. Applying to Rome the same epithets the prophets had earlier used to castigate Babylon, he invoked its history as proof of the frailty of all things human.[5]

Parallel but also conflicting traditions were articulated by pagan authors, both Greek and Roman. Starting in the third century before Christ, with the work of Theocritus and other bucolic poets of the Hellenistic world, the pastoral mode emerged as an implicitly critical response to city life. The pastoral current ran deep in Latin literature, finding classic expression in the odes of Horace and in Vergil's *Eclogues*, where the countryside symbolizes distant and innocent virtue, 'far from the strife of arms'. Although these poets did not concern themselves explicitly with the city itself, the satirist Juvenal, writing in the second century A.D., denounced Rome as a hotbed of corruption. 'What can I do in Rome? I never learnt how to lie', he wrote, going on to refer to 'that clique in Rome who affect ancestral peasant virtues as a front for their lechery'. Juvenal, like the pastoralists and like most other urban critics in later centuries, was of course a thoroughly urban man, who depended on the city for intellectual as well as material sustenance, but he left it to others to celebrate the urban virtues.[6]

Paeans of praise for particular urban places are not at all difficult to find in the literature of classical antiquity. According to Thucydides' version of the funeral oration delivered by Pericles in 431 B.C., the Athenian polis constituted a model of civilized morality, embodying both liberty and community and displaying both 'daring and deliberation'. It deserved devotion, and it compelled respect. Pericles' speech is customarily regarded as a defense of democracy, but it can also be read as a precursor of later evocations of civic pride. Among Latin authors, the glorification of Rome not only as the home of the national gods but also as the center of civilization (note, in passing, the derivation of the word itself from *civitas*, meaning 'city-state') recurred repeatedly, reaching its climax during the Augustan period in the *Aeneid* of Vergil and in Livy's *History*. As Lidia Storoni Mazzolani writes, 'The *Aeneid* sets out to show how its [Rome's] greatness was foreordained in heaven. Livy's *History* celebrates the valour of the makers of Rome, and narrates the gradual rise of the City in a style which blends mysticism with fatalism'. Vergil and Livy propounded a teleological view of history according to which the city that had become the capital of a great empire had been destined from the outset to exercise a beneficent rule that would endure forever. This was the view to which Augustine's was diametrically opposed.[7]

Men of the nineteenth century could also reflect upon much more widespread and explicit comments on urban life that had been made by many writers in the relatively recent past. The eighteenth century certainly witnessed a greater awareness of cities than the centuries immediately preceding it. Carl Schorske has suggested that, for men of the Enlightenment, the city represented 'civilized virtue'. The evidence for this view is familiar enough. Early in his career, Voltaire lauded London as the 'rival of Athens' because of the respect it displayed for talent, and he soon generalized its virtues to the modern city as such. Rewarding industry as it provided pleasure, the city worked toward both intellectual and aesthetic perfection. Adam Smith had greater reservations about urban life, but he still saw cities as places that offered freedom and order, creating a nation in which men were both more equal and more prosperous.[8]

Among men of letters, perhaps the least ambivalent city lovers were James Boswell and Samuel Johnson, both devoted denizens of the English metropolis. Boswell thrilled to London's pulsating variety, which he compared 'to a museum, a garden, to endless musical combinations'. The streets, crowds, and sights of the city intoxicated him, infusing him with energy he could feel nowhere else and providing him with a theater in which to discover and display his own personality. Johnson, the lover of London *par excellence*, prized the capital not only for the diversity of its pleasures but also for two other reasons. It chastened the ambition and humbled the pride of all men who had an inflated sense of their own importance, and it offered companionship and a sense of community to Johnson himself, who was haunted by a fear of solitude.[9]

Currents of opinion that ran counter to these views were already very much in evidence during the century of the *philosophes*, and they became still more apparent under the impact of romanticism. François Quesnay and other Physiocrats in France and physicians and other students of public health in Germany, such as Christoph Wilhelm Hufeland and Johann Peter Süssmilch, leveled the same charges against cities from a demographic standpoint that had been made in the preceding century by two English statisticians, John Graunt and William Petty. In their view, high urban death rates meant that further increases in the percentage of the population living in cities would inevitably sap the wellsprings of natural vitality by diminishing a country's only true wealth: the quality and quantity of its inhabitants. Among better known thinkers, Rousseau stands out in Europe owing to the intensity of his denunciations of Paris, which he branded in *Emile* a 'city of noise, of smoke, and of mud'. Paris was a 'moloch' that fed greedily on blood supplied by the provinces and corrupted those whom it did not kill. After Rousseau's death, two of his disciples, Restif de la Bretonne and Sebastien Mercier, continued to castigate the French capital as an example and a source of moral degradation, with Mercier, in his panoramic *Tableau de Paris*, elaborating an apocalyptic vision of the collapse of the city almost on the eve of the great Revolution. In the United States, also during the 1780s, Thomas Jefferson began to articulate a highly influential American version of the anti-urban creed. He asserted that 'the mobs of great cities add just so much to the support of pure government, as sores do to the strength of the human body' and that democracy could flourish only in a society that consisted primarily of rural freeholders.[10]

But it was in England that critical sentiment asserted itself most forcefully. Throughout the eighteenth century, London inspired oppressive horror among many of the major English authors. When one considers the writings of Daniel Defoe, Alexander Pope, and Henry Fielding, among others, it is clear that Boswell and Johnson hardly typified the literary response to city life in their age. Around the turn of the century, in the works of William Blake and William Wordsworth, the sense of gloomy foreboding and alienation became especially pronounced as the romantic poets gave voice to the misery they observed and the loneliness they felt while walking among their fellow urbanites. Blake, in 'London' (1794), saw in every face 'marks of weakness, marks of woe', and Wordsworth, in *The Prelude* (1805 version), expressed part of his disenchantment with London as follows: 'Above all, one thought/Baffled my understanding: how men lived/Even next-door neighbours, as we say, yet still/Strangers, not knowing each the other's name' (VII, 115-118). This feeling that proximity to large numbers of other human beings entailed personal isolation from them was to recur more and more frequently as cities themselves grew in size and complexity.[11]

The evolution of urban consciousness

Starting in the third decade of the nineteenth century more and more writers began to address themselves to specifically urban phenomena — to the problems posed and the possibilities offered by city growth. The shifting overall balance between country and city and the emergence of larger and larger cities impinged with ever deepening impact on the consciousness of thoughtful observers of the contemporary world.

The centrality of the city to the problems of modern society meant that it elicited concern and comment from a wide range of authors. During most of the nineteenth century, clergymen who had been assigned to urban parishes, medical doctors who treated city dwellers, and others who were professionally involved in questions of public health played an especially important part in alerting the public to the dangers inherent in the crowded conditions of rookeries and slums. So too did numerous authors of descriptive books and essays to whom the most precise occupational label that can be attached is 'publicist', although many of them doubtless derived their income from sources other than their writing. Practitioners of social realism in the writing of fiction brought the anguish experienced by some urbanites to the attention of an even wider audience. Critics of cities, occasionally including even the novelists, but also defenders obtained much of their ammunition from statisticians, who provided more and more information about their societies that referred specifically to the urban sector.[12] Aside from economists, scholars who would be designated today as 'social scientists' did not confront the city directly in their work until late in the nineteenth century. Urban sociology, conceived and pursued as a distinct subdiscipline, first emerged in the twentieth century. Its leading exponents attempted to comprehend urban processes without necessarily passing moral judgements upon them, but they inevitably dealt with the quality of urban life.

Several other groups of men wrote about cities at a much lower level of generalization. Architects and city planners became especially important in the early twentieth century, elaborating a vision of the city as an entity susceptible to rational control and future betterment. So too did local officials, many of whom proposed further urban improvements while at the same time expressing pride in what they had already accomplished. Finally, there were the local historians, few of whom had much if any standing in the historical profession. As we shall see, they almost always cultivated a view of the past that exuded affection, pride, and confidence.

We start our consideration of the thoughts of these writers by beginning with the British in the second quarter of the nineteenth century and treating their views of their own towns up to about 1880. The enormous gap between urban growth in Britain and the development of cities elsewhere during this period makes separate consideration of the British experience imperative. The first work of any substance to take the problems of cities in general as its central theme, written by Thomas Chalmers, began to appear in Scotland in 1821.[13] The British evinced greatly heightened interest in cities in the 1830s and 1840s, devoting intense scrutiny to Manchester as well as to London. There were still relatively few books about 'the city' as a general phenomenon, but, continuing into the 1850s, many articles in the leading reviews and in less well known magazines treated the theme of 'town and country' or more limited aspects of the urban scene. Moreover, travel literature, works of social description and analysis, and the novels of Charles Dickens and Elizabeth Gaskell focused on cities too.

The next two chapters treat writers from France, Germany, and America during roughly the same period covered for Britain. European authors such as Alexis de Tocqueville and Friedrich Engels were both fascinated and horrified by English cities, which they frequently regarded as indicators of what the future might hold in store for their own countries. Paris, after a period of about thirty years in which it had almost dropped from sight in French literature,[14] began once again to imprint itself forcefully on public consciousness, not only in the works of novelists and poets (Honoré de Balzac, Victor Hugo, Charles Baudelaire) but also in the great studies of urban pathology produced by hygienists and other social reformers. Germans remained relatively inattentive to their own cities throughout the early and middle decades of the century. In the United States, however, leading writers such as Ralph Waldo Emerson and Herman Melville, together with many lesser lights, were beginning to grapple much more intensively with urban phenomena.

The core of my study concentrates on the years 1880-1918. Starting around 1880, there was a great upsurge of inquiry into and thought about the conditions of urban living, first in Britain and soon thereafter in the other three countries, and these interests continued unabated in all of them at least through the early part of the twentieth century. In Britain, London moved clearly to center stage. Its impoverished under-class drew sustained attention not only from social investigators such as Charles Booth but also from novelists such as George Gissing and from liberal reformers such as Charles Masterman, who publicized their ideas in the leading magazines as well as in books. Many British clergymen continued to inveigh against urban wicked-ness, but Canon S. A. Barnett, together with others who participated in the settlement house movement, evinced a strong sense of hope that emerged from recent urban progress, as did Patrick Geddes from the standpoint of city planning. In France, the late nineteenth century was the period when Emile Zola rose to prominence as one of the modern period's premier city novelists and when scholars such as Emile Levasseur and Paul Meuriot sought to assess the impact of urban growth in an economic perspective.

Germany experienced an extraordinary heightening of its urban conscious-ness. Massive studies of many facets of urban life were published by the reformist Verein für Sozialpolitik, and a flood of articles on the *Grossstadt* in all its aspects appeared in periodicals, including several newly established journals that concentrated exclusively and explicitly on urban affairs.[15] Demographers became obsessed with the relations between urbanization and the declining birth rate, and both clergymen and poets called attention to psychic and moral conflicts. Just after the turn of the century, Dresden hosted a well publicized German City Exhibition. Subsequently, more and more celebrations of municipal progress in a large number of German cities found their way into print. Both critics and advocates of the city — and those in between — continued to focus in great detail on the changes that were occurring in the urban milieu. In contrast to Britain and France, where the city seemed to be receding from consciousness in the years immediately preceding the First World War, Germany produced more and more writing about urban life with every passing year.

A similar situation obtained in the United States, where rapid urbanization and its consequences provided recurrent topics for publicists and scholars. In 1890, Jacob Riis exposed the squalid conditions in the tenements of New York. Before the century ended, Adna Weber produced what is still the standard treatise on urban growth in Europe as well as America. Around this time, several specialized journals treating municipal affairs first made their appearance,[16] and there was a rash of studies by reformers and political scientists on the problems and accomplishments of city governments, including books by Jane Addams, Frederic C. Howe, and many others. In Theodore Dreiser, the United States could boast of an urban novelist whose stature approached that of Zola, if not that of Dickens.

The volume of what was written in Europe and America during the four decades that spanned the year 1900 and the parallels between the ideas expressed in different countries were such that it makes little sense to deal with each national experience in turn. My chapters on this period will therefore focus on general themes. We shall start with those moments at which men and women portrayed or at least mentioned the big city's blemishes. A survey of the articulate awareness of material deprivation will lead to an analysis of parallel fears with regard to the biological present and future of the urbanite and his family. It will also help to set the stage for a much lengthier exploration of a cluster of anxieties that centered on the city's moral, political, and cultural defects. We then listen to expressions of admiration and hope, which came both from some writers who offered praise in place of criticism and from many others who offered praise in addition to criticism. Some of the authors treated in Part Two will thus reappear in new contexts in Part Three, as we consider first the general points that seemed to militate in the big city's favor and then the much more specific perceptions of communal efforts and communal progress in particular places at the levels of both voluntary and municipal activity. Each chapter dealing with the years between 1880 and 1918 will emphasize similarities that cut across national boundaries, while at the same time pointing out those differences that seem most worthy of note.

During the interwar years, national differences once again became quite striking, and the chapter on that period therefore focuses on these distinctions. We shall have relatively little to say about Britain and France. Britain had become so heavily urbanized that the problems of the city were almost coextensive with the problems of society as a whole. Cities no longer stood out in the way they had earlier as peculiar places that needed to be scrutinized and evaluated separately from the rest of the nation. Englishmen did continue to reflect on the life of their cities, especially London, about which they evinced a growing grimness, but their earlier intensity of feeling had clearly abated. The French, whose real importance in the discussion of urban themes had already come to an end shortly after the turn of the century, had very little at all to contribute aside from the brilliant ideas of Le Corbusier in the area of city planning.

In Germany, however, the trend that had been evident before the war continued, and cities became increasingly controversial, eliciting more and more comment. But if there was a debate, it was decidedly one-sided. For many writers, cities became symbols of all that was worst in modern civilization. The denunciations of the cosmopolitan *Weltstadt* by Oswald Spengler were echoed in countless books and essays by other right-wing enemies of the Weimar Republic and reiterated by leading ideologists and social scientists in the Third Reich. The promising initiatives in the direction of an urban sociology that had been undertaken earlier in the century were largely discontinued.

Like Germany, the United States produced a flood of urban writing, but most of it indicated quite different approaches and sentiments from the ones that were asserting themselves in Central Europe. Lewis Mumford, the single most important critic of cities to appear during the twentieth century, and several others who shared his views were quite capable of excoriating 'megalopolis' in the manner of Spengler, but they did so for purposes that diverged sharply from those of the German anti-urbanists. In addition, there was noticeably more thinking in America than in Germany that can be described as generally positive, including many of the perceptions of a growing cadre of urban sociologists. Led by Robert Park and his colleagues at the University of Chicago, these scholars kept up a steady flow of evenhanded works on all aspects of urban society that was quite unparalleled in Europe. It also implied ultimate acceptance of the modern city.

As we encounter the thinking of the men and women referred to above and of several hundred other authors whose books and essays appeared during the years 1820-1940, we shall examine a great variety of intellectual responses to urban growth and the big cities it produced. The urbanization of Western society generated an enormous amount of inquiry, research, reflection, and debate. The big city was hailed proudly and criticized sharply. Awareness of the cities' inadequacies and their dangers was frequently linked to nostalgic defenses of tradition and sometimes to a desperate advocacy of authoritarian politics. But many criticisms led to progressive reforms, which themselves offered substantial grounds both for pride in some city dwellers' recent achievements and to optimism about their future prospects. It is the complex interplay among such crosscurrents of thought and feeling and between urban ideas and urban experiences that constitutes the basic theme of the rest of this book.

Part One

Urban Themes in England and Elsewhere, 1820–1880

2

Victorian Cities in the Eyes of the British

In early and mid-nineteenth-century Britain, the phenomena associated with city life generated widespread interest and often bitter controversy. Try as some of them might, the Victorians could hardly ignore the dense centers of population that were springing up in their midst. The city as a general phenomenon, particular cities in their entirety, and more specific aspects of town life received extensive treatment in a voluminous and widely read body of writing. Urban themes came to the fore in governmental reports, medical treatises, sermons, essays that appeared in leading magazines, and popular works of history, travel, and description.

The Victorians' thinking about their towns ranged from science to sophistry, from sober analysis to ideological partisanship. Here we encounter the first generation of men who perceived cities as both the vehicles and the symbols of modernity, with all of its problems and its promise. Few authors painted cities all black or all white. Most recognized that town life comprised both good and bad, and accordingly they displayed a certain ambivalence toward it. But the mixture of colors varied greatly from canvas to canvas, depending on a particular author's occupation or political and social ideology and on the period in which he or she was writing. Some observers depicted the urban scene in varying shades of medium to dark gray. It is with their perceptions that we begin, before turning later to cityscapes that were painted in brighter hues.

Indictments of industrial towns

Urban criticism proceeded on many fronts and took many forms. There was a vivid awareness among the Victorians — most noticeable in the 1830s and 1840s but still evident long thereafter — that urban overcrowding could and often did result in a terrible loss of human health and life. Numerous observers, especially medical doctors, saw the big city as a biological threat of the first order, and they sought with considerable success to focus public attention on the need for improved sanitation. At the same time, clergymen of the Church of England took the lead in criticizing the cities' moral health. They were joined in this effort by a wide range of other authors, including not only sanitary reformers but also men engaged in law enforcement and politics and the various publicists who wrote about high life and low life in London. Finally, there were the well known 'sages', whose works of fiction, cultural commentary and philosophical reflection expressed views of the city that incorporated both moral considerations and a sense of growing unease that was largely aesthetic.

William Cobbett's references to cities in his famous account of his travels in rural England during the 1820s proclaimed a deep hostility based in part on the belief that town life militated against a large and healthy population. Via his favorite metaphor for cities — 'wens' — the prolific publicist who combined political radicalism with rural nostalgia implied that they were tumors on the social organism. Moreover, Cobbett linked their growth to what he believed was an absolute decline in the number of English men and women. The decay of agriculture and the emptying of the countryside were in his view not simply signs of a geographic redistribution of the island's growing number of inhabitants. Instead, they highlighted the supposed fact that during Cobbett's own lifetime there had been no increase whatsoever in the size of the English population and that since the Middle Ages there had been an enormous decline. 'England', he wrote, 'was at one time, and that too, eight hundred years ago, beyond all measure more populous than it is now'. This preposterous belief was not widely shared at the time by other commentators on English society. It does, however, provide a point of entry into a set of concerns that were to become quite widespread during the two decades after Cobbett had completed his tours of the English countryside. Cobbett's scattered remarks on rural decay, the concomitant expansion of the 'wens', and overall depopulation contributed in a general way to a growing conviction that increased urban density seriously threatened the biological well-being of the nation by inflicting severe physical penalties upon the men and women who lived and, with increasing frequency, died there.[1]

Medical doctors played the leading role in alerting the public to the increasingly unpleasant facts about urban health, by relentlessly exposing the high rates of disease and death that prevailed among city dwellers relative to the non-urban population. They found themselves in a position to do so not only because of the changes that were occurring in urban society but also because of changes that were taking place in their own profession. The period from the late eighteenth century through the early nineteenth witnessed a dramatic growth in the number of British physicians. The University of Edinburgh, the center of medical education in Britain, trained only 213 medical graduates in the 1770s but 1139 in the 1820s, at the end of which the efforts of its professors were supplemented by those of the medical faculty at the newly established University College in London. The teaching of medicine at Edinburgh was the best in Britain from a scientific standpoint. Moreover, under the guidance of William Pulteney Alison, who taught there from 1820 to 1856, it emphasized the need to set medical problems within a broad social context, and this orientation bore fruit in the writings of many of Alison's students.[2] At the same time, a fundamental transformation was occurring in medical science itself. Physicians no longer regarded disease as 'a bundle of characters disseminated here and there over the surface of the body' but instead as 'a set of forms and deformations, figures and accidents and of displaced, destroyed, or modified elements bound together in sequences according to a geography that can be followed step by step'. This change from a topographical to an anatomical approach to illness strongly influenced students of public health and provided some of them with a paradigm for understanding not only sick individuals but also sick cities.[3]

Two physicians who practiced in northern industrial towns published notable books about urban health in the early 1830s. C. Turner Thackrah turned his attention to conditions in Leeds. Insisting from the outset on 'the superiority of agricultural laborers in health, vigour, and size' *vis-à-vis* the inhabitants of his city, he pointed out that ten years earlier the crude death rate in Leeds had been one in fifty-five, whereas in the nearby village of Pickering Lythe it had been only one in seventy-five. He reformulated this finding as follows, using a statistical strategy that was to become increasingly common as a way of making the facts of death come alive:

> . . . At least 450 persons die annually in the borough of Leeds, from the injurious effects of manufactures, the crowded state of the population, and the consequent bad habits of life! We may say that every day of the year is carried to the grave the corpse of an individual whom nature would have long preserved in health and vigour; every day we see sacrificed to the artificial state of society one, and sometimes two victims, whom the destinies of nature would have spared.

In most of the rest of his treatise, he methodically examined the job-related hazards to which each occupational group was exposed. He emphasized not only the noxious pollutants inflicted upon workers in the flax trade (a staple industry in Leeds), but also the physical impairments suffered by merchants and manufacturers as a result of lack of exercise and of 'inordinate application of mind, the cares, anxieties, and disappointments of commercial life'. Moreover, he stressed the ills suffered by all classes as a result of intemperance.[4]

The idea that urban life styles were deleterious to bodily health at all levels

---

1 Exterior of a Manchester cellar. This illustration and the one below it depict the sort of living conditions that helped to produce the sanitary problems decried by public health reformers in the 1830s and 1840s (source: George R. Catt, *A Pictorial History of Manchester* [1843], 37).

2 Interior of a Manchester cellar (source: as above).

of the social hierarchy was by no means peculiar to Thackrah,[5] but it was not
the particular point that most medical men had in mind when they wrote
about the ills of the city. In 1832, a more representative and far more
influential work than Thackrah's, written by James Phillips Kay (an
Edinburgh graduate), focused on the plight of the working classes in
Manchester. Having served earlier that year as the secretary of a special
committee that coordinated the work of several boards of health during the
cholera epidemic, he reported in a pamphlet on his visits to the worst areas of
the city and sought to place what he had observed in proper perspective. Kay
admitted that many of the evils afflicting the poor 'flow from their own
ignorance or moral errors', but he hastened to add that the workers could not
be held fully accountable even for their own faults, which were effects as well
as causes of the deplorable living conditions in which they found themselves.
Hordes of Irish immigrants had 'taught the labouring classes of this country a
pernicious lesson' through the example of their own moral turpitude. And
quite apart from the polluting presence of the Irish, working-class Mancunians suffered from 'prolonged and exhausting labour', which resembled 'the
torment of Sisyphus' and deadened their minds, wretched diets, and the
necessity of living 'in cottages separated by narrow, unpaved, and almost
pestilential streets, in an atmosphere loaded with the smoke and exhalations
of a large manufacturing city'. The lack of sewers beneath the streets and of
privies in the houses that lined them further exacerbated the filth to which
the workers were exposed, as did the offal that lay about because of the
absence of properly regulated slaughterhouses. These were not the only
causes of the distress that Manchester had just experienced, but they were
widespread and they were basic.[6]

These ills, Kay hastened to point out, were in no way intrinsic to the
commercial and manufacturing system itself, for which Kay expressed
enthusiastic admiration. He believed that 'the sudden creation of the mighty
system of commercial organization which covers this country, and stretches
its arms to the most distant seas', bore witness to 'the power and dignity of
man'. Its natural tendency was 'to develop the energies of society, to increase
the comforts and luxuries of life, and to elevate the physical condition of
every member of the social body'. But the evils that beset the working classes
were bound to impair the system unless timely measures were taken to cure
them.[7]

The largely qualitative indictments of the urban environment formulated
by Thackrah, Kay, and others pointed up the need for accurate and
comprehensive statistics that would illuminate the issues they had raised in
systematic and authoritative detail. The 1830s and 1840s witnessed a
widespread 'statistical movement' in Britain that grew in large part out of
rising anxiety about the state of the nation's bodily health. The first census of
England and Wales had been taken in 1800, national crime statistics had been
collected since 1810, and a statistical department had been set up at the Board

of Trade in 1832, but it was only with the founding of other institutions soon thereafter that the number gatherers shifted into high gear. Local statistical societies came into existence during the period in at least eight British cities, starting with Manchester in 1833, where Kay played a leading role. Londoners followed suit in 1834. Subsequently, societies sprang up in Glasgow, Bristol, Newcastle, Leeds, and several other provincial towns. Public health and the condition of the poor were recurring themes in the reports issued by these groups. Generally Whiggish in political outlook, their members favored *laissez-faire* and resisted factory legislation, arguing, as Kay had done in his pamphlet of 1832, that the main evils to be combated stemmed not from industry but from urbanization.

In 1837, statisticians achieved their greatest gain during the period. From that year, a General Register Office began to record official data for England and Wales concerning births, deaths, and marriages. The dominant figure in the operations of this bureau was a middle-level official, William Farr, who had trained as a medical doctor in Paris and London and begun to practice in the metropolis in 1833. His early interest in public health led him naturally to the study of population statistics, and the annual reports that he produced during a period of more than three decades relentlessly expounded his environmentalist views of the etiology of poverty and disease. Already in his first report he concluded that mortality increased with density, a view he was to refine but never to abandon during the rest of his career.[8]

The late 1830s were of special importance for the emerging consciousness of public health problems less because of the establishment of the General Register Office than because of developments that were occurring under the aegis of the Poor Law Commission, which had been entrusted by the New Poor Law of 1834 with the task of coordinating public assistance to the indigent. Since their inception, the new Poor Law Unions in almost every locality had appointed medical officers to supervise 'outdoor' medical relief, among them some of the most distinguished authorities on urban disease in the country (e.g., Richard Baron Howard of Manchester and William Duncan of Liverpool). Toward the end of the decade, the Poor Law authorities secured the services of three doctors whose investigations of disease in London placed them at the forefront of the nascent public health movement. One of the three was James Kay. The others were Neill Arnott and Thomas Southwood Smith, who like Kay had trained at Edinburgh. Southwood Smith had long enjoyed a high reputation as a student of public health and an advocate of sanitary reform, and his influence far surpassed that of Kay and Arnott. In his 'Report on Some of the Physical Causes of Sickness and Mortality ... Exemplified in the Present Condition of Bethnal Green and Whitechapel Districts' and in his 'Report on the Prevalence of Fever in Twenty Metropolitan Unions or Parishes during the Year Ended the 20th March 1838', he elaborated and substantiated his view of the sanitary economy of the town as the product of constant interchange between living organisms and their physical environment. The basic prerequisites for a healthy city paralleled those for a healthy human body — free circulation of fluids and air and the efficient elimination of waste products — and they were clearly absent from contemporary towns.[9] The first of these reports, together with reports by Kay and Arnott, was included in 1838 in the *Fourth Annual Report* of the Poor Law Commissioners. It reached a much wider audience than earlier Poor Law reports and thus helped to stimulate considerable public awareness of facts that until then had been familiar primarily to members of the medical profession.

At this juncture, our attention must shift away from the physicians to the one man who did more than any other in Britain or elsewhere in the century to heighten consciousness of the terrible losses of human life that were occurring continually in cities and towns. That man was Edwin Chadwick.[10] Having trained as a lawyer and served as an assistant to the Utilitarian philosopher Jeremy Bentham when a young man, Chadwick had been instrumental in the passage of the New Poor Law of 1834 and had been given major responsibility for administering its draconian provisions. He was too busy during the mid-1830s to think much about public health. But in 1838 he drafted the brief report that introduced the studies of London referred to above, and for well over a decade thereafter he devoted himself wholeheartedly to the cause of sanitation.

After the articles in the report of 1838 had been reinforced by an article of Southwood Smith's in the report of 1839, Bishop Blomfield of London moved in the House of Lords that an inquiry be made into the sanitary condition of the working classes, and the Poor Law Commissioners, to whom Chadwick was still Secretary, were ordered to undertake it. For the next two years, Chadwick was freed from his other duties so that he could give all his time to the investigation. After surmounting serious obstacles both in the government and in the Poor Law Commission, he completed his report by early 1842, and it appeared that summer under his name alone.

Chadwick surveyed not only the larger industrial towns but also smaller towns and rural villages, in Scotland as well as England and Wales, and he drew on a wide range of sources in order to marshal a great mass of vivid and unimpeachable evidence. Assistant Poor Law Commissioners and over one thousand Poor Law medical officers throughout the country were called upon to provide information about sanitary conditions in their districts. Investigators received detailed questionnaires that told them just what to look for. They were urged to adopt 'the most compendious mode of coming at the worst conditioned districts of a town', and they were told how to do so. For instance, they were urged to locate schools attended by sickly or stunted children and then to visit their homes, where they were to ask specific questions. For Scotland, where the administrative machinery created by the new Poor Law did not exist, Chadwick had to draw on the expertise of

especially knowledgeable doctors, ministers of the Kirk, and other distinguished citizens. To a lesser extent, he also depended on such men for
information about England and Wales, where individual physicians, prison
superintendents, model employers, factory inspectors, and other miscellaneous experts all made significant contributions. Moreover, he visited
several large towns himself and broadened his perspective by reading widely
in relevant works by such French authorities as A. J. B. Parent-Duchâtelet
and Louis-René Villermé.

Chadwick made his points both through the careful presentation of
statistics and through the use of gruesomely vivid descriptions. He sought at
the start of his report to convey the magnitude of the horrors he was writing
about as forcefully as possible by means of the following calculation:

> . . . From the fact, that of the deaths caused during one year in England and
> Wales by epidemic, endemic, and contagious diseases, including fever, typhus,
> and scarlatina, amounting to 56,461, the great proportion of which are proved to
> be preventible, it may be said that the effect is as if the whole county of
> Westmorland, now containing 56,469 souls, or the whole county of Huntingdon-
> shire, or any other equivalent district, were entirely depopulated annually, and
> were only occupied again by the growth of a new and feeble population living
> under the fears of a similar visitation. The annual slaughter in England and
> Wales from preventible causes of typhus which attacks persons in the vigour of
> life, appears to be double the amount of what was suffered by the Allied Armies
> in the battle of Waterloo.[11]

Approximately the first half of the report documented the extent of this
preventable illness and early death and linked it to defective drainage,
inadequate water supplies, and overcrowded housing.

Chadwick admitted that the problems were not confined to towns. They
also plagued the countryside.[12] But they were clearly most acute among city
dwellers, and the most memorable evidence in the report testified to the
endemic filth and misery in what would later come to be known as urban
slums. Consider, for instance, the following excerpt, which Chadwick quoted
at length, from a report on Liverpool by Dr. William Duncan:

> In consequence of finding that not less than 63 cases of fever had occurred in one
> year in Union-court Banastre-street (containing 12 houses), I visited the court in
> order to ascertain, if possible, their origin, and I found the whole court
> inundated with fluid filth which had oozed through the walls from two adjoining
> ash-pits or cess-pools, and which had no means of escape in consequence of the
> court being below the level of the street, and having no drain.... The house
> nearest the ash-pit had been untenanted for nearly three years in consequence of
> the filthy matter oozing up through the floor, and the occupiers of the adjoining
> houses were unable to take their meals without previously closing the doors and
> windows.[13]

It was urban conditions like these — not poverty as such and certainly not industry — that undermined the nation's health.

Although Chadwick was obviously distressed over the needless loss of human life, he did not share Cobbett's fear that urban growth implied a stagnant or a declining population. In fact, his anxieties pointed in just the opposite direction. He challenged the Malthusian view that unsanitary conditions in cities served as a 'positive check' on too rapid population growth, arguing instead that disease bred poverty and that poverty encouraged high birth rates, thus exacerbating the problem of overpopulation. 'In such [crowded] districts', he wrote, 'the fact is observable, that where the mortality is the highest, the number of births are more than sufficient to replace the deaths, however numerous they may be'.[14]

Chadwick was an indignant optimist, and much of what he had to say suggested that the prospects for towns were not at all unfavorable. One of his most important achievements was to document variations in the death rate within towns from one district to another, showing that some were every bit as healthy as the best agricultural counties. Nor was the urban insalubrity he had depicted inevitable. It could be overcome through the judicious introduction of sanitary reform. He did not spell out specific proposals at great length, but he insisted strongly on the need for effective removal of sewage by suspension in water, which was to be conveyed in glazed, circular drains. He also called for legislative and administrative uniformity throughout the nation, so that the imposition of proper standards would not vary from one locality to another.[15]

It was essential for Chadwick's purposes that his report be widely disseminated, so that maximum influence would be exerted on public opinion. Issued officially as an unwieldy folio paper of the House of Lords, it would have remained quite inaccessible had Chadwick not arranged to have it published separately in a very large quarto edition. Somewhere between 10,000 and 100,000 copies of this edition were either sold or given away. Even if we take the lowest estimate, it is clear that the sales far exceeded those of any other official document up to that time. Both *The Times* and *The Morning Chronicle* carried leading articles on the issues the report raised, and the conservative *Quarterly Review* published a long essay that expressed strong sympathy for Chadwick's efforts and his message. Chadwick had shown unmistakably 'that the physician and the engineer are the head and the hand professionally most competent to undertake the cure' of urban pestilence, and there was no excuse for failing to rely on their expertise. Chadwick had also displayed his own 'benevolent feeling towards the poor and the suffering'.[16]

Chadwick's findings were supplemented and his suggestions were supported from several sides during the years after 1842. More and more publicists, such as Robert Seeley, a promoter of evangelical and philanthropic movements, took up the cause of sanitary reform. In 1844, he wrote,

'Manchester and Glasgow, with their vice and their diseases, cannot keep up their own populations. Cut off supplies of fresh labourers from without, and these towns, in sixty years, would be without inhabitants'. Four things were necessary to remedy this deplorable situation: 'paved streets, covered sewers, ventilation, and a supply of water'.[17] That same year, a parliamentary Health of Towns Commission published the first of two reports (the second was to appear in 1845) that took up where the earlier *Report of the Select Committee on the Health of Towns* (1840) had left off. Robert Slaney, the chairman of the Select Committee, was a prominent member of the Commission too,[18] but Chadwick, though not a member at all, drafted the greater part of the Commission's reports. Chadwick, along with Southwood Smith, also assumed an active role in the Health of Towns Association, a pressure group that began to agitate for reform in 1844. Because he was a civil servant, he felt that he should not hold formal membership in the Association, but he provided plentiful advice to those who did belong, many of whom produced books and pamphlets for the purpose of keeping public attention focused on the need for remedial action. William Augustus Guy contributed a pamphlet titled *Unhealthiness of Towns: Its Causes and Remedies* (1845) that explained the general purposes of the Association. Hector Gavin produced one on the *Unhealthiness of London, and Necessity for Remedial Measures* (1847), and many other works with similar titles appeared during these years.

After the 1840s, in part as a result of the passage of the first Public Health Act by Parliament in 1848,[19] there was a marked decline of public concern over the health and longevity of townsmen. To be sure, William Farr's annual reports continued to document the discrepancy between town and countryside in the area of physical well-being. In 1863, he showed that during the period 1851-60 a total of 327,354 deaths had occurred in England and Wales in excess of the number that could have been expected had the towns been as healthy as the countryside. The gap was greatest by far, both as a total number and as a ratio, among children under five years of age, 203,520 of whom had succumbed to the insalubrious conditions of urban life.[20] These were needless deaths, which represented preventable mortality on a still awesome scale. There were occasional moments during these years when other medical men sought to alert their fellow citizens to the continuing threat posed by urban growth. John Edward Morgan, a physician in Salford and the Honorary Secretary of the Manchester and Salford Sanitary Association, read a paper at the Social Science Congress in Sheffield in 1865 which he titled *The Danger of Deterioration of Race from the Too Rapid Increase of Great Towns*. His statistics showed 'that the prospects of life are nearly twice as favourable to the dwellers in rural districts as to their brethren in the towns', and Morgan doubted that sanitary improvements could ever close the gap completely. Balthazar Foster, a professor of medicine in Birmingham, delivered a similar lecture a decade later under the title *How We Die in Large Towns* at the local Temperance Hall in a course of Penny Sanitary Lessons for the Working Classes. His message was not quite so grim as Morgan's, but he pointed out that deaths from preventable disease were two and one-half times as frequent in towns as in rural areas and that during the first five years of life nearly three times as many children died in towns as in 'the healthy districts'. On the whole, however, the voices of such men were raised and heard much less frequently during the third quarter of the century than they had been in the period of heroic effort by Chadwick and his disciples. Their calculations had by this time lost much of their power to shock, and they did little to arouse or sustain the kind of public outrage that had been so clearly evident two decades earlier.[21]

Anxieties pertaining to bodily health were paralleled by similar and frequently linked concerns with regard to urban morals and the condition of urban society. Numerous authors complained loudly that town life was undermining not only the urbanite's physique but also his character. The inhabitants of great towns, they argued, displayed all too little in the way of either self-control or devotion to the well-being of a larger community.

Many medical doctors feared an upsurge of personal depravity and the breakdown of social cohesion, some making clear connections between these maladies and physical ones. Immorality was identified frequently as a powerful contributor to physical illness, most convincingly in the case of alcoholic drink, which provided one of the prime targets for social reformers throughout the Victorian period.[22] But the physicians were equally inclined to indict the wretched physical environment and the diseases it engendered as major culprits in the etiology of urban wrongdoing. In any case, whichever was the cause and whichever the effect, threats to physical and moral well-being were regarded as intimately linked facets of urban life. Kay pointed out this connection in the very title of his work on Manchester, with his reference to the moral as well as the physical condition of the city's workers. In much of the second half of this work, he dwelt on excessive drink, high crime rates, and the lack of both religion and education.[23]

Chadwick and the medical men who helped him to assemble his great report insisted strongly on the harmful impact of poor sanitary conditions on the character of urban men and women. The following sentences convey the gist of Chadwick's message:

> The familiarity with the sickness and death constantly present in the crowded and unwholesome districts, appears to re-act as another concurrent cause in aggravation of the wretchedness and vice in which they are plunged. Seeing the apparent uncertainty of the morrow, the inhabitants really take no heed of it, and abandon themselves with the recklessness and avidity of common soldiers in a war to whatever gross enjoyment comes within their reach.

Education would not suffice to counteract such influences. Chadwick believed that until the physical environment was ameliorated 'moral agencies have but a remote chance of success'.[24]

A far more comprehensive critique of urban society issued between Kay's and Chadwick's reports from the pen of Peter Gaskell. Little is known about Gaskell beyond the fact that he had secured certification as an apothecary and a surgeon. But despite his personal obscurity his study of the working classes was to be used extensively by Friedrich Engels, and it deserves to be considered as a major statement of the moral case against industrial urbanization.[25]

Gaskell prefaced his analysis of contemporary conditions with a long paean to the world of the domestic laborer who had lived on the land or in a village in the years before about 1760, painting an idyllic picture that was suffused with nostalgia.

> These were, undoubtedly, the golden times of manufactures, considered in reference to the character of the labourer. By all the processes being carried on under a man's own roof, he retained his individual respectability, he was kept apart from associations that might injure his moral worth, and he generally earned wages which were not only sufficient to live comfortably upon, but which enabled him to rent a few acres of land.... The circumstances of a man's labour being conducted in the midst of his household, exercised a powerful influence upon his social affections and those of his offspring.... His children grew up under his immediate inspection and control.... The same generation lived age after age on the same spot, and under the same thatched roof, which thus became a sort of heirloom, endeared to its occupier by a long series of happy memories and home delights ... and, in the end, they crowded the same narrow tenement in the quiet and sequestered church-yard, suffered to moulder in peace beneath its fresh and verdant turf, and swept over by the free, the balmy, and the uncontaminated breath of heaven.[26]

It was against this backdrop that Gaskell depicted the life of the manufacturing population under the industrial system that had developed in the city. He asserted that the greatest misfortune to befall the working man was 'the breaking up of ... family ties, the consequent abolition of the domestic circle, and the perversion of all the social obligations which should exist between parent and child on the one hand, and between children themselves on the other'. This process might be mitigated among industrial workers who lived under the close supervision of their employers, but such situations seldom obtained in the towns, where evil influences therefore ran rampant. As a result, there was not only a marked increase in sexual promiscuity but also greater drunkenness, more irreligion, and more crime. Finally, Gaskell directed fully as much vituperation against another phenomenon that had just begun to appear in the urban-industrial world, the trade union, whose moral influence he labeled 'exceedingly pernicious'. For all of these reasons, Gaskell looked toward the future with unconcealed anxiety. He feared an explosion, and he had little if any idea of how to prevent it.[27]

A quarter of a century later, another medical doctor took up the theme of urban morals from a somewhat different standpoint. John Shaw wrote not a sociological treatise but rather a vivid personal account of his travels with city and town missionaries. What struck him was less the gap between town and country than the enormous contrasts that had opened up within the town itself. In the area around Oxford Street in London, elegant shops were located only a stone's throw from 'back slums, inhabited by people so lost to modern morality and civilization, and so little allied in architecture, manners, and mode of life with their neighbours with whom they are in actual contact, that they may be compared to the wildest colony of savages, transplanted by an act of conjuration from the centre of Africa'. The comparison between the English slum dweller and the non-European savage, which was to recur more and more often in the late nineteenth century, dramatically underlined the yawning gulf between proper society and a large segment of the masses in the English capital.[28]

It was men like Shaw's travelling companions who articulated most fully and sharply the argument that city life undermined the morals of city dwellers. Clergymen were the moral critics *par excellence*. Their professional vocation led them quite naturally to denounce deviance from received canons of right conduct and to urge those who had engaged in it to return to the straight and narrow path. They felt a special obligation to carry out their task with regard to the city because this was the place in which the traditional institutions and rites they administered were being most strongly challenged by the forces of modern secularism. At the same time, many of them were increasingly sensitive to the whole range of social forces that militated against virtue among the faithful as well as among the unfaithful. In their preaching and in their writing, they thus went well beyond the ethical conduct of the isolated individual and the degree of his relationship or non-relationship to the Churches, examining and indicting the quality of urban society across the board.

For an early clerical critic of town life, one can do no better than to begin with Thomas Chalmers, a leading minister of the Scottish Kirk and a theologian whose high repute extended throughout the United Kingdom. Having moved in 1815 from the small parish of Kilmeny in Fife to one in Glasgow that was ten times larger, he was transferred five years later to another parish in Glasgow that was both the largest and the poorest in the city. He began shortly thereafter to publish a lengthy study of both the religious and the secular, or 'civic', aspects of town life.[29]

The first major work published anywhere in the century that explicitly identified and analyzed big cities as generically linked phenomena, it quite naturally placed heavy emphasis on precisely those problems that had occupied Chalmers most directly in his own work. Foremost among these was the difficult task of bringing the urban masses into lasting contact with organized Christianity. Surveying the state of religious observance in the urban setting, he concluded that 'a mass of heathenism' had attained to an enormous magnitude and density in Scotland's large towns. The basic reason for this sorry state of affairs was that too few churches served too big a population and that in large parishes, the ministers found it simply impossible to keep track of the members of their flock.[30]

The threats to the influence of the Kirk were paralleled by a more general lack of social cohesion in urban society as a whole. The social groups inhabiting the major centers of commerce were morally isolated from one another to a degree quite unprecedented in smaller provincial towns. Chalmers did not wish to be counted among the opponents of business and industry, but he insisted that in places like Glasgow the relation of manufacturers to their employees was 'greatly more an intercourse of collision, and greatly less an intercourse of kindliness, than is that of the higher orders in such towns as Bath, or Oxford, or Edinburgh'. As a result, to put it mildly, the two groups were 'mutually blind to the real cordialities and attractions which belong to each of them', and there was a constant danger of 'political restlessness'.[31]

Despite Chalmers' priority in time, it was clergymen of the established Church of England who voiced the greatest alarm about the conditions and the conduct of life in urban society. Many, preferring life among country squires for themselves to life among shop-owners or worse, were upset by the reality or the mere prospect of having to change their own bases of operations from their native grounds to *terra incognita*. To an even greater extent, they were distressed by the difficulties their Church was encountering in its efforts to build up a constituency among the great mass of newcomers to English towns. Part of the problem was the Anglicans' failure to build as many new churches as were needed to keep pace with the growing urban population. Much less active in this regard than their rivals, the Dissenters, they were able to provide sittings for only about one-fifth of the urban population by mid-century. Although the country as a whole was slightly more than half urban, only a little over a third of the Church's sittings were located in the towns. But it was also becoming clear that even when adequate accommodation was provided city dwellers still remained aloof. Various bits of statistical evidence suggested this conclusion in the 1830s and 1840s, and the unpleasant truth toward which they pointed was made undeniably clear in 1854, when the sections of the 1851 census pertaining to religious worship were finally released. They showed that on census Sunday less than half of the population of England and Wales had attended a religious service and that almost half of this number had gone to Dissenters' chapels. The situation looked especially bleak in the cities. In Manchester, for instance, only about a third of the population attended any religious service, and only a third of this minority went to Anglican churches. Statistics for other large towns followed much the same lines, revealing that even in the most densely crowded areas Anglican churches were often half empty. Urbanization was pushing the established Church away from the center of English society, and its clergy recognized that fact full well.[32]

Anglican anxiety came to the surface in its most extreme form in a

particularly wrathful sermon that was preached and published in 1844 by
James Shergold Boone, minister of St. John's Church in the Paddington
district of London. He gave his sermon in connection with Bishop
Blomfield's efforts to provide additional churches and clergymen for the
metropolis by means of a special fund to be accumulated for that purpose.
Like other ministers, he observed that precisely because of the centrality and
the influence of the big city in modern society, it was all the more vital for city
dwellers to be animated by a religious spirit. A powerful empire could
scarcely afford to find itself in a situation where its capital was given over to
the forces of darkness.[33]

This, however, was exactly the threat that Boone conjured up. His words
eloquently recalled the books of the Old Testament, with their denunciations
of Babylon and Nineveh, of Sodom and Gomorrah:

> The very extent of edifices, and the very collection of vast masses of human
> beings into one spot, humanity remaining what it is, must be fraught with moral
> infection.... Cities are the centres and theatres of human ambition, human
> cupidity, human pleasure. On the one side, the appetites, the passions, the
> carnal corruptions of man are forced, as in a hot-bed, into a rank and foul
> luxuriance; and countless evils, which would have elsewhere a feeble and
> difficult existence, are struck out into activity and warmth, by their mere contact
> with each other. On the other side, many restraints and safeguards are
> weakened, or even withdrawn.... In cities, there is a complication of evils:
> external forces co-operate with inward desires, in tainting, defiling, poisoning
> the character; in at once sharpening and perverting the intellect, and producing
> that crooked cleverness, the opposite and worst enemy of wisdom, which only
> renders its possessors more dexterous in sin and self-deception.

In Boone's view, the city fostered immorality both because it loosened
traditional restraints that had earlier militated against vice, thus giving free
play to base instincts, and also because it spread wicked temptations before
irresolute and unsupervised men and women.[34]

In such a place, in Boone's eyes, churches were absolutely necessary for the
preservation of a bare minimum of order and decency. No other agency of
social control could replace them. Boone exhorted his listeners to reflect upon
the blessings that would accrue from a vigorous program of church-building.
'In a word', he wrote, 'churches will create church-goers; and church-goers
will create churches'. But it was clear, although Boone did not say so
outright, that the very forces which made church attendance desirable would
severely hamper efforts of the sort he had in mind.[35]

In addition to jeremiads against the city such as Boone's, Anglicans also
offered more carefully reasoned and moderate criticisms that pointed to the
need for social reform within it. These writings reflected a general tendency
among leaders of the Church, starting in the 1830s, to speak out in favor of
legislative efforts to help the poor and downtrodden. Whereas earlier
churchmen had given little credence to positive action by government as a
means of alleviating social ills (Chalmers, for instance, had been a strong

proponent of economic self-help) now they turned increasingly away from *laissez-faire* in order to support the regulation of child labor, other factory legislation, and public health laws. Bishop Sumner of Chester (named Archbishop of Canterbury in 1848) and Bishop Blomfield, formerly adherents of hands-off liberalism, were coming to the realization that it was not enough simply to build more churches and preach more sermons. Spiritual endeavor would avail little in the absence of determined efforts to improve the degrading physical conditions that hardened the heart of the urbanite to the message of the Gospel. Their reasoning and their aims were obviously conservative. They supported social reform in order to strengthen their Church and at the same time to fortify the state to which it was bound against the threats of socialism and Chartism, but the fact that a far-reaching change was coming about in their whole approach to urban society cannot be denied.[36]

Two less highly placed clergymen who wrote about cites during the middle decades of the century elaborated some of these general concerns in more specific detail. Thomas Nunns, Curator of the St. Bartholomew Chapel in Birmingham, wrote an open letter to a leading Tory with a reputation for benevolent paternalism in which he lamented the low state of urban workers everywhere. The welfare of the whole community was intimately linked to that of its humblest members. It was, he wrote, 'impossible to live in a large town ... and to mix with all classes, without being forcibly impressed, that the lower orders are so large a class, and so influential, as very materially to affect, ay, and to go very far towards forming, the character of the community at large'. Anticipating the pride that was to become much more evident in his city several decades later, he argued that conditions there were relatively good compared to those in other towns. The fact that even Birmingham left so much to be desired was therefore especially troubling. Early and indiscriminate employment of boys and girls in the same workshops, lack of regard by the masters to the well-being of their employees, and the deficiencies of education in general all contributed to 'a degraded, a vicious, and a turbulent population'. To remedy this situation, he advocated factory legislation and more schools, in addition to the building of more churches and the recruitment of more clergymen.[37]

Charles Kingsley, the curate of Eversley in Hampshire, was also a novelist, historian, and miscellaneous writer who devoted his considerable literary energy and somewhat less abundant talent to the cause of Christian social reform. In his novel *Alton Locke* (1850), he explored the distress of the working classes in London in the 1840s and the Chartist agitation it had helped to engender. Kingsley used the hero of the novel as his instrument for driving home the message that revolution was not only impolitic but also immoral, but in his view the poor still had real grievances that deserved redress. Later in the decade, he spelled out his thoughts about cities in general more explicitly in a lecture on 'Great Cities and Their Influence for

Good and Evil'. After recalling the riots he had witnessed in Bristol when a boy, he asserted that 'the social state of a city depends directly on its moral state, and ... on the physical state of that city, on the food, water, air, and lodging of its inhabitants'. Social relationships, morality, and the physical environment were all linked to one another, and they all cried out for improvement.[38]

Men engaged in law enforcement or politics did not for the most part reflect as broadly on cities as did clergymen, but they had just as much reason to ponder the implications of urban growth for social control. The dangers of individual lawlessness and collective protest in urban settings intruded directly into the day-to-day experience of such men, and some of them sought to communicate their anxieties about these threats to a broad reading public. Archibald Alison, the son of a Scottish clergyman and a student of the law, was the sheriff of Lanarkshire when, in the early 1840s, he published a general treatise on population in which he excoriated cities on moral as well as demographic grounds. 'It is there', he wrote, 'that vice has spread her temptations, and pleasure her seductions, and folly her allurements: that guilt is encouraged by the hope of impunity, and idleness fostered by the frequency of example'. The result was contagious corruption, which manifested itself in illegitimacy, in drink, and in crime. During the 1850s, the versatile Alison turned his attention to the history of Europe since 1815. Unlike most historians at the time, he reflected extensively on social as well as political developments, and urban problems again came to the fore. He sought here to link society and politics by showing that the passion for democracy was to be found chiefly among townsmen, 'among whom numbers, closely aggregated together, have awakened a feeling of strength, and increasing wealth has engendered the desire for independence'. Throughout Europe, the rise of the town had been central to the outbreak of revolution in recent decades.[39]

Sir Charles Shaw, after serving as police chief of Manchester, described the residents of industrial cities as 'the debris, which the vast whirlpool of human affairs has deposited here in one of its eddies, associated, but not united; contiguous, but not connected'. One result of the attenuation of social bonds was the growth of crime. In Manchester, he asserted, more than seven times as many prisoners had been apprehended in 1840 as in 1825. The breakdown of social control indicated by such statistics did not simply threaten the tranquility of the manufacturing districts. Whatever happened there would affect society at large, and positive steps (e.g., reduction of working hours and implementation of sanitary reforms) had to be taken to prevent injury to the whole nation.[40]

Robert Slaney, a liberal M.P. between 1826 and 1841 and again between 1847 and his death in 1862 and a prominent member of the Health of Towns Association in the mid-1840s, injected a still stronger emphasis on reform into his writings about the urban poor. The nation as a whole had made great strides forward since the beginning of the century, but the working classes were in many respects worse off than before, both relatively and absolutely. Physical evils had given rise to moral ones, and the result was rising discontent. 'Do we wonder', he asked, 'that their minds are soured, and that they are ready to listen to bad advisers, and to look to short remedies?' Slaney feared that unless the 'extensive evils' were attended to speedily they would 'be the cause of great suffering to multitudes, of danger to the peace of the country and to the property of its inhabitants'. To say this was by no means to reject the city but rather to underline the necessity of improving it for the sake of the entire country.[41]

Journalists, publicists, and other authors of works of social description depended heavily upon urban newspapers, magazines, and publishers to print their essays and books, and they depended equally upon the urban middle classes to buy and read them, but many turned a highly critical eye nonetheless on the places in which they lived and worked. There is no point in trying to catalogue all of the occasional pieces with a negative thrust that were written during these years on such themes as 'town and country', 'town versus country', and so on, many of whose authors remained anonymous. The most feasible way to begin to approach these writers is to focus on a small number who concentrated on London.

Two highly prolific writers of popular books stood out in the 1830s and 1840s. Robert Mudie could hardly have announced his intentions more clearly than he did when he gave his study of the metropolis the title *London and the Londoners: Or a Second Judgement of Babylon the Great*. Mudie's denunciation of the capital was as biblical in its thrust and tone as if it had been written by a clergyman. The 'perfect disorder' of the city's inanimate components seemed in his view to be at least matched if not surpassed by the incomprehensibility of — and moral chaos in — the city as a whole. Preoccupied with their own affairs, Londoners ignored the needs of their fellow citizens, and the result was 'desolation, where every street is a crowd; the world around, and yet comfort from no lip, and pity from no eye'. Consequently, while the rich indulged their penchant for profligacy at pleasure spots such as Vauxhall Gardens, the poor sought to redress their grievances through theft and robbery.[42]

James Grant, another popular author, wrote repeatedly about many aspects of life in London. Less censorious than Mudie, he was fascinated by the metropolitan color and excitement that provided him with subjects about which to write. But although he made his case more moderately, the basic point was still the same. In this vast entity, 'a little world in itself', sharp contrasts between social groups whose members shared little in common — least of all sympathy with one another — were the rule. Men were oblivious of their fellows. 'The teeming population on the pavement all pass each other with as much indifference as if they had not eyes in their heads, or were so many inanimate objects moved by machinery. They seem as if they did not belong to the same species, or as if it were a crime to take cognisance, in any way, of each other, as they pass along'. Those who lived in the fashionable districts knew little if anything about the deep distress that prevailed among the poor. Grant admitted that London exhibited 'the extremes of virtue' along with its many vices, but on the whole he gave much more attention to the shadows than to the lights of London life.[43]

In the 1850s and the early 1860s, three other journalists assembled critical books about London society from articles that had originally appeared in magazines and newspapers. Their works were even less cohesive than those of Mudie and Grant, but they revealed a much sharper eye for the textures of lower-class life. George Godwin, who edited the foremost British architectural journal, *The Builder*, collected some of the writings he had previously published in that magazine in two volumes: *London Shadows: A Glance at the Homes of the Thousands* (1854) and *Town Swamps and Social Bridges*(1859). These books illuminated the darker corners of the metropolis, showing how poor residential and sanitary conditions of the sort detailed by Chadwick more than a decade earlier had produced moral as well as physical pestilence and the breakdown of social organization. Crime, unemployment, poverty, disease, superstition, and alcoholism were all related aspects of the general urban morass.[44] John Hollingshead, a popular writer on many subjects, collected ten letters he had published in the *Morning Post* in *Ragged London in 1861* (1861). His essays examined the living conditions of the poor in all parts of the city, including ragged schools, model lodging houses, and charitable institutions, and then provided abundant evidence of 'metropolitan social degradation'.

The year that witnessed the appearance of *Ragged London* also saw the publication of the first three volumes of one of the greatest of all the nineteenth-century studies of urban society, a work that is still mined assiduously by social historians: Henry Mayhew's *London Labour and the London Poor*. They consisted largely of articles that had first appeared between 1849 and 1850 in the *Morning Chronicle*, although a fourth volume (published in 1862) consisted mostly of new material. Mayhew made no effort to survey all of London society. Nor did he attempt to investigate even the working classes in their entirety. He undertook instead to depict, in encyclopedic detail, the life styles of 'street sellers, street buyers, street finders, street performers, street artisans, [and] street labourers'. Combining copious statistics with seemingly endless case studies, he provided a panoramic view of the customs, the language, the religion, and the politics of the hundreds of thousands of men, women, and children who worked out of doors and frequently lived like nomads, without any fixed abode. In his pages, the reader could safely brush up against costermongers and rag-pickers, Jewish pedlars and chimney-sweeps, organ-grinders and dock-laborers, cab-drivers and vagrants, prostitutes and thieves. His massive tomes were descriptive rather than analytic, and they failed to develop a coherent theme, but they did evince deep dissatisfaction with the lot of the urban lower classes. Although many of their members appeared via Mayhew's skillful vignettes to be resourceful and vibrant personalities, the main point he wanted to make was that their 'misery, ignorance, and vice, amidst all the immense wealth and great knowledge of "the first city of the world"' was a national disgrace. It was hardly surprising that Mayhew's together with Hollingshead's, prompted one reviewer to refer to 'the drawbacks ... the depravity, and ... the weak shamelessness of the city life of the nineteenth century'.[45]

In addition to the numerous and mostly undistinguished individuals whom we have encountered so far, a handful of leading thinkers and social novelists contributed their efforts to the critique of urban life. The great 'sages' of the Victorian period, who sought to imbue their contemporaries with moral wisdom and a taste for righteousness, and other authors of literary works whose reputations have survived the years in which they were written, seldom grappled directly with urban themes. Some, especially imaginative writers, commented on the city at best indirectly, or simply avoided it. There were nonetheless numerous occasions when the literature they produced revealed the impact of the great controversies that raged about them — and when they brought their own refined sensibilities to bear on the towns of their time.[46] Many of these writers combined a growing awareness of social problems with a special sensitivity to the big city's cultural and aesthetic defects. Moreover, much of their discontent also evinced a good deal of nostalgia for earlier and supposedly better times. These were the writers who formulated the classic indictments of the Victorian industrial city.

In the early part of the period, the conservative poet and historian Robert Southey articulated a backward-looking version of discontent that was redolent of romantic nostalgia for the Middle Ages. His *Sir Thomas More: Or Colloquies on the Progress and Prospects of Modern Society*, a fictional dialogue between one Montesinos (a spokesman for modern ideas) and the ghost of the sixteenth-century statesman, invoked tradition and authority against the ills of urban modernity. Through More, he asserted that ordinary workers were far worse off in the industrial city than their forefathers had been in the countryside. 'They are worse fed', he judged, 'than when they were hunters, fishers, and herdsmen; their clothing and habitations are little better, and, in comparison with those of the higher classes, immeasurably worse'. Moreover, independence from their superiors had been purchased at the price of 'the loss of kindly feelings and ennobling attachments'. London was not only 'the seat of intellect and empire' but also 'a wilderness wherein they, who live like wild beasts upon their fellow creatures, find prey and cover', and Southey feared the day when the streets of the metropolis might erupt like a volcano. The reason for this state of affairs in his view was not the mere size of the city but the fact that it was animated by the pursuit of material gain and the spirit of greed. It symbolized, in short, a commercial way of life that Southey held in utter contempt, preferring instead to look back fondly on the putative goodness of simpler and more generous times.[47]

A much greater writer and critic of the age, Thomas Carlyle, approached the city still more circuitously a few years later in his *Sartor Resartus*, a work written under the influence of German romanticism that treated the life and thought of an imaginary Professor Teufelsdröckh. Carlyle concentrated his thoughts on the city in this work in a few pages that treat an imaginary town whose very name, Weissnichtwo (meaning literally Know-not-Where), enables it to serve as a symbol of towns everywhere. As Teufelsdröckh looks down upon the city, he sees 'all that wasp-nest or bee-hive' and witnesses its inhabitants in 'their wax-laying and honey-making, and poison-brewing, and choking by sulphur'. He is revolted by smoke and noise, luxury and poverty, corruption and violence: 'all these heaped together, with nothing but a little carpentry and masonry between them'. Like Southey, Carlyle castigated greed, competition, and class struggle among people who were 'crammed in, like salted fish in their barrel; or weltering, shall I say, like an Egyptian pitcher of tamed vipers, each struggling to get its head above the others'. Here was a classic statement of the view that urban sinfulness manifested itself not just in the moral laxity of the poor but more generally in the selfishness displayed by almost everyone.[48]

The real city figured no more prominently in most poems or novels than did Weissnichtwo in *Sartor Resartus*, but in the work of two novelists who wrote around mid-century it was omnipresent and extraordinarily vivid, its moral failings delineated in exquisite and heart-rending detail. Elizabeth Gaskell, the wife of a Unitarian minister, wrote from first-hand experience when she produced a searching depiction of the urban milieu, *Mary Barton: A Tale of Manchester Life* (1848). The central themes of the book were poverty and class conflict in the cotton capital of the north between 1839 and 1841. Gaskell wrote,

> It need excite no surprise then to learn that a bad feeling between working-men and the upper classes became very strong in this season of privation. The indigence and sufferings of the operatives induced a suspicion in the minds of many of them, that their legislators, their magistrates, their employers, and even the ministers of religion, were, in general, their oppressors and enemies; and were in league for their prostration and enthrallment. The most deplorable and enduring evil which arose out of this period of commercial depression ... was this feeling of alienation between the different classes of society.

Through the story of John Barton, his family, his friends, and his middle-class antagonists, Gaskell made these conflicts immediately intelligible. She did not reject the industrial city as such. In fact, her portrayal of Alice Wilson demonstrated the hollowness of nostalgia for the lost world of the country-side. But in this novel (though not in her later *North and South*, to which we shall turn shortly), her overall view of the city in which she lived was decidedly gloomy. She earnestly hoped and believed that her fellow Mancunians could escape from the moral and social predicament in which they found themselves, but her conclusion suggested that some of them would have to cross the Atlantic in order to do so.[49]

Charles Dickens admired Gaskell but of course surpassed her, both in the range of experience he could encompass and in his imaginative power, which ensured that his novels would reach an enormous audience and do more than any others to shape men's consciousness of the Victorian city. London provided the setting for large parts of almost all of Dickens' novels, and he evoked its houses and its shops, its prisons and its theaters, its weather and its river, and above all its people on the basis of an intimate knowledge possessed by few if any other writers. Walter Bagehot wrote aptly of Dickens, 'He describes London like a special correspondent for posterity'. Dickens was drawn to the metropolis and to a lesser extent to other cities as subjects, and he evinced a strong personal attraction to London throughout most of his adult life, but increasingly his fascination with the city had to be understood in terms of what he himself called 'the attraction of repulsion'. The exuberant joy in beholding the urban spectacle displayed in the early *Sketches by Boz* (1836-37) and the acceptance of the city implicit in *Nicholas Nickleby* (1839) and *Dombey and Son* (1848) gave way after mid-century to a darker view of London that had also asserted itself in some of Dickens' other early works, notably *Oliver Twist* (1838). In that view, London was a mysterious labyrinth, physically and morally isolated from the rest of the world, a city of desolation and death. Dickens signalled his growing pessimism when he wrote in 1851 to Edward Bulwer Lytton, 'London is a vile place.... Whenever I come back from the country now, and see that great heavy canopy lowering over the treetops, I wonder what on earth I do there except on obligation'. In *Bleak House* (1853), London was indeed a vile place, its evil attributes powerfully symbolized by poisonous fog. In *Little Dorrit* (1857), the city appeared to be a similarly hostile environment, inimical to all forms of life. Its grimness is repeatedly evoked via images of the wilderness, the desert, the prison, and the tomb. And in *Our Mutual Friend* (1865), Dickens created an aura both of darkness and of wastefulness through his rendering of the Thames and his use of images of dust-heaps.[50]

Dickens had little to say about the newer industrial cities, except in *Hard Times* (1854), which was set in the imaginary Coketown. This town, an exaggerated and distorted version of Manchester, took on even more fearful dimensions than London at its worst. The creation of the likes of the cruel and hypocritical Josiah Bounderby, it displayed physical aspects that bore vivid witness to moral ugliness and soul-destroying monotony. As Dickens put it on the famous opening page of Chapter 5 (Bk. I),

> It was a town of red brick, or of brick that would have been red if the smoke and ashes had allowed it; but as matters stood it was a town of unnatural red and black like the painted face of a savage. It was a town of machinery and tall

chimneys, out of which interminable serpents of smoke trailed themselves for ever and ever, and never got uncoiled. It had a black canal in it, and a river that ran purple with ill-smelling dye, and vast piles of buildings full of windows where there was a rattling and a trembling all day long, and where the piston of the steam-engine worked monotonously up and down like the head of an elephant in a state of melancholy madness. It contained several large streets all very like one another, and many small streets still more like one another, inhabited by people equally like one another, who all went in and out at the same hours, with the same sound upon the same pavements, to do the same work, and to whom every day was the same as yesterday and tomorrow, and every year the counterpart of the last and the next.

Here was the Dickensian view of urban life at its gloomiest and most apocalyptic — a view that has deeply influenced countless later commentaries on the industrial city.

For the years after Dickens had finished his last major work, the most searching critics of town life among leading men of letters were Matthew Arnold and John Ruskin. Both of these writers, deeply revered as guides to right thinking and good conduct during their own lifetimes and long thereafter, were sorely troubled by the whole thrust of the civilization that was emerging in the modern town. Arnold, in his classic *Culture and Anarchy* (1869), displayed little tolerance for the middle-class Philistines and the working-class Populace of England's cities, who lacked both discipline and refinement. His response to the modern city was essentially a cultivated man's rejection of what he saw as ubiquitous disorder and boorishness, endemic in society as a whole but particularly offensive in the crowded towns where men thought first and foremost about getting and spending. He wrote with obvious scorn about London's 'unutterable external hideousness ... with its internal canker of *publice egestas, privatim opulentia*' and contrasted it with 'the beauty and sweetness' of Oxford, which he cherished as a guardian and exemplar of the great cultural tradition.[51]

Ruskin, probably the most influential of all the Victorian sages, referred repeatedly to cities in his denunciations of the modern world, and in so doing he summed up — albeit only in bits and pieces — the whole tradition of nostalgic social and cultural criticism that had begun with the early romantics and persisted through the writings of Southey, Carlyle, Arnold, and many of the social novelists. Like Arnold, he excoriated both greed and ugliness, regarding the second as a product of the first and both as hallmarks of the commercial and industrial city. In a lecture delivered at the Town Hall in Bradford in 1864, he told his audience that their architecture, with its chimneys 'more mighty and costly than cathedral spires', had been dedicated to their 'great Goddess of "Getting-on"', and he implied that its aesthetic merits were not even worth discussing. The following year, at the Working Men's Institute in Camberwell, he echoed Dickens' description of Coketown when he referred to 'that great foul city of London there, — rattling, growling, smoking, stinking, — a ghastly heap of fermenting brickwork, pouring out poison at every pore'.[52]

Ruskin went beyond merely castigating the city for its physical ugliness and indicted it for its injurious impact on the life of the mind. In a late essay (1881), he attributed the supposed morbidness of modern fiction to 'the hot fermentation ... of the population crowded into large cities', and he voiced the fear that the 'trampling pressure' and 'pollution' of the 'staggering mass that chokes and crushes' would melt him into mud. Ruskin thus asserted in his inimitable and highly influential prose that quantity was inimical to quality and that in the city it worked to the constant detriment of artists and thinkers, who were both its critics and its victims. Ruskin was no Tory. He did as much as any English thinker to prepare the way for socialism. Nonetheless, he was a romantic anti-urbanist, whose values were rooted very much in the past and whose hostility to the modern town grew in large measure out of the feeling that city life in the present threatened to flatten his own heightened sensibilities and those of other men who inhabited his cultural universe.[53]

Some of what the urban critics, especially the cultural sages, had to say about Victorian towns suggested an aversion to big cities as such. It seemed to imply a romantic desire to recapture the world of the small town and the countryside, or in some other way to turn back the social clock. But complaints about contemporary towns did not have uniformly conservative implications. Most, though by no means all, of those who spoke harshly of the urban present drew their readers' attention to urban ills for the purpose of encouraging them to seek urban remedies. Many of the Victorian men and women who wrote about the various deficiencies of the towns they inhabited did so precisely because they fervently believed that these places could indeed be made more livable. They sought not to escape the town but to improve it. In this sense, much of the commentary that was clearly negative shared a great deal in common with the case for the defense.

The case for the defense

Although the most familiar names in the history of high Victorian culture offered a view of their cities that was generally somber and sometimes critical almost to the point of despair, numerous other writers spoke out in favor of the urban society emerging in their midst. It was inevitable that their voices should be raised and heard and that the city should become a subject for lively debate, not simply a target for criticism and scorn. Men and women were, after all, flocking to the towns in great numbers. Whether they did so on balance more because they were repelled by conditions in the countryside or because they were attracted by what they thought awaited them in the town is a question that need not concern us here. The main point is that there seemed to be a *prima facie* case for the defense of the towns that rested in the first place — though by no means exclusively — on the simple fact of their extraordinary growth. The rapid increase of the urban population bore effective witness to some sort of magnetic quality that could not be based on misinformation and illusion alone, and in the eyes of many observers it held out the hope of progress rather than the threat of decline.

Among the earliest and most vocal defenders of British towns were liberal writers who highly valued the economic growth and material progress that urbanization helped make possible. They rightly recognized the close links among the city, industry, and commerce, and they welcomed the expansion of all three as the harbinger of a better life for the great bulk of the nation's inhabitants. They might admit the existence of short-term drawbacks, but they regarded the long-term prognosis as distinctly favorable to the wealth and health of their fellow citizens.

Thomas Babington Macaulay, the brilliant Whig essayist who was soon to become an M.P. and later to win great renown as Britain's leading historian, articulated this viewpoint effectively in 1830 in his famous review of Southey's *Colloquies*. He derided Southey for failing to substantiate his views with any facts whatsoever, and he went on to point out that the countryside suffered from far greater poverty than was to be found in areas where industry had taken hold. Macaulay admitted that death rates still stood higher in the towns than in the country, but he pointed out that the urban-rural difference had declined markedly since the eighteenth century, and he argued that urban progress in this regard was attributable to the increasing national prosperity being produced by and in the growing industrial cities.[54]

The themes of material prosperity and physical health were taken up subsequently by the statistician George R. Porter. Porter displayed great satisfaction when he wrote about the buildings that had been constructed and the public works that had been undertaken in London and other English towns during the recent past. Waterloo Bridge, the Houses of Parliament, and Bethlehem Hospital, among other projects, would entitle the men of his day to be remembered for 'the splendour, the durability, and the practical utility' of the works that had engaged their energies. Much the same boast could be made by leading citizens in other towns. 'Hardly any one of the large manufacturing and trading towns of the kingdom can be mentioned which does not afford this proof of the existence and the employment of increasing wealth'. Like Macaulay, he pointed out that although mortality in the city was high relative to the countryside, the long-term trend was promising. Crude death rates had declined in Manchester from 1:25 in 1750 to 1:49 in 1830, and in the county of Middlesex (much of which was included in London) from 1:35 in 1801 to 1:53 in 1840. These improvements in the vitality of urban populations proved that men who crowded together in factories were by no means condemned to live miserably and briefly.[55]

The urban economy — like many other facets of town life — found its most enthusiastic advocates among men who wrote about the virtues of individual cities rather than about the advantages of cities in general. An historian of Nottingham, an early center of hosiery manufacturing in the Midlands, celebrated the commercial development of that town by asserting at the outset of his work that 'in industry and useful invention' it equaled any other in Britain. Nottingham's greatness lay primarily in its trade, which brushed off 'the rust of barbarism' and replaced 'the rude customs of seclusion' with 'politeness of behaviour' by begetting 'refined wants' and fostering 'the germs of invention'. Henry Smithers, who described the institutions and the economy of Liverpool, proudly proclaimed, 'Liverpool offers few examples of those venerable ruins which mark the devotions or the superstitions of our ancestors. Like Tyre, it owes its fame to its commerce, and that but of comparatively recent growth; nevertheless, the infant Hercules hath already acquired gigantic stature'. He admitted that according to recent census reports crude death rates in Liverpool far exceeded those in England and Wales as a whole, but these statistics did not seriously embarrass him. In the first place, conveniently overlooking immigration, he argued that in view of the rapid increase of population the reports were probably inaccurate. Then he shifted his position, maintaining that if there was a high death rate it could be attributed largely to 'extraneous causes' (in particular the great influx of immigrants!). 'All these circumstances combined', he wrote, 'account for the too great ratio of mortality in Liverpool, without at all impugning the doctrine of the healthfulness of the place'.[56]

Sir George Head, on his travels through numerous commercial and industrial cities in 1835, dispensed his praise even more effusively. He was fascinated by the technological marvels he could observe everywhere he went. Describing a tunnel under Liverpool that led to the Edge Hill railroad station, he wrote, 'This vast subterranean excavation, a mile and a quarter in length ... through the bowels of the earth, and below the site of a populous town, is a truly wonderful performance'. Along the waterfront, 'the beauty and symmetry of the arrangements which prevail among the warehouses' impressed him similarly. In Leeds, the machinery in a cloth factory led him to compare the building to 'a temple, dedicated by man, grateful for the stupendous power that moved within, to Him who built the universe'. In a machine-building factory, he was overcome with a 'feeling of veneration'. There could be 'no spectacle more grateful to the heart of an Englishman than ... to observe the features of each hard-working mechanic blackened by smoke, yet radiant with the light of intelligence'. Like his more famous contemporary, Andrew Ure (author of *The Philosophy of Manufactures*, 1835), he discerned no misery or fatigue in the faces of the workers, even among the children. 'I saw around me', he assured his readers, 'a crowd of apparently happy beings, working in lofty well-ventilated buildings, with whom a comparison could no more in fairness be drawn with the solitary weaver plying his shuttle from morning to night in his close dusty den, than is the bustle and occupation of life with soul-destroying solitude'. So much for the putative joys and benefits of working and living in the countryside when compared with the opportunities afforded by the industrial town.[57]

The passages just quoted make it quite clear that men such as Head prized their cities for many reasons other than purely material ones. They saw the urban economy and other aspects of city life as forces for moral uplift and social progress, which were to elevate the urbanite well above the retrograde status of the countryman. But Head did not develop this theme to any great extent, leaving the task instead to a trio of liberals who reflected on cities in more general terms in the early 1840s.

William Cooke Taylor, the son of an Irish manufacturer, was a Whiggish writer on historical, political, and other topics, who went to Lancashire after the onset of the commercial crisis of 1842 to study the area's industries and the life of its workers. He reported on what he saw in a collection of letters whose publication was sponsored (behind the scenes) by the Anti-Corn Law League, which had been agitating for several years for abolition of the high tariffs on imported grain.[58] His work was in part an exercise in political propaganda, but it offered much more than that, providing a sensitive and well-informed picture of city life in a large part of the industrial north. It was in the same genre as Head's earlier book but far more penetrating in its observations and judgements of the urban scene.

Taylor did not turn a blind eye to the sufferings of urban workers or to the other problems presented by urban growth. Having written earlier on topics such as crime, poverty, overcrowding, and pollution in London and Glasgow as well as Manchester,[59] he had no wish to deny the existence of such evils now. His initially unfavorable impression of Manchester and other manufacturing towns seemed to persist throughout much of what he wrote in 1842. He confessed that one could not 'contemplate these "crowded hives" without feelings of anxiety and apprehension almost amounting to dismay'. The urban population constituted 'an aggregate of masses, our conceptions of which clothe themselves in terms that express something portentous and fearful', and he spoke of it as 'an ocean which must, at some future and no distant time, bear all the elements of society aloft upon its bosom, and float them — Heaven knows whither'. Taylor laid bare the source of many of the city's greatest difficulties when he referred to the spatial subdivision of Manchester 'into districts in which relative poverty and wealth form the demarkation of frontiers. The rich lose sight of the poor, or only recognise them when attention is forced to their existence by their appearance as vagrants, mendicants, or delinquents'.[60]

But in so far as Taylor criticized the city, he did so primarily in order to defend the factory and thus to attack the Corn Laws. Poverty and high death rates in the cities resulted not from industrialization or even from defects in the towns themselves but rather from the influx of migrants and especially from the artificially high cost of bread. Once that indefensible impediment to working-class well-being was eliminated, the manufacturing population would prosper in every way under an inherently beneficial system of production. Such criticism of the city was tactical, not fundamental, and it had nothing to do with aristocratic and traditionalist hostility to modernity as such. It accepted both the inevitability and the desirability of an urban-industrial world.[61]

Despite the passages in which Taylor wrote about the especially good fortune of those workers who labored in rural mills in the area outside Manchester (e.g., in the villages of Turton and Egerton),[62] he had much to say that pointed up the advantages of life in the larger town. In his opening letter, he observed that the workers, even in seasons of extreme distress, resisted every effort to send them back to the agricultural districts whence they had come. The industrial worker, he noted, 'faces famine rather than return to the farm'. Taylor did not argue that the worker made this choice for any reason other than the hope of once again obtaining relatively high wages, but it is significant that two pages later he praised Mancunians not only for their businesslike qualities but also for their 'zeal for religion, charity, and science'. He was deeply impressed not only by the literary and scientific institutions that catered to the middle classes but also by the lyceums, which united the advantages of temperance reading-rooms and schools for adults. For only twopence per week, operatives could use a library and attend lectures and occasional parties at which they imbibed both tea and ideas. These men and their families were certainly no less moral than than the members of 'the most primitive agricultural population'. Despite the lingering tendency to regard the life of the savage as more natural and therefore more virtuous than that of the civilized man, the facts proved that towns and townsmen enjoyed moral superiority. Factories in particular, in Taylor's view, exerted a strongly beneficial influence, with the result that, 'in soundness of moral principle and propriety of moral conduct', the operatives who worked within them equaled 'the average of any other class or order in the British empire'. The divergence between this view of the city and the one espoused only a few years earlier by Peter Gaskell was nearly total.[63]

In 1843, Edward Baines strengthened the defense in another report on social conditions in 'the manufacturing districts', the widely used term that by now served as a designation for the most densely populated areas in the kingdom outside the metropolis. Baines was a typical middle-class representative of northern urban culture and a proud spokesman for the dominant values of the places in which he had been raised. Born in Leeds, he was educated at a Dissenters' grammar school in Manchester, and he remained active in the affairs of the Congregational chapel in his native city for many years after he returned there. While still a young man, he became the editor of the *Leeds Mercury*. Like Taylor, he propagandized in favor of mechanics' institutes and factories and against the Corn Laws. He was an ardent liberal, whose editorial position enabled him to address a much larger audience than the readership for Taylor's *Notes*.[64]

Baines vehemently rejected what he regarded as the distorted and malicious aspersions cast upon the industrial areas by supposedly well-intentioned reformers. With Lord Ashley in the lead, they had painted a bleak picture of life in the manufacturing towns in order to intensify their campaign for legislation that would, in Baines' view, unfairly and injuriously regulate the relationships between factory-owners and their employees. The debate about factory legislation, along with the one about free trade, was crucially important to mid-nineteenth-century liberals, and it led Baines quite naturally to use every weapon in his arsenal.[65]

On this occasion, he undertook a defense not of the factories themselves but of the larger communities in which they had arisen. His main point was that the inhabitants of the centers of industry stood superior to the inhabitants both of London and of the countryside according to any and all criteria of moral excellence. Evidence that supposedly proved excessive criminality in Leeds was not at all representative of the community as a whole. Far from committing a disproportionate number of offenses against the law, young people employed in the factories seldom came before the local magistrates, and, Baines pointed out, the city had not experienced a riot of any kind since 1807. Turning to the manufacturing towns as a group, he presented statistics that showed more sittings *per capita* in churches and chapels than in London and an abundance of Sunday schools and day schools as well. Asserting confidently that this evidence fully vindicated the voluntary principle in the area of education, he admitted that there was 'much ignorance and moral evil amongst us' but went on to declare that it was 'mainly of a character which no Government and no laws can reach'. In any case, the religious and educational institutions that had sprung up as a result of the 'spontaneous zeal and Christian principle of the inhabitants' had maintained the population of these towns at a level of right thinking and good conduct that compared quite favorably with the rest of the country. Drawing up the final balance, he wrote,

> Comparing these seats of Manufactures, then, either with the great Metropolis of the land, — with the selectest portions of Westminster, in the very presence of the throne, the legislature, the aristocracy, and the hierarchy, — with the Arcadias of Dorsetshire and the South, — and I may add, even with the learned shades of Oxford, — I maintain, that we have no need to blush or hang our heads, whether you make the comparison in regard to Education, Morality, Religion, Industry, or Order.

Men who denied this proposition, Baines charged, did so not because they could demonstrate clear-cut offenses against social and moral order but rather because they rightly detected and wrongly loathed the 'taint' of religious dissent, which inclined them to condemn the manufacturers' religion, their education, and all the rest of their good works as well.[66]

The links between religious dissent and liberalism on the one hand and an affirmative attitude toward urban civilization on the other appear quite clearly in the career of a contemporary of Baines', a man to whom Baines referred frequently and favorably in his own pamphlet. Robert Vaughan, also a Congregationalist, had accepted a call to serve as minister of a church in Kensington in 1825 and had become professor of history at the University of London in 1834. While in London, he established close contacts with leading Whigs and succeeded in drawing men of high social standing to his services. In 1843, he became president and professor of theology in the Lancashire Independent College in Manchester, where he gave his inaugural address on the topic of 'Protestant Nonconformity'. The fact that the Nonconformist Churches had done relatively well compared with the Church of England in the large towns doubtless explains a large part of the enthusiasm for urban society that Vaughan displayed so exuberantly in his *Age of Great Cities: Or, Modern Society Viewed in Its Relation to Intelligence, Morals, and Religion* (1843) — a book that stands out as the most sweeping and impassioned statement of the urban ethos to appear anytime in England or anywhere in the century.[67]

Vaughan's range extended far beyond Taylor's and Baines', reaching back to antiquity and out to the European continent. In his view, cities had played a leading role in the drama of human progress from early times up to the present. They had served as 'centres of vast experiments in the history of society', and he sought to place them on as large a stage as he could. The rise of cities, far from symbolizing and reinforcing man's alienation from God, reflected 'the designs of Providence'. It was, Vaughan wrote, 'as much a part of the purpose of the Creator with regard to man, that he should build towns, as that he should till the land'. Man, he continued, was 'constituted to realize his destiny from his association with man, more than from any contact with places', and as he pursued that destiny in the city he did the Lord's work as well as his own.[68]

The intellectual stimulation that individuals derived from living in close proximity to one another provided the key to the city's beneficence in general. 'The picturesque ... may be with the country', Vaughan declared, 'but the intellectual ... must be with the town'. Only through association could 'the aptitudes of the human mind' attain their full potential. Urban intellectual superiority had demonstrated itself long ago in the physical sciences. The remaining monuments of Thebes, Persepolis, Athens, and Rome were 'so many mutilated treatises on the science of the ancients', and many mechanical inventions bore witness to urban intellect in the present. Cities similarly fostered 'just and enlightened views in relation to political science', encouraging men to familiarize themselves with public affairs and thus strengthening the principle of popular rule at every level of government. Disputing the cultural pretensions of the landed aristocracy, Vaughan asserted that urban wealth provided the *sine qua non* for artistic excellence:

'... the successful patronage of the fine arts depends less upon the existence of noble families, than upon the existence of prosperous cities'. So too with regard to literature. Cities had produced not only the affected literature of aristocrats prevalent in Periclean Athens, Augustan Rome, and Paris and London during the reign of Louis XIV but also a more robust popular literature, dating from the Reformation, and a reading public to consume it. 'Great cities ... have now raised a large portion of our people from their former state of ignorance and sensuality, to their present measure of acquaintance with letters and with the means of mental improvement'.[69]

Vaughan understandably devoted much more of his attention to 'popular intelligence' than to the sciences and high culture. Instrumental though the cities were in his eyes for the creation of ideas, it was their part in the diffusion of ideas that impressed him most, and he went on at some length to praise them for their schools and their other educational institutions. These facilities, together with the general ambience created by the sheer numbers of inhabitants colliding fruitfully with one another, sharpened men's wits and thus contributed continually to 'greater general intelligence'.[70]

The march of intellect, in Vaughan's view, made men more virtuous as well as more acute. Knowledge and morality went hand in hand, and as men became better educated they became more assiduous and effective in the practice of righteousness. They learned, as he argued in his chapter on political science, not only how to win freedom but also how to use it wisely and well. Far from lapsing into tumult and chaos, they happily combined liberty with order. Vaughan admitted the existence of moral plague spots on the face of the city. He recognized the 'hazard of infection' to which the pure were exposed in crowded towns. Man's natural tendency was 'to imitate the evil rather than the good', and he seemed to have every inducement to do so in places where temptations beckoned and restraints slackened. But Vaughan denied that factory operatives were on the whole any more depraved than agricultural workers, and he sought to combat fears of urban lawlessness by portraying them as evidence of that very intelligence which was conducive to social improvement. The belief that the incidence of crime had grown did not rest on an upsurge of bad behavior but rather on more precise definitions of criminal acts and on heightened awareness of evils that had formerly remained hidden from public view. In this regard, better roads and more newspapers had been decisive. In any event, enhanced intelligence would re-establish the necessary equilibrium between material and moral improvement. 'The sphere of our responsibility', he confidently asserted, 'widens with every increase of intelligence, wealth, and association; but it does not widen as opening new sourcs of temptation, more than as presenting new considerations on the side of resisting temptation'.[71]

Vaughan summarized his hopeful view of the harmonious interrelationships between right thinking and good conduct in the world of the city as follows:

If large towns may be regarded as giving shelter and maturity to some of the worst forms of depravity, it must not be forgotten that to such towns, almost entirely, society is indebted for that higher tone of moral feeling by which vice is in so great measure discountenanced, and for those voluntary combinations of the virtuous in the cause of purity, humanity, and general improvement, which hold so conspicuous a place in our social history. It is not only true that from cities good laws, liberal arts, and letters, have, in the main, their origin, but no less true that spontaneous efforts in the cause of public morals, and in aid of the necessitous ... are found almost exclusively among citizens. ... Our conclusions on this subject, therefore, will not be just, except as we place in one view with the evils which are generated by the state of society in large towns, the good also which only that condition of society is found competent to call into existence.

In this view, the city's greatest virtue was that it created within itself the intellectual and moral energies necessary to remedy its own worst failings. It regulated and corrected itself, eliminating its dysfunctions almost automatically as it advanced from one equilibrium to another. [72]

Although Baines admitted almost no urban defects, Taylor, Vaughan, and other spokesmen for the city could not and did not deny that the urban landscape was marred by serious social problems. They preferred to minimize them, but their eyes and ears were open, and by mid-century at the latest they certainly knew about unsanitary drainage, overcrowded housing, and the decline of religious observance. These conditions made it clear that much work had to be undertaken to make the town as favorable to life and virtue as it ought to be, but they were not at all disheartened, believing that the problems were manageable and that the job could and would be done. As one anonymous author put it, the important thing was not to dwell overly long on the admittedly awful circumstances of life for many urbanites but rather to note 'the fact that attention is awakening to these evils'. In a similar vein, the liberal publisher Charles Knight, in the preface to his multivolume panorama of London, admitted the existence of 'crime and ignorance, and suffering and sorrow, in such an immense city, as well as propriety, and elegance, and comfort, and pleasure'. But he hastened to add that by depicting 'what we are and what we were' he would 'indirectly show how the condition of every Londoner is to be ameliorated; and how, by diminishing ignorance, we may diminish crime; and, by cultivating innocent pleasures, do something to drive out unlawful excitements'. London, after all, had been 'a city of progress from its first foundation', and Knight saw no reason to suppose that it would not continue to stride forward in the future. [73]

There was, moreover, widespread acceptance of the view that by stimulating its inhabitants' mental faculties the town functioned as a self-correcting system, constantly working to eliminate whatever difficulties it might be experiencing during particular phases of somewhat too rapid growth. The Whig statesman who reviewed Taylor's and Vaughan's books, among others, for the influential *Edinburgh Review* indicated his belief in this idea when he wrote that privations and suffering were not inevitable in great cities and other centers of manufacturing. On the contrary, the progress of industry produced 'peculiar facilities for their mitigation and removal', and improvement in general occurred far more readily in the town than anywhere else. Through competition, the town fostered intelligence, and intelligence fostered virtue. Another reviewer was much more critical of Vaughan. Nonetheless, he ended by stating, 'It is one of the peculiar advantages of cities, that they supply the lover of his race with the means of ... improving ... the moral wealth of the multitude. The electric properties of benevolence and sympathy, not less than of emulation and courage, are drawn out by the rapid contact of masses'. On this point, he and Vaughan agreed fully.[74]

During the third quarter of the century, numerous writers argued not only that cities possessed the potential for progress but also that they had demonstrated the fact of progress by dealing effectively with their various ills and that they therefore deserved ever increasing respect. As Britain emerged from the most traumatic phase of the industrial revolution, as the 'hungry forties' gave way to a period of renewed prosperity, and as the political threat presented by Chartism disappeared, criticism of the city receded in favor of the more hopeful views espoused by Vaughan and Baines. Britain's 'age of equipoise'[75] was a time in which the city, along with modern society as a whole, looked better and better to more and more people. The great sages and cultural critics — Carlyle, Dickens, Arnold, and Ruskin — continued to hurl their verbal thunderbolts. But they did so in large measure to protest against an increasingly widespread sense of contentment with the state of industrial-urban society and a belief that the British, foremost among nations in this realm, held the lead in most if not all others as well.

One can detect manifestations of this pervasive optimism and confidence with specific regard to the city in many works published at or shortly after mid-century. Harriet Martineau, a popular economist and moralist of Unitarian upbringing and liberal persuasion, looked back in 1850 on the last few decades with plainly evident satisfaction. The Municipal Corporations Act of 1835 had done much to eliminate the inequities and corruption prevelant under the old system of self-government, and great improvements had occurred in sanitary arrangements. 'Now', she wrote, 'we have People's Parks, here and there; we have Baths and Washhouses for the poor.... We have not yet achieved the wholesome and profitable drainage of towns, and ventilation of the houses therein, and the abolition of burial of the dead among the homes of the living; but we have a firm hold of the idea and the purpose; and the great work is sure to be done'. Charles Kingsley, in a lecture advocating urban reform to which we referred earlier, expressed his gratitude for the work that had already been done since about 1830 by the upper classes to improve their towns. Their efforts served as a reminder of the fact that 'crowded city life can bring out human nobleness as well as human baseness'.[76]

Similar views found expression in the 1860s. Charles Knight, the self-made publisher, admitted that the urban population had been wretchedly housed around 1840, but his point in saying this, far from reopening old wounds, was to emphasize the enormous strides forward that urban society had made in the interim. The poor were now cleaner both in life and in death, and as a result everyone lived longer. Popular education had improved, and so too had relations between those at the top and those at the bottom of the social hierarchy. Two advocates of Christian Socialism and working-class political rights argued later in the decade in connection with the debate about further parliamentary reform that workers in the great manufacturing towns had progressed enormously since 1832 in a whole host of ways. They had benefited from public health and other protective legislation, from laws that restructured local government, and from the spread of libraries, museums and schools, as well as from their own efforts to develop economic cooperatives and trade unions. The authors' main point was less to celebrate urban progress as such than to substantiate the workers' claims to a measure of political enfranchisement commensurate with their newly attained level of prosperity and culture, but their survey of working-class improvement still evinced considerable pride in the mid-Victorian city.[77]

Such pride usually found expression less in terms of urban life in general than with regard to the evolution of particular cities. Industrial and commercial towns in the north and in the Midlands such as Manchester, Liverpool, Bradford, Leeds, Sheffield, and especially Birmingham stood out as places where enormous changes for the better had taken place since the 1840s. As a result of both economic prosperity and incipient efforts by local authorities to ameliorate and compensate for the worst effects of early overcrowding, these towns appeared in an increasingly favorable light. Numerous local authors celebrated such places for the ways in which their citizens had contributed to equipoise by pursuing improvement and for many other virtues as well. In works of fiction, description, and history that spoke to a large audience of ordinary middle-class readers, they reflected and contributed to an unsophisticated but widespread sense of civic loyalty. Many cities were of course praised for much the same achievements and qualities, and there is no need to recount exhaustively what was written about all of them, but there were differences of emphasis from one town to another, and it is essential in any case to consider what was said about a few of them in some detail. There is no other way to appreciate fully the extent and the intensity of the urban sentiment.

Manchester enjoyed markedly better publicity than it had received in the 1830s and 1840s. Elizabeth Gaskell did her part to improve its image in her second major city novel, *North and South* (first published in Dickens' *Household Words* in 1854-55). In part an effort to satisfy the critics who charged that she had maligned Manchester and its manufacturers in *Mary*

Barton, the novel contrasted the quiet life in the parsonage of Helstone and the luxurious life in London with the dynamic world of Milton, a cotton manufacturing city that represented her home town. Through the story of Margaret Hale, born and bred in the south and imbued at the outset with its prejudices against commerce and industry, and John Thornton, a stubborn, hard-headed employer, Gaskell sought to show that a decent social order and a good life could indeed flourish in the industrial city. Margaret's movement away from her early preconceptions provides one of the novel's major themes. Toward the end, she tells a worker who contemplates a move to the south to work on a farm, 'You would not bear the dulness of the life; you don't know what it is; it would eat you away like rust'. At the same time, Thornton becomes more sympathetic to the legitimate grievances of his workers, reluctantly accepting their right to organize and strike. His final success, after much effort and misfortune, at wooing Margaret symbolizes the belief that the values of north and south could also be married, with capitalism being softened by compassion inside the industrial city.[78]

Other local authors praised Manchester less hesitantly and more directly, recording with still more pride the progress the city had made during and after the second quarter of the century. The case of Robert Lamb is particularly instructive, inasmuch as he, like Gaskell, had focused in 1848 on urban poverty. In 1853, he saw the city in a much more favorable light. He celebrated Manchester not only for its commercial dynamism and its political liberalism but also for its churches, its schools, and the mental accomplishments of even its poorest citizens (referring in this connection to the portrayal of Job Legh in *Mary Barton*). 'We are', he concluded, 'a go-ahead sort of people.... The engine "Manchester" now and then runs off the rail, it is true; but it is soon right again, and away it goes'. A decade later, he continued with the mechanical metaphor, comparing Manchester to 'one of its engines, often working with smoothness and precision, but sometimes breaking loose and spreading consternation and ruin'. Because of the American Civil War, Manchester was suffering at that point from a commercial depression, but Lamb concentrated on the general betterment — moral as well as economic — that the workers had experienced in recent years. The 'fine spirit' the workers were exhibiting in the face of the current adversity showed how far they had advanced since the days when labor disputes had not infrequently resulted in violent riots.[79]

Also in the 1860s, an historian of Manchester, William Fordyce, extolled 'the moral, social and political progress of a great city'. He admitted in passing that the workers did not yet receive enough education. According to a report in 1855 by the chaplain in the Preston House of Correction, one-fourteenth of the working-class males in Lancashire had run afoul of the law in a single year, and only 2 percent of those imprisoned could read and write, but Fordyce believed that since then 'the exertions of better-class teachers' and 'numerous sanitary and other improvements' had greatly elevated the workers' moral status. His publisher conveyed the overall thrust of his book quite accurately when he wrote,

> Manchester has attained a proud pre-eminence as a seat of manufactures of the first importance to the trade of the empire, and the support of an intelligent, industrious and immense population; and in all things connected with great speculations, popular movements, and true progress, Manchester may justly claim to be second to no city in the world.

Some men had felt similarly a generation earlier, but their optimism had been challenged by the revelations of James Kay and other social reformers. Now a relatively benign view of Mancunian society seemed much more credible.[80]

To the west of Manchester, the port city of Liverpool received laudatory treatment at the hands of Thomas Baines, the brother of Edward and the editor of the *Liverpool Times*. In his massive history of the city, Baines focused on commercial developments, but he celebrated much more than the growth of the economy. Referring to Chadwick's complaint in 1847 about the cost of the new St. George's Hall, he admitted that nearly £200,000 had indeed been spent 'in adorning the town with one of the noblest buildings of modern times', but he also insisted that two or three times that amount had gone into various improvements calculated to promote better public health. He argued, recalling Smithers' earlier excuses for Liverpool's high death rates, that given the ease with which destitute Irish could reach the city, Liverpool would never be as healthy as other, more fortunate towns, but he emphasized that everything practicable to improve the situation would be done. A few years later, in a descriptive work that surveyed all aspects of contemporary life in the city, he reiterated these points. He described 'some of the finest public buildings, and ... the handsomest range of offices, which exist in any town in the empire' and then went on to congratulate the town fathers for 'the most unremitting care ... in removing every nuisance dangerous to the public health'. Moreover, making a point that appeared frequently in other town histories and descriptions, he voiced great satisfaction with the city's charitable institutions, which were 'calculated to meet every form of bodily distress and every moral evil, which is capable of being mitigated by the action of benevolence'.[81]

To the east, in industrial Yorkshire, the woolen manufacturing towns of Bradford and Leeds and the capital of cutlery, Sheffield, all received similar encomiums. An historian of Bradford, updating a work on that city published a quarter of a century earlier, looked back on the urban past with pride and contentment, seeing in it the promise of an ever happier future. 'Where, within the memory of most of even middle-aged native inhabitants, the noisy rooks made their nests', he wrote, 'buildings, warehouses, rivalling in size and splendour the far-famed palaces of Venice, rear their proud fronts'. This allusion to Renaissance Italy, a common tactic among spokesmen for provincial towns, helped to legitimate Bradford culturally as well as economically, although most of what followed with regard to progress outside

3 Victoria Hall in the Leeds Town Hall. Constructed in the 1850s, the Leeds Town Hall was one of the great monuments of mid-Victorian civic pride (source: *Building News*, IV [1858]).

the spheres of commerce and industry referred to relatively mundane improvements having to do with matters such as sewage disposal, public utilities, and the Mechanics' Institute. Thomas Baines wrote about Bradford in a similar vein a few years later. He lauded the city for establishing new schools, for opening a free library, and for building model lodging houses, baths, and hospitals. He discerned an enormous change for the better in the life of the city during the third quarter of the century. 'Those who knew Bradford twenty years previously could hardly recognize it in 1873', he commented, 'the changes in the intervening period having been great and numerous'.[82]

In his remarks on Leeds, where intense local pride had already given rise in the 1850s to one of the most widely celebrated of the Victorian town halls, Baines waxed still more eloquent. Increasing opportunities for profitable employment had generated the 'wonderfully rapid increase of numbers ... drawing multitudes together to this spot from other districts, sustaining the people in comfort, and promoting marriages'. In addition to the town hall, the city could boast improved streets and bridges, a better police force, and a vast array of newly founded or expanded cultural institutions. Echoing Vaughan, Baines wrote,

> ... Great cities and towns have always been nurseries of intelligence, from the time of Tyre, Athens, and Florence, which were seats of knowledge and the fine arts, as well as of trade and commerce. The cities and towns of England have produced many men of eminent learning and great literary and scientific attainments, as well as numerous inventors and promoters of the useful arts. Leeds has had its fair share of men of this description; and now that intelligence and education are so widely diffused amongst the populations of our large manufacturing cities and towns, there is every reason to hope that the number will increase.[83]

The progress of Sheffield did not excite Baines' enthusiasm as much as developments in either Bradford or Leeds, but it figured prominently in a book by a local author, who again updated an earlier work of urban history. He pointed proudly to the high wages, comfortable houses, and good diet enjoyed by the city's artisans. The 'honourable rise in life, through industry and perseverance' that many of them had experienced were 'but epitomes of the history of the town itself'. Sheffield had advanced of late in every respect, even culturally, despite the fact that in such a busy town it 'would be unreasonable to look for any marked cultivation of literature and art'. The Literary and Philosophical Society, a subscription library, and new schools all provided signposts for the march of intellect.[84]

Birmingham commended itself to natives and outsiders alike for several reasons, and its progress stimulated an enormous outburst of pride and admiration. As a center of the metal-finishing trades and of machine-building, it displayed extraordinary industrial dynamism, which fascinated contemporary observers. John Doran, in an essay written to highlight an upcoming meeting in Birmingham of the British Association for the Advancement of Science, emphasized that 'healthy labour, and not Royalty' had made it 'one of the most remarkable cities in the land. Labour and the sons of labour have done it all'. Even in prehistoric times, residents of the area 'made nails with their fingers, and could drive them into planks with their knuckles'. As a result of the ingenuity and energy displayed by inhabitants of the city in more recent years, Birmingham had justly gained a reputation as 'queen of the sounding anvil' and the 'great toy-shop of

Europe'. It furnished an enormous number of indispensable items: spoons, buttons, pins, guns, and so on, almost *ad infinitum*. According to Doran, Birmingham had given Prince Albert the idea for the Industrial Exhibition of All Nations that was held in the Crystal Palace, where its manufacturers won great fame for many of their products.[85]

As Asa Briggs points out, the industrial structure of Birmingham, with its large number of small factories and workshops, tended to dampen class conflicts between workers and employers, producing a greater measure of social peace than was to be found in towns such as Manchester, where the average employer had many more employees. But while it had enjoyed a comparatively high degree of social tranquility, Birmingham had by no means stagnated politically. To the contrary, it had given powerful impulses to the cause of liberalism. As John Alfred Langford wrote in his chronicle of the city's institutional life, 'From the commencement of the agitation, which ended in the passing of the Reform Bill of 1832, to the present time, Birmingham has taken the foremost rank in the political history of the country.... Her influence has also, during that period, been undeviatingly in favor of liberal government'. Local support for the removal of Jewish disabilities, for abolition of the Corn Laws, and for further extension of the suffrage, as well as for public education (through the activities of the National Education League) all gave Birmingham a legitimate claim to gratitude from liberals everywhere.[86]

In the 1860s and 1870s, a gospel of civic activism flourished in Birmingham. Propagated in large part by two Nonconformist ministers, George Dawson and Robert William Dale, the municipal ideal emphasized the obligation of the citizen to serve his community and the need for the city government to further the well-being of all the town's inhabitants. The teachings of these and other men came to fruition in the mid-1870s. After the 'economy' group lost control of the town council to politicians whose views reflected the progressivism of the city's big businessmen and after Joseph Chamberlain, a screw manufacturer who had entered local politics, became mayor of the city, Birmingham experienced a series of far-reaching innovations that soon gave it the reputation of being 'the best-governed city in the world'. During Chamberlain's three years in office, between 1873 and 1876, the city government, in his words, 'engaged in a great struggle to promote the welfare, health, and happiness of the population'. It gained control of the gas system, appropriating the profits from that monopoly for other public purposes. It took over the water system, primarily for sanitary reasons. And it undertook a large 'improvement scheme' in the center of the city that involved extensive land acquisition, clearance of old buildings, and construction of new ones. These breakthroughs constituted seminal examples of what would later become known as 'municipal socialism'.[87]

Such reforms helped to generate the massive municipal history that began to appear two years after Chamberlain gave up the mayoralty in order to become an M.P. They also provided more than sufficient justification for the pervasive sense of accomplishment that it conveyed. The author, John Thackray Bunce, compared the condition of the city in 1878 with the situation in 1838, when the town had received its charter of incorporation, and saw an enormous change for the better. By the end of those four decades, an expanded municipal government had 'supplied omissions, remedied defects, created public spirit, and given form and purpose alike to individual and corporate action'. The city could look back on its past 'with honest pride'. The 'true communal spirit' had manifested itself in fine public buildings, in clean streets, in washhouses, in parks, and in libraries, schools, and museums, as well as in the public monopolies of gas and water. All these things were parts of 'the vast machinery of local administration ... equal ever to new duties imposed, never refusing new services required'. In Bunce's view, the town government was a machine with a heart, conferring benefits on citizens of all classes and responding to no special interests.[88]

Robert Dent implied a similar view when he wrote at the end of his history,

> ... If the reader has marked the steady improvement in every department of our public life, he will have felt that, like the great Apostle of the Gentiles, the Birmingham man may claim with truth to be a 'citizen of no mean city'.... He will feel that it is no small honour to be able to say, 'I, too, am a Birmingham man'.

Dent saw in the evolution of public policy a generous spirit that had attained epic proportions. His history evinced civic pride at its zenith in Victorian England. What he and others had to say about Birmingham represented the most intense enthusiasm for the municipal achievements of a particular city to be found anywhere in the nineteenth century. Nonetheless, the civic spirit in the Midlands metropolis represented the intensification of a more wide-spread phenomenon that was manifesting itself in many other towns as well.[89]

Finally, London. An administrative hodgepodge that lacked any real cohesion until the London County Council was established in 1888, it did not merit municipal histories of the sort bestowed upon incorporated towns like Bradford and Birmingham. Moreover, the vast size of the under-class portrayed by Mayhew and others tended to dampen the buoyant optimism that was so clearly evident elsewhere. But despite the enormous social problems that continued to plague the metropolis, popular writers still displayed great affection for what one of them, George R. Emerson, called 'this wonderful aggregation of humanity — this immense town growing so certainly and so rapidly'. In Emerson's eyes, London was far more than one of the largest and most densely populated cities in the world. It was also 'one of the oldest and most memorable; in itself an epitome of the nation of which it is the metropolis'. George Augustus Sala, a regular contributor to *Household Words* who wrote over forty books, took his readers on a literary tour of the city that began at Covent Garden Market at 6.00 a.m., proceeded to banks, docks, and auction rooms, stopped at fashionable clubs and parks, included several theaters as well as a late debate at the House of Commons, and concluded with a masked ball and the arraignment of prisoners at night at Bow Street Magistrates Court. He sought to portray 'the monster London in the varied phases of its outer and inner life, at every hour of the day-season and the night-season ... the giant sleeping and the giant waking ... in his mad noonday rages, and in his sparse moments of unquiet repose'. Although he repeatedly pointed out the sharp contrasts between wealth and poverty and between virtue and vice, his main themes were the variety, vitality, and color of London life. The city offered a mysterious and marvelous spectacle, exciting both amazement and devotion. In Sala's words, it was a 'shrine ... rich in relics', which would amply repay the literary pilgrimage he offered his readers.[90]

Walter Thornbury, author of much the largest work on London since the collaborative effort coordinated by Knight in the early 1840s, made a similar effort to whet his readers' appetites by describing it as 'a city every street and alley of which teems with interesting associations, every paving stone of which marks ... the abiding-place of some ancient legend or biographical story'. He celebrated the metropolis for its great crimes as well as its noble virtues. London epitomized not only the nation but also all humanity, and this representative quality attracted him more than any other feature of the great city. 'Her miles of red-tiled roofs', he observed, 'her quiet green squares, her vast black mountain of a cathedral, her silver belt of a river, her acres and acres of stony terraces, her beautiful parks, her tributary fleets, seem to me as so many episodes in one great epic, the true delineation of which would form a new chapter in the History of Mankind'. This kind of panegyric, like Sala's, eloquently summarized the advantages of almost all aspects of life in the metropolis from the standpoint of the author in search of a fruitful subject that would hold the interest of a large reading public. It recalled Dickens' fascination with the city without imparting much if any Dickensian gloom. London was literally spectacular, continually stimulating the story-teller and thus enriching the lives of his readers, wherever they might happen to live. This quality alone provided more than enough justification in Thornbury's eyes for the existence of the great metropolis.[91]

As we saw earlier, anti-urbanists and other writers continued to indict the cities for their faults throughout this period. During the years between 1850 and the mid-1870s, John Ruskin was at the height of his powers as the century's leading critic of urban culture. But the works written by large numbers of less memorable authors, such as Sala and Thornbury, suggest that by 1880 the reputation of London and of Britain's other large cities had improved quite considerably compared with what it had been several decades

4 The spectacle of London. An author and an illustrator celebrate the vitality and diversity of the great metropolis (source: Walter Thornbury, *Old and New London*, I [1872], 1).

LONDON AS IT WAS AND AS IT IS.

WRITING the history of a vast city like London is like writing a history of the ocean—the area is so vast, its inhabitants are so multifarious, the treasures that lie in its depths so countless. What aspect of the great chameleon city should one select? for, as Boswell, with more than his usual sense, once remarked, "London is to the politician merely a seat of government, to the grazier a cattle market, to the merchant a huge exchange, to the dramatic enthusiast a congeries of theatres, to the man of pleasure an assemblage of taverns." If we follow one path alone, we must neglect other roads equally important; let us, then, consider the metropolis as a whole, for, as Johnson's friend well says, "the intellectual man is struck with London as comprehending the whole of human life in all its variety, the contemplation of which is inexhaustible." In histories, in biographies, in scientific records, and in chronicles of the past, however humble, let us gather materials for a record of the great and the wise, the base and the noble, the odd and the witty, who have inhabited London and left their names upon its walls. Wherever the glimmer of the cross of St. Paul's can be seen we shall wander from street to alley, from alley to street, noting almost every event of interest that has taken place there since London was a city.

before. At this point, the defenders appeared to have the upper hand. The continuing popularity of the liberal belief in the essential validity of a process that seemingly stemmed from individual choice was increasingly supplemented by a well-founded feeling that the towns themselves had more to offer than ever before. Having experienced enormous changes for the better since the relatively grim days of the 1830s and 1840s, Victorian cities enjoyed a high degree of affection and esteem among a great many if not most of the men and women who commented on them in print during the century's third quarter.

3

The City Observed by Continental Europeans

Views of Britain from abroad

Between the end of the Napoleonic wars in 1815 and the mid-1840s, dozens of individuals from France and Germany visited Britain and described what they saw during stays that ranged from only a few weeks to a year or more, and many others also wrote about contemporary society across the English Channel. Many of the travel accounts, like earlier reports that had begun to appear in the late eighteenth century, primarily recorded industrial and topographical details. Others seldom rose above the level of a rather dull diary. But starting in the 1820s authors increasingly provided their readers with more penetrating views of urban society in a country whose cities, they realized, far surpassed those of continental Europe both in size and in dynamism.

Visiting and writing about British cities gave Frenchmen and Germans a means of beginning to assess urban life more generally. Towns in England and Scotland could be looked at with an eye to their differences from towns elsewhere, thus highlighting Britain's peculiarity, but they could also be seen as examples of social phenomena that knew no national boundaries. Britain fascinated many observers because it manifested, in an exaggerated fashion, processes and problems already evident to a lesser degree or soon to make their appearance in other countries as well. It appeared to be a social laboratory, in which men had undertaken a vast experiment that might instruct and benefit foreign as well as domestic observers. To take careful stock of contemporary Britain provided a way of anticipating the urban future and of sorting out one's feelings about the kind of social order that seemed to await not only England but also Europe as a result of city growth.

Evaluations of urban society in Britain both reflected and helped to define foreign ideological orientations. Liberals tended to look on British cities favorably. To be sure, continental liberals as well as English ones sometimes drew attention to the ills of the city precisely in order to vindicate industry. According to this line of argument, the misfortunes of the working classes stemmed less from the conditions under which they labored than from the environment in which they lived. On the whole, however, the ideologies of urban critics from across the Channel were well to the left of the political and social center. The rising strength of socialism on the European continent added a noticeably more radical flavor to the discussion of British towns by Frenchmen and Germans than was to be found in the writings of their British contemporaries.

Through the early 1830s, those Frenchmen who visited Britain devoted considerably more attention to social conditions in general and to urban life in particular than did their relatively few German counterparts. Sick of revolution and imperial rule within their own country, they saw Britain as the embodiment of orderly freedom and progress. Regarding cities, they tended to focus on and to praise London, a city in which, quite naturally, they spent a disproportionate share of their time.

Consider what several of them had to say about the quality of life in the British capital. Georges Crapelet viewed the workers as being 'frugal and industrious' and the shopkeepers and other businessmen as being both highly independent and morally trustworthy. He rejected the charge that commercial success had degraded the English character. To the contrary, it had equipped Englishmen with 'not only the power but also the firm resolve to be just'. The Baron Charles d'Haussez remarked with amazement on the great difference between London and Paris. 'In London there is a crowd without confusion — a bustle without noise — immensity with an absence of grandeur'. Numerous bridges, docks that sheltered thousands of vessels, and gas lights along the streets all partook of 'the animation imparted by the movement of a numerous, active, and busy population'. He also noted admiringly that there were few other capitals in which robberies were less frequent or so soon discovered and punished and in which there were 'fewer collisions between the different classes of society'. The comparison with the French capital, which had just experienced another revolution a few years earlier, was so obvious that it did not need to be made explicit. The young Gustave d'Eichtal, a disciple of the positivist philosopher Auguste Comte, also marveled at both the technology and the society he observed in the metropolis. He wrote, 'Much has been said about the excellence of English machinery, and I think the finest machine is the populace of London. Here everything is done with as little friction and loss of time as possible'. He noted much vice and poverty on a tour of Houndsditch, but he also remarked on the great amount of meat consumed by better-class workers, and on the whole he offered a decidedly favorable view of metropolitan life.[1]

Liverpool also attracted both attention and praise, functioning as another symbol of the English virtues of enterprise and freedom. Edouard de Montulé saw in the port city of 77,000 inhabitants 'the expression of the condition of England'. Its appearance, its development, and its commerce formed 'a miniature image of what England presents in the large'. Because of its importance as an outlet for manufactured goods, Liverpool was certain to keep on growing rapidly, thus highlighting the difference between 'the industrial spirit of the English' and the stodgy inertia that prevailed in France. Jerome Adolphe Blanqui commended the city not only for its commerce and wealth, but also for the beneficent uses to which that wealth had been put, including the new town hall, libraries, reading rooms, schools, and churches. He emphasized that the achievements in which the citizens could take most pride had not depended upon support from the state. They had resulted from voluntary initiatives by individuals. The city had proved that 'if one permits a great nation to act freely, one must expect achievements worthy of her'. In Blanqui's eyes, Liverpool presented compelling testimony to the moral as well as the economic efficacy of social liberalism. Free men in a free city grew in numbers and in righteousness quite spontaneously.[2]

In the 1830s and 1840s, several changes became noticeable in the pattern of continental perceptions of British cities. Germans as well as Frenchmen commented thoughtfully on urban society, rising increasingly above their earlier levels of observation. Views of London became more diverse, evincing more negativity than had appeared earlier. And attention shifted away from London to the smaller cities of the industrial north, which served more and more as the symbols of contemporary society.

London continued to elicit some praise from its foreign visitors. A liberal professor of history, Friedrich von Raumer, regarded the 'remarkable and imposing' size of the city as a quality that bespoke not only 'wealth growing out of the most varied and complicated activity, which demands and exercises both body and mind', but also 'the security of property, widely diffused and deeply rooted amid these masses'. Like earlier observers, he emphasized profound stability as well as restless dynamism. Significantly, he used an organic metaphor to make his point, comparing London to an oak tree, whose deep roots enabled it to endure much longer than the lowly mushroom. In this perspective, size became a guarantee of longevity rather than a harbinger of upheaval. Theodor Fontane, later to become Germany's most distinguished novelist, felt in 1844 that London was 'a miniature or quintessence of the whole world'. He wrote enthusiastically about 'the humming, restless activity' that pulsated all around him, comparing the crowds in the streets to swarms of bees and to 'a sea in which individuals are like drops of water' before concluding simply that the city was 'magnificent and unique.'[3]

In contrast, other authors portrayed London in much darker colors. Two French writers undertook searching examinations of metropolitan society in which they sought to expose the underside of life for the great majority of the capital's inhabitants. Flora Tristan, a utopian socialist who was drawn to the teachings of Charles Fourier and Robert Owen, based her book on London on several visits to England between 1826 and 1839. At the very start, in a chapter on 'la ville monstre', she indicated her critical intentions by emphasizing the enormous contrasts presented by the major geographical subdivisions of the metropolis: the commercial 'City', the aristocratic West End, and the vast territories to the northeast and the south inhabited by often impoverished workers. These contrasts appeared in all the great capitals, but they were 'more shocking in London than anywhere else'. The rest of the work offered a series of impressions of London life, ranging from the slums of St. Giles to the race tracks at Ascot. Tristan focused on class struggle — which in her view pitted the workers against the aristocracy rather than against the bourgeoisie — on the still small socialist movement, and on feminism. Markedly Anglophobic in places, she combined her criticism of London with more general statements of her utopian socialist beliefs concerning the need for social change everywhere in Europe, and her book was well received by socialists in both England and France.[4]

Shortly after the appearance of Tristan's work, a liberal journalist by the name of Léon Faucher reported at length on London (and on other British cities too) for the influential *Revue des deux mondes*. Echoing Robert Vaughan, he referred to his time as 'the age of great cities', and he observed that England deserved the attention of thoughtful men precisely because it alone presented 'a range of experience broad enough to permit study of the problems weighing upon modern society'. His essays on the metropolis, like Tristan's, emphasized the sharp contrast between the splendor of the West End and the City on the one hand and the misery that prevailed in areas such as Whitechapel and St. Giles on the other. Faucher pointed out that these splits appeared in other British cities too and also in the countryside, but they seemed worst of all in the capital. In any case, he contended that London had become far too big. Invoking the authority of Rousseau, he suggested that living there was 'fatal to the vigor of the body and to the purity of morals'.[5]

A German visitor to London about the same time, one August Jäger, made more of an effort to survey the city as a whole, but he still painted a verbal picture that emphasized its less attractive features. Warning against the excesses of 'Anglomania', he pointed on the one hand to 'moral decay, the commercial spirit, deceit, egoism, and evil of every sort' and on the other to second-rate academic institutions, poor artistic taste, and a generally low level of cultural attainment. In the big commercial city, overriding concern with practical utility degraded men both morally and spiritually. Jäger suggested at some points that he was focusing on specifically English traits, but he also indicated that the evils that concerned him obtained in big cities everywhere and that they posed an especially serious threat in London primarily because that city contained so many more inhabitants than any other. 'Just as London is the biggest and most populated city', he wrote, 'all the vices indicated here and many others as well manifest themselves to the highest and most shocking degree'.[6]

Criticism of Britain's emerging urban society came to the surface most clearly in connection with the same industrial cities that appeared to contemporary Englishmen as the foci of problematic change and disruption. Manchester seized the imagination of native and foreign observers alike far more than any other provincial town, but several other centers of manufacturing also attracted extensive attention. These cities were experiencing much the fastest growth at the time, and they therefore seemed clearly to possess the greatest paradigmatic significance. While London could never be replicated, the burgeoning towns of Lancashire, Yorkshire, and the Midlands presented social models that seemed directly relevant to men who sought insight into the problems that might be awaiting their own countries in the not too distant future. For this reason, as well as because of the current emphasis on the difficulties of industrial society among Englishmen themselves, foreign observers turned their attention increasingly to areas outside the metropolis.

Two travelers in the mid-1830s gave their readers brief but suggestive glimpses of the industrial city. The great French liberal, Alexis de Tocqueville, shortly after his famous trip to the United States, went to England for five weeks, and a year and a half later he went again for a stay of several months that included a visit to Ireland. In the notes he wrote during his second tour, he took a dim view of two cities, referring first to Birmingham as 'an immense workshop, a huge forge, a vast shop', in which one saw 'only busy people and faces brown with smoke'. Nothing was audible 'but the sound of hammers and the whistle of steam escaping from boilers', and everything was 'black, dirty, and obscure'. But Birmingham seemed almost harmless in comparison with Manchester, which Tocqueville visited a few days later. Here he saw chaos and worse. 'Everything in the exterior appearance of this city', he observed, 'attests the individual powers of man; nothing the directing power of society. At every turn human liberty shows its capricious creative force'. Devoted though Tocqueville was to individual freedom, he could not accept the conditions to which it had led in the industrial city. Huge factories, surrounded by wretched and haphazardly scattered dwellings, bore witness to the prevalent disorder. The 'fetid, muddy waters, stained with a thousand colors by the factories they pass', that ran in one of the town's streams made it appear to be 'the Styx of this new Hades'. The black smoke that covered the city further intensified Tocqueville's impression that, in entering 'this damp, dark labyrinth', he had passed through the gates of Hell. So too did the sounds he heard and the demeanor of the people he passed in the streets.

> The footsteps of a busy crowd, the crunching wheels of machinery, the shriek of steam from boilers, the regular beat of the looms, the heavy rumble of carts, those are the noises from which you can never escape in the sombre half-light of these streets.... Crowds are ever hurrying this way and that in the Manchester streets, but their footsteps are brisk, their looks preoccupied, and their appearance sombre and harsh.

Tocqueville recognized that Manchester could boast of great prowess as a center of production, but he concluded his general assessment of the city by writing that in it civilized man was being 'turned back almost into a savage'.[7]

Friedrich von Raumer, later that summer, wrote less one-sidedly and more prosaically about both of the towns on which Tocqueville had commented, but he still came to essentially negative conclusions. He admitted that workmen in Manchester received higher wages and generally lived better than their counterparts in Germany and insisted that many complaints about factories were unjustified, but then, after attacking child labor, he went on to describe conditions in Germany as 'more simple — more natural and healthful'. Germans did not produce as much cloth, but they produced 'more thoughts and feelings'. As he approached Birmingham, he too conjured up images of Hell. 'As far as the eye can reach all is black, with coal mines and iron works; and from this gloomy desert rise countless slender pyramidal chimneys, whose flames illumine the earth, while their smoke darkens the heavens'. He then went on to make a general observation that suggested a tendency more noticeable among Germans than among Frenchmen to evaluate the city according to essentially cultural criteria. He complained in concluding his discussion of the towns he saw outside London that they seemed thoroughly lacking in individual character when compared with one another. Pointing to 'a certain similarity and repetition' in what he had seen, 'from exchanges to prisons, and from soft cotton to hard iron', he implied that he had eventually become bored. 'If', he continued, 'I compare a series of English and German towns, the former are far superior to the latter in extent, wealth, activity, and population, but inferior in peculiarity of character and decided contrast'. Only Oxford and Edinburgh struck him as exceptions to this overall assessment of the British urban landscape.[8]

During the early 1840s, several Europeans commented on industrial urbanism in Britain at much greater length than either Tocqueville or Raumer, providing accounts of Victorian cities that rank as at least minor classics of social reportage and analysis. One was a liberal, one a democratic radical, and two were socialists, but they shared a common sense of sympathy for the urban working classes, and they sought through their books to communicate that sentiment to their readers.

The outstanding Frenchmen were Léon Faucher and Eugène Buret. Faucher wrote extensively not only about London but also about Liverpool, Birmingham, Leeds, and Manchester, all of which struck him as unhealthy, immoral, and thoroughly disagreeable places in which to live. Like other observers, he was fascinated by Manchester, 'a diligent spider ... in the centre of the web ... an agglomeration the most extraordinary, the most interesting, and in some aspects the most monstrous, which the progress of society has presented'. He saw the city as an almost wholly industrial entity, whose inhabitants paid little attention to literature or art. In this way, it exemplified the Benthamite standard of utility, but endemic poverty and other social ills made it appear to be anything but a well regulated community. Suffering as it did, like other manufacturing towns, from 'that unnatural co-existence between labour and misery, between the excess of vice and the excess of activity' and more particularly from 'the wide-spread physical and moral degradation of the labouring classes', Manchester was a 'reproach upon the public conscience'. Faucher was careful, like William Cooke Taylor, to distinguish between industry, which he favored, and the industrial city, which he did not. He believed that the manufacturing system was passing through a transitional phase, at the end of which England would find a new equilibrium, and that in an ideal future factories would operate in the countryside, leaving the towns free 'for the concentration of commerce and luxury, literature, science, and the fine arts'.[9]

A few years before Faucher's trip, Eugène Buret, also a journalist, won a competition sponsored by the Academy of Moral and Political Sciences in France, which offered 5,000 francs for the best manuscript on the theme of 'misery, its manifestations and causes in different countries'. Buret used his prize in part in order to travel to England and to gather the documentation he needed to turn his study into a much longer treatise. Evincing broad sympathy for socialist ideas, he identified the amoral economics of the liberals as the basic cause of working-class distress. 'Absolute *laissez-faire*', he argued, 'is worth no more in an industrial system than in a political system; its true name is anarchy'. Modern industrial cities, with their 'floating population ... this mass of men whom industry summons, whom she cannot employ constantly, whom she always holds in reserve at her mercy', exemplified this anarchy all too clearly, and British cities suffered especially from social ills. All of the big ones — not only London but also Manchester, Liverpool, Leeds, Glasgow, Edinburgh, and others — had vast quarters whose 'horrible appearance' was much more difficult to describe than the wealthier parts of these 'opulent' cities. Outside London, Manchester drew more of Buret's attention than any other city. Although he seems to have visited it, most of what he had to say came directly from the book on the working classes published almost a decade earlier by James Kay. Buret did not add much to Englishmen's knowledge of their own cities (and his book, unlike several other travel accounts, was never translated), but he did help greatly to familiarize his countrymen with what was happening across the Channel.[10]

Two German counterparts to Buret and Faucher were Johann Georg Kohl and Jakob Venedey, both of whom traveled widely in industrial England. Kohl, who wrote extensively about his trips to other parts of the world as well, had little to say about London but a great deal to report about the Midlands, Lancashire, and Yorkshire. Like other Germans, he emphasized the ugly monotony and the other cultural defects of many of the towns he visited. 'A large portion of Birmingham', he wrote, 'might be described as a wilderness of houses, all equally ugly, an ungainly mass, unbroken by a single building of a pleasing exterior'. The city displayed 'nothing but a dull, and endless succession of house after house, and street after street'. Leeds, 'like its brethren, Sheffield, Manchester, and the other great manufacturing cities of England', could 'boast of no interesting antiquities, or historical associations', and like them it was 'a dirty, smoky, disagreeable town'. But both Birmingham and Leeds and especially Manchester alarmed Kohl because of much more serious defects than their aesthetic failings. He saw there large numbers of people who lived a nomadic existence as they wandered about, 'making a precarious income, sometimes by begging and selling trifling articles, and sometimes by various frauds and depredations'. He saw factory workers whom the advance of machinery had, in his eyes, ground down 'into the abyss of wretchedness and degradation'. And he called attention to huge increases in the frequency of crime and to large numbers of houses of prostitution and taverns. Kohl was fascinated by Britain's technological virtuosity, which prompted him at one point to celebrate England as 'this most wonderful country of a truly wonderful age', but his readers found little to admire in his accounts of British towns.[11]

Venedey, a radical democrat who had campaigned for political reform in Germany, met with Chartists as well as industrialists in England, and in his report on what he saw and heard he highlighted the human costs of industrial progress. Men became parts of machines in the hellish factories in which they labored. In Leeds, he noted the paucity of and the low level of local interest in such cultural institutions as theaters, concert halls, and libraries. Manchester was far from dull, displaying contrasts aplenty. 'The shops, the banks, the Athenaeum, the stock exchange, and many hotels and private houses in the main streets', he wrote, 'recall Paris and London, whereas the poorer areas remind me of the most wretched areas of Dublin'. But Venedey focused more clearly on urban poverty and suffering than on any aspects of the city in which Mancunians could take much pride, and he concluded by warning his readers to shun the unbridled materialism that had subjected England to 'golden misery'.[12]

None of the foreign observers of British cities discussed so far wrote about them with nearly as much passion or insight, and none achieved anything like as great an impact, as the young German who went to England in late 1842 and stayed there until mid-1844 to work in a branch of his family's cotton firm. Friedrich Engels, born into a staunchly Pietist family in the textile town of Barmen, was sent to Manchester by his industrialist father so that he would be separated from the radical company he had been keeping in Berlin and Cologne. The elder Engels hoped that his son would stay out of mischief in England and that he would complete his training as a businessman. Young Friedrich welcomed the opportunity to study at first hand a country that he already regarded as the likely leader in a future social revolution. He worked during most of his stay as a clerk in the offices of Ermen and Engels, but he still had ample spare time in which to walk the streets of the city, to meet Chartists, socialists, and other working-class leaders, and to read widely in contemporary British writings about social and economic questions. Some of what he learned appeared in a number of articles he wrote during his stay for several continental newspapers and for Robert Owen's *New Moral World*. But the ideas that had been germinating in Manchester did not come to fruition until after his return (via Paris, where he first met Karl Marx) to Barmen. There, during a period of about half a year, he wrote the astonishingly precocious work that later appeared in English under the title *The Condition of the Working Class in England*.[13]

In many respects, Engels' book recapitulated earlier and contemporary complaints about the damage to human beings purportedly wrought by the rise of industrial capitalism. Seeking to pillory the bourgeoisie to which he himself belonged for its callous enslavement and exploitation of the 'proletariat', he devoted his attention in large part to the areas in which working-class suffering was most readily apparent, the industrial cities. His long chapter on 'The Great Towns', judged by one of his severest critics as well as by one of his most enthusiastic champions to be among the finest things he ever wrote, provided an extraordinary combination of careful analysis and fervent denunciation.[14]

After several pages on London, in which he dwelt on 'the disintegration of society into individuals, each guided by his private principles and each pursuing his own aims' and on 'the demoralizing influences of poverty, dirt and low environment', Engels took his readers quickly through the slums of half a dozen other towns before finally settling down in Manchester. Here, the sense of chaos and misery adumbrated in his remarks on London reached overwhelming proportions. Engels argued that the spatial splitting apart of the city into a series of belts that mirrored its antagonistic classes and the presence of elegant shopfronts along main thoroughfares made it all too easy for the bourgeoisie to 'sanctimoniously ignore the existence of their less fortunate neighbours'. The city was fragmented geographically as well as socially in such a way that the middle classes could simply eliminate the workers from their consciousness.[15]

Engels' feeling that he had fallen into the midst of 'disorderly confusion' became especially pronounced in his account of his wanderings through the working-class quarters. 'Turning left from the main street that is still Long Millgate', he recalled, 'the visitor can easily lose his way. He wanders aimlessly from one court to another. He turns one corner after another through innumerable narrow dirty alleyways and passages, and in only a few minutes he has lost all sense of direction and does not know which way to turn'. After describing many more such places, he wrote,

> I may sum up the impressions of my visits to these districts by stating that 350,000 workers in Manchester and the surrounding districts nearly all live in inferior, damp, dirty cottages; that the streets are generally in a disgraceful state of filth and disrepair, and that the lay-out of the dwellings reflects the greed of the builder for profits from the way in which ventilation is lacking. In a word,

> the workers' dwellings of Manchester are dirty, miserable and wholly lacking in comforts. In such houses only inhuman, degraded and unhealthy creatures would feel at home.

Numerous other passages in this chapter and in later ones made it clear that in Engels' view large numbers of men and women inhabiting these houses had indeed sunk, both physically and morally, to the degraded level of their domestic surroundings. Excessive drinking, child neglect, suicide, sexual irregularity, and crime all testified to the devastating effects of life in the industrial city.[16]

Although Engels viewed the urban milieu at least as grimly as any of his contemporaries, he also affirmed the city as an agent of liberation from the very fetters it had helped to forge. In a sense, he shared Robert Vaughan's conviction that the city would spontaneously generate the cures necessary to remedy its own worst maladies. But whereas Vaughan looked to the beneficial effects of middle-class culture, Engels eagerly awaited the revolutionary impact of heightened working-class consciousness. 'If', he argued, 'the concentration of population in urban centres furthers the expansion of middle-class power, at the same time it leads to an even more rapid development among the working classes.... In this way the great cities are the birthplace of the working-class movement'. For Engels, it was only by passing through the urban crucible that the proletariat could form itself and transform society.[17]

Engels' book, published at a time of growing anxiety about social distress in Germany, was widely reviewed and quoted, and it was reprinted three years after it had first appeared. Official commentators in Prussia and most other conservatives regarded it not as a revolutionary threat to the *status quo* but as a piece of ammunition they could use in order to defend the monarchy against liberal demands for constitutional reforms and parliamentary government. Only the authoritarian but benevolent rule of the Prussian king, they argued, could defend German workers from the fate that had befallen their English brethren at the hands of the English middle classes. Socialist and other left-wing journals praised Engels loudly, for reasons that obviously differed from those of the conservatives. So too did the liberal (but socially reformist) historian, Karl Biedermann. On the other hand, writers who represented the views of businessmen saw that Engels' criticisms of English society could be applied to German industrialists and the cities they were helping to build too. It came as no surprise that a newspaper in his home town, the *Barmer Zeitung*, gave him an especially unfavorable review.[18]

After the 1840s, continental writers showed diminished interest in British society. Books about Britain continued to issue from the pens of Frenchmen and Germans throughout the rest of the century, but fewer and fewer of them evinced the urgent concern with Britain as a social laboratory that had appeared so frequently in the earlier literature. In 1850, a French democrat,

Alexandre Ledru-Rollin, translated and edited a collection of official documents that pertained to various social ills in England. A few years later, a conservative German social reformer, Viktor Aimé Huber, published an account of his recent travels that included lengthy discussions of working-class life in many British cities. But when the great French critic and historian, Hippolyte Taine, published the notes he had made on several trips to England between 1861 and 1871, he focused for the most part on upper- and middle-class life in and around London. He did not ignore Manchester and the working classes, but he relegated them to the background, and he did not treat any other industrial towns at all.[19]

Two points may help to explain this change in the intellectual landscape. First, the lessening of social tensions within England, while it nourished a more benign view of urban civilization among Englishmen, tended simply to undercut all interest among foreigners. Frenchmen and Germans had flocked to Britain for over two decades in large part because they saw there not only promise but also problems, and as the difficulties stemming from the early phases of the industrial revolution abated so too did the desire among foreigners to make sense of the British experience. Equally important was the fact that the novelty of the economic and social changes that had originated in Britain had begun to wear off. As France and Germany started to compete with Britain in the race to industrialize, writers in those countries became increasingly concerned with their own urban societies. It is to the evidence of such interest that we now turn.

Paris in the eyes of the French

Frenchmen wrote far more about Paris than about any other French city or about cities in general. Of course, every country tended to dwell on the affairs of its largest city, especially if that city enjoyed the status of a national capital, but the French delimited their range of vision much more narrowly than observers in any other nation. The reasons are not hard to find. Paris had always been considerably larger than other French cities, and the gap was growing rapidly during the nineteenth century. Moreover, not only because of its size but also because of the high degree of administrative centralization within the French state, Parisian influence over the political and cultural life of the nation as a whole had grown to enormous proportions. As a result, Frenchmen who sought to understand urban life concentrated on a single urban entity to an extent that would have been unthinkable in Britain, let alone Germany or the United States.

As in Britain, numerous observers investigated and commented critically on the quantity and quality of life among the lower classes, particularly with regard to public health and morality. Medical doctors here too played a leading part in alerting the nation to unhealthy urban conditions. One Claude

Lachaise, in his *Topographie médicale de Paris* (1822), emphasized traditional considerations having to do with factors such as sunlight, wind, and humidity, but he also wrote about the harmful effects of dense population, relating lack of sun and fresh air to congested housing and narrow streets. A few years later, the great medical and social investigator, Louis-René Villermé, began to publish his statistical studies of mortality, one of which correlated death rates in different districts of Paris with varying levels of prosperity. His methods were still quite primitive by later standards of demographic analysis (failing, for instance, to take account of age-specific mortality), but he found parallels between death and poverty that are still judged to be basically valid. One French historian of statistics has written, 'These articles by Villermé ... can be seen as decisive events in the fusion of three distinct conceptual universes: hygiene, statistics ... and the systematic study of the social world and its evolution'. A third medical man who contributed greatly to the study of urban public health was A. J. P. Parent-Duchâtelet, who, together with Villermé and others, established in 1829 the influential *Annales d'hygiène publique et de médecine légale*. A member of the Board of Health in Paris, he concerned himself mainly with sewerage, but he also wrote about the disposal of dead horses (a major problem at the time in towns) and health in factories, and along with Villermé he provided much data that Edwin Chadwick used for purposes of comparison in his great report on sanitary conditions in Britain in the 1840s.[20]

Parent-Duchâtelet made his greatest contribution to urban studies less in the area of physical health than in the area of moral health. His great work on Parisian prostitution stands as a nineteenth-century classic of empirical social inquiry. In the introduction to the first volume, he clearly indicated the close connection in his own professional experience and in his sense of his own professional identity between material and moral filth. Distancing himself from the excessive delicacy of those who had expressed repugnance at his willingness to concern himself with fallen women, he replied,

> If I have been able, without scandalizing anyone at all, to penetrate into the sewers, handle putrid matter, pass part of my time in dumps, and live after a fashion in the midst of all that is most abject and disgusting among groups of men, why should I blush to approach a sewer of another sort (a sewer filthier, I admit, than all the others) in the well-founded hope of doing some good while examining it in all its aspects?

Prostitution appeared in such a passage to be just one part of the larger urban morass. Houses of ill fame and the women who worked there functioned as additional conduits that carried their filth into and out of the vast urban cesspool. Parent-Duchâtelet did not seek to construct theories that would explain what he described. He provided tables that might have permitted correlations between the frequency of prostitution in different parts of the city and the density of these areas, but he made no attempt to draw any clear conclusions from these statistics. Perhaps the major conclusion of the whole work, hardly surprising and certainly not at all encouraging, was that prostitution 'exists and will always exist in big cities, because, like begging and gambling, it is an industry and a resource against hunger'. It was, he seemed to be saying, a natural feature of an unnatural place.[21]

The other great opus on the subject of urban immorality, published only a few years after Parent-Duchâtelet's, issued from the pen of Antoine-Honoré Frégier, a department chief in the Prefecture of the Seine. In a long book that received a prize from the Academy of Moral and Political Sciences, Frégier treated 'the dangerous classes of the population', ostensibly including big cities in general but actually limiting his attention to Paris. He felt that a careful examination of the capital would help greatly to illuminate the relationships between criminality and the city as such, 'in the midst of which corruption spreads more easily [than in the countryside]'. The Parisian example could go a long way toward enabling the reader to obtain an accurate conception of 'the vicious and delinquent agglomerations which agitate in the metropolises and in the substantial cities of countries other than France' as well as in French cities other than Paris itself. Frégier proposed to analyze evildoers of all sorts, including elegant swindlers who operated at the upper levels of polite society and ne'er-do-wells from respectable middle-class homes. But as he proceeded in his analysis he focused continually on impoverished workers in such a way that the adjectives 'dangerous' and 'laboring' became almost synonymous. Vice and poverty were inextricably linked, and they pervaded the great bulk of the Parisian population.[22]

The ramifications of lower-class misery in urban settings received their fullest treatment in two works published in 1840 by Villermé and by Eugène Buret, both of whom looked well beyond the confines of the French capital. Villermé, in his great survey of the physical and moral condition of French textile workers, had next to nothing to say about Paris. Instead, he focused on towns such as Lille, Lyons, Mulhouse, and Rouen. Charged with the task of investigating working-class living standards by the same Academy that had honored Frégier and was to honor Buret, Villermé displayed a fundamentally antisocialist bias that reflected much better than Buret's outlook the conservative views of his fellow academicians. He sought to prove that the socialists had exaggerated the extent of the ills induced by industrialism and that whatever working-class hardships did exist were to a large extent self-inflicted.[23]

Villermé's explanations for what he saw carried less weight than his descriptions of the conditions themselves, which provided abundant evidence of social suffering over which the workers seemed to have little if any control. One of the most famous passages in the work depicted the cellars inhabited by the poorest workers in Lille. In these dark and crowded quarters, which contained only the barest minimum of furniture, many of the city's laborers were literally piled on top of one another. In many of the beds, Villermé wrote, 'father, mother, old people, children, adults crowd together, heaped up.... The reader will complete the picture, but ... his imagination must not recoil from any of the disgusting mysteries that take place on these impure couches, in the heart of darkness and intoxication'. Similar if somewhat less shocking situations were observable in other cities, leading Villermé to conclude that textile workers who lived on the land, where they could combine weaving with agricultural work, enjoyed a much healthier and more virtuous life than those who had flocked to the towns.[24]

Buret, whose study of working-class misery included Paris and other French cities as well as England, argued that phenomena such as poverty, disease, prostitution, and crime had not reached such great proportions in his own country as they had across the Channel. Inasmuch as France had not progressed as far as its neighbor in the area of industrial development, it suffered from much less social distress. 'England', he wrote, 'has experienced the social war of industry much longer than we have, and it must therefore count a larger number of wounded and dead'. Moreover, he believed that because of the more equitable distribution of land effected in France during the Revolution, the French people would never experience the hardships into which the English had 'plunged'.[25]

Nonetheless, Buret discerned great suffering at home as well as abroad, and he found it primarily in urban centers. Basing his remarks on an analysis of statistics pertaining to indigence in six dozen of the largest French towns, he concluded, 'Misery increases with the population.... The more numerous the armies, the bloodier the battles.... The hospitals of the populous towns are like the ambulances which march behind the great armies'. Buret did not really analyze and certainly did not espouse class conflict, but his combination of military and medical metaphors clearly implied a view of the city as a place in which the struggle to survive continually took a heavy toll in human life and happiness. Pointing to sharp contrasts between urban wealth and urban squalor, he went on to write, 'Perceived poverty, that which is conscious of itself, the distress that lays claim implacably to the assistance of public charity, is pretty nearly the privilege of the cities'. In Paris, the gap between opulent luxury on the one hand and destitution on the other had reached its zenith. Poverty remained well enough hidden so that visitors to the city did not have to confront it, but in the *ateliers*, the hospitals, the workhouses, and more generally in the older quarters far away from the city center, wretched misery was painfully evident. Although economic and social conditions varied less within French towns outside Paris, Buret also subjected them to harsh criticism. In fact, he seemed to believe that in absolute terms the smaller industrial cities suffered most of all from social misery. 'Despite the regulations of the police and despite the precautions taken by local authorities', he wrote, 'each industrial city creates in its heart a Little Ireland'. Lille ranked as the worst city in this respect, but, drawing on Villermé, Buret commented negatively on the smaller towns of Mulhouse and Rheims as well. Finally, unlike Villermé, he argued that French (as well as

English) misery stemmed from fundamental defects in the workings of society that could only be remedied through radical departures from economic liberalism. Solutions to urban problems necessitated far-reaching (though non-violent) changes in the structure of society as a whole. Buret, like Engels, evaluated the city from a socialist standpoint, without, however, calling for a proletarian revolution.[26]

Throughout the 1830s and 1840s, many French writers echoed the insistence by these social investigators on the physical and moral insalubrity of the French capital. As Louis Chevalier has shown quite convincingly, close connections developed between the social scientific perceptions of the city and the perceptions purveyed by publicists and particularly by leading novelists. The *Journal des Débats* and the *Globe* commented extensively on Villermé's studies of the Parisian population, as well as on demographic studies by others, starting in the mid-1820s. In the 1830s, the Vicomte de Launay exclaimed,

> How ugly Paris seems after one has been away for a year.... How one stifles in these dark, damp, narrow corridors which you are pleased to call the streets of Paris! One would think one was in an underground city, so sluggish is the air, so profound the obscurity.... And the thousands of people live, bustle, throng in the liquid darkness, like reptiles in a marsh.

In 1848, Victor Considérant, a disciple of the socialist Charles Fourier, looked up from the streets, but what he saw was just as grim, and his thoughts about it were even more depressing.

> Look at Paris: all these windows, doors and apertures are mouths which need to breathe — and above it all you can see, when the wind is not blowing, a leaden, heavy, gray-and-blueish atmosphere composed of all the foul exhalations of this great sink. This atmosphere is the crown on the great capital's brow; this is the atmosphere that Paris breathes; beneath it Paris stifles.... Paris is a great manufactory of putrefaction, in which poverty, plague and disease labor in concert, and air and sunlight barely enter. Paris is a foul hole where plants wilt and perish and four out of seven children die within the year.

Another writer of the period observed, 'Those who have something to hide come to Paris. They see the labyrinths of its streets and the depravity of its morals, and they plunge into it as into a forest.... The nearly 900,000 persons thronging it are prey to a corruption twice as bad as that of the 31 millions surrounding them'. One could go on, courtesy of Chevalier, at much greater length quoting such passages from writings by many little-known authors, all of whom expressed and strengthened a widespread belief that Paris suffered from an irremediable malaise that stemmed directly from its rapid growth and its inflated size.[27]

Both the social and the physical condition of Paris during the period of the Restoration and the July Monarchy was best captured for posterity in the works of three social novelists, two of whom were unquestionably great artists as well as careful observers. The greatest of the three, Honoré de

Balzac, depended on Paris as a setting for his fiction just as much as Dickens depended on London. With Dickens and with Nicolai Gogol, according to Donald Fanger, Balzac was one of 'the first fully to realize the potentialities of the metropolis as a subject for fiction'. Many passages in the novels that comprise his multivolume *Comédie humaine* (first published between 1829 and 1847) indicate detailed awareness of the findings of the social investigators who were active while he was writing. Balzac described life and death in the capital with a high degree of fidelity to the often unpleasant facts as they had been recorded in the best works of empirical social science available at the time. As Chevalier puts it,

> Mortality, fertility, economic situation, social group, criminality: all these problems Balzac defines by estimates or proportions which, though sometimes inconsistent, denote an attention to official or generally accepted numerical data, expressing at the very least the inability of the novelist — like the historian — to describe social developments save by assessing and expressing them in terms of figures.

Sickness and death from diseases such as cholera and smallpox, among others, figure prominently in Balzac's *oeuvre*.[28]

Balzac's works also emphasize social pathology in general and criminality in particular. In his *Etudes philosophiques* (1834), speaking through Félix Davin, Balzac wrote concerning Paris,

> Here genuine feelings are the exception; they are broken by the play of interests, crushed between the wheels of this mechanical world. Virtue is slandered here; innocence is sold here. Passions have given way to ruinous tastes and vices; everything is sublimated, is analyzed, bought and sold. It is a bazaar where everything has its price, and the calculations are made in broad daylight without shame. Humanity has only two forms, the deceiver and the deceived.

The moral world that Balzac both described and indicted consisted largely of members of the urban upper and middle classes who sought relentlessly to satisfy their craving for money and pleasure. In so doing, they thought only of themselves, making human solidarity, even at the level of the family, virtually impossible. Balzac made that point most sharply in his account of family relationships in *Le père Goriot* (1835). In this novel the old and indulgent father is cruelly exploited by his ungrateful daughters, and other parent-child relationships appear in a similarly unhappy light. In the early novels the main form of criminality was theft, and criminals were mostly larger than life individuals, such as Vautrin. But as he grew older, Balzac evinced a growing tendency to regard not only callousness but also the worst forms of lawlessness as quite ordinary phenomena, which permeated Parisian society. Theft gave way to murder, and crime in general became an emanation from the masses that expressed their degraded social condition. Balzac thus began to approach the newer view (espoused among others by Frégier) according to which urban criminality characterized a large portion if not the great bulk of urban society as a whole.[29]

5　Violence in the streets of Paris. The illustration draws the reader's attention to
the darkness and the evil that pervade a highly influential work of urban fiction (source:
Eugène Sue, *Les mystères de Paris*, rev. ed., I [1843], 4).

The works of fiction that explored the Parisian underworld most thoroughly were two enormous novels, Eugène Sue's *Mystères de Paris* (1842-43) and
Victor Hugo's *Les misérables* (begun in the early 1840s, published in 1862).
Sue wrote in lurid and sensational detail about life among the lowliest of the
city's inhabitants. In his eyes, Paris was a murky labyrinth, a place in which
intricate conspiracies were hatched and terrible deeds were done by men
whom he described as 'barbarians as far outside civilization as the savage
tribes portrayed so well by [James Fenimore] Cooper'. Sue noted the
importance of heredity in producing these savages, but, motivated by strong
humanitarianism, he sought to turn the attention of the upper classes to the
ravages wrought by the urban environment. Eagerly devoured by a mass

public at the time (the novel was one of the first to appear originally as a series of installments in the daily press), Sue's work had an enormous influence both at home and abroad.[30]

The links and the parallels between Sue and the much greater Hugo are quite clear. Having inspired Sue via the richly descriptive passages in his historical *Notre Dame de Paris* (1831), Hugo received back from his fellow novelist ample repayment in kind. His passionate concern in *Les misérables* with the fate of society's victims bore witness to Sue's literary example, as did many of the particular human types and situations he delineated. The familiar story of the hunted convict Jean Valjean, sentenced as a young man to the dreaded galleys because he had stolen a loaf of bread for his starving family, need not be retold here. What most needs to be emphasized about it at this juncture is that it served as the focal point for Hugo's depiction of the misery that pervaded all parts of the city about which he wrote, excepting only the convent in which Valjean finds refuge with his quasi-daughter Cosette and the houses inhabited by old Monsieur Gillenormand and the other frivolous legitimists with whom he associates. And even Gillenormand suffers, owing to the decision by his idealistic grandson, Marius Pontmercy, to break with his family and cast his lot with the young revolutionaries who stage the futile insurrection of 1832. Hugo used various images to convey a sense of the evil that lurked beneath the surface of polite Parisian society. 'Paris', he wrote, 'is a maelstrom in which everything is lost; and everything disappears in this whirlpool of the world as in the whirlpool of the sea'. He also commented,

> Cities, like forests, have their dens in which hide all their vilest and most terrible monsters. But in cities, what hides thus is ferocious, unclean and petty, that is to say, ugly; in forests, what hides is ferocious, savage, and grand, that is to say beautiful. Den for den, those of beasts are preferable to those of men. Caverns are better than the wretched holes which shelter humanity.[31]

Much the most memorable sections of the novel recount Valjean's long trek through the sewers, with the wounded Marius on his shoulders. Here, in passages that were certainly influenced by the sanitary treatises of Parent-Duchâtelet, Hugo created a powerful image that rendered the city figuratively as well as literally from below. The sewer was 'the conscience of the city', stripping away all its pretenses. 'In this lurid place', Hugo wrote, 'there is darkness, but there are no secrets.... All the uncleanness of civilization, when once out of service, falls into this pit of truth'. Having surveyed Paris toward the start of his first great novel from the pinnacle of a cathedral, he now wandered beneath it in subterranean passages, the dead and the discarded contents of which remorselessly reproduced and exposed the unhappy world of those who lived above them.[32]

Neither Balzac nor Hugo could by any stretch of the critical imagination be regarded as anti-urban, let alone anti-Parisian. Like Dickens, they worked in a relationship of creative tension with the city, admiring and reveling in it even as they exposed and castigated its faults. In one of his early comments on Paris, Balzac had exclaimed, 'O civilization! O Paris! Admirable kaleidoscope, which, always agitated, shows us these four baubles: man, woman, child, and old person, in so many forms that its pictures are innumerable! O marvelous Paris!' A few years later, in his novel *Ferragus*, he again celebrated the city as a source of rich diversity and aesthetic delight, this time evoking its poetic qualities: 'O Paris! Whoever has not admired your somber landscapes, your bright vistas, your deep and silent culs-de-sac, whoever has not heard your murmurs between midnight and two o'clock in the morning, knows nothing of your true poesy, nor of your great and bizarre contrasts'. The sense of vastness, variety, and fascination conveyed in these passages was reinforced by some of the other metaphors Balzac used to refer to the city. Sometimes he labeled it a 'cauldron' (cuve), sometimes an 'ocean', in both cases implying a rather different attitude from the one he suggested when he called it a 'monster'. In short, Paris awed and inspired Balzac more than it disgusted or repelled him.[33]

Hugo expressed his love for Paris in *Les misérables* still more clearly. Alluding briefly to the fact that he had lived in exile since breaking with Louis Napoleon in 1851, he wrote affectionately about the old Paris he had known in earlier years — a Paris that was disappearing as a result of the emperor's ambitious schemes of urban renewal. Paris was 'the ceiling of the human race ... an epitome of dead and living manners and customs ... a synonym of Cosmos'. But it was more than just a spectacular variety show or a repository of the past. Paris, he wrote,

> builds up in every mind the ideal of progress; the liberating dogmas which it forges are swords by the pillows of generations, and with the soul of its thinkers and poets have all the heroes of all nations since 1789 been made.... The smoke of its roofs is the ideas of the universe. A heap of mud and stone, if you will, but above all a moral being. It is more than great, it is immense. Why? Because it dares.

Here was a view of Paris as a city that had stored up vast moral capital by playing a great and glorious role on the stage of world history.[34]

The delight in and devotion to Paris that competed strongly in the writings of Balzac and Hugo with their vivid awareness of pervasive immorality and suffering appeared more clearly in the works of numerous other authors, all but one of whom were admittedly far less well known than either of the two great novelists. These other men, on the whole, contributed rather less ambiguously to the elaboration and perpetuation of a distinctly generous and sympathetic view of the capital — one that emphasized its energy, its grandeur, and its beneficence. None was a novelist. Some were belletrists, others historians or social scientists. These were the men who most effectively counteracted the depictions of urban misery among the working classes and the dangerous classes presented by the empirical social investigators and the general sense of social malaise expressed by the social novelists.

One can do no better in considering the views of these writers than to begin with the long poem titled simply *Paris* that the romantic philosopher-poet Alfred de Vigny wrote in 1831. This work exemplifies a new poetic conception of the city that manifested itself in a large body of verse between the revolutions of 1830 and 1848. (Pierre Citron has located eighty-four poems from the period that treat Paris as a whole or some general aspect of the city, compared with only six from the years 1820-30.) Paris emerged from this poetry as a living being, an organism animated by spiritual forces. Even when it was compared with the sea or a volcano rather than with a lion or with Hercules, it displayed dynamism, and usually, as in the view of Vigny, it deserved devotion. Using an abundance of biblical metaphors, Vigny propagated a vision of Paris as not only a living but also a sacred entity. God himself had marked out the limits of the city, and if He should somehow order its destruction the exterminating angel 'would tremble in committing a second deicide'. Paris was holy not so much because of the revolutions it had accomplished as because of its spiritual achievements: the ideas it had disseminated and the light it still radiated. Images of recently installed gas street lamps served to reinforce the sense of Paris as a source of moral enlightenment. Moreover, biblical images of a fiery furnace suggested not only light but also the more active forging of 'a totally new world by this flame'. Some passages in the poem took an agnostic position on the matter of whether this new world would be better or worse than the old one. Vigny did not know for sure whether what the city represented was good or evil, but it was splendid in any case. As Citron has written, 'The bet [by Vigny] is implicit: it is in favor of the only illuminated path open, with its risks, to the human race. Paris is the symbol of the only hope possible for humanity: that of the progress of thought. Paris is a danger that must be run'.[35]

Jules Michelet, the greatest of the French romantic historians and an archivist and professor until he lost his official positions in 1851 because he refused to swear allegiance to Louis Napoleon, was well situated to mythologize Paris for a large audience of attentive readers. During the 1830s and 1840s and after the middle of the century, he expressed more often and more effectively than any other writer the view of Paris as a special place that deserved the heartfelt devotion of men everywhere. In his journals and in other early writings he rhapsodized about its sweetness and its charm. He called it his 'house', presenting it as a maternal refuge, and unlike Balzac and Hugo he never used pejorative imagery to represent the city in its entirety. There was, he wrote, 'no city more beautiful, more complete, more humane'. He even celebrated 'the sacred mud of the metropolis of the world', in which was mixed the sweat of earlier generations of heroic Parisians. The beauty and holiness of Paris appeared not so much through observation of the present (and Michelet had little to say about contemporary urban society) as through imaginative contemplation of the past. What made Paris worthy of devotion in Michelet's eyes was its glorious history, the traces of which were everywhere in evidence. Scenes of and monuments to heroism abounded, from the Champ de Mars to the Panthéon and the Invalides. Like Vigny and Hugo, Michelet romanticized Paris as a place that had been the conscience of the world and the leader in the pursuit of progress. As he wrote in the second volume of his *Histoire de la Révolution française* (1847), Paris was 'this astonishing crucible' in which ideas were continually created and men were transformed. Because, as he wrote elsewhere, it had guided humanity, it was 'the universal city of the world'.[36]

Much the same spirit evident in Michelet's writings appeared in a work by one of his lesser contemporaries, the prolific if undistinguished Alphonse Esquiros. Writing in the mid-1840s, Esquiros described the city of his own day as a place that encapsulated a glorious past in an imposing present. 'Paris', he wrote 'is an idea in the framework of stone. This encyclopedic city conserves and augments incessantly within its walls the store of all human knowledge and all useful discoveries'. It did so not only through its museums and its academic institutions but also through a host of physical monuments, which pointed to the history of the nation and beyond that to the progress of the world. He wrote that 'the successive augmentation of Parisian civilization' offered 'an image of the movement and formation of all peoples'. To tour Paris was 'to grasp in microcosm within the confines of one city the human events which the law of progress brings about in the large throughout the whole world'. Few French authors would have disagreed.[37]

After Baron Haussmann, during the early part of the reign of Napoleon III, had begun his vast projects of urban modernization and beautification — laying out new streets and widening old ones above ground and improving sewers and water mains below ground — many men looked even more favorably on the French capital. By the end of the 1850s, memories of the turbulence and bloodshed that had occurred in 1848 were fading, and there was growing emphasis on the progress the city had experienced under the aegis of a technologically innovative despotism. A popular historian, in a text intended for use in public schools, told his young readers that Paris was 'the heart of France' and 'the hearth of civilization, which radiates from there throughout the Empire and is going to spread to all of Europe'. It was 'the most beautiful, the richest, and the most flourishing city of the universe'. Already far advanced by mid-century, it had progressed still further under the tutelage of Napoleon III. Alfred Legoyt, an economist and civil servant, wrote glowingly a few years later, in the earliest general assessment of urbanization by any French author, about the enormous strides forward the city had taken during the preceding decade and a half. One might harbor reservations with regard to the desirability of some of the public works the imperial government had sponsored, but 'Paris transformed' had to be considered a splendid achievement: 'a work of great utility, great benevo-

6 The rebuilt Rue de Rivoli in Paris. Begun under Napoleon I, the construction along this elegant street was completed during the Second Empire under the direction of Baron Haussmann (source: *Paris nouveau et ses environs* [1857]).

lence, and great political prescience'. New parks and baths as well as other sanitary improvements had made the population healthier, and new schools, churches, and other public buildings had improved Parisian life in other ways, providing an example of 'hygienic and moral' betterment that other French cities would do well to emulate.[38]

Between 1870 and 1905, Maxime Du Camp, another prolific author who ranged widely in his many writings, published nine editions of a vast survey of Parisian life in which the city similarly appeared as an admirable example of enlightened administration, both public and private. The title of the work, with its references to organs and functions, already suggested the general view of Paris as a harmonious system conveyed by the study as a whole. Owing in large measure to the transformation it had experienced since mid-century, Paris offered not only a fascinating display of perpetual motion and nervous energy but also the miraculous spectacle of a vast 'body' whose constituent parts all contributed to the well-being of the whole. Du Camp mixed his metaphors, referring in one sentence to 'administrative organs' and to 'the different wheels of such a vast, such an ingenious mechanism', but both sorts of imagery indicated the same feeling. They expressed succinctly his view of the city as a place in which the ordinary citizen could rely with confidence on the smooth functioning of urban institutions: the post offices and the railways, the courts and the prisons, the hospitals and the schools, the banks and the theaters. 'Paris', he assured his readers, 'can rest in peace; while it amuses itself and while it works, while it sleeps and while it wakes, its innumerable guardians arrange the elements of its life without respite and take care of everything so that nothing, whether necessary or superfluous, is lacking'.[39]

The last words on Paris during the years of the Second Empire belong to one of the greatest of all the French writers whom the city engaged at that time, the early modernist poet Charles Baudelaire. He was the quintessential urbanite. His literary stature *vis-à-vis* others who grappled with the city rested, however, not on what most of his readers would have regarded as praise for Paris but rather on the ways in which he unified widely divergent attitudes toward urban experience within the framework of his own artistic vision. In the verses first published together under the heading 'Tableaux parisiens' in the second edition of *Les fleurs du mal* (1861) and in the later poems published after his death in 1867 both as *Petits poèmes en prose* and as *Le spleen de Paris*, Baudelaire enunciated a view of the city that combined extreme revulsion and fervent affirmation.

Baudelaire's distinctive achievement as an urban poet was to immerse himself in the wretchedness and misery of the city and at the same time to celebrate the city precisely for the very worst of its defects as a stimulus to aesthetic creativity. He began his poem 'The Little Old Women' with the lines 'In sinuous folds of cities old and grim,/Where all things, even horror, turn to grace,/I follow, in obedience to my whim,/Strange, feeble, charming creatures round the place'. Other poems, about prostitutes and gamblers, blind men and beggars, recorded his sense of the urban milieu as a place where physical and moral degradation provided the raw material that enabled the artist to enlarge and enhance his aesthetic sensibilities. Since sickness was so much more interesting than health, the city was endlessly fascinating. The epilogue to *Le spleen de Paris* articulated this view with the utmost clarity. Looking down on Paris from on high, Baudelaire saw it as 'Hospital, brothel, purgatory, hell, prison,/Where every enormity blooms like a flower', and he went on to conclude, 'I love you, infamous capital! Courtesans and bandits, such are the pleasures you often offer,/Which the vulgar herd cannot understand!'[40]

The artist had to pay a high price when he delighted in the city in this manner. Whatever sympathy he might feel and express for society's outcasts, he inevitably separated himself from his fellow man and thus renounced the possibility of participating in an integrated social whole. The city thus became the place where the sensitive artist experienced particularly acute isolation from ordinary people, even as he passed by and mingled among them. Baudelaire's fascination with Paris was not unrelated to the sentiments voiced by earlier writers, such as Balzac and Vigny, but his fundamental antisociability pointed much more clearly to the decadent aestheticism of the *fin de siècle*, for which his work served as a brilliant example and a fertile source of inspiration.

Two features of French urban thought during this period deserve special emphasis by way of summary. One is the virtual absence of critical thinking that looked toward the past. France had no Southey or Ruskin, let alone a Wilhelm Heinrich Riehl (about whom, more shortly). To be sure, there were quite vocal conservatives during the period of the Restoration (1815-30), but they had little to say about the city. In later decades, the reassertion and elaboration of ideas descended from the Revolution led Frenchmen away from pre-urban traditionalism, the conservative social values of Balzac being perhaps the major exception to this generalization. Consequently, as in the case of French writing about cities in England, criticism by Frenchmen of urban society in their own country was more likely to be associated with ideologies of the left than with those of the right. A second noteworthy feature stemmed from the centrality of Paris in the overall French experience of urban life. Although the French capital received its fair share of adverse publicity from social investigators and social novelists, it tended on the whole to elicit both fascination and respect, especially after about 1850. The historic significance of Paris as a stronghold for the forces of progress in the past and the technological and administrative advances of the city in the present, together with the city's vibrant diversity and color, imparted an increasingly favorable quality to French urban thinking during the century's third quarter.

The city between tradition and modernity in Germany

The economic, social, and political backwardness of Germany relative to Western Europe throughout at least the first half of the nineteenth century meant both that the Germans displayed rather little interest in specifically urban phenomena and also that what they did have to say about cities frequently revealed peculiarly German concerns and attitudes. The Germans, though just as attentive as the French to the British paradigm of industrial urbanization, experienced urban growth at their own pace and in their own manner, responding to the city in ways that often diverged from the responses of men in neighboring countries. The period between the 1840s and the late 1870s already witnessed the articulation of some of the extreme positions for and against the city that were to become increasingly characteristic of much of the German debate in later years, and the way in which the debate was conducted pointed clearly to the continuing effects of German retardation. In contrast to the situation in France, there was a great deal of both urban and anti-urban nostalgia. Progressive pro-urbanists often justified cities with reference to a quite distant past, and many critics evinced unmistakable conservatism.[41]

German anti-urbanism — not just criticism of this or that blemish on the face of the city but more fundamentally anti-modernist hostility to the big city as such — found an early and a forceful spokesman during the 1850s in Wilhelm Heinrich Riehl. Riehl was a Bavarian journalist and university professor, whose social and political conservatism reflected the fears felt by many other intellectuals during the years after the revolutions of 1848-49.[42] In a multivolume sociological and ethnographic treatise on contemporary Germany, he depicted cities both as symbols and as sources of the worst aspects of the modern world. When he wrote, 'Europe is becoming sick as a result of the monstrosity of its big cities', he had in mind a wide range of maladies. Urban development entailed the loss of national character, the growth of social, psychological, and political instability, and numerous cultural ills. Like the capital cities constructed by German princes during the eighteenth century, which had been modeled on Versailles, German cities of the nineteenth century increasingly resembled foreign prototypes, such as Paris and London, rather than the distinctively German cities of earlier centuries. 'The originality of German urban life' was disappearing as big cities rid themselves of 'every distinguishing feature of nationality' and became 'the abode of a leveling cosmopolitanism'.[43]

The loss of a stable social order, firmly based on the maintenance of the traditional *Stände* (nobility, peasantry, *Bürgertum*) and on the family caused Riehl even greater concern. After pointing out that cities depended for their growth (if not for their very survival) on a migratory surplus from the countryside, he painted a grim picture of the urban social scene. Urban populations consisted increasingly of a rootless proletariat whose members came to the big city in hope of making easy fortunes and were quick to move on when opportunity appeared to beckon. The new proletarians had broken loose not only from the system of social estates but also from familial ties. An urbanite lived in solitude, and the 'fragmentation' from which he suffered increased in direct proportion to the size of the city he inhabited. Even when city dwellers did reside with their families, Riehl asserted, domestic life lacked much of the meaning it had in the countryside. The urban home, unlike its rural counterpart, no longer served as a place of regular religious worship for family members. Indeed, city households were 'devoid of all religiosity'.[44]

The multitude of stimuli offered by great metropolises, which were 'gigantic encyclopedias of the customs, the art, and the industry of all civilized Europe', threatened the psychic well-being of the individual and the political stability of the nation. Having gone to the city in search of broader horizons, young people were less likely to acquire maturity than to become 'intoxicated, confused, and discontented' as a result of their new experiences.

What worried Riehl most about the confused discontent of the young urban proletarians was the likelihood that in conjunction with the social disintegration prevalent among the rest of the Fourth Estate it would lead to renewed political turmoil. Unlike the highly conservative peasant, the typical lower-class urbanite was all too likely to be animated by a 'revolutionary spirit' that led him in search of 'theoretically phantasized novelty'. Having been won over to the socialist and communist slogans propagated by uprooted intellectuals, the proletariat sought to dominate not only the city but also, using the city as its base, the whole country. The growing power of the urban masses thus threatened the very foundations of civilized society.[45]

Riehl also objected sharply to other aspects of the modern urban scene, especially the physical ugliness of cities and the kind of cultural life they promoted. Recently built urban housing amounted to little more than 'proletarian barracks'. It had been designed by speculators to meet the immediate needs of solitary individuals at the lowest possible cost and was totally devoid of the ornamental features that might appeal to a family over the long run. Modern city streets were similarly lacking in aesthetic appeal. In contrast to the more picturesque streets of the past, with their curves and turns and variations in the size of buildings, a broad, straight 'parade street', such as the new Ludwigsstrasse in Munich, looked like 'a lifeless academic model'. Flanked by unbroken lines of oversized buildings, none of which reflected the scale or the tastes of an individual family, the Ludwigsstrasse symbolized 'the leveling tendencies of the modern money economy'. Finally, Riehl maintained that big cities hindered the 'spiritual concentration' necessary for the emergence of great artists and thinkers, that they fostered 'blasé and frivolous taste' among the consumers of culture, and that they led to the displacement of the craftsman's art by industrial technology. For all these reasons, Riehl predicted without regret or apprehension that modern cities would ultimately collapse.[46]

Riehl stood pretty much alone in Germany during the mid-nineteenth century as a general interpreter of urban life, but several other authors helped in varying ways to reinforce one or another of his anti-urban sentiments. Loud echoes of Riehl's social and political conservatism were clearly audible in an article on cities that appeared in the 1860s in the political encyclopedia edited by the reactionary Prussian publicist, Hermann Wagener. The author admitted that large towns had their virtues, mainly in the areas of cultural and economic development, but he quickly turned to 'the shadowy side, religious and political corruption, social misery, and the revolutionary pursuit of innovation'. The cities were 'the fermenting element in the state, through which the division of labor continually fragments and reshapes society', and they were 'the source of all the evils that accompany the division of labor: one-sidedness, centralization, the weakening of authority, pauperism, sensuality, the craving for change, and so on'.[47]

A spirit of traditionalist anti-modernity also appeared in the works of a prolific and widely read novelist from northern Germany, Wilhelm Raabe. In his *Die Chronik der Sperlingsgasse* (1857), *Der Hungerpastor* (1864), and *Meister Autor* (1874), among numerous other works that continued to appear on into the 1890s, Raabe voiced the sense of disillusionment and loneliness he had felt as a university student in Berlin after moving there from the much smaller city of Magdeburg. Especially in his early novels, Raabe also expressed strong sympathy for the plight of the urban poor, much in the manner of Eugène Sue, but his deepest affections were reserved for humble introverts and dreamers who thrived in the cosy security of small-town surroundings. As he grew older, he became increasingly critical of modern mechanization, materialism, rootlessness, and aimlessness, all of which he perceived in excess in the big city, and he evinced an ever stronger attachment to the *Kleinstadt* as a *heile Welt* that provided a refuge and a safeguard for the spiritual life.[48]

Other authors who criticized the urban scene during the 1860s and 1870s did so from a standpoint that implied acceptance of the necessity of the city and emphasized the need to remedy its defects rather than to reject it. Carl Friedrich Reichardt, an architect in Hamburg, denounced the failure by planners to deal sensibly with the physical chaos inherited from the Middle Ages. Only if there were 'a total transformation of the small, self-contained, uncomfortable, and unhealthy medieval city into its opposite, the rationally designed, salubrious, and open modern big city', would cities become tolerable places in which to live. In the 1870s, there was growing awareness of an urban housing problem as a result of the sudden influx of migrants from villages and the countryside and the shortage of new accommodation. Indeed, so far as I know, the first German work of any kind — either a book or an essay — that contained the word *Grossstadt* in its title was a book by a reform-minded countess who viewed the big cities in terms of their *Wohnungsnot* ('housing deficit'). She insisted that the moral improvement that was essential for the more general betterment of working-class living conditions would only take place if the workers were given larger, healthier, and more pleasant dwellings. About the same time, Heinrich Bettzeich, a journalist, linked the housing problem to the phenomenon of urban crime. He was searching for possible remedies that might be available to the 'forces of salvation' in their struggle against 'the titanic forces of destruction and annihilation' represented by 'the dangerous classes'. Toward this end, he advocated the elimination of slums together with the construction of lower-density housing in previously undeveloped areas on the outskirts of big cities, where the benefits of the city and the countryside could be combined.[49]

These criticisms contrasted sharply with expressions of civic pride that were just as deeply rooted as small-town and rural conservatism in the German past. Many German cities had, it must be remembered, become highly developed during the Middle Ages and the early modern period, and their inhabitants could look back on a long urban history with a considerable sense of collective achievement. Such pride was especially evident in towns that had enjoyed the status of Imperial Free Cities (*Reichsstädte*) before the territorial reorganization carried out under the guidance of Napoleon in 1803, only a handful of which continued to enjoy political independence thereafter. The senate of Frankfurt am Main, one of the fortunate few, received evidence of this sentiment in a letter from the city's most famous son, the poet Johann Wolfgang von Goethe. He wrote in the 1820s that there was 'no glimpse into history more beautiful than the one that teaches us how the cities of Germany formed highly significant entities through action, integrity, and dependability, and ... [how they] gained great advantages as they spread life and commerce'. Accordingly, it was 'of the greatest importance for the thinking man to belong to such corporations'. The still independent Hanseatic cities of the far north also fostered a highly positive urban self-consciousness, whose roots reached similarly far into the past. The author of a history of Hamburg that appeared in the 1840s exemplified this attitude when he wrote that belonging to a city was just as important as belonging to a state (in Hamburg of course the city was a state) and that the story of the urban past would show the citizenry 'how the city became great and rich through its own efforts, how it became independent, and how it has maintained and will maintain itself'. Hamburg had 'a beautiful history, full of the means to encourage energy, freedom, communal spirit, and civic virtue'. About the same time, a clergyman in nearby Bremen wrote a long history of his city that praised the rugged independence and other virtues displayed by men there during their glorious past. Meanwhile, a schoolteacher in Nuremberg, which had been incorporated into the kingdom of Bavaria earlier in the century, wrote in a guidebook intended for visiting academics about the city's traditional position as 'a midpoint of commerce and art [and] a refuge for learning' and asserted that its decline from its earlier greatness stemmed from external forces rather than from any factors that reflected internal weaknesses. Many similar statements by other authors who wrote about these and other cities could be amassed quite easily. Numerous spokesmen for towns that had experienced their golden age in centuries past looked back with enormous satisfaction but also with nostalgia on a history of political autonomy, of commercial prosperity, and of artistic excellence, much of which was still evident in fine old houses, churches, and town halls.[50]

Men who sought forward-looking political changes sprang to the city's defense in more general terms. Their urban enthusiasms directly reflected the intensity of the struggle in which they found themselves in their efforts to modernize the entrenched and outdated system of authoritarian rule represented before political unification by several dozen state governments in the area of the German Confederation.

On the far left, the radical publicist Ernst Dronke incurred the wrath of the Prussian government in the mid-1840s by writing a book about Berlin

7   The old Leipzig Town Hall. Built in the mid-sixteenth century, this fine Renaissance *Rathaus* served in the mid-nineteenth both as a reminder of a glorious past and as a center of civic activity (source: *Leipzig: Ein Führer durch die Stadt und ihre Umgebungen* [Leipzig, 1860], 144).

that identified a wide range of social ills. He regarded widespread crime and prostitution in the capital as forms of social protest against 'the immorality of inequality' in general and against the exploitation of the proletariat in particular. But he also prized Berlin as 'the city of intelligence', a place in which contemporary ideas were discussed critically and the clash of rival ideologies produced a fruitfully heightened political consciousness. 'Life in a big city', he wrote, 'is always stimulating, precisely because it is many-sided, and I have often heard intelligent men say that they could not live in any other city'. Just as ideas competed against one another, so too did individuals and social groups, and although this competition often had unpleasant and unfair consequences it also benefited society by undermining the privileges and barriers characteristic of the old regime. Titled aristocrats in particular found it more and more difficult to assert their traditional prerogatives in the big city, and others, who would have felt unduly inhibited by customary codes of conduct and 'philistine prejudices' had they lived in a small town, experienced a refreshing sense of personal freedom. 'On the streets and elsewhere in public, everything surges and rushes together', Dronke wrote, 'high and low, rich and poor: no one is limited by anyone else. Only within the houses do caste-like differences still assert themselves'. Dronke's view of the big city by no means overlooked urban blemishes: social injustice was one of his central themes. But, like Engels, he saw urbanization as a stimulus to the process of progressive change that would hopefully lead to far-reaching amelioration of those very defects.[51]

Moderate liberals, led by the politically influential professors who played a crucial role at the Frankfurt Parliament in 1848-49, articulated an urban ethos more wholeheartedly and propagated it more effectively. In the middle decades of the century, they derived great confidence from the political strength they had accumulated in cities and towns, where many of them translated their local prestige into honorary municipal offices and where their vote totals significantly surpassed the levels they attained statewide. Such considerations fostered the belief among liberals that the growth of cities heralded the future victory of progressive politics in society at large. They expected that as urbanization proceeded and as the urban *Bürgertum* grew in strength cities would become more and more potent agents of enlightenment and liberation, weaning the rural masses from political apathy and accustoming them to the rights and responsibilities of free citizenship.[52]

The liberals often made their case by talking just as much about the past as about the present or the future. A revealing statement of the liberal view appeared in 1843 (the same year that saw the appearance of Robert Vaughan's similarly optimistic *Age of Great Cities in England*) in an article written by a leading south German political theorist and parliamentarian, Carl Theodor Welcker, for the famous *Staats-Lexikon*, an encyclopedic and highly influential compendium of liberal thought. In his discussion of cities and city government, Welcker wrote, 'Life in cities awakens, unifies, and protects the higher aspirations, industry, commerce, [and] civilization in general.... Man becomes strong and educated only through close ties with his fellow men. Therefore, urban life distinguishes and furthers a higher cultural level among nations'. He went on to assert that Germany owed its cities a debt of gratitude for the role they had played from the outset in protecting the country both from feudal power and from anarchy and in fostering the ideas of civic freedom and representative government. Alluding to the notion of a Germanic political tradition of local liberty that had established itself in Anglo-Saxon Britain as well as in Germany itself, he contended that without the freedom German cities had enjoyed in the Middle Ages and for centuries thereafter the widely admired British constitution would never have evolved as it did and that German constitutionalism would be stymied in the present.[53]

Historians in the 1850s commented in a similar vein on the vital functions medieval cities had performed in nourishing the ideas of personal freedom and equality before the law. 'The flowering of the cities', wrote one Friedrich Wilhelm Barthold, 'broke through the sterile, rigid block into which feudal rule had transformed early German freedom', and what the cities had won for themselves at that time (though largely lost in subsequent centuries) would eventually become the property of the whole nation. Another historian, the prominent liberal Karl Biedermann, wrote admiringly about medieval cities as places 'where a large number of energetic, industrious, and clever men were collected at one point and found in firm solidarity a certain means of resisting illegitimate oppression'. He did not make any explicit references to the liberating functions of cities in the present, but the contemporary ramifications of his admiration for the urban virtues of the past were clear enough just the same.[54]

The reorientation of German political thought that occurred subsequently as a result of Otto von Bismarck's success in unifying German militarily between 1864 and 1871 — the waning of earlier liberal ideas in favor of a more authoritarian nationalism — began to be reflected in the 1870s in books that celebrated Berlin as a Prussian and a German capital. Julius Faucher, a journalist, insisted proudly that the *Reichshauptstadt* fully deserved to be ranked with Vienna, Paris, and London. It had not quite passed the million mark, but it would do so soon, and that gave cause to rejoice. Faucher contended that Berlin still lagged behind other capitals in many of its communal institutions and especially in its cultural life, but he clearly viewed it as a young city on the way up. Robert Springer, another publicist, lauded Berlin effusively in a popular work of history and description that identified the city in its title as 'the German imperial city'. He admitted that Berlin had its problems — especially in the area of housing — but what he emphasized was the way in which its progress from early times up to the present paralleled the ascent of the Prussian state to which it belonged.

> There thus emerged from a fishing village an imperial city — from insignificant and scattered fishermen's cottages the capital of an internally strong, extensive, populous, politically important state, glittering with masterpieces of architecture and sculpture, distinguished for artistic zeal and intellectual culture, for academic learning, for the flowering of commerce and industry, for the higher progress of social life.

In this view, the city became an emblem of national prosperity and power. Urban culture functioned as an adornment of the state and as proof of its vitality, while the liberating effects of city life were at best alluded to only briefly.[55]

In Germany, unlike Britain and to some extent France, there did not seem to be any discernible movement toward greater acceptance of the city as such between the 1840s and the 1870s. What happened was that the urban advocates shifted their emphases from political freedom to political power. Critics of cities were neither more nor less noticeable to any great degree than they had been several decades earlier. This situation reflected the fact that urban themes in general still attracted a good deal less attention here than they did elsewhere. The great debate about the *Grossstadt* was not to begin in earnest until the 1890s, when men with views such as those of either Welcker or Springer found themselves very much on the defensive as they confronted the heirs of Riehl and Wagener.

4

Anxiety and Hope in the United States

American writers in the mid-nineteenth century still devoted less attention to urban phenomena than their more highly urbanized brethren in Britain, but they displayed at least as much sensitivity to the city as the French and rather more than the Germans. By 1840 at the latest, they were becoming increasingly aware that an urban future awaited their country. As George Tucker, a professor of moral philosophy at the University of Virginia, wrote in a work on the history of the American economy and the American population, published in 1843, 'Whatever may be the good or evil tendencies of populous cities, they are the result to which all countries, that are at once fertile, free and intelligent, inevitably tend'. The rapid urbanization that marked the next quarter of a century led E. L. Godkin, editor of the prestigious *Nation*, to observe in 1869, 'The influence of cities is now almost all-pervading. They draw to them the most energetic and enterprising of the population, the greatest talent as well as the greatest wealth, the soberest and steadiest and most intelligent, as well as the most ignorant and vicious'.[1]

In their efforts to understand the emerging world of the big city, Americans, like Frenchmen and Germans, looked abroad. Though primarily concerned with the English urban experience, they also reflected occasionally on urban conditions elsewhere in Europe. But because of geographic distance, because of the vast qualitative differences that separated cities in the new world from cities in the old, and because of the sectional conflict between North and South, Americans who thought about urban problems were much more heavily preoccupied than the French and the Germans with developments at home.

Criticisms of cities at home and abroad

Although Thomas Jefferson had castigated cities as 'pestilential sores' and although several outbreaks of cholera later pointed up the unhealthiness of many American towns, medical men in the United States did not evince a great deal of interest during this period in urban sanitation. In so far as mid-nineteenth-century America witnessed an articulate public health movement in any way comparable to the efforts of Edwin Chadwick, Thomas Southwood Smith, and their followers in Britain or of Louis-René Villermé and A. J. P. Parent-Duchâtelet in France, what it saw was largely the work of John H. Griscom and a few others in New York. Griscom, the city's chief health officer starting in 1842, enlarged part of one of his early reports and used it as the basis for a famous lecture in 1844 (published as a pamphlet the following year) on the *Sanitary Condition of the Laboring Population of New York*. In this and in later writings, Griscom displayed a level of concern with public health that was quite atypical of the American medical profession at large. Motivated by a strong belief that the pursuit of cleanliness was a moral and a religious obligation, he emphasized the unhealthiness of urban life with a view to encouraging city dwellers to make their habitats as salubrious as possible. He believed that public health reform would cure not only physical illnesses but also the moral decay that followed inevitably in their wake. 'From a low state of general health', he argued, 'whether in an individual or in numbers, proceed diminished energy of body and mind, and a vitiated moral perception, the frequent precursor of habits and deeds, which give employment to the officers of police, and the ministers of justice'.[2]

Griscom's contemporary and fellow New Yorker, Robert M. Hartley, though not a physician, similarly linked and combated both physical and moral ills. As a principal organizer and a long-time director of the New York Association for Improving the Condition of the Poor, he too derived a sense of urgency not only from his awareness of physical filth (which he recorded, for instance, in a treatise published in 1842 on the dire consequences of unsanitary methods of producing milk for urban consumption) but also from his deeply religious values. His awareness of the links between poor health and low morals led him to ask rhetorically at one point with regard to the purchase of tainted milk, 'Are you not bound by the most powerful obligations to wash your hands from all participation in so great an evil?' His metaphor here neatly linked physical cleanliness and moral purity.[3]

As in Britain, the men who excoriated the city most explicitly for its deleterious impact on the quality of men's morals were Protestant clergymen. A particularly good example of religiously based anti-urbanism appeared in a book written by John Todd and published in 1841 under the title *The Moral Influence, Dangers and Duties Connected with Great Cities*. Having come to grief during the late 1830s as a result of his efforts to establish and maintain a new Congregational church in Philadelphia, he used his book as a vehicle for publicizing what he saw as the wider implications of his own misfortune. Feeling on the basis of first-hand experience that 'if there be a spot on earth full of pitfalls and death-holes it is the city', he denounced cities in general as 'gangrenes on the body politic', as 'greenhouse[s] of crime', and as centers of 'all that demoralizes and pollutes'. Todd catalogued one urban vice after another: prostitution, 'licentiousness', gambling, theater-going, and failure to observe the Sabbath and to heed parental wisdom. He sharply contrasted the city with the countryside, much in the manner of Peter Gaskell. In the country, men were benignly bound by continuous traditions, which rooted them in the ways of their ancestors. But in the city, according to Todd, 'our attachments ... are to things in general.... The waves roll too rapidly to allow us to love anyone very strongly'.[4]

Similar criticisms appeared in a book about New York published nearly two decades later by the Reverend Amory D. Mayo, who attacked the city vehemently as a place in which the struggle for personal success damaged the bodies and minds of winners and losers alike. He presented his indictment of the urban milieu as follows:

> All dangers of the town may be summed up in this: that here, withdrawn from the blessed influence of Nature, and set face to face against humanity, man loses his own nature and becomes a new and artificial creature — an unhuman cog in a social machinery that works like a fate, and cheats him of his true culture as a soul. The most unnatural fashions and habits, the strangest eccentricities of intellect, the wildest and most pernicious theories in social morals, and the most appalling and incurable barbarism, are the legitimate growth of city life.

Again, the country and the city functioned as the sharply contrasting locations and symbols of innocent virtue and worldly vice.[5]

The nineteenth-century American who criticized cities most probingly was Ralph Waldo Emerson. Having trained at Harvard Divinity School and served briefly as pastor of a Unitarian church in Boston, he brought the moral sensitivities of a clergyman to the phenomena of urban life. But both the nature of his career during most of his adult life, which he spent as an independent essayist and lecturer, and the subtle complexity of his ideas make it sensible to think of him less as a minister than as the leading American counterpart to the great philosophical and literary sages of Victorian England (one of whom, Thomas Carlyle, became his close friend in the 1830s).

Emerson was by no means a thoroughgoing anti-urbanist in the manner of a John Todd, a Robert Southey, or a Wilhelm Heinrich Riehl, but much of what he wrote in his essays, journals, and letters — roughly between the mid-1830s and the early 1860s — certainly conveyed anti-urban sentiments. Having expressed personal dislike for the city in 1834 by moving to the semi-rural village of Concord, he wrote much thereafter that provided a moral and an aesthetic justification for his choice of residence. In his lecture of 1844 on 'The Young Americans', he asserted,

> The cities drain the country of the best part of its population: the flower of the youth, of both sexes, goes into the towns, and the country is cultivated by a so much inferior class.... Whatever events in progress shall go to disgust men with cities and infuse into them the passion for country life and country pleasure, will

render a service to the whole face of this continent, and will further the most poetic of all the occupations of real life, the bringing out by art the native but hidden graces of the landscape.[6]

Emerson distinguished between country and city, exalting the former at the expense of the latter, in related but differing ways elsewhere. Writing in the manner of the transcendental philosopher, he contrasted the two as follows in 1839:

> The City delights the Understanding. It is made up of finites: short, sharp, mathematical lines, all calculable. It is full of varieties, of successions, of contrivances. The Country, on the contrary, offers an unbroken horizon, the monotony of an endless road, of vast uniform plains, of distant mountains, the melancholy of uniform and infinite vegetation; the objects on the road are few and worthless, the eye is invited ever to the horizon and the clouds. It is the school of the Reason.

Here was a romantic view of the city as an artificial environment that schooled the intellect but starved the imagination — a place in which philosopher-poets such as Emerson could expect to learn much about the inventions of their fellow men but not to feel deeply or to think well.[7]

Emerson also contrasted the country and the city with regard to religion and morals. In his essay 'Worship', he warned, 'In our large cities, the population is godless, materialized, — no bond, no fellow-feeling, no enthusiasm. These are not men, but hungers, thirsts, fevers and appetites walking'. And in 1854 he entered the following observation in his journal:

> Rest on your humanity, and it will supply you with strength and hope and vision for the day. Solitude and the country, books, and openness, will feed you; but go into the city — I am afraid there is no morning in Chestnut Street, it is full of rememberers, they shun each other's eyes, they are all wrinkled with memory of the tricks they have played, or mean to play, each other, of petty arts and aims all contracting and lowering their aspect and character.

In such passages, Emerson associated himself clearly with the repugnance for urban living that had been expressed earlier by his romantic predecessors in Europe.[8]

Hostility to cities appeared repeatedly in the works of mid-nineteenth-century novelists, both major and minor, whose literary creations provided powerful counterparts in the realm of the imagination to the philosophical misgivings voiced by Emerson. The greatest of the American novelists painted some of their darkest urban scenes in books and stories that dealt wholly or in part with cities in Europe, thus supporting a view of the United States as a country that remained relatively uncorrupted by the ills that beset the older nations across the Atlantic. James Fenimore Cooper set his most markedly anti-urban novel, *The Bravo* (1831), in Venice, which he depicted as a center of intrigue and corruption. Frequent images of mazes and masks served to underline the point that in such a place one could seldom trust in appearances, which deceived and trapped the innocent individual. Edgar

Allan Poe treated Venice, Paris, and London in several of his stories, in each case portraying the big city as a sinister place where violent deeds were perpetrated by mysterious men under the cover of dark and ominous shadows. He exploited the urban milieu most intensively in 'The Man of the Crowd' (1840). In this story, London, the largest of all cities, provides the perfect setting for a tale that dwells on the themes of alienation and crime. Herman Melville, in his largely autobiographical *Redburn* (1849), takes his protagonist through the labyrinthine slums of 'sooty and begrimed' Liverpool, where he observes in horror the depths of misery and degradation. In the same book, the gaudy gaiety of London serves to highlight rather than to offset the urban suffering observed to the north. Nathaniel Hawthorne, who had earlier recorded his distaste for the 'mushroom' towns with their 'straggling suburbs' that were 'denaturalizing' the countryside and imposing the 'cold plan' of a gridiron upon older urban areas in industrial England, expressed his moral anxieties about the city most forcefully in *The Marble Faun* (1860). This novel is set in 'sickly Rome', a city characterized by 'evil scents', 'hard harsh cries', 'guilty shadows', and 'evil streets', to name only a few of the expletives that Hawthorne employed to characterize the urban milieu.[9]

Although these writers directed their harshest criticisms against the cities of old Europe, they also feared that European evils might well reach American shores. Negative attitudes toward urban society in the United States emerge clearly from many of Cooper's works. His best known novels, comprised in the Leatherstocking series, constitute one of the classic expressions of the anti-urban myth of the American frontier. These books celebrate primal wilderness as the locus of freedom, which they contrast with the constraint and alienation imposed by the towns. The protagonist of the series, Natty Bumpo, repeatedly indicts cities for their materialism, their triviality, and their deceptiveness. Natty does not always speak for Cooper, but his message comes through loud and clear nonetheless. In other novels, Cooper looked favorably on only one American city, Albany, a place he described in terms that emphasized its close links to the land and its non-modernity. Poe expressed his anxieties about and his revulsion for the city in America in 'Mellonta Tauta' (1849), in which New York, a city almost wholly dedicated to wealth and fashion, is destroyed in the year 2050 by an earthquake. Moreover, in 'Some Words with a Mummy' (1845), Poe lamented, 'I am heartily sick of this life and of the nineteenth century in general. I am convinced that everything is going wrong'. In this context, 'everything' clearly included urbanization. Hawthorne focused in 'My Kinsman, Major Molineux' (1832) on the terror experienced by a country boy who comes to Boston to search for an affluent relative and on 'a sensation of loneliness stronger than any he had ever felt in the remotest depths of his native woods'. In 'The New Adam and Eve', Hawthorne brought Adam and Eve back to Boston after all of its inhabitants had disappeared and showed them wandering through the streets as a way of emphasizing the artificiality of urban civilization and the price that urban men had paid for their 'revolt against nature'.[10]

The most searching critique of an American city in any of the imaginative works by major American authors appeared in Melville's *Pierre* (1852). Early in the novel, Melville contrasts the country, where Pierre is born and raised, and the town, to which he moves, as follows: ' ... the country is not only the most poetical and philosophical, but it is the most aristocratic part of this earth, for it is the most venerable.... Whereas the town is the more plebeian portion; which, besides many other things, is plainly evinced by the dirty unwashed face perpetually worn by the town'. The circumstances that lead to Pierre's departure from his ancestral home make it difficult to regard the rhapsodic evocation of bucolic joy and innocence in the opening chapters as anything but a parody of pastoral conventions, but Melville's account of the tragic hero's arrival in New York conjures up a vision of unmistakable horror. Pierre's bitter remark to Isabel succinctly summarizes the coldness and lack of fellow feeling in the city: 'Milk dropped from the milkman's can in December, freezes not more quickly on those stones, than does snow-white innocence, if in poverty it chance to fall in these streets'. A few pages later, as Pierre re-enters the police station where he has temporarily left his traveling companions in what he had thought would be safe keeping, he experiences the depths of an urban hell: 'frantic, diseased-looking men and women of all colors ... leaping, yelling, and cursing', their voices 'interlarded now and then, with the foulest of all human lingoes, that dialect of sin and death, known as the Cant language, or the Flash'. By the end of the novel, the deaths of Pierre, Isabel, and Lucy seem quite inevitable, and they underline the inhumanity of the big city.[11]

The evidence of pro-urban optimism

Although Morton and Lucia White have effectively used these novels and stories, along with some of the passages quoted above from works by Emerson, to substantiate their view that anti-urbanism predominated in the intellectuals' responses to the city during the period leading up to (and also following) the Civil War, several of the men who wrote them viewed cities positively as well as negatively. The most careful student of Emerson's ideas about urban life has provided abundant evidence that the transcendentalist philosopher held high hopes for cities, seeing them not so much in an antithetical as in a dialectical relationship to what lay outside them, and even the Whites recognize the difficulty of compressing his thought within the confines of anti-urbanism pure and simple. In his accounts of his travels to England, Emerson frequently voiced his fascination with and his admiration for the English metropolis. Like other intellectuals, he valued that city particularly for the ways in which its heterogeneity liberated men from dull routine and forced them to develop their capacities for independent thought and action. In his essay on 'Culture' (1851), he wrote,

> Cities give us collision.... We must remember the high social possibilities of a million of men. The best bribe which London offers to-day to the imagination is that in such a vast variety of people and conditions one can believe there is room for persons of romantic character to exist, and that the poet, the mystic and hero may hope to confront their counterparts.[12]

Emerson expressed his urban sympathies most fervently a decade later in a lecture titled 'Boston' (1861), which depicted the city of his birth as 'the town which was appointed in the destiny of nations to lead the civilization of North America'. Looking back at the history of this remarkable center of intellectual energy, he saw the parallel fulfillment of both the individual and his community through the creative use of freedom. In his conclusion, as he considered Boston in relation to other American cities, Emerson readmitted it to the world of nature via the following use of organic metaphor:

> And thus our little city thrives and enlarges, striking deep roots, and sending out boughs and buds, and propagating itself like a banyan over the continent. Greater cities there are that sprung from it, full of its blood and name and traditions. It is very willing to be outnumbered and outgrown, so long as they carry forward its life of civil and religious freedom, of education, of social order, and of loyalty to law.

Approaching the end of his career as a lecturer, Emerson viewed the city more benignly than ever.[13]

There is evidence in the works of other major writers that they too regarded the city with ambivalence rather than outright hostility. Cooper seemed to move toward greater acceptance of the city by mid-century. He declared in 1851 in his book *New York* that he did not 'believe any more in the superior innocence and virtue of a rural population than in that of the largest capitals'. He recognized the 'incentives to wrong-doing in the crowded population of a capital town', but he insisted that 'there are many incentives to refinement, public virtue, and even piety, that are not to be met with elsewhere'. The theme of reconciliation with the city was developed in fiction by Hawthorne in *The Blithedale Romance* (1852), based in large measure on the author's own experience at the famous Brook Farm. The narrator and central character, Miles Coverdale, recounts his departure from Boston in order to participate in a communal experiment on the land, where he has been disillusioned by the discovery that the drudgery of rural labor is not offset either by social harmony or by personal freedom. In the end, he has returned to the city, which he has come to appreciate for its delightful variety of human life. 'Whatever had been my taste for solitude and natural scenery', Coverdale concludes, 'yet the thick, foggy, stifled element of cities, the entangled life of many men together, sordid as it was, and empty of the beautiful, took quite as strenuous a hold upon my mind. I felt as if there could never be enough of it.'[14]

It is even easier to modify the Whites' view of the American intellectual scene by considering the thought of less well known writers who wrote at much lower levels of intellectual and literary sophistication. Numerous clergymen realized that the city had come to stay and urged men to make the best of it. Before the middle of the century, two Unitarian ministers in Boston strongly rejected the notion that cities were inherently un-Christian. Joseph Tuckerman asserted that dedicated effort could make them the centers of the 'purest and highest religious and moral influence, of the highest intellectual culture, and of the greatest advancement of the arts and sciences'. William Ellery Channing spoke for himself as well as his friend when, in eulogizing Tuckerman, he proclaimed 'his deliberate conviction ... that great cities need not be haunts of vice and poverty; that ... there were now intelligence, virtue and piety enough, could they be brought into united action, to give a new intellectual and moral life to the more neglected classes of society'.[15]

Edward Lathrop, a Baptist minister in New York, wrote optimistically in 1851 that 'the power of modern cities ... is greatly augmented by the increased facilities which the present age affords for multiplying, as well as diffusing the elements of social and moral progress'. The city, he believed, could become the 'grand centre' of American religious life. 'The prosecution of the work of universal evangelization', he argued, 'must be advanced or retarded, in just the degree that the combined and centralized influence of large cities, is enlisted in the cause of the world's social and religious amelioration'.[16]

The Reverend Edwin H. Chapin, in works such as *Moral Aspects of City Life* (1851) and *Humanity in the City* (1854) expressed similar hopes that urbanization would ultimately contribute to men's moral betterment. The city, he believed, was 'not an abnormal world ... not a world outside the divine sphere' but rather 'the great appointed sphere of human endeavor'. Town life was admittedly unsettling, inasmuch as it forced men to confront choices and make decisions, but herein lay its great moral value. As Chapin put it,

> The city reveals the moral ends of being, and sets the awful problems of life.... When men are crowded together, the good and evil that are in them are more intensely excited and thrown to the surface.... Innocence may thrive in the sweet air of the country, but ... that which is strongest and noblest in our nature is illustrated in the city.... The city is a great school for principle, because it affords a keen trial for principle.[17]

One of the fullest defenses of urbanization by an American author, a work whose scope and spirit suggest comparison with Robert Vaughan's *Age of Great Cities*, was a survey of city growth undertaken in a lecture in 1855 by Henry Tappan. Tappan, the chancellor of the University of Michigan as well as a clergyman, considered the themes of urban religion and morality within the broader framework of the history of all human capabilities under the stimulating impact of contact and cooperation among men. 'There can be no question', he stated, 'that the association of men in cities is favorable to the highest development of humanity'. Economically, intellectually, and morally men had benefited from the wider possibilities offered by the urban way of life. That was the lesson of ancient history and also of more recent experience in modern Europe. 'The same causes', he asserted, 'which make cities the centres of intelligence, enterprise, and education, must go to make them, also, the centres of religious and benevolent influence'. Tappan admitted that preoccupation with the pursuit of material gain, especially in commercial cities, might undermine the urbanite's character, but in his eyes the appropriate way to guard against this danger was to cultivate love for the city among leading citizens, thus inducing them 'to embellish, enrich, and elevate it with whatever contributes to the finest culture and the purest pleasures of our being'. This was his prescription and his hope for the place in which he was lecturing, the city of New York.[18]

A still less finely nuanced — and in many respects quite misleading — view of the urban scene appeared in a good deal of the pulp fiction produced for the mass reading public. There was an enormous outpouring of favorable sentiment with regard to urban growth in a great many of the more than 300 novels published between 1820 and 1870 that were set in New York, Boston, or Philadelphia and in many works of fiction set in other cities too. Numerous novels of scant interest to students of literary art reveal a great deal about urban consciousness among ordinary members of urban society. Works of popular fiction, such as Robert St. Clar's *The Metropolites: Or Know Thy Neighbor* (1864) and Horatio Alger's *Ragged Dick* (1868), depicted the city as a promising place of nearly unlimited opportunity. Here, it appeared, the migrant from the countryside or from abroad could strive effectively to make his mark with full confidence that ultimately hard work and virtuous conduct would receive their just rewards. The authors of these books, in the words of the historian who has studied them most closely, 'etched an urban landscape pocked with moral crevices yet dominated by vistas of economic, social, and intellectual plenty'. They also communicated a view of the city as a place which, by 1870, could take legitimate pride in its police and fire departments, in its communal efforts to relieve distress, and in its expanded facilities for education and amusement. Appearing well before the great improvements in municipal administration ushered in by the progressives around the turn of the century, this view was decidedly premature, to say the least. Together with emphasis on the supposed abundance of individual opportunity, it tended to inhibit rather than to encourage more far-reaching efforts in the direction of social and political reform.[19]

The least ambiguous and most exuberant support for cities appeared during this period in the works of other authors who also wrote for a popular audience but through different channels and with mostly different towns in mind. Advocates of commercial expansion, these men sang the praises of and

8 A view of Cincinnati from across the Ohio River. Cincinnati was a booming center of commerce in the Middle West, whose rapid growth in the mid-nineteenth century evoked pride and admiration among city boosters (source: Geo. E. Stevens, *The City of Cincinnati: A Summary of Its Attractions, Advantages, Institutions and Internal Improvements* [Cincinnati, 1869], 26).

prophesied a splendid future for the newer cities of the West and the South, addressing their readers for the most part via popular periodicals. One author suggested in 1853 that 'a magician's wand appears to be summoning vast marts of commerce from the blue waves of the ocean, and beautiful villages from the bosoms of the forests'. He asserted that no development served better than the growth of cities 'to illustrate the wonderful progress of our country in industrial pursuits, social refinement, and true national greatness'. Focusing first on Brooklyn and then turning to Rochester and Buffalo, he celebrated the last of these cities as 'this modern Tyre upon the American Mediterranean Seas'. In conclusion, he told his readers, 'Look westward of the Alleghanies [sic], and greater wonders meet the vision'. J. B. D. De Bow, the editor of the New Orleans-based *Commercial Review of the South and Southwest* (popularly known as *De Bow's Review*), had predicted a few years earlier that in fifty years there would be 'at least twenty cities westward of the Alleghenny mountains with a population of half a million ... each'. He added, 'If such a thought does not awake in our bosoms true conceptions of the prospective greatness of our country, we know not what will', leaving no doubt in his readers' minds that he looked forward to this development with great pleasure.[20]

One of De Bow's more wide-ranging and thoughtful authors was Jessup W. Scott, who wrote under the influence of theories of urban development of the sort contained in the works of the German geographer Alexander von

Humboldt and popularized in America by the explorer William Gilpin. As applied to North America by Gilpin and Scott, Humboldtian geography implied that the region of the Great Lakes and the Mississippi River provided a perfect setting for future urban development. A favorable climate and a network of waterways meant that cities would grow rapidly in this area according to natural laws that could be grasped rationally by the student of society. In Scott's case, scientific understanding of nature's plan combined with personal good fortune to foster a highly benign view of the consequences of urban growth. Having become wealthy speculating in real estate in Toledo, Ohio, Scott found it easy to believe that cities were 'among the most remarkable phenomena of human progress', and he viewed the future of an urban Midwest with gleeful optimism. He wrote in 1853,

> In our central plain will, probably, grow up the hugest aggregations of people in the world. Before it reaches the density of England, it will contain one or more cities numbering ten millions.... The imagination can conceive nothing more imposingly grand than this march of humanity westward, to enter into possession of 'time's noblest Empire'. No logical induction ... can be clearer to our mind, than that here will come together the greatest aggregations of men in cities — outrivalling in splendor as in magnitude, all which past ages have produced.

Such a view of urban growth was clearly much more positive than the subtler appreciations of urban culture voiced by Emerson, the ambivalence toward urban morals expressed by many clergymen, and the somewhat checkered if ultimately positive images propagated by popular novelists. Scott's utter lack of hesitancy reflected the high expectations of material prosperity in such places as Chicago, St. Louis, and Kansas City — places that looked very much to the future rather than their brief past.[21]

Other authors, including still more contributors to *De Bow's Review*, advocated an urban South. Despite a general tendency among leading southern intellectuals to disparage urban industrialism as a northern threat to hallowed southern traditions, there was growing recognition in the South during the 1840s and 1850s that cities had a vital role to play everywhere. George Fitzhugh, a leading spokesman for slavery, made the general case for the city in one of his contributions as follows:

> In the earliest dawn of human history, we find men engaged in building cities as the first act in colonizing and settling new countries. So universal with civilized races has been this procedure, that it must be a matter of instinct and necessity, rather than of choice, taste or judgement. Cities are but human hives and honeycombs, and as much the natural residences of men as the latter are of bees.

An anonymous contributor urged in 1847 that energetic measures be undertaken to help New Orleans to win 'not the second or third rank, but front rank in commercial importance over every other city in the world'. An influential North Carolinian, Hinton R. Helper, argued in his *The Impending Crisis and How to Meet It* (1857) that southerners could ill afford to leave

9 Broadway in New York. With affectionate humor, the artist depicts the main street of New York City as a place filled with human vitality. His work shares much in common with the verses of Walt Whitman (source: *Harper's Weekly*, August 27, 1859).

urbanization to the industrial North, and growing numbers of men who lived in his region agreed with him. As David Goldfield has pointed out, the deepening sectional crisis led many southerners to look for the defense of their way of life not simply to the plantation but also to the commercial and industrial city, which was to serve as a bulwark against northern 'economic and political aggression'.[22]

Although the great majority of writers who wholeheartedly praised cities in mid-nineteenth-century America were quite undistinguished either as thinkers or as artists, one major author stands out among them, and he deserves the last word. Walt Whitman, newspaperman and poet, opened himself sympathetically to all aspects of human experience. He was a democrat both ideologically and artistically, and his writings ring with enthusiasm not only for nature but also for the city, with its teeming masses and its physical and social heterogeneity. In 'Salut au Monde!' (1856), he mused, 'I see the cities of the earth and make myself at random a part of them,/I am a real Parisian,/ I am a habitan of Vienna, St. Petersburg, Berlin, Constantinople', and so on, naming more than two dozen other cities around the world before proclaiming, 'I descend upon all those cities and rise from them again'.[23]

It was New York, which Whitman frequented during many of his most productive years, that excited his greatest enthusiasm. Generally attractive images of that city dominate many of his best short poems and portions of several longer ones, and it is these that have established his reputation as the pre-eminent spokesman for urban life among American men of letters. In 'A Broadway Pageant' (1860), he wrote, 'When million-footed Manhattan unpent descends to her pavements/... I too arising, answering, descend to the pavements, merge with the crowd, and gaze with them'. And in 'Manahatta' (1860), he concluded his celebration of the city by writing about 'A million people — manners free and superb — open voices — hospitality — the most courageous and friendly young men,/City of hurried and sparkling waters! City of spires and masts!/City nested in bays! My city!' A decade later, he expressed comparable sentiments in prose in a lyrical passage that was to appear subsequently in his *Democratic Vistas*, a passage occasioned by his return to New York and Brooklyn after a long absence. He referred glowingly to 'the splendor, picturesqueness, and oceanic amplitude and rush of these great cities', where 'costly and lofty new buildings', 'endless ships', 'tumultuous streets', and 'the heavy, low, musical roar' all fascinated him. Through his 'esthetic conscience' he gained here 'continued exaltation and absolute fulfilment'.[24]

Like Baudelaire, Whitman valued the city above all for the stimulation he derived from it as an artist, but unlike his French contemporary he liked most of what he saw as well as the experience of perceiving it. There are criticisms of the city in Whitman's works, especially in *Democratic Vistas*, but Whitman nowhere evinces Baudelaire's sense of estrangement and loneliness in the urban milieu. The spectacle that delighted him was the pageant of productively restless humanity, not of men and women engulfed by sickness and suffering.

Whitman's fascination with the vitality of New York reflected the sentiments of large numbers of his fellow Americans. To be sure, a marked streak of anti-urbanism was one component of transcendental literature and philosophy. But even Emerson evinced enthusiasm as well as distaste for city life. Moreover, a multitude of lesser writers were clearly enamored of the urban America they knew and looked forward eagerly to an urban future. Many clergymen and popular novelists, together with contributors to commercial magazines such as *De Bow's Review*, hoped and believed that the newer cities of America would avoid the pitfalls and tribulations that beset their forerunners across the Atlantic. Their writings call into serious question the familiar view that American intellectual energies were directed overwhelmingly during these years against the course of urban development. At a minimum, it is quite clear that Americans were just as favorably disposed toward their cities as Europeans were toward theirs, and a good case can be made that the balance of opinion was more favorable in the United States than it was anywhere else.

Part Two

**Perspectives on Urban
Ills, *1880–1918***

5

Awareness of Urban Poverty

After several decades during which optimism about the ability of urbanites to surmount their various problems had been in the ascendant, there occurred during the late nineteenth century a reawakening of concern over the condition of the urban lower classes. Starting roughly between 1880 and 1890, many observers of the urban scene began to voice a heightened awareness of poverty in the midst of plenty. In their view, material deprivation among the poorer classes in the cities had not simply failed to disappear in accord with the earlier expectations of urban optimists; it had also in many cases become much worse and certainly more noticeable, owing to the sheer increase in the numbers of men and women who were crowding into the already overpopulated cities of Europe and America. Moreover, the social and moral consequences that resulted from such deprivation seemed more threatening than ever. As in the earlier part of the century, the British took the lead. During the 1880s, the 1890s, and the first few years after the turn of the century, many publicists and clergymen and a few social scientists dealt exhaustively with the problem of urban poverty, primarily though not exclusively in London. A smaller number of men on the European continent displayed similar concern, while in the United States the investigation of urban poverty proceeded at a rapid pace throughout the years leading up to the First World War. Parallel developments occurred in each country in the realm of imaginative literature, where the practitioners of social realism amplified the messages of the social reporters in novels and in verse. Addressing a broad public in ways that made what they had to say readily intelligible and relentlessly unsettling, both the purveyors of facts and the creators of fiction propagated somber truths regarding urban life that deeply colored much other writing of the period about cities and their prospects.

The exploration of unknown England

As Asa Briggs has observed, London was in certain respects to the late nineteenth century what Manchester had been half a century earlier: the city that symbolized more than any other the crucially important urban developments occurring at the time. Briggs remarks quite rightly that London's problems 'dominated all British discussions of the city in the late-Victorian period'.[1] The centrality of London to men's awareness of city life appeared most clearly in the great flood of writing about living standards among the urban lower classes, whose plight became a major topic of public concern in the early 1880s and remained one for two decades. Most British writers viewed the problems associated with poor housing, low wages, and unemployment from the standpoint of the metropolis, with its huge population of overcrowded and underfed men, women, and children. At the same time, these sorespots appeared to be the most noteworthy if not the dominant features of the capital as a whole. Particularly in the 1880s and 1890s, they were the aspects of metropolitan life that imprinted themselves most forcefully on the consciousness of articulate urban observers.

Several factors contributed to the reorientation of thinking about London after 1880. A depression in 1879, followed by several years of indifferent trade and a much more severe slump in the period 1884-87, exacerbated the long-term decline of older industries such as shipbuilding, certain branches of metalworking, and garmentmaking, thus intensifying endemic underemployment among men and women who worked in these trades to the point of severe and chronic unemployment. Faced with a decline in their real income, these people and others had to contend with a chronic shortage of working-class housing in the inner industrial areas of the city. Finally, there was the emergence of socialism and of other collectivist movements, which constituted an increasingly powerful challenge to the traditional liberal belief in the beneficence of *laissez-faire* and in the responsibility of the poor for their own misfortunes. Their thinking and agitation prodded more moderate men to look critically at the urban milieu with an eye to identifying real and potential causes of popular discontent.[2]

Although the condition of the London poor had been treated repeatedly in numerous writings ever since the 1840s, it emerged much more clearly as a major issue in the year 1883. The central concern in the thinking of a large number of authors who appeared in print then and shortly thereafter was the shortage of decent housing that the great mass of workers could afford to inhabit. This was regarded as the crucial urban problem of the day. Whereas earlier critics of physical defects in the urban environment, writing under the influence of Chadwick and his fellow sanitary reformers, had concentrated on inadequate sewers and drains, the newer critics focused more particularly on the size and quality of the places in which the workers lived. They linked the deplorable condition of the metropolitan under-class, especially in East London, not to noxious effluvia emanating from streets and privies, which had been vastly improved since Chadwick's day, but rather to the great gulf

between the reality of working-class houses and the Victorian image of a happy home.

Several months after the popular journalist George Sims had published a series of disturbing articles in June of 1883 in the *Pictorial World* on 'How the Poor Live', a short pamphlet bearing the title *The Bitter Cry of Outcast London* marked the real opening of the new phase of public interest in urban poverty. The pamphlet was published under the auspices of the London Congregational Union, and although its authorship used to be in some question, there is little doubt now that Andrew Mearns, secretary of the Union and formerly a minister in Chelsea, conceived and wrote it. Mearns sought to encourage his readers to evangelize slum dwellers, and his opening pages voiced the by now familiar fear among clergymen that the Churches were losing the allegiance of the great bulk of the urban population. But Mearns quickly directed his attention in his efforts to account for non-attendance at church by the poor toward 'the condition in which they live'. The very idea of going to church had 'never dawned upon these people', primarily because of the quality of domestic life in the environment of the slum. The poor lived in places 'compared with which the lair of a wild beast would be a comfortable and healthy spot ... pestilential human rookeries ... where tens of thousands are crowded together amidst houses which call to mind ... the middle passage of the slave ship'.[3]

The impact of *The Bitter Cry* gained greatly from the publicity it received in the popular *Pall Mall Gazette*, whose editor, W. T. Stead, used it as a powerful weapon in his campaign against urban slums. He summarized the pamphlet extensively just after it came out, and he published two editorials that mentioned it explicitly. In his view, 'the crying scandal of our age' was 'the excessive overcrowding of enormous multitudes of the very poor in pestilential rookeries where it is a matter of physical impossibility to live a human life'. In the sensational style of the popular journalist, he wrote about 'reeking tenements', 'the stunted squalid savages of civilization', and 'the foul ulcer of London'.[4]

For several years thereafter, a flood of pamphlets and articles on the London poor inundated the reading public. The articles by the statesmen Lord Salisbury and Joseph Chamberlain on workers' housing that appeared later in 1883 (the first in the *National Review*, the second in the *Fortnightly Review*) enjoyed widespread attention at least in part because of the controversy started by Mearns. Other writers, many of whose essays also appeared in the leading liberal reviews, were much more deeply indebted to their anonymous predecessor. Such indebtedness can be discerned most

10   Destitution on a London sidewalk. This photograph depicts an impoverished and exhausted old woman in St. Giles who was known as a 'crawler' and a young child for whom she cared as best she could while its mother worked in a coffee shop. Both were denizens of 'outcast London' (source: Adolphe Smith and John Thompson, *Street Life in London* [1877], 117).

clearly in the many cases where the author incorporated phases such as 'bitter cry' or 'outcast London' in the title of his work. The article by Brooke Lambert, 'The Outcast Poor, Esau's Cry', was an obvious case in point. Another was an essay by a clergyman, George Sale Reaney, on 'Outcast London'. Published in 1886, just after a highly critical and widely noticed report by a special Royal Commission on the Housing of the Working Classes, it summarized a viewpoint that had by now become quite common among commentators on urban life. Drawing sharp contrasts both between London as a whole and 'those thriving towns of the north' and between the west and east ends of the metropolis itself, he insisted that much of London constituted 'the most neglected portion of the whole empire' and that it functioned as 'the human dustbin of the whole population'.[5]

Mearns also made a strong if indirect impression on another religious leader whose fame as a social critic was to surpass that of any of the other clergymen writing at the time: General William Booth, founder of the Salvation Army. Having concluded, as a result of the Army's failure to make significant inroads in working-class districts, that moral reformation necessitated improved living conditions, he signaled his conversion to social reform in 1890 in his enormously influential book, *In Darkest England and the Way Out*. Partly written by Booth's close friend, W. T. Stead, the book included passages at the end of the first chapter that were taken almost verbatim from the first editorial in the *Pall Mall Gazette* in which Stead had hailed *The Bitter Cry*.[6]

Most of Booth's book outlined his proposals for eliminating poverty by means of work colonies in the city, on farms, and overseas and also by means of various other programs sponsored by the Army, but a long opening section presented a general view of the conditions that cried out for remedial action. More forcefully than any of his predecessors, Booth drew the parallel between slums at home and jungles abroad. Having already suggested it in the title of his book, he went on to delineate it explicitly as he answered the following rhetorical questions: 'As there is a darkest Africa, is there not also a darkest England? Civilisation, which can breed its own barbarians, does it not also breed its own pygmies? May we not find a parallel at our own doors, and discover within a stone's throw of our cathedrals and palaces similar horrors to those which Stanley has found existing in the great Equatorial forest?' The English slum resembled the African jungle in 'its monotonous darkness, its malaria and its gloom, its dwarfish de-humanized inhabitants, the slavery to which they are subjected, their privations and their misery'.[7]

During the 1880s, the theme of poverty began to appear more frequently not only in journalistic exposés but also in social novels. Many of these books focused on East London: the vast and unlovely territory beyond the Tower that included areas such as Whitechapel, Spitalfields, Bethnal Green, Poplar, and the Isle of Dogs. Working-class life in these neighborhoods provided the basic subject matter for Walter Besant's *All Sorts and Conditions of Men*

(1882), for Israel Zangwill's *Children of the Ghetto* (1892), for Arthur Morrison's *Tales of Mean Streets* (1894) and *A Child of the Jago* (1896), and for a host of other novels published during the last few years of the century. These books all helped to define East London as a potent symbol of urban poverty.[8]

The best written and most penetrating fiction about the hard lives of the metropolitan masses dealt, however, with other parts of the city. It came from the pen of George Gissing, the outstanding representative of literary naturalism in Britain and one of a handful of late nineteenth-century novelists whose works possess something of the same value for historians as that contained in so many works from the 1840s and 1850s. Born into a lower middle-class family in a medium-sized town in Yorkshire, he experienced severe poverty himself both in Chicago and in London during the late 1870s. His own life in the slums as he struggled to support himself and the former prostitute, now an alcoholic, whom he had married after suffering imprisonment for thefts committed on her behalf gave him plenty of raw material for his novels, the first of which, *Workers in the Dawn*, appeared in 1880.[9] In a later novel, *Demos: A Story of English Socialism* (1886), he conveyed his sense of the grim hopelessness of life in large parts of the British capital in passages such as the following:

> On the south is Hoxton, a region of malodorous market streets, of factories, timber-yards, grimy warehouses, of alleys swarming with small trades and crafts, of filthy courts and passages leading into pestilential gloom; everywhere toil in its most degrading forms; the thoroughfares thundering with high-laden waggons, the pavements trodden by working folk of the coarsest type, the corners and lurking-holes showing destitution at its ugliest.[10]

It was in *The Nether World* (1889), whose title aptly indicates the depressed grimness of the areas in which the action of the book takes place, that Gissing explored slum life in London most fully and depicted the hellishness of urban poverty most brutally. A powerful examination of the misery and the moral and physical collapse among urbanites that resulted from seemingly hopeless destitution, it deserves recognition as the most effective portrayal of poverty by any British novelist of the late nineteenth century. Throughout the book, Gissing presented men and women who were trapped by physical circumstances over which they had little if any control and who suffered accordingly. Wherever one went in Clerkenwell, the part of London where most of the action takes place, one encountered 'multiform evidence of toil, intolerable as a nightmare'. Many of the buildings in the area stood out as powerful reminders of the passive misery experienced by large numbers of the people who lived within their confines. 'What terrible barracks, those Farringdon Road Buildings!' Gissing exclaimed. 'Vast, sheer walls, unbroken by even an attempt at ornament; row above row of windows in the mud-coloured surface ... murky openings that tell of bareness, disorder, comfortlessness within'. As one passed by them in the night, it required a strenuous effort of imagination 'to picture the weltering mass of human weariness, of bestiality, of unmerited dolour, of hopeless hope, of crushed surrender, tumbled together within those forbidding walls'. Gissing's almost totally unrelieved pessimism was underlined once again at the very end of the novel, which he concluded with a reference to 'those brute forces of society which fill with wreck the abysses of the nether world'.[11]

The popular writing about poverty that appeared in such great profusion during the 1880s stimulated Charles Booth (no relation to William) to undertake and complete the greatest of all the nineteenth-century works in the area of urban studies, his massive *Life and Labour of the People in London*, which appeared in seventeen volumes between 1889 and 1903. Having worked during his young adulthood entirely in the shipping trade, Booth began in middle age, without the benefit of academic training, to devote much of his considerable intellectual energy to social investigation. He did so in large part out of a desire to test what he suspected were wildly exaggerated assertions by others about the extent of real destitution among the urban masses. There is no evidence except for statements by some of his later colleagues that Booth was motivated specifically by *The Bitter Cry*. Moreover, it seems doubtful that Henry Hyndman, founder of the Social Democratic Federation, played nearly as important a part in triggering Booth's inquiry as his recollections of a meeting with Booth in 1886 have long led historians to believe. But Booth certainly saw his project as a means of clarifying what seemed to him to be a great deal of confusion about the true condition of urban society. As he wrote in the first volume of his survey,

> East London lay hidden from view behind a curtain on which were painted terrible pictures: — Starving children, suffering women, overworked men; horrors of drunkenness and vice; monsters and demons of inhumanity; giants of disease and despair. Did these pictures truly represent what lay behind, or did they bear to the facts a relation similar to that which the pictures outside a booth at some country fair bear to the performance or show within?

This was the question Booth sought to answer.[12]

Employing a large team of assistants (including the young Beatrice Potter, later to become the wife of Sidney Webb), Booth embarked upon an exceedingly ambitious effort to portray the quality of life among all elements of the London population, first in the East End and then in other parts of the metropolis as well. He was influenced both by his practical experience as a businessman and by a positivist conviction, shared by many others at the time, that only scientific methods could provide the answers to the most important questions that confronted contemporary society. Having joined the Royal Statistical Society in 1885, he believed fervently in the necessity of numbers, referring at one point to his 'resolution to make use of no fact' to which he could not 'give a quantitative value'. His sources and methods, however, included not only reports by school board visitors, the census, other statistical data, and sampling techniques, but also studies of institutions and individuals and his own observations and impressions.[13]

The result of Booth's labors was not in any sense a work of theory but rather a sprawling compendium of information that displayed the fruits of its author's dogged empiricism. The survey as a whole was divided into three separately titled but overlapping series: one on *Poverty*, another on *Industry*, and a third on *Religious Influences*. The first series employed two approaches, 'dividing the people by districts and again by trades, so as to show at once the manner of their life and of their work'. Using numerous maps and tables, Booth and his co-workers showed how eight social groupings (listed in ascending order from 'A. the lowest class of occasional labourers, loafers, and semi-criminals' to 'H. upper middle class and all above this level') were distributed both among the city's various regions and among some of its occupational groups.[14] The second series focused on the relations among poverty, occupational distribution, and crowding. The third, arranged geographically, dealt with 'the action of organized religion in all its forms', with that of 'other organized social and philanthropic influences', with the public authorities, and with a number of social conditions that had received insufficient attention in the first two series (providing information on 'housing and health, on drink, prostitution and crime, on marriage and on thrift').

Booth felt real satisfaction at discovering that truly grinding poverty was not as extensive as many people had thought before he began to publish his findings. He was 'inclined to think that if an inquiry, such as the present, had been made at any previous time in the history of London, it would have shown a greater proportion of depravity and misery than now exists, and a lower general standard of life'. Even in East London, the lowest of the low amounted to only a little over 1 percent, and for the city as a whole they amounted to only 0.9 percent. The statistics for class B ('the very poor — casual labour, hand-to-mouth existence, chronic want') were 11.2 percent and 7.5 percent. Findings such as these led Booth to comment, 'The hordes of barbarians of whom we have heard, who, issuing from their slums, will one day overwhelm modern civilization, do not exist. There are barbarians, but they are a handful, a small and decreasing percentage: a disgrace but not a danger'.[15]

But Booth's survey also contained results that tended to militate against a favorable view of urban society. By including among the poor those classes to which he assigned the labels C and D ('those whose earnings are small, because of irregularity of employment, and those whose work, though regular, is ill-paid'), Booth came up with total percentages of 34.2 (East London) and 30.7 (the entire city). The most fortunate of these people, while by no means destitute, were still engaged in 'an unending struggle, and lack[ed] comfort', and their life style was to be distinguished clearly from that of 'the regularly employed and fairly paid working class'. Booth summarized the statistics on poverty in the East End with evident grimness, writing that 'when we count up the 100,000 individuals, the 20,000 families [in classes A and B], who lead so pinched a life among the population described, and remember that there are in addition double that number who, if not actually pressed by want, yet have nothing to spare, we shrink aghast from the picture'. Moreover, in Booth's view, the great majority of all those whom he classified as poor suffered from poverty not because of 'questions of habit' such as drunkenness or lack of thrift but instead because of what he called 'questions of employment' or 'questions of circumstance' (e.g., large families or illness). To be sure, Booth's scheme of classification did not take account of the possibility that factors such as irregular earnings and illness might stem from drink or other bad habits, but the important point is that his explanations for poverty seemed to support an environmentalist view of the problem rather than one that focused on defects of character among the poor themselves. It was the structure of urban society, rather than individual irresponsibility, that accounted for urban poverty.[16]

Booth's main interest lay in the accumulation and orderly presentation of facts, not in the devising of solutions. 'If', he wrote, 'the facts thus stated are of use in helping social reformers to find remedies for the evils which exist, or do anything to prevent the adoption of false remedies, my purpose is answered'. He asserted that he had not intended to put forth any suggestions of his own and that he had made a few along the way only 'with much hesitation'. He justified the role he had defined for himself by suggesting that 'the qualities of mind which enable a man to make this inquiry are the least of all likely to give him that elevation of soul, sympathetic insight, and sublime confidence which must go to the making of a great regenerating teacher'.[17] Booth did strongly advocate two major reforms. In the survey, he proposed an extension of the Poor Law so that it would provide for labor colonies outside London. These were supposed to draw off the members of class B, thus relieving much of the pressure in the job market on class C. Elsewhere, he repeatedly proposed the establishment of old-age pensions by the state, which were in fact to be implemented on a small scale less than a decade after the survey was completed. But the greatest need was still the acquisition of more facts, and with this imperative in mind he concluded hopefully that 'the spirit of patient inquiry is abroad; my attempt is only one of its children'.[18]

Booth's survey attracted an enormous amount of favorable attention. Many reviewers praised him for having illuminated his subject in a way that a broad reading public could readily comprehend, even though very few people would read his work in its entirety. As one of them put it, 'It is a volume that would reflect credit on any Government department in Europe, while at the same time it would run a dead-heat with any book on the lists of Mr. Mudie or Messrs. Smith [popular booksellers]'. Another wrote, 'His is a splendid achievement, both in conception and in carrying out; and if any man deserves the thanks of the public, it is the author of the work before us. He has let us see exactly how we stand, and that is the essential preliminary to finding a remedy for any ill in the body politic'.[19]

There was considerable relief among some writers at discovering that the problem of poverty was less bad than had been expected.[20] Nonetheless, many of Booth's contemporaries and most men who wrote about him in later years placed great emphasis on the negative implications of what he had to say. Robert Gregory, Dean of St. Paul's Cathedral, wrote that it was 'painful to feel assured, that such misery and wretchedness exist, and that all efforts seem powerless to remove it, though they may lessen it'. Benjamin Kidd, the eminent social philosopher, commented that Booth had revealed 'what is perhaps the most noteworthy aspect of the life of the masses in such a centre of our civilisation, namely, the enormous proportion of the population which exists in a state of chronic poverty'. Moreover, he emphasized that London was by no means unique in this respect. 'Other European cities have a like tale to tell. Even when we turn to the great centres of population in the New World we find the same conditions of life reproduced; the same ceaseless competition, the same keen struggle for employment and for the means of existence; the same want, failure and misery meet us on every side'. Such writers helped to focus public attention not just on the great strides forward in ameliorating poverty that had been accomplished since Henry Mayhew's time but also on the enormous tasks that remained to be finished and on the ways in which bad conditions in London were paralleled by comparable defects in urban society more generally.[21]

One of the men uppermost in Booth's mind when he referred to 'the spirit of patient inquiry' was Benjamin Seebohm Rowntree. Like Booth, Rowntree turned to social investigation after having acquired practical experience in the world of commerce. Educated as a chemist at Owens College in Manchester, he entered his family's cocoa and confectionery business in York in 1889, soon became responsible for labor relations, and a few years thereafter became a director of the firm. Inspired by Booth's example, he decided in the late 1890s to undertake his own survey of York, with a view to determining whether the incidence of poverty was as great in a medium-sized provincial town (population about 76,000) as in the imperial capital. Published under the title *Poverty: A Study of Town Life* (1901), the survey ranks with Booth's as a classic work of empirical sociology. Rowntree advanced methodologically beyond Booth in several ways, considering the opinions of physiologists and dieticians with regard to nutritional standards and making more systematic use of family budgets. Moreover, instead of relying on middle-class bureaucrats as intermediaries, he collected information directly from every wage-earning family in the city (11,560 households, accounting for 46,754 individuals) about housing, occupations, earnings, and numbers and ages of children.[22]

After ascertaining the amount of income a typical family (mother, father, three children) would need per week in order to maintain 'merely physical efficiency', Rowntree calculated on the basis of his survey data that nearly 10 percent of the population could not meet this minimum standard and therefore lived in 'primary' poverty. One of the most eloquent passages in the book described the condition of those whose income barely sufficed to keep them above the primary poverty line if they spent it carefully all the time. Beginning with the observation that 'a family living upon the scale allowed for in this estimate must never spend a penny on railway fare or omnibus', Rowntree went on to list all the other things that people living on the margin of poverty had to regard as luxuries: newspapers, concerts, postage stamps, contributions to churches, chapels, sick clubs, and trade unions, toys, candy, tobacco, beer, and pretty clothes. He concluded grimly, 'Should a child fall ill, it must be attended by the parish doctor; should it die, it must be buried by the parish. Finally, the wage-earner must never be absent from his work for a single day'.[23]

Although only one-tenth of the citizenry was in want because of insufficient income, close to another two-tenths were mired in 'secondary' poverty. The families suffering from this condition were those 'whose total earnings would be sufficient for the maintenance of merely physical efficiency were it not that some portion of it is absorbed by other expenditure, either useful or wasteful'. When Rowntree discussed the causes of secondary poverty in detail, he assigned the greatest importance to drink, followed by betting, gambling, and poor housekeeping, but he did not really blame the poor for their own fate, as the following passage makes clear:

> ... They [the causes of secondary poverty] are themselves often the outcome of the adverse conditions under which too many of the working classes live. Housed for the most part in sordid streets, frequently under overcrowded and unhealthy conditions, compelled very often to earn their bread by monotonous and laborious work, and unable, partly through limited education and partly through overtime and other causes of physical exhaustion, to enjoy intellectual recreation, what wonder that many of these people fall a ready prey to the publican and the bookmaker?[24]

Rowntree pointed out that the percentage of those living in primary or secondary poverty in York came to almost precisely the same figure at which Booth had arrived for classes A, B, C, and D in London (27.84 versus 30.7). This finding led him to conclude more generally that 'from 25 to 30 percent of the town population of the United Kingdom are living in poverty'. Rowntree expressed none of Booth's occasional relief at discovering that urban poverty was no worse than this. He regarded such widespread want in 'this land of abounding wealth' as 'a fact which may well cause great searchings of heart', and he challenged his readers to find workable remedies for the painful conditions he had so painstakingly depicted.[25]

The period after the first few years of the century saw much less writing about poverty in London in particular and in British cities more generally

than had appeared during the preceding two decades
not so much that objective conditions had improve
rather that by now the facts had become all too famil.
dissatisfied with the *status quo* were accordingly directed
of basic problems and more toward the details of p\
solutions.

Nonetheless, reformers and social scientists continued at least c
to remind their readers of the poor living conditions that persisted an.
lowest strata of the urban population, especially in the older areas neai
centers. A contributor to the *Westminster Review* asserted concerning th.
slums, 'If the conditions are not worse now than they were in 1901 they are
probably no better'. He insisted that 'the perfection or imperfection of an
individual or a class is more dependent on environment than on any other
influence' and that there was 'no greater social curse at the present time than
the herding of the people in insanitary sub-divided tenements'. Similarly, an
economist who, just before the First World War, surveyed the course of
English urban history throughout the preceding century, concluded that 'in
the very large industrial centres, and to a smaller extent in most industrial
centres, a considerable portion of the population is living under physical and
moral conditions which are almost as bad as those which obtained fifty years
ago'. Despite the economic and social progress experienced by the upper
sections of the working classes, a large lower section was still trapped in
central slums where the quality of life remained stationary at a miserably low
level. 'The problem of dealing with these central slums', he wrote, 'has
become more difficult with the lapse of time, and any solution vastly more
expensive; but it is crying Peace where there is no Peace if the social
legislation of the last century is pronounced a success, when it has only been a
very partial success'.[26]

Studies of misery and poor housing on the European continent

With only a few exceptions, there was a real dearth in late nineteenth-
and early twentieth-century France of the sort of writing about urban poverty
that had appeared in that country during the 1830s and 1840s and was
appearing in England in great profusion. One man stood head and shoulders
above the rest as an observer of lower-class life in the French metropolis: the
great exponent and practitioner of literary naturalism, Emile Zola. His
novels, most of which treated the fictitious Rougon-Macquart family during
the decades of the Second Empire, provided a panoramic view of Parisian life
that constituted in effect a late nineteenth-century 'human comedy', comparable in many ways to Balzac's achievement half a century earlier.

The work in which Zola most fully explored the depths of misery among
the urban poor was his masterful *L'assomoir* (1877). The book focused on a
small working-class area in the northern part of Paris and on the dreary and

graded lives of the people who inhabited it. At the outset of the novel, Zola created a strong impression of debilitating meanness by describing the best room in a hotel inhabited by the central character, Gervaise, her children, and their father Lantier, who was soon to run off with another woman.

> She [Gervaise] sat there on the bed under the tattered and faded chintz canopy hanging from a rod tied to the ceiling with string. And through her tear-dimmed eyes she looked slowly round the miserable furnished room, at its walnut chest with one drawer missing, three cane-bottomed chairs and little grease-stained table with the cracked water-jug standing on it.

After continuing in this vein, Zola went on to describe the exterior of the hotel as 'a tumble-down two-storey building, painted purple halfway up, with rotting, rain-sodden shutters'. The main theme of the novel, as Zola explained in his preface, was 'the inevitable downfall of a working-class family in the polluted atmosphere of our urban areas'. Although Zola believed that the Rougon-Macquart line was to some extent predisposed to evil ways because of heredity, he placed greater emphasis on the deleterious effects of the environment in which its members lived. As he traced the seemingly inevitable descent of Gervaise's husband Coupeau and then of Gervaise herself into ultimately fatal alcoholism, what he did was to underline the destructive consequences of poverty for working-class Parisians.[27]

Two decades later, the last of Zola's series *Les trois villes* (3 vols, 1894-98), *Paris*, provided a much broader view of the French capital, but Zola again opened by describing a working-class area: 'the eastern portion of the city, the abodes of misery and toil ... submerged beneath ruddy steam, amid which the panting of workshops and factories could be divined'. As the central character, the Abbé Pierre Froment, looks toward the horizon, he sees 'a chaos of stone, studded with stagnant pools ... a Paris of mystery, shrouded by clouds, buried as it were beneath the ashes of some disaster, already half-sunken in the suffering and shame of that which its immensity concealed'. A few pages further on, Zola commented that new middle-class houses in Montmartre 'lent a yet more sombre and leprous aspect to such of the old shaky buildings as remained, the low pot-houses with blood-coloured walls, the cities of workmen's dwellings, those abodes of suffering with black, soiled buildings in which human cattle were piled'. This was an area in which 'filth and destitution brought terrible sadness to the heart'. Much of the action in Paris takes place among the well-to-do, but Zola still insisted on laying bare the miseries of the Parisian poor.[28]

Aside from Zola's novels, the most notable explorations of the urban underworld in France came from the pen of a politician and writer of noble descent, one Othenin d'Haussonville, who contributed frequently in the late 1870s and early 1880s to the moderate and respected *Revue des deux mondes*. Having begun with a long series of articles in which he focused on abandonment, vagabondage, sickness, begging, and delinquency among Parisian children, who 'as in almost all other big cities' were 'prey to many temptations and sufferings',[29] Haussonville moved on to take up the theme of *la misère* in the capital more generally. 'When', he lamented, 'one thinks of Paris in particular, this city of joy and pleasure and of festivals which we inhabit, hardly a day, an hour, or a minute does not mark some suffering....' Haussonville also lamented the fact that for several decades studies of poverty had appeared only rarely. Pauperism, he believed, had remained approximately constant since 1869, despite a great increase in the general level of economic well-being. The material deprivation that resulted from low wages, sickness, old age, misconduct, and overly large families cried out for exposure, and Haussonville turned to the task with diligence and sympathy, though with considerably less analytic precision than either Booth or Rowntree.[30]

Beyond the articles by Haussonville, there was little else in the *Revue* to compare with the numerous essays on poverty in London that appeared in similar British journals. Nor was a survey of urban poverty that remotely approached the work being done across the Channel published anywhere else.[31] There were several studies of the working classes, most of whose members were at best far from prosperous. Some of the authors of such works built on the example of empirical research set by Frédéric Le Play in his seminal *Les ouvriers européens* (1855), but like their predecessor they had little to say about the specifically urban dimensions of their subject.[32] The same held true of most authors who discussed and tried to answer 'the social question'.[33] The exposure and criticism of poverty among the lower classes was at best only loosely linked to the phenomenon of urban growth. To be sure, opponents of urbanization frequently buttressed their arguments in favor of efforts to keep men and women from leaving the countryside by pointing out that migration to the city reduced the wages of urban workers and drove up their rents.[34] This argument did not, however, rest on or help to generate an especially large or otherwise memorable body of writing about urban poverty *per se*.

In Germany, the rapid development of an industrial economy and an urban society elicited much greater interest in the problems besetting the lower-class inhabitants of cities than appeared in France. Still, the level of articulate concern remained well below what could be discerned in Britain. There was no controversy such as the one that had surrounded *The Bitter Cry of Outcast London*, nor were there any works on urban poverty that compared in scope or impact with the studies by Booth and Rowntree. Observers of German cities certainly recognized that many of these places left a great deal to be desired from the standpoint of the ordinary people who lived there, but their criticisms of primarily material deprivation were more limited and less widely noticed than the ones voiced by their counterparts across the Channel. In part, this deficiency resulted from the continuing — and in many respects worsening — gap between the educated middle classes and the workers. This split tended to undercut not only broad political alliances along the lines of the British Liberal Party but also middle-class social reformism and the efforts that would have been required in order to provide it with an intellectual underpinning. But inattention to poverty also stemmed, as we shall see later, from a continuing German tendency to dwell heavily on the city's biological, moral, and cultural defects rather than on its economic and material ones.

Among Germans who did write about living conditions among the working and lower classes in the big cities, none laboured more diligently or produced more impressive monuments of empirical social research than various contributors to the long series of publications sponsored by the Association for Social Policy (Verein für Sozialpolitik). Founded in 1872 by reform-minded university professors, other civil servants, and a few industrialists, the Association was led by such well known economists as Gustav Schmoller, Adolf Wagner, and Lujo Brentano, all of whom were in revolt against the principle of *laissez-faire*. They and their fellow Socialists of the Lectern (*Kathedersozialisten*) sought strenuously during the 1870s to win support in informed and responsible circles for policies of social reform through active intervention by the state. But thereafter, in order to assuage internal tensions, they turned the Association into a more purely academic group, which published learned studies of various social and economic questions and provided (usually every other year) a forum at which the policy implications of these works could be discussed. In the 1880s and 1890s, the Association emerged as the leading center of survey research in the German Empire, but its studies of workers focused on rural labor and on workers engaged in trade, in peddling, in shipping, and in transport rather than on urban-industrial workers. It appears that because of the anti-socialist legislation in force between 1878 and 1890 the factory proletariat was regarded as too controversial for the Association to handle.[35]

The Association did confront urban questions directly in several volumes that dealt with what had been emerging for some time as unquestionably a major social issue: the *Wohnungsfrage*, or housing question. Two volumes published in 1886 indicated in their title where and for whom the housing question had become most acute: for the poorer classes in the big cities.[36] Altogether, these works contained eighteen contributions. Thirteen, written by local experts engaged for the most part in municipal government, provided copious statistics on individual cities. One summarized the statistics for a number of cities, two dealt with foreign countries (England and France), and two focused on possible legislative remedies. The mayor of Frankfurt am Main, Johannes Miquel, clarified the main thrust of most of the descriptive studies when he declared at a meeting of the Association in September of 1886,

> I believe it has been clearly proved that for the needy classes of the people in the big cities there is a constant housing shortage to a greater or lesser extent,

frequently and regularly brought about by the absence or insufficient number of small apartments but always by the disproportionately high rents for decent smaller apartments and by the resulting recourse to unhealthy areas and overcrowding.

When, he continued, one considered not only the dreary statistics pertaining to size, density, and prices but also, among other evils, 'the absolute unhealthiness of a large number ... of badly ventilated, damp rooms ... [and] the absence of courtyards and toilets', one could only conclude that poor housing was one of the darkest aspects of modern society. Whether one regarded the matter from the standpoint of social progress, of political security, or merely of human sympathy, it was obligatory to combat the lack of decent dwellings energetically.[37]

A decade and a half later, the Association brought out four volumes on housing in Germany, Austria, and eight other countries. Aside from long articles on Berlin and Vienna, the focus was not so explicitly urban as in the earlier studies, but the problems of the urban population remained upper-most in the minds of all the contributors. Again, the detailed reports provided the basis for discussion and debate at a meeting of the Association, this one held at Munich in September of 1901. Carl Johann Fuchs performed the task of summarizing the results of the just published surveys. He asserted that since 1886, despite numerous theoretical solutions for the difficulties that had faced German city dwellers, their housing problems had either remained the same or become worse. Highlighting some of the salient data in the statistical chapter by Hugo Lindemann,[38] he pointed out that in Berlin the number of dwellings with only one heated room had risen from 152,000 in 1885 to 203,000 in 1895. Between 1880 and 1895 the number of persons living as lodgers in dwellings owned or rented by others had increased from 59,000 to 95,000, with the result that nearly one-quarter of all families in the capital were accommodating outsiders in their midst, and in Leipzig and Munich such overcrowding was even worse, reaching the level of 30 percent in the one city and 31 percent in the other.[39]

After the turn of the century, increased efforts were made to publicize the facts of life at the lower levels of the urban hierarchy through channels that would reach a much broader public than the one constituted by people who had the stamina to plow through the weighty tomes published by the Association for Social Policy. One such channel opened up as a result of the efforts of Hans Ostwald, a skilled worker and a prolific publicist.[40] He mobilized several dozen other writers, lawyers, and medical doctors (but apparently no university professors) for the purpose of producing a vast, fifty-volume panorama of urban life that appeared between 1905 and 1908 under the title *Grossstadt Dokumente*. Most of the books in this series dealt with Berlin, although a few treated Vienna, Hamburg, or big cities in general. They certainly did not dwell exclusively on urban suffering. In his preface to the first volume, Ostwald insisted that big cities possessed a definite 'cultural value' and that he intended to bring out their good as well as their bad sides. Nonetheless, many of the authors, whether with an eye to prodding their readers in the direction of social reform or (at least in a few cases) more in order to titillate them, did concentrate on things grim and sordid. Ostwald himself wrote about homeless vagabonds in Berlin. Several of the other contributors also dwelt on the problems of poor or nonexistent housing and of economic deprivation more generally. One Max Winter wrote about homelessness in Vienna. Ernst Schuchardt wrote an account of six months spent in a workhouse. Finally, Albert Südekum, editor of the Social Democratic *Kommunale Praxis* and a socialist member of the Reichstag, wrote a general study of 'big-city housing misery' in which he asserted that poor living quarters were the most oppressive of all the conditions that afflicted urban workers. In the view of all of these writers, far too many working-class Berliners and inhabitants of other big cities in Central Europe lived in a domestic environment that was appallingly bad and growing better much too slowly if at all.[41]

Another channel for the expression of popular views concerning urban life was opened up by Paul Göhre. As a young theology student, he spent three months in 1890 working incognito in a tool factory in Chemnitz and living among his fellow workers. His account of his experiences, published the following year, provided a fascinating and sympathetic view of laboring life in a major industrial town, treating not only the world of work but also many aspects of life outside the factory. Göhre wrote about skilled workers, for whom he had come to feel considerable respect, not about a destitute and demoralized *Lumpenproletariat*. Nonetheless, much of what he had to say about 'the material condition' of his fellow workers emphasized the meanness if not the poverty of their lives, especially with regard to domestic arrangements. 'It is difficult', he wrote, 'to call the interiors commonly occupied by our working people by the name of homes. Or may we indeed so designate a two-windowed room with an adjoining one-windowed recess, which cannot be heated?' In Göhre's experience, 'this and nothing more' constituted the abode of a large proportion of the workers' families, and in cases where the apartments exceeded this size a mother, father, and several children were likely to share their quarters with one or more lodgers. His descriptions of such places, together with his analysis of the ways in which not only crowding but also long working hours undermined familial solidarity, made his book an enormously popular as well as perceptive essay in firsthand social reporting about city life.[42]

Göhre's work also served as an inspiration for real laborers whom he began to enlist after the turn of the century in his effort to present to the public a series of authentic working-class autobiographies. Five such works appeared under his editorship between 1904 and 1911. Several of them, along with a massive survey of working-class attitudes undertaken by another worker, Adolf Levenstein, helped greatly to acquaint educated Germans with facets of urban life that had been as unfamiliar to most of them as conditions among African savages.[43]

Statistical information of the sort contained in works sponsored by the Association for Social Policy and more qualitative data of the sort conveyed by the *Grossstadt Dokumente* series and the workers' autobiographies was combined in another popular work that explored city life quite broadly, this one written by a professional economist. Adolf Weber, presenting a course of lectures to a group of schoolteachers in Bonn, surveyed the whole range of social problems that confronted the inhabitants and the governments of German big cities. He celebrated cities for the contributions they had made to economic progress and prosperity, and he asserted that on the whole the incomes of urban workers sufficed for a tolerably good life. Nonetheless, he still recognized genuine defects in the quality of urban life from an economic and material standpoint. In particular, he emphasized the persistence of residential overcrowding and excessive rents, the severity of urban unemployment, and the great extent of urban poverty. None of these difficulties, with the exception of the housing shortage, seriously affected more than a minority of the population, but they were all exacerbated by the sharp contrasts between poverty and wealth and the fact that many men had fallen into the one from the other. Weber retained a basic commitment to economic liberalism, which he supported in part by blaming the poor for their own misfortunes and suggesting better education as a major remedy, but he also recognized forces over which they could exercise little or no control.[44]

Germany failed throughout this period to produce a major urban novelist, but many of the country's best poets as well as an enormous number of relatively obscure ones described and interpreted the darker sides of city life in a large body of verse that came to be widely known as *Grossstadtlyrik*. Whereas the closest counterparts among novelists to the urban fiction of Gissing and Zola were the works about Berlin written by the distinctly minor Max Kretzer and Michael Georg Conrad's similarly second-rate panorama of Munich,[45] German urban poetry attained levels of precision, power, and popularity that far surpassed what could be discerned in the contemporary history of this genre in any other country.[46]

Much, though by no means all, of this writing took up the themes of poverty and material deprivation. Images of the big city as a place in which ordinary people experienced demoralizing want and suffering appeared repeatedly in the naturalistic poetry of the 1880s. Led by Arno Holz, the brothers Hart, and Karl Henckell, all of whom lived in or near Berlin, the naturalists wrote their poems in order to shock middle-class readers and to evoke sympathy from them for the urban proletariat. Embracing a non-Marxist brand of 'free socialism', they viewed their writing in large part as a form of quasipolitical philanthropy. Some of their basic attitudes toward urban life appear in Holz's poem, 'Ein Andres' ('Another Person'), which recounts the fate of a young mother lying in a sparsely furnished room on the sixth floor of a workers' tenement house. She is sick with fever. Three children sit numbly by her side as her husband sinks into a drunken stupor. A physician who serves the poor, summoned by neighbors, comes upon the scene at the end, only to exclaim, 'Weep, children! I was called too late./Your mother has already died'. Henckell, in his 'Berliner Abendbild' ('A Picture of Berlin in the Evening'), took up a similar theme in more general terms when he lamented, 'No one inquires about your pain,/No one hears another's heart-beat,/No one cares if you're sick and weak,/Everyone's after his own gain'.[47]

Although it was the naturalists who explored the subject of urban deprivation most directly and fully, a vivid sense of the city as a physically and emotionally painful place for many of its inhabitants resonated in much of the poetry written subsequently by the symbolists and the expressionists. Rainer Maria Rilke, generally regarded as the greatest German poet of the twentieth century, wrote of the cities in *Das Stundenbuch* (1905),

> There men live, badly and hard,/In cellar rooms, their gestures full of fright,
> More fearful still than helpless sheep./Outside, the earth awakens and breathes,
> But they barely exist and know it not./Children grow up on window sills,/
> Who stay forever in the shade./And they don't know that followers call,/
> Telling of freedom, wind, and joy./They must be children, young and sad.

In these lines, a perceptive observer of the urban scene conveyed a general sense of urban malaise at least in part by focusing specifically on people whose lives in the city were especially narrow and mean. This is not to say that Rilke's poem is 'about' poverty. Its range of implication and sentiment is far too broad to be encompassed by a topical category of that sort. But it did reflect, and help to crystallize, a feeling among many German authors that numerous city dwellers inhabited an environment that provided them at best with few comforts and little joy.[48]

Descriptions of the deprived in America

The closest and most numerous parallels to the perceptions of urban poverty articulated in the late nineteenth century by British observers appeared not on the European continent but in the United States. Large sectors of the burgeoning cities of America had been *terra incognita* for most thinkers and writers not only because of growing economic and social stratification but also because of their huge and rapidly growing populations of foreign-born immigrants. But these conditions, together with rising labor unrest, a developing social conscience among Protestant clergymen and other reformers, and the influence of thought about cities in Europe, stimulated wide-ranging efforts by large numbers of Americans to expose critically the dark underside of the urban world. Like their counterparts in Britain, these writers sought to shock their fellow citizens by enlightening them, first with lurid details and then increasingly with systematically gathered data, about the brute facts of life in the lower depths of their big cities.

The man whose writing did the most to stimulate concern with poverty in America during the first part of this period — and a good deal to stimulate English thinkers too — was Henry George, the author of *Progress and Poverty* (1879). A self-taught social philosopher who had worked at various trades and then turned to journalism in San Francisco, George wrote his treatise in order to win adherents to his scheme for taxing the 'unearned increment' gained by landowners as a result of rising rents. This seemed to him to be the only effective way to counteract a pattern according to which the rich grew richer while the poor grew poorer, a pattern most clearly evident in the big city. The controversy that surrounded George's work made men increasingly aware of the poverty that existed throughout America but most obviously in the densely settled urban areas, and it helped to generate much of the detailed writing about economic want that followed his book. George himself did not concentrate explicitly on cities and mentioned them only in passing, but he wrote about a fundamental urban problem, and the social critics who came after him focused more and more clearly on material deprivation within specifically urban settings.[49]

In the 1880s, urban poverty still received a good deal less attention in the United States than it was getting at the time in Britain, but the level of articulate concern was clearly rising. Writers for *Harper's Weekly* continued the efforts they had been waging in the 1870s to publicize poor housing in areas of New York known by such colorful names as Bottle Alley and Ragpicker's Court. Helen Campbell wrote a series of articles on sweatshops for the *New York Daily Tribune* (published as a book in 1887 under the title *Prisoners of Poverty*) in which she showed how competition in the needle trades forced even well-intentioned employers to mistreat their workers.

Shortly thereafter, Edward Bellamy brought out his novel, *Looking Backward* (1888), a work comparable in its impact on men's views of contemporary society to the book by George that had appeared a decade earlier. Toward the end of the novel, Julian West returns in a dream from the utopian world of the year 2000 to the Boston of the 1880s in which the book opens. He perceives the city quite differently from the way in which he had viewed it when he actually lived there. 'The squalor and malodorousness of the town struck me', he tells the reader, 'from the moment I stood upon the street, as facts I had never before observed'. He goes on to describe some of the conditions that remained all too real for most Bostonians — who, unlike the fictional narrator, could not escape from their time and place — as follows:

> From the black doorways and windows of rookeries on every side came gusts of fetid air. The streets and alleys reeked with the effluvia of a slave ship's between-decks. As I passed I had glimpses within of pale babies gasping out their lives amid sultry stenches, of hopeless-faced women deformed by hardship.... Like the starving bands of mongrel curs that infest the streets of Moslem towns, swarms of half-clad brutalized children filled the air with shrieks and curses as they fought and tumbled among the garbage that littered the courtyards.

In this 'Inferno', West encounters a 'festering mass of human wretchedness' so vast and horrible that it seems temporarily to be the stuff of truth rather than of memory and imagination, despite a temporal gap of over a century.[50]

No one did more after George and Bellamy to heighten public anguish over the condition of the urban poor than Jacob Riis. Having grown to young adulthood in the small and isolated town of Ribe in Denmark, Riis emigrated to the United States in 1870. Thereafter, he held a succession of jobs in different parts of the country for several years before discovering his vocation in the late 1870s as a reporter for the *New York Tribune* and the Associated Press Bureau. With a beat that included the Police Department, the Board of Health, and the coroner's office, he operated from a room located in the midst of an East Side slum. After writing numerous articles about slum life during the 1880s, Riis traveled in 1888 throughout the state of New York giving an illustrated lecture to church groups on the theme 'The Other Half, How It Lives and Dies in New York'. An article published the next year in *Scribner's Magazine*, 'How the Other Half Lives', served as the basis for his first book, which appeared in 1890 under the same title. Inspired in large part by the literary example of Charles Dickens, whom he much admired, Riis produced a work comparable in its impact to Andrew Mearns' *Bitter Cry of Outcast London* (1883), although at the time it appeared it was naturally paired instead with William Booth's *In Darkest England* (1890). Like Mearns and Booth, Riis took his readers on a literary tour through an urban underworld, and his influence fully equaled theirs, far exceeding that of any of the American social reporters who had preceded him.[51]

As Riis surveyed the life styles of the various groups of immigrants who constituted the great majority of New Yorkers at the time, he concentrated on the debilitating effects they all experienced as a result of the conditions that prevailed in tenement housing. His plentiful anecdotes and his occasional statistics served to reinforce his basic argument that most of the 'ever-increasing multitude' who lived in the city suffered both physically and morally from their cramped and rundown habitats. Riis denied that 'the whole body of the population living in the tenements ... or even the larger part of it, is to be classed as vicious or as poor in the sense of verging on beggary'. But the unfortunate people who lived there were 'truly poor for having no better homes; waxing poorer in purse as the exorbitant rents to which they are tied, as ever was serf to soil, keep rising'. He devoted special attention to the fate of the children. As he guided his readers through a typical dwelling inhabited by the poor, he wrote, 'Listen! That short hacking cough, that tiny, helpless wail — what do they mean? ... The child is dying

11 Gotham Court on New York's Lower East Side. This was a typical courtyard behind a tenement inhabited for the most part by recent immigrants (source: Jacob Riis, *How the Other Half Lives* [1890] frontispiece).

with measles. With half a chance it might have lived; but it had none. That dark bedroom killed it'.[52]

The rest of the 1890s, a period of continuing economic depression and social discontent, saw the appearance of numerous essays in popular magazines and books aimed at a broad reading audience, all written with a view to increasing the citizenry's awareness of the kinds of facts Riis had done so much to publicize in *How the Other Half Lives*. *Scribner's Magazine* printed a dozen articles in 1892 and 1893 under the general title 'The Poor in Great Cities', including not only a contribution by Riis on 'The Children of the Poor' and another titled 'Among the Poor of Chicago' but also studies of London and Naples.[53] *The Arena*, edited by Benjamin O. Flower, printed a host of articles on urban poverty, typified by Helen Gardener's 'Thrown in with the City Dead' (1890). Her harrowing account of conditions on Blackwell's Island, to which the city government of New York consigned its lunatics, some of its prisoners, and its pauper dead, provided an excellent early example of urban muckraking. So too did Flower's own book, *Civilization's Inferno: Or Studies in the Social Cellar* (1893), which represented an attempt to do for the slums of Boston what Riis's work had done for those of Manhattan.

At the same time, men active in religious circles intensified their efforts to arouse the social conscience of the Christian faithful. The 1890s were the decade when the 'social gospel', a program for positive reform that had originated from the efforts of Charles Loring Brace, Richard T. Ely, and Washington Gladden among others, came of age. The Protestant clergymen who spread it during these years repeatedly called attention to the urban problems that in their eyes made urban reform a moral imperative. Louis A. Banks, a Methodist minister in Boston, wrote a series of sermons on the disgusting conditions in the city's sweatshops that appeared under the deliberately provocative title *White Slaves: Or, the Oppression of the Worthy Poor* (1891). Gladden, pastor of a Congregational church in Columbus, Ohio, showed a broader awareness of poverty in a review article in which he drew attention to the work of Riis and, at much greater length, that of Charles Booth. 'The facts', he wrote, 'are far worse than most intelligent Americans suspect, and there is need of thorough investigation'.[54]

The last decade of the century also saw a marked upsurge of concern about the urban poor in the realm of imaginative literature. A multitude of poets whose names have long since passed into oblivion castigated the modern city for a whole host of defects, some of the most obvious of which appeared in the slums. As one poet put it, 'In cities densely populated/The poor are apt to dwell,/And to describe their misery,/Is more than tongue can tell'. Another emphasized the wretchedness experienced by the poor by contrasting it with the urban opulence they could see around them. He wrote,

In a great, Christian city, died friendless, of hunger!
Starved to death, where there's many a bright banquet hall!

> In a city of hospitals, died in a prison!
> Homeless died in a land that boasts free homes for all!
> In a city of millionaires, died without money!

Sentimental verse of this sort made no great contribution to the nation's storehouse of art, but it did add to men's awareness of social realities in the cities in which more and more of them were living.[55]

The literary men whose writings provided the best depictions of life among the urban poor were, as in Britain and France, the social novelists. William Dean Howells, unquestionably one of the leading men of letters in America during the last two decades of the century, descended from the upper-class world of Boston that provided the settings for *The Rise of Silas Lapham* (1885) into working-class areas of New York in *A Hazard of New Fortunes* (1890). In that book, after leaving Boston to live in the metropolis, Basil March and his wife pass accidentally through a place marked by 'a poverty as hopeless as any in the world, transmitting itself from generation to generation and establishing conditions of permanency to which human life adjusts itself as it does to those of some incurable disease, like leprosy'. Most of the novel treats the lives of the well-to-do, but the world inhabited by the poor remains ever present. A few years later, in a nonfictional work of urban description, Howells wrote that although the tenement districts in New York seemed at first glance to possess a picturesque gaiety, to really plunge into them was 'to inhale the stenches of the neglected street, and to catch that yet fouler and dreadfuller poverty-smell which breathes from the open doorways'. He continued in the same vein, referring to 'children quarrelling in their games … like the little savage outlaws they are … the work-worn look of the mothers, the squalor of the babes, the haggish ugliness of the old women, the slovenly frowziness of the young girls'. His utopian novels, *A Traveler from Altruria* (1894) and *Through the Eye of the Needle* (1907), expressed similar views, revealing an anti-urban streak that became ever more pronounced as Howells advanced in years.[56]

Urban poverty played a still more central part in the novels written by a younger generation of literary naturalists, such as Stephen Crane's *Maggie: A Girl of the Streets* (1893). Crane described part of the environment in which a girl from the tenement districts grows up, becomes a prostitute, and ultimately takes her own life in passages such as the following, which have secured his reputation as a penetrating observer of life in the slums:

> … From a careening building, a dozen gruesome doorways gave up loads of babies to the street and gutter. A wind of early autumn raised yellow dust from cobbles and swirled it against an hundred windows. Long streamers of garments fluttered from fire-escapes. In all unhandy places there were buckets, brooms, rags and bottles. In the street infants played or fought with other infants or sat stupidly in the way of vehicles. Formidable women, with uncombed hair and disordered dress, gossiped while leaning on railings, or screamed in frantic quarrels. Withered persons, in curious postures of submission to something, sat smoking pipes in obscure corners. A thousand odors of cooking food came forth

to the street. The building quivered and creaked from the weight of humanity stamping about in its bowels.

Having experienced poverty in New York himself as a starving freelance writer while he was writing *Maggie*, Crane succumbed to tuberculosis at the age of twenty-nine in 1900, but before his death he published a second urban novel, *George's Mother*, and two short stories ('The Men in the Storm' and 'An Experiment in Misery') that presented the city in a similarly dark light.[57]

The greatest representative of naturalism and the most impressive novelist of the city in America, Theodore Dreiser, was unquestionably one of the closest students of urban poverty during the early years of the twentieth century. The son of an immigrant, Dreiser had suffered from poverty himself as a small-town boy before he witnessed it in the lives of others as a newspaper reporter in Chicago, St. Louis, Cleveland, Pittsburgh, Buffalo, and New York. Like Crane and like George Gissing in England, he created his fictional portrayals of urban misery on the basis of personal experience as well as observation. He knew that the possession or lack of money made an enormous difference in the ways people acted and in the treatment they received from others and that poverty entailed doing without all sorts of things that human beings needed if they were to enjoy decent lives.[58]

Dreiser's first and greatest novel, *Sister Carrie* (1901), reveals many traces of his own life, beginning with the arrival of Carrie Meeber in Chicago as a young woman. Seeking a niche for herself in the city, she quickly discovers that it does not treat the newcomer generously. She longs for 'wealth, fashion, ease — every adornment for women', but she experiences sharp disappointment as a result of her inability to find any work other than the exhausting, unhealthy, and unremunerative labor in a sweatshop. She manages to make a go of her life only by becoming the mistress of a traveling salesman, Charles Drouet. At this point, the world of the poor is left behind, but it reappears after the action shifts to New York, to which Carrie moves reluctantly as the mistress of the initially prosperous George Hurstwood. His difficulties finding a job there in the book's closing chapters provide a parallel to Carrie's troubles earlier, but instead of surmounting them he is overcome by them. He sinks deeper and deeper into destitution that is all the more striking because of the way in which Dreiser contrasts it with the good fortune that comes to Carrie as she becomes a famous actress. Dreiser's account of Hurstwood's gradual entry into a world populated by 'the class that sits on the park benches during the endurable days and sleeps upon them during the summer nights', consisting of men who are 'all pale, flabby, sunken-eyed, hollow-chested', is the most memorable depiction of the process of economic decline and personal disintegration in an urban environment anywhere in American literature.[59]

Subsequently, Dreiser took up the theme of poverty in the midst of plenty again and again. Robert Bremner has observed that 'the annals of the Gerhardt family [in *Jennie Gerhardt*, 1911] read like a case record prepared by a charity agent'. The novel carefully studies the Gerhardts' family budget, showing how they barely keep their heads above water until Mr. Gerhardt is injured in an accident at work. It is in order to stave off the necessity of choosing between begging and starving that Jennie, like Carrie before her, accepts the advances of a male benefactor. Many sketches of the poor also appear in Dreiser's book *The Color of A Great City*, written in New York between 1900 and 1915. Short pieces on topics such as 'Bums', 'On Being Poor', 'The Toilers of the Tenements', 'The Bread-Line', 'A Wayplace of the Fallen', and 'The Bowery Mission' testify to his continuing fascination with the lives of those who had descended to — or never risen above — the bottom rungs of the urban hierarchy.[60]

In the meantime, a more consciously quantitative and analytical body of writing about urban society had begun to appear and to attract attention. It came from men and women for whom heart-rending description and moral pleading did not go nearly far enough to satisfy their desires for scientific knowledge and understanding. These were the writers who, especially after the turn of the century, did the most to illuminate the conditions of life among the urban poor.

Economists and statisticians were ideally situated to undertake thorough studies of urban problems along the lines of those sponsored in Germany by the Association for Social Policy, and as in Germany poor housing claimed much of their attention. The economist Marcus T. Reynolds drew together an enormous amount of data on the conditions experienced by tenement dwellers from state labor bureaus, boards of health, housing commissions, and charity organization societies in a work on *The Housing of the Poor in American Cities* that received a prize from the American Economic Association in 1892. Reynolds carefully set forth extensive statistics in order to demonstrate the intensification of overcrowding, the increase of rents relative to incomes, and the moral as well as physical evils that stemmed from these developments. E. R. L. Gould, a statistician for the United States Department of Labor, provided comparable information and expressed similar views a few years later in his work, *The Housing of the Working People*.[61]

Despite the quantitative expertise of men such as Reynolds and Gould, the most numerous and influential examples of empirical analysis of the urban poor were written not by professional social scientists but rather by men and women who had worked closely with those about whom they wrote. Foremost among them were people who had familiarized themselves with lower-class life at first hand through charitable work in the social settlements that began to spring up in American cities during the late 1880s in imitation of Toynbee Hall, established in East London earlier in the decade.[62]

Among the numerous college and university graduates who settled in the slums with a view to improving the poor through close contact with them, none exerted greater influence not only locally but also nationwide than Jane Addams and her co-workers at Hull House in Chicago. Half a dozen years after the Chicago settlement had opened, they brought out an influential collection of essays under the title *Hull-House Maps and Papers*.[63] It offers an excellent example of the detailed investigations of slum life under way among many settlement workers around this time. In her preface to the volume, Addams emphasized that most of the contributors had devoted their energies during their years in residence at Hull House 'not towards sociological investigation, but to constructive work'.[64] Nonetheless, in addition to several essays on charitable work in general and on the work done at Hull House in particular and a pair of rather impressionistic pieces on the Bohemians and the Italians, there were detailed studies of wage-earning children, of wages and expenditures in the clothing industry, and of the Chicago ghetto. Perhaps the most notable parts of the volume from a sociological viewpoint were the maps of nationalities and wages. The wage map, based on some of the data for Chicago accumulated by Florence Kelley in connection with the Special Investigation of the Slums of Great Cities undertaken in 1893 by the United States Department of Labor, signified the group's scientific aspirations especially clearly by displaying the same colors used by Charles Booth on his maps of London. Booth was also acknowledged explicitly as an exemplary researcher and a man who inspired others to go beyond him.[65]

A few years later, residents and associates of the South End House in Boston wrote a set of essays that appeared under the title *The City Wilderness* (1898). These settlement workers surveyed the lives of the people around them in a spirit similar to that of their colleagues in Chicago, focusing on 'toilsome monotony' and on 'the effects of unwholesome surroundings in childhood, joined with the cramping necessities of adult life'. In their view, the men, women, and children whom they had encountered lay 'at the mercy of great social forces which move almost like the march of destiny'. Like the residents of Hull House, they regarded involuntary poverty as a central and inescapable fact in the lives of a large portion of the urban population.[66]

Shortly after the turn of the century, others who had participated in settlement work during the 1890s helped to produce major studies that once again focused on poor housing. Robert Hunter, a former resident of Hull House and the secretary of the Chicago Board of Charities, chaired a special committee of the Chicago City Homes Association that investigated tenement life in that city. He reported in 1901, '... Housing conditions are growing steadily worse, and ... the slum now building is likely to repeat the history of those in other cities.... The night of the double-dealer, the worst of all tenements, is enveloping the West as yesterday it blackened the East'. Photographs, bar graphs, maps, and tables in great abundance served to highlight overcrowding, poor sanitation, and 'social pathology'.[67]

About the same time, an investigation of housing that was to exert a much greater influence on later social research began in New York. Although carried out by a state commission, it resulted largely from impulses generated by the New York City Charity Organization Society, which in 1898 had established its own Tenement House Commission, a group that included

12   A model of a dumb-bell tenement in New York. This model was used in an influential exhibition mounted by reformers in 1900 in order to publicize the evils of slum housing (source: Robert W. DeForest and Lawrence Veiller, eds., *The Tenement House Problem*, I [New York, 1903], 10).

among its members E. R. L. Gould and Jacob Riis. Lawrence Veiller, who had earlier worked as a volunteer in a New York settlement house, organized a vast exhibition on tenements that opened under the Commission's auspices in the spring of 1900, replete with over a thousand photographs, many detailed maps, tables, and charts, and papier-maché models of slum blocks. These displays demonstrated not only the widespread lack of outside light and ventilation but also the close correlation between housing conditions on the one hand and pauperism and disease on the other. They also revealed that buildings even worse than those in the older slum districts were springing up at the rate of several thousand a year in the newer areas of the city.

Veiller's highly effective efforts to show that working-class families were less well housed in New York than in any other city in the civilized world led Governor Theodore Roosevelt to create the New York State Tenement House Commission, on which Veiller served as secretary. The report submitted by Veiller and by Robert W. DeForest, a lawyer, chairman of the C.O.S., and also chairman of the state commission, incorporated much of the data assembled for the earlier exhibition and far exceeded in scope Hunter's report on Chicago. In their introduction they asserted,

> The tenement districts of New York are places in which thousands of people are living in the smallest space in which it is possible for human beings to exist — crowded together in dark, ill-ventilated rooms, in many of which the sunlight never enters and in most of which fresh air is unknown.[68]

The other contributions, some written by Veiller, one by Gould, and others by various technical experts, called attention to specific defects in the tenements then under construction and to the ways in which they bred social as well as physical disorder. Full of recommendations that were soon put into effect by state legislation, DeForest and Veiller's report impressively demonstrated the practical utility of research that was not only well-intentioned but also methodologically sophisticated. As Robert Bremner put it, 'The lesson of the tenement-house investigation seemed to be that the path to reform lay through research'.[69]

Research into the condition of the urban poor became ever more widespread and systematic. The year 1905 saw the formation of a Charities Publication Committee that included both Addams and Riis. The Committee functioned as an editorial board for the magazine *Charities and the Commons*, which fused the organs of the New York C.O.S. and the settlement house movement. Under the direction of Edward T. Devine and Paul U. Kellogg, the new journal printed two special issues during its first year, one titled 'The Negro in the Cities of the North', the other titled 'Next Door to Congress'. The latter, a report on housing, health, education, and child labor in Washington, D.C., aroused considerable public interest.

This interest encouraged the Committee to accept a suggestion by an official of a juvenile court in Allegheny County (Pennsylvania) that it undertake a similar study of the steel-making city of Pittsburgh. Headed by Kellogg, a staff that included Florence Kelley and Robert Woods carried out the field work for the survey in 1907 and 1908 with generous financial support from the Russell Sage Foundation, whose president was Robert DeForest. The *Pittsburgh Survey*, published between 1909 and 1914, was the greatest of all the urban surveys undertaken in America before the First World War, a work that more nearly approximated Booth's study of London than anything else published at the time in any country. Six substantial volumes treated wages, working conditions, budgets and domestic life in the steelworkers' homes, health and sanitation, crime and the administration of justice, playgrounds and recreation, schools and other institutions, and additional topics as well.

The facts presented in the survey gave little reason for anyone in the city to feel much satisfaction. It emerged clearly that many Pittsburghers worked up to twelve hours per day, that wages were calculated according to the needs of single men rather than to those of responsible heads of families, and that the wages of women averaged between one-half and one-third of what the men received. The extraordinary pressures of work, the prevalence of preventable diseases, and the high toll of industrial accidents all undermined family life and contributed to social pathology in other ways as well. Pittsburgh stood out as an American Coketown, a city in which short-range and shortsighted considerations of costs and profits by the agents of absentee capitalists wreaked havoc in the lives of the great mass of the population. Jane Addams regarded the survey as a major source of 'the veritable zeal for reform' that swept through the United States during the years when it was published, and many other reformers found ammunition in its pages. Its influence, however, rested not on any polemical qualities but instead on the honest and reliable way in which it presented factual information to men and women who knew that sound knowledge was indispensable for achieving the better future they sought for the cities in which they lived.[70]

The *Pittsburgh Survey* appeared at the end of a period of three decades during which countless authors on both sides of the Atlantic had described, analyzed, and protested against urban poverty. Especially in Britain and in the United States, and to a lesser extent in France and Germany, economists, sociologists, novelists, clergymen, and a variety of social reformers (most notably people who were active in settlement work) provided abundant documentation of want in the midst of plenty. Slum housing, low wages, and unemployment struck numerous men and women as all-too pervasive features of city life, not only in East London and on the Lower East Side, but also in many other urban areas, from Berlin, Paris, and York to Boston and Chicago. In their view, the denizens of urban slums suffered from unacceptably low levels of material well-being that stemmed not from their own inadequacies as individuals but instead from the economic and physical environment in which they lived. Slum dwellers were certainly not seen as constituting the bulk of the urban population. But the impoverished lower classes appeared nonetheless to pose an urban challenge of enormous and undeniable magnitude. Although in an absolute sense most urban workers were clearly far more prosperous around 1900 than their forebears a generation or two earlier, the persistence of large — and in some cases growing — pockets of poverty was one of the major themes in urban thought during these years. Much of what these writers had to say echoed the rising chorus of protest by socialists against industrial capitalism, but only a handful of them belonged to the socialist camp. What one encounters here by and large is a diverse series of efforts by moderately progressive members of the middle classes to publicize problems of the urban sector that they regarded as essentially soluble within the confines of a capitalist economy.

6

Fears of Physical and Demographic Decline

The intellectual climate fostered by men such as Charles Booth, Emile Zola, Hans Ostwald, and Jacob Riis in their empirical and literary descriptions of overcrowded housing in mean streets and other facets of urban poverty stimulated a wide range of criticisms and anxieties. Two of the clearest implications of much of what they wrote were that deleterious physical surroundings produced inferior physical specimens and that such city dwellers could not maintain a stable let alone a growing population on their own. Many observers, particularly but by no means only in the ranks of the medical profession, voiced deep fears that the continued growth of cities posed an ominous threat to the health, the size, and even the eventual survival of the populations living in the countries in which this process was occurring. Their warnings echoed similar concerns expressed by public health reformers around the middle of the century. The late nineteenth-century critics focused, however, not simply on high death rates *per se* — the incidence of mortality having greatly declined since the days of Edwin Chadwick, A. J. P. Parent-Duchâtelet, and John Griscom — but also on the sickliness of those who did not die and on what they regarded as an unfavorable ratio of deaths to births. Moreover, they did so in a manner that indicated greatly heightened awareness of the social and political implications of the trends about which they were alarmed. Critical observations with regard to urban health and demography led to a widening range of related concerns. They simultaneously incorporated the growing awareness of material deprivation and suggested the presence of some of the moral and ideological sentiments to which we shall turn more directly in the chapter after this.

Health and population problems in England and France

In England, the belief that the rise of the city portended the decline of the city dweller found repeated expression during the 1880s, shortly after the upsurge of concern over the plight of 'outcast London'. The man who did the most to draw public attention at this time to the tribute in human health and numbers exacted by a great city from many of its citizens was James Cantlie, a surgeon and a medical educator who worked in London hospitals. In his frequently cited lecture, *Degeneration amongst Londoners* (1885), he argued that because of overcrowding in the metropolis the air there lacked ozone and most inhabitants could not derive the benefit they needed from vigorous exercise. What Cantlie labeled 'urbomorbus' or 'city disease' afflicted urbanites at all levels of the social hierarchy. 'Everyone in their inner conscience', he wrote, 'knows and believes that town air is bad, that everyone working in it must suffer after a time in health and stamina; and that person must be blind who does not observe the effect on children born and brought up in towns, even if they belong to the upper or middle classes'.[1]

Cantlie recognized that the most severe damage resulted from the 'insanitary environment of the poorer classes of the community',[2] but poor health by no means afflicted them alone. It took its toll throughout the city, producing a 'puny and ill-developed race', incapable of surviving for more than three generations. Cantlie asserted that he had succeeded only after much effort in finding a handful of people living in the metropolis with some grandparents as well as both parents who had also been Londoners. He described one of them as follows: 'Height 5 feet 1 inch; age 21; chest measurement 28 inches. His head measure around the eyebrows is 19 inches (nearly 3 inches below the average); measured across from tip of ear to tip of ear, 11 inches (1½ below the average). His aspect is pale waxy; he is very narrow between the eyes, and with a decided squint'. Cantlie observed with regard to the next generation, 'I have never come across the children of any such [specimen], and I believe it is not likely I ever shall. Nature steps in and denies the continuance of such; and weakness of brain-power gives such a being but little chance in this struggling world'.[3]

Other medical men added their voices to the chorus of despair. J. Milner Fothergill, a prolific writer on medical matters, gave an address in 1887 to the Anthropological Section of the British Association for the Advancement of Science. In his paper he asserted, 'It has long been recognized that town populations have a tendency to deteriorate.... Look at the denizens of large towns! You see them small in bone, light in muscle, short in stature; with chest measurements small in all directions. They constitute, indeed, another race'. As he went on to elaborate upon his ideas a few years later, he emphasized that the migrant from the countryside to the city made a choice that entailed fateful consequences for his family's future. 'They are certainly more affluent than their country cousins; but they are town dwellers, and thereby, a doomed race. Without infusions of new blood in a few generations they die out; while their country cousins remain a fertile folk'. Townsmen suffered not only from bad housing, air, water, and food, from lack of exercise, and from other conditions that directly weakened their bodies but also from constant overstimulation of their psyches. This produced both intellectual precocity and 'a tendency to have neurotic troubles'. In Fothergill's view, 'the highly strung neurosal woman' was generally a product of town life. Such a woman, 'liable to migraine ... plagued with indigestion ... subject to rheumatism' and afflicted by a host of other disorders that stemmed from her overwrought state of mind, could, he implied, hardly be expected to raise a large and healthy family. For many reasons, those born and bred in towns were therefore 'a dying race'. The town was 'like a huge dragon preying on mankind'.[4]

J. P. Williams-Freeman wrote in a similar vein a few years later, stating that

> The child of the townsman is 'bred too fine', it is too great an exaggeration of himself, excitable and painfully precocious in its childhood, neurotic, dyspeptic, pale, and undersized in its adult state, if it ever reach it. The females, too, although possibly prolific, are not good mothers, sometimes giving a large quantity of feebly nourishing milk, sometimes producing none.

The combination of psychic and physical degeneration led, it seemed, to much higher death rates in densely settled areas than in the countryside. Citing statistics provided by the Registrar General, Williams-Freeman pointed out that as soon as there were fewer than two acres per inhabitant in any census district mortality increased directly with density, ranging from 20 per thousand in areas where there were 1.4 acres per inhabitant to between 27 and 34 in areas where there was only 0.1 acre. Such evidence indicated that all those who could afford to do so ought

> to look upon urban London as we do upon India, or the Straits Settlements, as a rich but unhealthy locality, where, with due care and precautions the well-to-do can remain during the working period of their lives in fair health and comfort ... but where children can only be brought up with great risk both to health and life, and where all attempts to settle permanently from generation to generation only result in rapid falling off, both physical and moral, and in early extinction of the race.

The city as a whole would remain dependent on rural to urban migration for constant replenishment of its ranks, without which it would die out in two or three generations. Unfortunately, however, it would continue to fulfill its demographic needs by attracting 'the pick of the youth, both physically and intellectually', thus encouraging 'a survival of the unfittest by elimination of the best'.[5]

Clear parallels to the warnings voiced by these medical doctors appeared in the writings of other men who wrote about cities from somewhat different vantage points. Arnold White, a prolific publicist, expressed deep dismay over high death rates and 'the general reduction of stamina all round from the generic poison of overcrowded centres'. Reginald Brabazon, a liberal philanthropist and social reformer, conjectured, 'If we could isolate the city, and could prevent all intermarriage with the country, the degeneration in the physique of the inhabitants of the former would probably be so marked as to horrify the public, and would arouse a sense of national danger which would command the attention of Parliament and the country'. Brabazon admitted the difficulty of proving urban degeneration statistically, but he asserted that 'it is only necessary for an intelligent man or woman to walk through the slums of our great towns in order to assure himself or herself, beyond all question or doubt, that the physical condition of the people in these crowded districts is, to say the least, unsatisfactory, and one of which no Englishman can be proud'. Brabazon's references to national danger and national pride pointed toward his concluding remarks about the implications of poor health for Britain's prosperity and security. Physical strength was essential for success *vis-à-vis* other nations 'in the peaceful contests of everyday life as in wars', and Britain could not hope to compete effectively if its workers were weak both in body and in intellect as a result of living in a deleterious urban environment.[6]

Robert Blatchford, an enormously popular writer who advocated a blend of socialism and imperialism, attacked urbanization a few years later by pointing an accusing finger at 'unhealthy work, vile air, overcrowding, disease, ugliness, drunkenness, and a high death-rate', and more specifically at rural-urban differences in the health of recruits for the army. Like Brabazon, he emphasized the harm inflicted by urban conditions on the nation as a whole. Poor working-class health was both morally offensive and wasteful. 'Cast your eyes ... over the Registrar-General's returns', he urged, 'and imagine if you can how many gentle nurses, good mothers, sweet singers, brave soldiers, and clever artists, inventors, and thinkers are swallowed up every year in that ocean of crime and sorrow, which is known to the official mind as "the high death-rate of the wage-earning classes"'.[7]

Around the turn of the century, alarm about the health of Britain's city dwellers reached its peak. The impetus for the upsurge of concern with the urban milieu as a source of physical degeneration came quite clearly from political considerations of the sort suggested by Brabazon and Blatchford. Britain's inability to bring the Boer War to a speedy and successful conclusion focused the attention of many intellectuals and politicians on the need to enhance the country's 'national efficiency'. Having already begun to feel anxiety as a result of the rising power of Imperial Germany, they saw the course of the conflict in South Africa between 1899 and 1902 as an ominous indication that the strength of the British nation was indeed declining relative to that of much of the rest of the world.

What most frightened many observers was the discovery that large numbers of urban workers were unfit for military service. Rumors to this effect began to circulate soon after the military disasters that occurred during the first six months of the war. In 1901, two writers sought to make some of the most troubling facts more clearly and generally understood. Arnold White, in his *Efficiency and Empire*, reported that three out of five men who had attempted to enlist in the army at the Manchester depot in 1899 had failed to pass the physical examination. B. Seebohm Rowntree, in his study of poverty in York, noted that between 1897 and 1900 out of 3,600 volunteers at the military depots in York, Leeds, and Sheffield, 26.5 percent had been rejected as unfit and an additional 29 percent had been accepted only provisionally. After several articles about the problem of inadequate military manpower had appeared in leading magazines in 1902 and 1903, the government established an Interdepartmental Committee on Physical Deterioration. The Committee held hearings, gathered evidence, and in 1904 published a report that confirmed earlier assertions by men such as White and Rowntree. The report retold the dreary tale of working-class infirmity and linked it clearly to disease, malnutrition, and poverty. It indicated the existence of unsanitary conditions and harmful misconceptions about healthy living in the countryside too, but it focused primarily on the problems facing townsmen, further darkening the already grimy image of the environment in which they lived.[8]

Concern over the political implications of physical changes in the British population was kept alive subsequently by two sorts of arguments. On the one hand, there was continued attention to what Cantlie described in 1907 as 'the degeneration, inevitable to dwellers in large cities'. But his fear that Britain might one day lack enough 'sons to carry on the work of Empire' also rested on awareness of a decline in the number of births. In order to meet Britain's needs overseas, each family had to produce five children. Cantlie did not provide statistics on urban as opposed to rural birth rates, but he clearly perceived the city as a place that failed to contribute its fair share of fresh blood to the social organism. Charles Masterman, a leading liberal reformer, also feared that falling fertility, both among the workers and among those above them, might well lead to a cessation of demographic growth, and he asked plaintively,

> Is the vitality of the race being burnt up in mine and furnace, in the huddled mazes of the city? And is the future of a colonising people to be jeopardised, not by difficulties of over-lordship at the extremities of its dominion, but by obscure changes in the opinion, the religion, and the energies at the heart of the Empire?

Trends in the cities seemed to indicate that the answer to these questions was 'yes'.[9]

In France, anxiety about the overall size of the population was readily apparent during these years. Beset by an extremely low birth rate throughout the nineteenth century, Frenchmen were increasingly concerned after 1870 about the slowness of their numerical growth. In light of the extremely rapid increase in the number of Germans, France's demographic stagnation loomed as an ominous portent of continuing decline and repeated humiliation in years to come. The fact that in the early 1890s the total number of deaths in

France had actually surpassed the number of births was an especially great cause for alarm.

Around this time, several social scientists expressed considerable consternation about the ways in which France's population problems might be exacerbated by the rise of the big city. Writing under the influence of the more general concerns referred to above, they sought to show that urbanization entailed not only damage to the bodies of those most directly affected by it but also too many deaths and not enough births.

Arthur Bordier, a professor of anthropology as well as a medical doctor, considered urban health and urban demography together in a general treatise on 'the life of societies', and the conclusions he drew were most alarming. Writing shortly after the publication of Cantlie's lecture on degeneration, he too emphasized the harmful effects of 'atmospheric conditions unfavorable to health'. They produced an array of illnesses, such as tuberculosis and typhoid fever, which he labeled 'malaria urbana'. After commenting critically on urban poverty, on overcrowded housing, and on urban rates of syphilis and alcoholism, he turned to demographic phenomena. He focused first on low natality, which he attributed to a variety of inhibiting factors: 'fatigue from work or from worldly pleasures, hygienic defects, lack of exercise, too much cerebral centralization of organic energies'. Such conditions created a situation in which, whereas 313 legitimate births resulted from every 100 marriages in all of France, in the Department of the Seine the number fell to 241. On the other side of the ledger — and here Bordier's analysis related more directly to his remarks on urban disease — mortality in the cities was relatively high. At age twenty, he reported, 6,114 persons survived out of every 10,000 who were born in all of France, whereas only 4,313 survived in the Department of the Seine. Bordier concluded, 'From these diverse demographic conditions it turns out that the population of Paris, if it were not renewed through immigration and if it were forced to rely upon itself, would rapidly die out'.[10]

In the 1890s and later, several men helped to substantiate charges of the sort made by Bordier in works that provided a great deal more in the way of hard statistical data. Emile Levasseur, a distinguished economist, showed that in the years 1872-86 every 1,000 Parisian women between the ages of fifteen and fifty produced only 89 children per year, whereas the average per 1,000 for all French women was 105. If one considered only married women, thus subtracting the large number of Parisian bastards from the reckoning, the contrast became still more striking: 129 versus 181. On the other hand, Parisian mortality was far too high, averaging 24.8 annually per 1,000 for the years 1876-85, compared with 22.5 for all of France, even though the capital possessed a disproportionate number of adults in the prime of life. For almost every age group, Levasseur pointed out, the incidence of death stood much higher in Paris than in the rest of the country, the discrepancy reaching its most shocking extent in the case of children between the ages of one and five (58.2 per 1,000 versus 30.3 in 1886.[11]

Several other writers added their voices to the chorus of complaint. Levasseur's student, Paul Meuriot, provided comparable statistics a few years later not only for Paris but also for many other cities both inside and outside France, all of which together implied the demographic inferiority of the urban centers to the less densely populated countryside. Like Bordier, he suggested that if left to its own devices Paris would eventually die out. About the same time, another student of population trends, Henri Lannes, argued that even in the short run migration into the cities led both to decreasing natality and increasing mortality for the nation as a whole. The only way to make France more productive demographically was to slow down the pace of urban growth by finding ways to keep the peasantry on the land. Over a decade later, a young economist complained in his doctoral thesis that poor urban housing was 'bad for the human race'. The lack of light and air in the dwellings of the working classes caused maladies that were unknown in the countryside and created a situation in which mortality threatened to outstrip the creation of new life.[12]

There was noticeably less concern about the specifically urban dimensions of hygienic and demographic trends in France than in England, and far less than in Germany. The strident warnings of men such as Bordier and Lannes were distinctly subordinate parts of a much larger pattern of anxiety about the slow increase of the French population as a whole. Many Frenchmen expressed great distress over the indisputable fact that overall population growth in their country had greatly diminished since the earlier part of the century, but it was not the custom to blame this clearly undesirable development on the rise of the city. The real problem according to most demographers was, as one analyst put it, that birth rates had declined faster than death rates everywhere in France, on the land as well as in the towns.[13] In so far as further urbanization could be expected to intensify an existing demographic problem that had already become quite serious, it loomed as a potential danger of great magnitude to the French nation. But in contrast to Englishmen and Germans, French writers who were concerned about population trends tended to focus on the demographic deficiencies of the entire country instead of on the shortcomings of the city.

The city as a threat to the Volk in Germany

Fears concerning the physiological and demographic impact of city life found expression in an especially extreme manner in Germany. A large number of German authors displayed an almost obsessive anxiety about the likely impact of continued urban growth on the health and especially on the size of the population of their country. The explosive increase of the urban sector in the German Empire during the closing decades of the century seemed to these men to be fraught with danger for a whole host of reasons. Many of their concerns, as we shall see later, emerged from deeply emotional value judgements and had little if anything to do with empirical observations. In their analysis of demographic trends they sought to substantiate their case against the city on the basis of hard facts, not just personal preferences. Nonetheless, they frequently leapt beyond the data they had in hand, spinning grand theories and making moral pronouncements that reflected anti-urban ideology rather than any dispassionate attempt to contribute to social knowledge. Nowhere more than in Germany did the discussion of population statistics grow out of and lead back into basic questions of social organization and national power.

What has come to be known in Germany as the 'social biology theory of urbanization' began its rise to prominence late in the 1880s with the publication of an enormously influential work of partly empirical and partly speculative demography by a previously obscure statistician from Munich named Georg Hansen. Hansen developed at great length some of the bases of what was to become one of the most pervasive and compelling lines of attack against the city among German anti-urbanists of all sorts: the contention that urban populations could not reproduce themselves for more than a few generations and that if left to themselves they would become extinct. The city dwellers were 'caught in a continual process of decline.... If, nonetheless, the cities remain and even grow ... this increase is only made possible through a constant influx of the surplus rural population'. Hansen admitted that the urban working classes more than reproduced themselves, but in his view the surplus that resulted from their demographic behavior was more than offset by the low birth rates among middle-class families. It was, he argued, only the stream of fresh blood from the countryside that permitted the cities to survive, let alone to grow. Without the rejuvenating support provided by migratory peasants, cities would be doomed. Moreover, even with such an influx, the danger remained that urbanization would diminish the relative strength of the *Mittelstand,* thus depriving the nation of the superior qualities its members might be expected to pass on to their offspring. Hansen did not have many statistics regarding the decline of middle-class birth rates at his disposal, and he did not develop his ideas concerning their possible implications for German society very clearly, but he gave his readers reason enough to regard the city as a place in which the most intelligent and capable components of the social order were steadily losing ground to an ever expanding proletariat. The fact that most of Hansen's statistics were quite limited and that they seldom proved what he thought they did scarcely diminished the impact of his work, which became a standard text for later critics of the big city.[14]

Hansen's arguments were amplified in a number of writings by Otto Ammon, a publicist and private scholar who was deeply influenced by Pan-Germanism and social Darwinism. Writing a kind of popular social anthropology, Ammon sought to make the anti-urbanism of Hansen more accessible to the general public and to sharpen its impact. Ammon fully shared Hansen's belief that urban families tended to die out, disagreeing with his mentor only in his assertion that the process might take three or four rather than just two generations. He added to the case against the city by arguing that those who migrated there were racially superior to the peasants who remained behind on the land. Men and women with long, thin heads, which signified typically Germanic 'qualities of the soul', were proportionally more numerous among migrants than among those who stayed in the countryside, where the high percentage of round heads indicated the numerical strength of originally Asiatic elements. The racially superior migrants rose to positions of social superiority within the cities, only to suffer the inevitable penalties attached to membership in the urban elite: the nervousness induced by mental labor and a whole host of vices which, together with the physical diseases endemic in urban places, led to 'degeneration' and a loss of reproductive power. Ammon admitted that death rates were highest among the urban lower classes, but he contended that the birth rates among the upper classes were so low that their share of the population always tended to decline. Quite clearly, cities posed an even more far-reaching threat than Hansen had supposed: their continued growth would ultimately deplete the basic racial stock that was the fundamental source of Germany's strength as a nation.[15]

After Hansen and Ammon had developed the main lines of a demographic case against urban growth, they received support from several groups of writers. Although medical men played a less important part in Germany than in England in stimulating public consciousness of the big city's population problems, some did add their voices to the chorus of anxiety. Ludwig Bauer, a physician who had worked for more than ten years among the lower classes of Stuttgart, showed in a book on urban growth and 'racial hygiene' that except for people over sixty years old death rates for all age groups stood higher in the cities than in the countryside. Urban mortality, he admitted, had declined in recent years, but owing to the fact that every major disease except for typhus was over-represented among city dwellers the ratio of urban to rural death rates had not improved significantly. Bauer strongly doubted that new public health measures or social legislation would do much to close the gap. 'The milieu remains', he wrote, 'and the burden will become still greater'. Bad working conditions, overcrowded housing, and a general environment that continually agitated urbanites and made it extremely difficult for them to relax and enjoy themselves by means of wholesome recreations all contributed to poor urban health, and they would continue to do so as long as people flocked into Germany's already bloated cities. A dentist in Dresden, contributing to a medical review, emphasized that the city penalized its inhabitants physically in all sorts of ways: by forcing them to do dangerous work, by giving them too much alcohol and not enough nourishing food, by making them breathe bad air, and by tempting them to engage in a wide range of harmful dissipations. He argued that statistics for

Dresden indicated the likelihood of a marked decline in the size of the population there within two generations if the city were forced to rely on its own human resources, and he denounced continuing migration to the cities as 'an enormous danger for the future of our entire German nation'. The rapid development of urban industry amounted to 'a plundering of the intellectual and bodily strength of the rural population', which would eventually rob industry itself of the fresh human blood it needed in order to keep its machines operating. Wilhelm Hanauer, in an article written for the social democratic periodical *Kommunale Praxis*, argued that apparently low death rates in the cities did not show that urban areas enjoyed hygienic superiority over farms and villages. One had to take account of age distributions, and in almost every city the incidence of mortality for specific age groups surpassed the corresponding rates for the countryside. Agricultural labor was healthier than work in factories, and housing and food were better outside the cities too. 'But what gives the land the greatest advantage over the city with regard to hygiene', he asserted, 'is the calm, moderate, and sober way of life of the inhabitants'. On the land, one did not experience 'the grinding haste in the struggle for existence, the pleasure-seeking and the craze for amusement by urbanites, the wear and tear on the nerves and the damage to public health from alcohol and syphilis'.[16]

Additional support for the theories of Hansen and Ammon came from social scientists who had a serious interest in vital statistics and sufficient expertise to discuss the controversies surrounding them with some degree of sophistication and authority. Carl Ballod, after abandoning his early pursuit of a clerical career, turned to economics and wrote a number of works in which he both refined and elaborated upon Hansen and Ammon's basic viewpoint. In the first of them, written for the seminar of the strongly pro-agrarian economist Max Sering, Ballod compared urban and rural vitality and sought to confirm a gap with regard to reproductive capacity in favor of the countryside, focusing primarily on low birth rates. He also argued that although urban death rates had declined as a result of sanitary improvements there was a real danger that they might rise again in the future because of overcrowding, conflicts among contending social and political groups, and an intensified struggle for survival. Later, he asserted that despite some improvements in urban sanitation there had been no significant rise in urban males' life expectancy. Moreover, he pointed out that the apparent self-sufficiency of many urban populations was an illusion. To be sure, crude birth rates might surpass crude death rates, but if these rates were corrected to take account of the over-representation in cities of men and women in the child-bearing age groups and the under-representation of the older age groups (both of which were temporary results of migration) then the cities' prospects could be seen as much less bright.[17]

Richard Thurnwald, an anthropologist, was another social scientist who argued that cities consumed more human beings than they produced and that they would probably continue to do so regardless of hygienic improvements. He, like many others, believed that the members of the urban elites faced especially dismal demographic prospects. '... It seems', he wrote, 'that the vital rhythm is slowing down among the intellectually active elements of the urban population, and although culture makes the life of the individual richer and more colorful, the cultural blossoms, barren of seeds, seem to be consumed in their own fire'. As a result, 'the neglected lower classes' steadily increased their share of the city, spreading 'physical and psychic evils'.[18]

Social scientists found the most compelling evidence that the big city militated against population growth in the statistics for Berlin. Georg von Mayr, a university professor in Munich who regarded Ammon's theories as interesting but unproven and unprovable, pointed out despite his generally favorable attitude toward cities that in the capital the overall birth rate between 1891 and 1900 had averaged 30.0 per thousand, whereas in Germany as a whole the figure had been 37.4. When one considered that women in their child-bearing years were over-represented in Berlin, it became quite clear that the city was not contributing anything like its fair share to the coming generation. Moreover, the deficit was growing. In 1894, Mayr reported, the number of births per thousand had exceeded the number of deaths by 10.3, but by 1900 the apparent margin of safety had fallen to 7.7, whereas in all of Prussia it had begun at 14.8, risen as high as 16.7, and fallen only to 14.3. Further calculations showed that such modest surpluses would not suffice to maintain a constant number of Berliners in the future. Between 1886 and 1896, birth rates had fallen short by about 10 percent of the level needed to keep up the population over the long run. Adolf Weber, a young economist, cited other statistics a few years later to the effect that between 1899 and 1902, for every 1000 married women under the age of fifty there had been 152 births in Berlin, 224 in other big cities, 256 in small towns, and 287 in the countryside; moreover, he showed that the fertility of women in Berlin was declining markedly year by year, having fallen by about 12 percent between 1901 and 1904.[19]

Felix Theilhaber formulated the most thorough demographic indictment of all in a work that won a prize from the Society for Racial Hygiene and appeared in 1913 under the title *Das sterile Berlin*. The German capital, he argued, provided 'the outstanding example of an inadequate increase of population'. Although the total number of inhabitants had grown between 1870 and 1912 by 254 percent, the total number of births per year had risen by only 23 percent. Theilhaber predicted that the 1,150,000 sexually mature Berliners alive when he was writing would ultimately produce at most 1,000,000 adults. A vitally important segment of the nation's capital, composed overwhelmingly of the families of professional men, civil servants, and the well-to-do, was not vital enough biologically, and it seemed to be well on the way toward extinction.[20]

Many of the men who supported all or part of the basic Hansen-Ammon line of attack were publicists and other writers who could not deal knowledgably with medical or statistical complexities. But their lack of professional expertise did not deter them from decrying what seemed to them to be quite obvious hygienic horrors and demographic threats, the seriousness of which had already been demonstrated by others. The relatively unsophisticated comments by such individuals, often appearing in brief magazine articles, showed that for numerous men a biologically based anti-urbanism had become almost a matter of faith.

The idea of demographic degeneration manifested itself frequently in writings by men who made no secret of their social and political conservatism. Heinrich Sohnrey, who in 1896 was to found a Committee for Rural Welfare, supported his extensive efforts to defend the agrarian sector of German society with arguments in which he borrowed heavily from the work of Hansen. Noting in 1894 that since Hansen had written his book the census of 1890 had revealed a drop (since 1871) in not only the relative but also the absolute size of the rural population, he voiced the fear that continued migration to the cities would exhaust the nation's *Volkskapital*. The necessary result of an ongoing depletion of Germany's human reservoirs would be 'chronic infirmity and decay' for the cities and for the nation. Reinhold Wulle, a staunch political conservative, wrote two decades later,

> The population of the big cities is not even capable of maintaining itself at a constant level. Urban families die out inexorably, and the urban population survives only because of constant transfusions from the countryside. In the industrial centers, new mass graves for our people are being dug every year, and no slick phrases can conceal them.

In this view, an urban Germany was almost certainly doomed.[21]

Men who wrote about social problems for Catholic publications displayed much the same anxiety concerning migration from the countryside and eventual demographic decline. Hans Rost pointed out in 1910 that according to the census of 1907 urban birth rates varied inversely according to city size and that a direct relationship obtained between urban growth and the marked decline of fertility since 1893. These facts reflected to some extent a diminution of infant mortality as a result of improved economic and hygienic conditions, but they also resulted from 'overly refined culture'. In the big cities, 'neo-Malthusian tendencies', supported by such irreligious groups as the Social Democrats, had made deep inroads, leading to 'unnatural lechery and immorality with regard to the sources of life'. Consequently, the cities did not display 'the vitality in the life process of the nation' manifested by the countryside, from which they steadily derived fresh energy. Matthias Salm believed that 'child-rearing and cattle-breeding take place in the country'. It was the land that provided the cities with 'missing human material'. An article of his ended with an especially somber summary of the demographic case against the big city, painting an apocalyptic picture of Germany's future as an urban nation:

> The rural population is the real fountain of youth for the entire nation, whereas the cities, which, like Kronos, devour their children, are the graves of the human race. To be sure, the more the urban population grows at the expense of the countryside, the more the blossoms of culture flower, but they are like the red cheeks of a dying consumptive. As soon as the rural population has been used up, the spiritual and intellectual level of the urban middle class will decline quickly, and general decay will begin.

Again, the future of an urban population seemed grim indeed.[22]

As in Britain, starting around the turn of the century a great deal of the criticism of urban demographic trends was closely linked to considerations of national power in a world of increasingly competitive nation states. Wulle warned that Germany faced neighboring countries to the east whose inhabitants hungered after its land. Russia, with its high birth rates, posed an especially severe threat. As a result, the German *Volk* found itself in 'a situation of struggle for its national territory', a struggle it could hope to win only if it remained healthy. Unfortunately, however, the development of the big city entailed 'an enormous weakening of our people'. The size and condition of Germany's armed forces gave special reason for concern. Sohnrey called attention in the early 1890s to statistics that indicated a huge discrepancy between the percentages of rural and urban young men who measured up to the army's standards of physical fitness: 90 percent compared to only 25 percent. Throughout the rest of the 1890s, many other defenders of the rural order, including some of Germany's most eminent economists, provided abundant evidence to the same effect. Rost, in 1910, presented figures that indicated a somewhat narrower gap, but it still emerged that whereas 60 percent of agricultural laborers were qualified to fight, only 30 to 40 percent of the young men from the big cities passed muster. To put it another way, although the big cities contained nearly one-fifth of the overall German population, they produced not quite one-seventeenth of the country's armed forces.[23]

During the First World War, Germans had all the more reason to take stock of their sources of military manpower, and they did not generally arrive at happy conclusions about the future. Carl Ballod emphasized not only the by now familiar facts pertaining to the physical condition of rural and urban military recruits but also the fundamental importance for national security of the overall numbers of Germans in the age groups eligible even to be considered for the army. The nation's immediate prospects seemed favorable. Ballod predicted, however, that the number of eighteen-year-olds would begin to decline in 1927 and that by 1934 it would fall from a high of 750,000 to 400,000. Although much of this drop would obviously be attributable to wartime disruption of normal family life, Ballod emphasized the long-term consequences of urbanization and the need to provide for an adequate fighting force in the future by counteracting them through an escape from urban 'walls of stone' and a return to more natural conditions beyond the reach of their debilitating influence.[24]

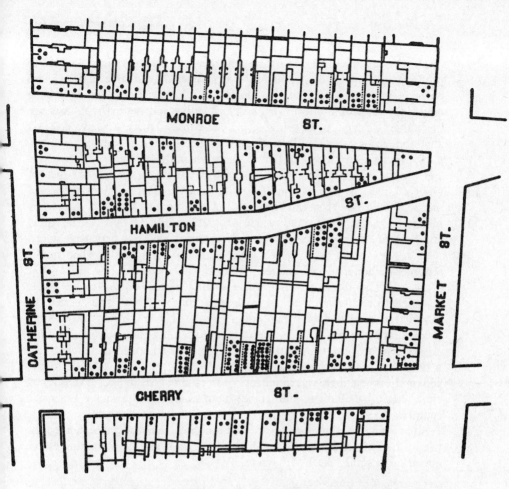

13 A map of tuberculosis in New York. Each dot represents one case in an area on the Lower East Side that was reported to the Board of Health over a five-year period. Only half the cases were generally reported (source: Robert W. DeForest and Lawrence Veiller, eds., *The Tenement House Problem*, I [New York, 1903], 12).

The limits of fear in the United States

This sort of pessimism found few adherents in the United States. To be sure, considerable anguish over low levels of urban health came to the surface in the studies of poverty undertaken by men such as Jacob Riis, Robert Hunter, and Lawrence Veiller. They continually called attention to the ill effects of overcrowded and unsanitary housing on men's bodies as well as their morals. Their complaints, however, seldom implied any real anxiety with regard to the long-term prospects of the urban population as a whole, and they did not lead to widespread acceptance of anything comparable to European theories of urban degeneration.[25]

A few medical men and social scientists sounded more apprehensive. A Canadian physician, Peter H. Bryce, in a paper read to the American Public

Health Association in 1914, lamented the failure of urban professional men to produce sons capable of stepping into their shoes. In the same vein, he went on to quote approvingly another doctor who had written, 'We have been crowding our people into towns, where bustling and nervous agitation are inevitable; we have been bringing up our babies (where we have any) on anything but mother's milk and by the employment of women in many industries have curtailed that family life in which the nervous child best lives and thrives'. Charles Henderson, a sociologist at the University of Chicago, observed that 'density of population ... tends to increase morbidity and mortality' and also that 'the attractions of pleasure and comfort' in the city militated against high fecundity. He wrote, 'The difficulty of securing quiet and retirement during pregnancy in a tenement house or expensive apartment residence is a factor of no slight significance, especially when public sentiment among women makes maternity ridiculous'. A few years later, Warren S. Thompson, a demographer at the University of Michigan, wrote an article titled 'Race Suicide in the United States', in which he decried the low birth rate among the urban upper classes. 'The well-to-do and wealthy classes have', he wrote, 'a higher average of ability than any of the other classes and are not contributing anything to the natural increase of the nation'. But such warnings were not sounded nearly as often as in Germany, and on the whole there was much less concern about the impact of the city on either health or demographic trends than in any of the major European countries.[26]

Adna Weber, author of a classic book that both analyzed and defended the rise of the city, commented explicitly on this fact, and his remarks deserve quotation at some length. He wrote,

> ... The problem of the concentration of population has with us scarcely any of the national significance that attaches to it in the crowded countries of Europe.... On the other hand, we have lately observed in both Germany and England a heated discussion of the evils of city life that enlisted the talents of eminent economists and public men. In Germany, the fundamental argument of the Agrarian party for its policy of extreme Protectionism was based on the alleged devitalizing effects of city life upon the national strength and vigor; to preserve which, they maintained, agriculture, the mainstay of a vigorous soldiery, must be made more profitable by means of high tariff duties. In England, national pride was touched to the quick by the decadence of its soldiery revealed in successive reductions of the physical standards for recruits for the South African War. The decadence was all but universally attributed to city life.... In the United States, it would require an unusually close observer to detect more than a trace of the fierce denunciation that in Germany and England has been heaped upon a public policy which allows the concentration of population, by migration from country to city, to go on unhindered.[27]

There were several reasons for the relative infrequency of European theories of degeneration in the United States. The one Weber emphasized was that American towns suffered far less from overcrowding than their European counterparts. Other reasons had to do with the still quite high birth rate in America as a whole, the continuing stream of immigrants from abroad, and the absence of neighboring countries that might have appeared to threaten America's pre-eminence in its part of the globe. Hygienic and demographic perspectives on the city differed markedly between the old world and the new primarily because there really was not as much cause for concern about the overall health and size of the population in the latter as there was in the former.

7

Critiques of Community and Culture

The big city aroused feelings of fear, disapproval, and distaste for many reasons beyond those having to do with the ill effects of the physical environment upon the least fortunate urbanites. The tendency — most marked in Germany but evident elsewhere as well — to berate the urban middle and upper classes for their failure to produce large families often implied a negative judgement upon those city dwellers' morals. Men and women who voluntarily refrained from large-scale procreation made manifest, according to this line of thinking, not so much a rational adaptiveness to the shortage of comfortable housing as the immoral selfishness and disregard for the needs of the community that, in varying degrees, marked the urban population as a whole. The conditions of city life seemed to many observers to threaten much more than the physical health of men's bodies. They also weakened the bonds that made for healthy and stable communities of values and interests, from the family and the locality to the level of the nation. Urban man, it was asserted, displayed distressing if not irremediable signs of self-centered egoism and unwillingness to subordinate his personal desires to the well-being of the whole. At the same time, chaos, disorder, and ugliness seemed to run rampant in the realm of cultural endeavor, producing an aesthetic aversion to the big city that closely complemented the denunciations voiced by censorious moralists and ideologues. This is not to equate such criticism of the city — any more than the awareness of urban poverty or the exposure of poor health — with rejection of the city as such. For some men, the city's assorted social and cultural ills did lead to despair and rejection, but discontent with one or another facet of urban civilization extended far beyond the ranks of the pessimists and the anti-modernists.

Denunciations and explanations of immorality

Everywhere during these decades, critics of urban society expressed anxiety over the impact of city life on the moral standards of individuals and on their modes of interacting with one another. Many discerned and denounced not simply the harmful impact of physical wretchedness upon the behavior of the lowliest of the low but also a more widespread undermining of the forces of communal control: the church, the family, and the neighborhood. In their view, urban conditions militated powerfully against the institutions and practices that had traditionally bound the individual to larger collectivities and subordinated him or her to their norms. These new circumstances uprooted the individual morally as well as physically. The urban situation fostered competitiveness, produced cold disregard for others, and stimulated materialistic desires for personal pleasure and gain. The results of these developments, pointed to with great and growing alarm, were crime, vice, and other forms of patently anti-social misconduct among men and women — especially young ones — who felt little if any restraint either from without or from within. Liberated from the watchful eyes of relatives, clergymen, and neighbors, modern urbanites could and would, it was asserted, exploit their newfound opportunities for socially destructive action to the fullest.

In Britain, as in most countries, the clearest statements of views such as these continued to come from Protestant clergymen. Religious practice appears to have been on the upswing during the period as regards the Church of England, and the Dissenting denominations experienced only a slight drop in their support in relation to the total population while continuing to add substantially to their overall membership. The urban variable as such does not seem to have had nearly as great an impact on religious observance as did social variations within the city, but the urban working classes and the poor did tend to withdraw from church life except in cases where they had reason to regard churchmen as conduits of material aid in times of distress.[1] This development converged with an awareness of other social problems that could not be ignored and the inertial force of earlier attitudes rooted in the teachings of the Bible. As a result, many clergymen saw the city as at worst a den of iniquity and at best a serious challenge that could be effectively countered only through constant vigilance.

Revulsion at both the irreligiosity of the urban lower classes and other evidence of low morals among city dwellers manifested itself clearly in writings about poverty such as Andrew Mearns' *Bitter Cry of Outcast London* (1883). Mearns shocked his readers by asserting that in the slums 'incest is common; and no form of vice or sensuality causes surprise or attracts attention'. For Mearns, the conduct of many lower-class Londoners made clearly manifest the corrupting effects of the physical environment in large parts of the big city.[2]

Other critical commentary on the urban milieu stemmed from an older tradition of religious denunciation, admonition, and exhortation. Horatius Bonar, minister of the Chalmers Memorial Church in Edinburgh and a prolific writer on religious topics, stated the traditional view in a series of missionary tracts directed at Parisian working men. 'Does God care for our Great Cities, or has he given them up?' he asked. These were questions that inevitably occurred 'to troubled, weary hearts, oppressed with the revelations of the enormous wickedness contained in these great centres of human evil'. The 'great Babylons, ancient or modern' admittedly displayed 'glory and beauty ... luxury and comfort ... monuments of art and genius, and skill, and power', but all of these rested on a foundation of sin, and those who overlooked it were forgetting 'the warning of Noah's days, and the doom of Sodom and Gomorrah'.[3]

John Thain Davidson, a Presbyterian who worked during most of his adult years as a minister in Salford and London and a prolific author of books directed at young people, reiterated these misgivings in a somewhat homelier fashion. In his book *The City Youth*, which went through numerous editions starting in 1886, he sought to provide the boy between ages sixteen and twenty who had recently arrived in a big city with 'a genial and useful Friend, who will ... put him on his guard against the moral dangers by which he is certain to be beset'. Davidson observed that 'the vastness and multitudinous-ness' of the modern metropolis enabled those who wished to do so to practice vice without fear of detection and punishment. 'Nowhere is it so easy to be a *homo incognitus* as in London', he wrote. 'You can bury yourself in the metropolis as completely as in an African desert, or an Indian jungle, or an American prairie. You can elude the gaze of all who know you'. At the same time, 'solicitations to vice' abounded. 'Every passion', he warned, 'has a tempter lying in wait for it'. Becoming increasingly declamatory, he wrote, 'Beneath the thinnest layer of outward decency, there is in this metropolis a seething mass of moral corruption ... a sodom in our midst that is sending forth pestilential effluvia on every side, and yearly swallowing up thousands of our youth to their eternal destruction'.[4]

Arthur F. Winnington-Ingram — the head of a settlement house, the Rector of Bethnal Green, and a future Bishop of London — gave a series of lectures at Cambridge Divinity School in 1895 in which he reported on the special problems facing the Church in great cities. Measurably more moder-ate and balanced than either Bonar or Davidson, he still emphasized the interrelationships between the urban milieu, low morals, and weak or non-existent adherence to organized religion in 'these monster growths of modern times'. The shortage of clergymen in relation to the size of the urban population, conflicts between social classes, the belief that the Church was a conservative ally of the upper classes, the pressures of work, pubs, gambling, and other 'excitements', as well as 'sickness and distress' and poverty of the sort documented by Charles Booth, all made the task of the urban clergyman difficult and demanding. In Winnington-Ingram's view, although unbelief was by no means confined to great cities, it assumed there, especially in working-class areas, 'a more organised and often more hostile form'. He observed, 'With Secularist lecturers at every street corner, and often Secularist talk in every workshop, one trembles for the faith of ignorant men and lads who cannot answer the questions raised'.[5]

No one in Britain did more during the years just after 1900 to publicize the ills of British urban society than Charles F. G. Masterman, whose writings about city life both echoed and added to the fears expressed by his clerical predecessors and contemporaries. A fellow of Christ's College, Cambridge, Masterman lived in London, where he participated actively in settlement house work and served as a member of the local Board of Guardians. In 1904-06 he served as a Liberal Member of Parliament, and he subsequently held several ministerial positions in the reforming governments of Henry Campbell-Bannerman and Herbert Asquith. His intellectual training, his personal involvement with the poor, and his commitment to political action fitted him admirably to perform the role of urban critic, and several of his studies constituted the most thoughtful expression of misgivings about contemporary cities published by anyone in Britain during the early twentieth century. The most notable of his works was a collaborative effort that he edited, *The Heart of the Empire: Discussions of Problems of Modern City Life in England* (1901), which contained contributions by nine other young liberal intellectuals in addition to Masterman, but he added several noteworthy pieces on urban life during the decade that followed.[6]

Although Masterman was highly sensitive to the urban population's physical problems, he focused more particularly on what he regarded as the moral degeneration then occurring as a result of the emergence of 'a new race ... this New Town type'. The second generation of urban immigrants, born and bred under metropolitan conditions, was not only 'stunted, narrow-chested, easily wearied' but also 'voluble, excitable, with little ballast, stamina, or endurance — seeking stimulus in drink, in betting, in any unaccustomed conflicts at home or abroad'. Still more ominous was 'the almost universal decay, amongst these massed and unheeded populations, of any form of spiritual religion'. Dependence upon alcohol and other vehicles of transitory excitement was exacerbated by the absence of 'a background to life — some common bond uniting, despite the discordance of the competitive struggle — some worthy subject of enthusiasm or devotion behind the aimless passage of the years — some spiritual force or ideal elevated over the shabby scene of temporary failure ... in our great cities today'.[7]

Masterman displayed much greater sensitivity to the full range of urban difficulties than most clergymen. He insisted on the importance of the Churches for the alleviation of contemporary ills not simply through the inculcation of personal virtue but also via a strengthening of the bonds of fellow feeling and broad social responsibility among men and women who were all too likely to remain indifferent to one another if left untouched by spiritual influence. In the absence of such guidance, next-door neighbors would continue to regard one another as strangers, walking their solitary ways 'in the midst of this human hive'. As matters stood, he lamented, 'We live and let live, finding sufficient difficulty in fulfilment of even that elastic creed: we do not greatly concern ourselves if our neighbours knife each other in the dark, or assail comfortable tradesmen who have wandered into the proscribed area'. This was, in Masterman's view, the low level of uncaring individualism to which urban man had been reduced by his anomic life in the mean streets of the English metropolis.[8]

One of the contributors to *The Heart of the Empire*, Reginald Bray, was especially close to Masterman, sharing two flats with him for eight years, and Bray's writings about urban life both reflected and amplified his friend's anxieties regarding urban morals. In his essay 'The Children of the Town', which he wrote shortly after moving out of a South London settlement house, and in his book *The Town Child* (1907), which appeared after he had spent several years as a member of the Committee on Underfed Children of the London County Council, he painted a detailed and somber picture of a limited but crucial aspect of urban society.[9]

Bray concentrated not on the physical but on the intellectual and moral impact of city conditions, emphasizing a variety of ways in which the urban environment impinged harmfully upon the psyches of youngsters. The urban milieu, he believed, created confusion. 'A mass of impressions', he wrote, 'are hurled at the observer, a thousand scenes sweep by him; but there is nothing to hold them together, nothing to produce a sense of order, nothing to give a perception of similarity. All is bewilderingly different'. The fact that almost everything the child encountered was man-made militated against any religious reverence for a suprahuman power. Lacking reverence for other human beings as well as for God, town children felt impelled as well as permitted to assert themselves competitively against one another whenever and however they could. 'Their acquaintance has brought home to them the truth that each man must depend on himself, that it is only by striving to forward his own interests that he can hope to share in the enjoyments of the town'. Physical circumstances played an important part in this development. Bray observed perceptively that

> Playthings and even the space for games are so limited in quantity that the enjoyment of the few restricts, if it does not destroy, the enjoyment of the many. In the parks a dozen games of cricket are carried on side by side within an area barely sufficient for one.... In the homes no one wants to do the same things, and every one wants his own way; a sister eagerly devouring a fairy-tale is given no peace by a brother who is anxious to play dominoes.... The objects of dear desire are few and the competitors innumerable; rivalry and dissension are the fruit.

Town children also absorbed a spirit of restless excitement simply from living among crowded multitudes. 'The concentrated power of the human element, when exerted to its full extent, creates the Hooligan; but it breeds excitement and dislike of any restraint in all alike who inhabit a large city'.[10]

Even among those who did not manifest obvious disorderliness, Bray detected a lack of steady commitment to the pursuit of worthy ideals, an inability to plan for the future and to take personal responsibility for the attainment of a better tomorrow. He believed that 'the aimless wandering of a child down the street' symbolized his whole attitude toward life. Unable to believe that his own efforts counted very much either for good or for ill in relation to the strivings of the masses by whom he was surrounded, the urban child saw life as a journey in which there was 'no particular destination to be reached, no special street to be crossed, no definite task to be worked through, and no final goal of all desire to be attained'. This, unfortunately, was the sort of person who would inherit the nation of cities that Britain had become.[11]

Critical commentary on the moral ramifications of urban growth was far less frequent and far less searching in France, but when it did appear it generally paralleled what was being written by British authors. In the absence of Protestant clergymen, articulate consciousness of urban misconduct manifested itself chiefly in writings by social scientists. Some of the harshest attacks came from men who wrote for the magazine *La réforme sociale*, which had been established in 1864 by the sociologist Frédéric Le Play as an organ for the dissemination of his peculiar mixture of conservative Catholicism, praise for patriarchal authority, and scientific method. An economic and administrative historian, Alfred Des Cilleuls, in a paper originally delivered at a meeting of the Association for Social Economics (also established by Le Play), addressed demographic and economic problems briefly and then turned at greater length to 'the large agglomerations' from the viewpoint of the moralist. His remarks offered a broad summary of many of the concerns that underlay the aversion to cities displayed by other representatives of the Le Play tradition. 'How many people in big cities', he exclaimed, 'live ... by exploiting the human propensity to compete against ... their fellow men!' Urban 'seductions' tempted a growing clientèle, and the 'rising flood of people eager to taste certain pleasures' engaged in 'unbridled rivalry' and lost both its 'physiological and its moral equilibrium'. Three results, he asserted, were increased rates of mental illness, of alcoholism, and of crime. Given the importance Le Play attached to the family as the basic cell of the social organism, Des Cilleuls' best statistics naturally bore on the incidence of illegitimacy and divorce, both of which, he showed clearly, increased directly with city size. He argued in addition that big cities contained more than their share of 'active instruments of demoralization', which exacerbated all of the specific maladies listed above. Books, newspapers, theaters, and other forms of entertainment all stimulated 'subversive ideas' and 'gross passions', substituting the ideal of instantaneous pleasure and blind ambition for the belief in loyalty to family and hard work. These were the main reasons why he labeled big cities as fundamentally 'undesirable' and urged that nothing be done that would in any way encourage further urban growth.[12]

At the turn of the century, the economist Louis Wuarin expressed deep misgivings about urban development in an article on 'the crisis of the countryside and the towns' that appeared in the middle-of-the-road *Revue des deux mondes*. Much of what distressed him had to do with the harmful economic consequences that resulted in rural areas from the absence of laborers who had abandoned the land, but he also emphasized the penalties that those who had fled brought upon themselves and others in their new environment by changing their place of residence. Having pointed out the ill effects of constant drinking in urban bars, he commented,

> There are, moreover, all sorts of spectacles ... the dissipation of festivals ... the thousand traps set for vanity and sensuality, the evil relationships having to do with business and pleasure that quietly lead the victim into the abyss. There are the vagabonds and the criminals who form a sort of secret society in order to thwart the power of the law. Just as one no longer finds the healthy air of the countryside in the populated centers, the moral atmosphere here is also polluted.[13]

Paul Meuriot assembled statistical data for several foreign countries as well as France that strongly supported Des Cilleuls' and Wuarin's general line of attack. No anti-urbanist himself, he could not deny that everywhere the cities undermined religious faith, fostered crime, illegitimacy, and alcoholism, and induced men and women to take their own lives to a highly disproportionate degree. The figures for suicide in Paris were especially alarming. It appeared that Parisians killed themselves four times more often than Frenchmen in general. This was the final result of the misfortunes and disappointments experienced by many people in a situation marked by 'the absence of traditional ties'.[14]

In Germany, moral disaffection with the urban milieu became increasingly evident, starting only a few years after the upsurge of biological and demographic concern. Here, the belief that the city worked to dissolve venerable traditions and to loosen desirable restraints became a basic article in the lengthening indictment of city civilization drawn up by conservative critics of modern society, and it permeated the thinking of many others as well.

As in England, it was Protestant clergymen who denounced the urban way of life most explicitly and most extensively for its deleterious impact on the religious and ethical standards of the previously faithful. Traditionally allied with the conservative forces in state and society to an even greater extent than their British counterparts, they perceived the big city as a milieu in which all their efforts to retain and guide their parishioners continually faced attack by the forces of secular individualism.[15]

Ludwig Heitmann spoke for many of them in the first volume of a long work titled *Grossstadt und Religion* when he lamented the 'slowly developing decomposition' occurring in cities. Big cities gave an impression of chaos rather than of organic growth. They were 'shapeless giants ... comparable to powerful vacuum cleaners, which swallow[ed] up men, organic cultural forms, and raw materials with irresistible mechanical force, in order to spit them out again, ground down, pressed into a new mold, and stamped with a factory trade mark'. Heitmann saw in 'the modern mass' only 'a wildly fluctuating chaos of human beings', whose social situation resulted from the 'atomization of life, this tearing apart of older social ties'. Among the 'traditional bonds' that suffered most severely under the impact of urban conditions were those that linked men to organized religion, which depended for their strength and continuity on the maintenance of a sense of communal solidarity. Like other clerics, Heitmann regarded the city as a place in which the forces of Christianity were inexorably placed on the defensive. In addition to weakening traditional religious ties, the city undermined the integrity of 'the innermost sanctuary of mankind, the familial community'. The inadequate living space provided in urban apartment houses and the growing tendency for women as well as men to work outside the home meant that 'familial solidarity and familial tradition' disappeared quickly in the metropolitan environment.[16]

Numerous clergymen voiced their support for one or another part of this general line of attack, and others spelled out some of the implications that seemed to follow from it. Otto Dibelius, later to become an Evangelical bishop, looked critically while still a young pastor in Danzig at the whole problem of church work in urban parishes. He reported in 1910 that everywhere in the cities there were fewer church weddings and burials and fewer baptisms than in the countryside. Seldom on a Sunday, he lamented, did more than 6 percent of the members of a big-city congregation attend church services, and often the rate fell to less than 1 percent. Dibelius admitted that the big city itself did not bear full responsibility for this state of affairs, but it had helped greatly to diminish men's power of resistance to the contemporary intellectual trends that pointed in the direction of free-thinking secularism. 'Morality and communal life, which sustain the individual in smaller places, fall away in the big city', he wrote. 'As a result, one support after another is removed from piety, until it finally collapses'. Friedrich Naumann, a pastor turned publicist who occupied an important position in the councils of reform-minded liberals, wrote that morality was 'nowhere weaker than in the big city'. The individual was no longer controlled from without. Whatever virtue might be discerned in the urbanite's conduct resulted from the influx of unspoiled migrants from the countryside, without whom the city would suffer 'inner bankruptcy'. The urban masses could not sustain either 'moral idealism' or 'a feeling of solidarity'. Consequently, family feeling tended to disappear, and so too did 'simple feelings such as sympathy and fairness'. Walther Classen, a former theology student who had turned to social work among young people in Hamburg, similarly bemoaned the weakening of familial ties as well as religious ones. He pointed specifically to facts such as the absence of fathers from their homes owing to long hours at work and the difficulty of finding times when parents and children could all sit down and eat meals together.[17]

Other clerics gave greater attention to the ways in which the diminution of moral and social controls gave self-assertive individuals the leeway they needed in order to act as they thought best or simply as they wished at any given moment, regardless of the consequences for their fellow citizens. Christian Rogge emphasized that men and women in the big city, no longer subject to constant scrutiny and surveillance by their neighbors, could in effect lead double lives if they wanted to. In any event, 'the intensified struggle for existence' inevitably led them to fight for their own survival and advancement with less and less regard to the fairness of their tactics. The competitive urban environment necessarily diminished 'the finer and more tender perceptions and feelings' and stimulated an unrelenting pursuit of material gain and sensual pleasure. It also bred 'masses of criminals' and 'an army of prostitutes and pimps'. Jakob Ernst charged that the big city was 'the school for pushiness'. Men who wished to pursue their own advantage at the expense of others had every opportunity to do so, and they usually availed themselves of it in the urban world. Accordingly, cold indifference toward others superseded the Christian virtue of love for one's fellow man, and 'all the demonic forces' ran rampant. He denounced the loose sexual practices that supposedly prevailed both among students in the upper levels of big-city secondary schools and among older people who frequented houses of prostitution. Even what was basically good in the big city could unfortunately serve immoral purposes: for instance, visits to art exhibits and similar cultural attractions might easily become pretexts for illicit rendezvous. Friedrich Schlegelmilch, a mission inspector in Berlin, having pointed to the familiar phenomena of irreligion and familial decay, bemoaned the disappearance of 'the feeling of decency, of moral obligation, in the swamp of big-city life'. For good measure, he added the following warning: 'Nowhere are there as many human wrecks as in the big city, as many bad men, whose trade it is to plunder their inexperienced neighbors, to familiarize them with shameful vices, and finally to hurl them into the abyss of despair'.[18]

These critical opinions reflected not only the institutional concerns of churchmen who worried about the receptivity of city dwellers to their moral guidance but also a much more broadly based and more widely shared sense of malaise and anxiety that pervaded much of German thought at the time. The fateful movement of ideas that has been labeled 'cultural despair' by one historian and 'the crisis of German ideology' by another had its roots in the period when Germany experienced its relatively sudden shift from country to city, and many of the writers who contributed to it made no secret of their loathing for the *Grossstadt*. Most of them did not write about big cities as such at any length, but they clearly regarded urban growth as a danger to the moral health of the German people. Cultural pessimists such as Paul de Lagarde, Julius Langbehn, and the neoconservative publisher Eugen Diederichs all felt deep doubts about the mores of metropolitan man.[19]

Several rungs below them on the intellectual ladder, the denunciation of urban ethics by conservative ideologues became more explicit and more vituperative. Heinrich Sohnrey repeatedly contrasted rural virtue and urban vice in his periodical *Das Land*. A typical article emphasized the many temptations and dangers to which country maidens were exposed after they migrated to the big city. Few were willing to endure the constraints of domestic service, and many turned instead to prostitution. Women's natural conservatism could flourish only 'in a domestic situation supported by strong morality'. Unfortunately, Sohnrey asserted, the big city destroyed 'the foundations of feminine character'. A less eminent writer, one Wilhelm Borée (pseudonymously known as A. l'Houet), attacked the city at length from the right for a whole host of moral defects. He depicted the *Grossstadt* as a place where men and women were led toward moral as well as physical degeneration. The absence of social controls played an especially important part in this destructive process. Borée argued that everyone knew everyone else in the countryside and that accordingly violations of accepted moral codes were publicized immediately. In contrast, city dwellers knew very few of those who lived around them. The individual urbanite was 'unknown, unsupervised, and uncontrolled'. Men came to the city largely 'to escape from home-town controls', and the anonymity of urban life gave them every opportunity to do so. This was the basic conservative view of the city in its simplest and most popular form: the belief that urban conditions militated against communal restraint and therefore gave free rein to the anarchic forces of willful and wicked individualism.[20]

Publicists of more progressive views said many of the same things, although their accents and their purposes differed markedly. In his panoramic survey, *Grossstadt Dokumente*, the left-leaning Hans Ostwald included many pamphlets that exposed urban men and women in Berlin and elsewhere in their worst light. He contributed studies of pimps and gamblers. Others whom he commissioned to help him wrote about homosexuality, lesbianism, prostitution, the white slave traffic, illegitimacy, criminals, young thugs, usurers, and urban vice in general. As a group, the contributors to the series certainly did not hate the city, but much of what they had to say conveyed an image of it as a place that currently fostered moral chaos.[21] The eminent architectural critic, Karl Scheffler, wrote in the same vein for the modernist journal, *Die Neue Rundschau*, reiterating the by then familiar equation of the big city and individual rootlessness. Both the family and the larger community suffered from the anarchic desire by urban newcomers to concentrate their energies overwhelmingly on the selfish pursuit of economic gain. 'To these people', he observed, 'the places where they work and live are almost

accidental; therefore, the city offers them no home [*nichts Heimatliches*], nothing symbolic, and no morally elevating sense of community can take root in them'. A conservative could not have said it better.[22]

Many social philosophers and social scientists helped to make the equation of urban growth and communal decline seem both plausible and intelligible even when they did not themselves denounce the developments they described. The major work of the sociologist Ferdinand Tönnies provides an outstanding case in point. Well before the most obvious manifestations of concern among clergymen, he had published his classic *Gemeinschaft und Gesellschaft* (1887), a difficult but nonetheless enormously influential work of social theory that could easily be read as a nostalgic study of the differences between rural and small-town 'community' and urban 'society'. Although Tönnies saw *Gesellschaft* as being represented most fully by the state, he identified the threshold that separated town and city as a crucial line of demarcation between the two sorts of entities and relationships he sought to contrast with one another. By no means a reactionary ruralist, he still betrayed a considerable debt to romantic traditionalism as he provided concepts and categories that would prove highly serviceable for conservative intellectuals in the future. The opening pages of his work contained passages such as the following, which immediately suggested feelings of loss as a result of the process of urban-industrial development: 'In *Gemeinschaft* with one's family, one lives from birth on, bound to it in weal and woe. One goes into *Gesellschaft* as into a strange country.... In contrast to *Gemeinschaft*, *Gesellschaft* is transitory and superficial. Accordingly, *Gemeinschaft* should be understood as a living organism, *Gesellschaft* as a mechanical aggregate and artifact'. As he continued, he related the rational and manipulative attitudes and conduct of men living in *Gesellschaft* to personal isolation and 'tension against all others', to individual selfishness, and to the decay of both religion and the family. Summarizing his ideas many years later, he equated his basic polarity with the dichotomies 'acquaintanceship and strangeness', 'sympathy and antipathy', and 'confidence and mistrust'. Tönnies clearly viewed the world of the big city as a place in which people like him, who had grown up in rural communities, were bound to feel a disquieting sense of alienation and estrangement from their fellow men.[23]

Georg Simmel similarly provided a finely nuanced analysis that laid bare the rootlessness of the modern urbanite and his solitude among his fellows. In a highly speculative essay that is widely recognized as a classic work of urban theory, he showed how men sought to defend themselves psychically against the urban pressures from without that threatened to deprive them of their individual autonomy and identity. In his view, they developed their con-

14 'The City': an expressionist painting by Jacob Steinhardt. Painted in 1913, this work conveys a powerful sense of urban disorder and anomie (original in the collection of the Staatliche Museen Preussicher Kulturbesitz, Nationalgalerie, West Berlin.

scious intellectual faculties instead of their emotions, displayed a veneer of
blasé sophistication, and acquired protective layers of reserve, indifference,
and aversion toward others — what Simmel called 'a mental strangeness and
repulsion'. One result of these tendencies was that 'under certain circumstances, one nowhere feels as lonely and lost as in the metropolitan crowd. For
here as elsewhere it is by no means necessary that the freedom of man be
reflected in his emotional life as comfort'.[24]

Other social scientists developed more pointed criticisms of the urban
community with more specific attention to particular urban maladies.
Richard Thurnwald, echoing the clergymen's fears of urban unscrupulous-
ness, wrote, 'In place of the effort to master nature, competition among men
has produced the desire to get ahead parasitically, through intrigue and guile.
In the city ... he counts as "fittest" who knows how to manage his fellow men
most cleverly'. The intensely competitive way in which men earned their
living in the cities gave rise to 'that urban morality, which glorifies the most
egoistic, inconsiderate, and racially destructive money-making, sanctions
parasitism, and capitulates before Byzantinism'. At the same time, Thurnwald presented evidence of higher suicide rates in cities than in rural areas
and of higher rates of alcoholism and sexual disease. Adolf Weber, in his
lectures on urban social problems, admitted sadly that in the *Grossstadt*
'moral filth' was rampant among young people. He quoted a leading Social
Democrat to the effect that 'whoever has the opportunity of getting to know
young people in the big city must ... be revolted by the brutality and
vulgarity of their manner of thinking and speaking'. He provided criminal
statistics showing that between 1898 and 1902 there were 152.4 convictions
per year per 10,000 adults in the big cities, compared with only 110.5 in the
rest of the Empire, other statistics that linked city size to divorce rates, and
additional figures showing approximately 50 percent more suicides *per capita*
in Berlin than in Prussia as a whole. Like the clergymen, he saw such
phenomena as outgrowths of a situation in which religious and familial
controls had become steadily weaker at the same time that 'selfishness' and
'egoism' flourished.[25]

Few Americans manifested the vitriolic dislike of urban living as such that
permeated much of the German literature written during these years, but
many men and women articulated a keen awareness of the moral blemishes
that disfigured the face of the American as well as the European city. Two
magazine articles by little known authors, published at either end of the
period, convey the basic elements of the anti-urban anxiety felt by some
moral critics with unmistakable clarity. George Washburn, writing at the
start of the 1880s about American cities for a British audience, lamented that
despite many efforts to improve New York that city was 'no better morally
than the great cities of Europe'. In fact, he believed that the moral differences
between the American metropolis and the towns and villages in its vicinity

greatly exceeded any contrasts between city and country that could be
discerned in Europe. This state of affairs resulted in large part from the influx
of foreign immigrants. 'The worst of the immigrants landed upon our shores
remain there', he observed, 'and there is no form of vice known in Europe
which they have not brought with them and domesticated in this city'. Even
beyond New York, 'pauperism, crime and all forms of irreligion' flourished
in urban settings, leading Washburn to conclude that the nation had 'more to
fear than to hope for in these great cities'.[26]

A little over three decades later, one G. S. Dickerman denounced the
continuing 'drift to the cities' in the *Atlantic Monthly*. The title of his article
suggested a chaotic and aimless quality in the whole process of urban growth,
and his comments on the impact of this growth sustained the impression of
dangerous disorder. Too many city dwellers displayed 'willingness to lie idle
rather than to undertake anything they do not quite like, to hang on charity
rather than to go where they are wanted and can be of use, with callous
incapacity for hearing any call of duty or feeling any thrill of interest at a
summons for help in an hour of somebody's crying necessity'. Saloons,
dance-halls, and gambling dens stimulated 'artificial appetites' instead of the
'moral worth ... religious sensibility ... [and] all the traits of a strong, upright
personality' cultivated by the circumstances that shaped life on a farm. Cities
would therefore always need the countryside for renewal in order to 'keep
them from relaxing into sensuality and sinking into decay'.[27]

To a greater degree in America than anywhere else, it was Protestant
clergymen who took the lead in publicizing the urban perils that threatened
the well-being of both the individual and society. This alarm resulted in large
part from their quite accurate perception that the rise of the city had placed
their Churches inexorably on the defensive and that its continued growth
raised serious if not insurmountable problems for the future. While the
Catholic Church prospered among the increasing numbers of urban workers
and their families, Protestant churchmen found themselves being pushed to
the margins of urban society. Awareness of this troubling trend colored their
whole outlook on the city and inevitably led many of them to depict it as a
cauldron of untamed and dangerous forces that was damaging the social as
well as the religious order of their country.[28]

No one did more to articulate a critical consciousness of the urban scene
than Josiah Strong, a Congregational minister from Ohio. During a period of
several years when he was working for the Congregational Home Missionary
Society, he wrote *Our Country* (1885), a widely read survey of the American
nation and the ills that threatened it. In this book and in *The Twentieth
Century City* (1898), written after more than a decade of service as secretary of
the American Evangelical Alliance, Strong portrayed the American city as a
hotbed of moral dangers that necessitated constant vigilance and vigor on the
part of all right-thinking citizens. Strong pointed with alarm to a number of
interrelated 'perils' that menaced the stability and future progress of the

American republic: immigration, 'Romanism', secularism, Mormonism, intemperance, socialism, and the concentration of great wealth, all of which, except for Mormonism, were intensified by the final peril, the American city. The city was the 'nerve center' but also the 'storm center' of modern civilization, and it had become 'a serious menace'. Because the cities contained such a large share of the country's foreign-born inhabitants, they had become strongholds of Catholicism, and for the same reason the saloon and 'the liquor power' had similarly extended their sway. The accumulation of urban riches bore witness to the materialistic worship of Mammon while at the same time making more starkly evident the wretched misery of the urban poor and arousing 'blind and bitter hatred' of the social system. The city was heaped high with 'social dynamite' in the form of 'roughs, gamblers, thieves, robbers, lawless and desperate men of all sorts', and 'skepticism and irreligion' abounded.[29]

Unfortunately, in Strong's view, the 'dangerous elements' who frequented these 'tainted spots in the body-politic' were not being combated effectively enough by the forces of social conservatism, which ought to have been represented by organized Protestantism. Precisely where it was needed most, the right kind of religious and moral influence was least evident. Strong presented a series of statistics on church accommodation in half a dozen large cities that all told the same story. The cities had only one-quarter to one-half as many Protestant churches as they ought to have had, given their size, and the situation was becoming steadily worse. In one area of Chicago, for example, Sunday school accommodation existed for only 2,000 out of 20,000 young people, whereas hundreds of saloons and other sources of commercial temptation lay in wait for the unwary. In Strong's opinion, it was no wonder that 7,200 boys and girls had run afoul of the police for various petty crimes during a single year. All these considerations, and others as well, led him to the conclusion that in the nineteenth-century city moral forces had not kept pace with material ones and that in the coming century only a mighty moral effort could save cities from 'the final doom of materialism'.[30]

Two years after the appearance of *Our Country*, another exposé of city life appeared with Strong's seal of approval. Originally prepared for the most part as a series of lectures for students at Andover Theological Seminary just outside Boston, Samuel L. Loomis' *Modern Cities and Their Religious Problems* reflected its author's urban experience both in America and in London, primarily in the form of a series of warnings. Loomis fully shared Strong's deep suspicion of Roman Catholicism and of foreign immigrants. The Catholic Church, 'emphatically the working man's church', had reared 'great edifices in the midst of the densest populations', and it kept them full with large congregations. The 'religion of Rome' was much better than no religion at all, but by making spiritual benefits a matter of barter, by fostering image-worship, and by keeping the faithful from direct contact with the word of God it had lowered moral standards, and its progress in the cities hindered the progress of the nation. The migrants, many of whom were Catholic, constituted an especially ominous danger. As Loomis put it,

> With some important exceptions those who come from foreign lands, both Catholics and Protestants, bring with them most crude and imperfect notions of religious truth. No Christian culture lies behind them. They have never breathed a Christian atmosphere. Ideas with which all Americans, whether of pious parentage or not, have been familiar from childhood, are strange to them. For at least one generation their language shuts them out from the influence of our churches. The whole method of our services, adapted to the cultured, Christianized elements of society, is so far above them that it fails to secure their interest and attention. When one of them strays into a church, the chances are that he finds nothing there for him.

Many working men also resisted the good influences of Protestant institutions because they regarded them as 'the churches of the capitalist'. For all of these reasons, Protestant religion was very much on the defensive in the American city.[31]

Among the worst of the predictable ills to which this religious situation contributed, according to Loomis, were drink, crime, pauperism, and anarchism. The 'filth, misery, ignorance, nameless vice, and unspeakable degradation' depicted in *The Bitter Cry of Outcast London*, to which Loomis (like Strong) referred in order to sharpen his warnings and strengthen their impact, showed the sad condition that large numbers of American city dwellers were approaching. These maladies were 'like a mighty storm-cloud' that cast a pall of gloom over 'the fever-sores of the land'.[32]

Concern over the integrity of the family, implicit in much of the religious literature but still subordinate to anxiety generated by the fate of the Churches, came to the surface more clearly in an article by an academic sociologist who sought to assess the impact of modern industry and city life within the domestic sphere. Charles R. Henderson, a professor at the University of Chicago, pointed to high death rates, to occupational diseases, and to the employment of women and children under unfavorable conditions as evils that militated against sound families in big cities. Comparatively low fecundity and 'communistic urban habits' (formed by experiences such as working in large factories, eating and traveling in crowds, and visiting common brothels), divorce, venereal disease, and prostitution all worked to loosen the bonds between husbands and wives and between parents and children. The situation was by no means hopeless. The various 'urban plagues' could be diminished and removed through 'concerted volition', but matters clearly could not be permitted to take their own course without grievous harm to a central component of a good society.[33]

The same year that saw the publication of Henderson's article witnessed the appearance of a book on a topic closely related to his by another Chicagoan, Jane Addams' enormously influential *The Spirit of Youth and City Streets* (1909). Praised extravagantly by William James in the *American*

Journal of Sociology, it added greatly to her already outstanding reputation as one of the nation's best informed and most sensitive observers of urban life. As another reviewer put it, 'Miss Addams is a prophet. She brings us messages from God'.[34]

Drawing on her many years of direct experience with slum children at Hull House and on the knowledge she had acquired as a leading participant in a successful effort to secure the establishment of the nation's first law court for juvenile offenders, she depicted the city as a place in which young people suffered constant exposure to temptations that almost inevitably proved too strong for them to resist. Addams pointed the finger of blame less at the absence of effective institutions for the control and suppression of the willful individual than at the city's lack of suitable outlets for the normal playfulness and pleasure-seeking of its boys and girls. She summarized her general argument when she wrote,

> Only in the modern city have men concluded that it is no longer necessary for the municipality to provide for the insatiable desire for play. In so far as they have acted upon this conclusion, they have entered upon a most difficult and dangerous experiment; and this at the very moment when the city has become distinctly industrial, and daily labor is continually more monotonous and subdivided.

The awakening senses of adolescents were strongly appealed to 'by all that is gaudy and sensual, by the flippant street music, the highly colored theater posters, the trashy love stories, the feathered hats, the cheap stories, the cheap heroics of the revolvers displayed in the pawn-shop windows'. Young urbanites felt attracted to these things because they craved color and excitement as vehicles of escape from the boredom that enveloped them at home and at work. They sought excitement in ways that harmed them as well as society in an entirely comprehensible 'protest against the dullness of life'. Moral disorder resulted not so much from rampant individualism as from the failure of the community to provide an environment that would nourish youth's best impulses and permit them to flourish naturally.[35]

The dangers of political disorder

Writers who expressed anxiety regarding the absence or weakness of moral bonds among supposedly isolated individuals frequently went on to make a more far-reaching criticism of the big city. They drew their readers' attention not only to personal alienation and pathological behavior by small groups of social misfits but also to the fragmentation of the larger society and the emergence of ominous threats to both the social and the political *status quo*. In the view of some liberals and of many conservatives, urban society was becoming spatially and socially segregated in ways that greatly intensified conflicts among classes and increased the probability of revolutionary attempts from below to overthrow established institutions, not only in the city but also throughout the country.

Such fears came to the surface most clearly in England in writings by reform-minded liberals, who conjured up the specter of revolution in order to gain support for their efforts to assuage what they saw as the root causes of urban discontent. George Reaney, during the years when concern over 'outcast London' was at its peak, warned in an article on this topic written for the *Fortnightly Review* that urban poverty was 'the open sore of a poisoned condition of national life'. He added solemnly,

> Socialism, physical-force Socialism is amongst us. The red cap of Continental revolutionary thought is passing along like a spectre of scenes not a century old.... The old faith in 'masters' is gone from the workshop; the old half-religious belief in the peer and the prince is under our feet; a deep, half-confessed sense of the injustice of life is becoming the living creed of men who curse the God of the churches and the rich.... They are thinking in silence to-day with a face that, so far as our culture and our policies are concerned, looks like that of a blind Samson. To-morrow they may grasp with their terrible might those strong columns upon which we have based and built our prosperity and freedom. Who knows what impulse may seize them, these inarticulate thousands and millions, when once they feel their own power?[36]

Charles Masterman voiced similar fears, but more subtly and with closer attention to geography as well as to social structure. He pointed out that in many of the large towns the different classes had moved steadily away from one another physically, with the result that total separation had occurred. 'In the towns of the North', he wrote, 'many of them built in valleys surrounded by hills, the wealthy and wise are found established round the rim of the crater; within, amid the smoke and clang of the factories and furnaces, are packed away the working populations'. In London, such segregation had become even more extreme. Proceeding from the ancient City, the center of commerce and finance, out to the west, one encountered 'the most lavish display of wealth and ostentation at present manifest in the world'. Elsewhere, however, the visitor to the metropolis saw 'miles of mean streets', inhabited by 'the pent-up, innumerable multitudes of the common people'. The belief that the urban masses constituted a potentially volcanic force and that their 'pent-up' grievances might one day erupt violently manifested itself repeatedly in Masterman's reflections on the problems of cities. Writing in the aftermath of popular disturbances during the Boer War, he referred apprehensively to 'the turmoil of the coming flood and the tramp of many footsteps'. After emerging from the underground railways 'like rats from a drain', the common people had surged through the streets, brushing off the police 'like an elephant dispersing flies'. Although they had done no real damage, their appearance indicated, for Masterman and for others, 'the fermenting, in the populous cities, of some new, all-powerful explosive'. This was one of the worst menaces emanating from 'the city Crowd'.[37]

Forebodings of the sort voiced by Reaney and Masterman were heard more frequently on the European continent, where fears regarding the future were nourished by memories of the past. Here, urban discontent had already led between 1789 and 1871 to violence on a far larger scale than anything experienced in the towns of modern Britain, and the growing political parties of the workers espoused markedly more radical ideologies than their fledgling counterparts across the Channel. Consequently, the specter of social disintegration and political revolution seemed measurably more ominous in the eyes of Frenchmen and Germans than it did in the eyes of the English.

The French had had the most tumultuous history in modern times of any European nation, and their capital had provided the setting if not the cause for its most memorable moments. As a result, even basically pro-urban moderates had to admit that urban conditions fostered popular unrest. Emile Levasseur observed succinctly,

> In the great agglomerations, passions ferment more. The working-class masses rise up and furnish flammable material that tempts the eloquence and the ambition of the tribunes. Political conditions become less stable. Although there used to be revolutionary troubles in the countryside, there were more of them in the towns.... Today, storms of this kind almost always break out in the capitals. France ... has been, since 1789, at the mercy of Paris, which makes and unmakes governments.

Paul Meuriot commented that the urban masses had always displayed 'a more tumultuous character' than other elements of society. Tradition exercised a weak grip on the numerous individuals who had migrated to the cities in which they lived, and the inhabitants of these places represented the spirit of 'desire' in contrast to the spirit of 'conservation' evident among peasants and villagers.[38]

These perceptions became clearer, and the language in which they were expressed became more strident in the comments on urban society and politics that issued from the pens of avowed conservatives and other defenders of the rural element in French life. Writing for Frédéric Le Play's journal, *La réforme sociale*, Louis Choisy lamented that the growth of the cities fostered both poverty and discontent. 'The competition for work drives down wages and augments unemployment', he charged. 'In order to occupy these unemployed laborers, the municipalities tend toward socialism.... The countryside becomes empty, and the towns suffocate: that is the brutal fact. Pauperism and socialism are the consequence'. Another author, in a doctoral thesis on rural depopulation, observed that the cities teemed with large numbers of people who lacked jobs and had become a menace to society as a result of being 'driven by need and misery'. He added, 'They permit themselves to be perverted rather quickly by the evil elements that have slipped into their midst'. Louis Wuarin commented, 'The existence of the industrial centers is feverish. Discord is frequent between employers and employees, and certain strikes resemble the outbreak of a civil war.

Moreover, residence in cities ... is conducive to agitation, to outbreaks. Crowds, it has been remarked, have a peculiar psychology, which does not always conform to common sense'.[39]

Wuarin's pejorative reference to 'crowds', like Masterman's to 'the city Crowd', occurred not long after the publication of Gustave Le Bon's book, *Les foules* (1895), which was soon translated into English as *The Crowd: A Study of the Popular Mind*. Though trained as a medical doctor, Le Bon had become a publicist who wrote about a wide variety of subjects, including anthropology and social psychology. An extreme conservative, he propagated racist doctrines along the lines of those espoused by Arthur de Gobineau, aristocratic elitism, and hostility to popular democracy. He referred to the coming age as 'the era of crowds', and he saw the crowd itself as a fickle source of destructive turbulence. Through association with one another, men in crowds developed a peculiar mentality that induced them to pursue objectives inimical to the well-being of society as a whole. Unwilling to accept any limitations upon their newly acquired strength, the crowds of the late nineteenth century (represented in particular by labor unions and popularly elected legislatures) sought 'nothing less than ... to utterly destroy society ... with a view to making it hark back to that primitive communism which was the normal condition of all human groups before the dawn of civilization'. The crowd could not reason, but it was quick to act, and its members refused to accept the rules and discipline that only a securely entrenched aristocracy of intellect could maintain. Le Bon nowhere mentioned cities as such, and he argued that a 'psychological crowd' could range in size from half a dozen men to a whole nation. Nonetheless, crowd formation seemed to have at least something to do with physical 'agglomeration', and it took little imagination to conclude that a crowd was more likely to form in the city than in the countryside. Le Bon's study could easily be read in any case as a hostile commentary on a society in which the urban masses were asserting their claims to a redistribution of social and economic goods (and in some cases political power) more insistently with every passing year.[40]

German thinkers manifested a still keener and more sustained awareness of the radical and disruptive forces at work within the urban milieu. The nineteenth century had produced political revolutions in their country only during the years 1848-49, but the widening gulf between the authoritarian forces of order and an increasingly powerful Social Democratic Party, whose members ostensibly accepted the teachings of Karl Marx, fueled the fears of many contemporary observers of city life. Ferdinand Tönnies pointed to some of the potential sources of social and political conflict in his analysis of the attributes of modern *Gesellschaft*. In contrast to traditional *Gemeinschaft*, the emerging society of the big city revealed 'many inner hostilities and antagonistic interests'. In his view, 'the antagonism between the rich or the so-called cultured class and the poor or the servant class' had always divided cities internally. The conditions of urban life in the present created a situation in which the multitudes felt that they could 'use their power only for a revolution if they want[ed] to free themselves from their fate'. He added, with undisguised trepidation, 'The masses become conscious of this social position through the education in schools and through newspapers. They proceed from class consciousness to class struggle. This class struggle may destroy society and the state which it is its purpose to reform'.[41]

Other writers, for the most part far more sympathetic to conservatism than the politically progressive Tönnies, echoed his general argument in a much more obviously ideological fashion. They indicted the big city as a primary source of disruptive influences that threatened to wreck the recently achieved unity of the German people. Beset by steadily growing fears that the harmonious equilibrium of the Empire and the *Volk* faced a potentially disastrous onslaught from the forces of revolution, they pointed to the urban variable as an obvious indicator of the rising tide of social and political change. Echoing Wilhelm Heinrich Riehl, to whose prophetic insights into city life he referred explicitly, one author who wrote shortly after Tönnies for the conservative journal *Die Grenzboten* predicted, 'The predominance of the big city will ultimately lead to the rule of the proletariat'. Heinrich Sohnrey expressed much the same viewpoint at greater length in the mid-1890s in a book whose title paired the flight from the land with social revolution. Rural to urban migration, by greatly strengthening the 'mass proletariat', jeopardized the very existence of the state itself. During the same decade, Otto Ammon coupled his criticisms of the big city for its biological defects with attacks that focused on Social Democracy and with praise of the peasantry as a bulwark of the traditional order.[42]

Over a decade later, such anxiety concerning urban social and political movements appeared again in the writings of numerous other authors. A Bavarian politician who represented agrarian interests, one Franz von Buhli, charged that in the *Grossstadt* men who had been 'uprooted' displayed both irritability and susceptibility to 'mass suggestion'. The inhabitants of big cities tended as a result to simplify all political questions, and consequently radicalism flourished in their midst. The 'radicalism of the masses', having already manifested itself long ago in Alexandria and more recently in Paris, clearly constituted a pressing danger in the present. Wilhelm Borée, a conservative publicist, asserted that in Germany the city had always resisted the claims of the state. 'The conflict between city and state is as old as Germany itself', he wrote. In his own time, urban populations undermined the state through their persistent hostility to the conservative values that were inseparable from true patriotism. Conservative clergymen added their voices to the refrain. Johannes Wapler warned that socialist agitation took root in the big city and spread from there to the countryside, while Christian Rogge wrote, 'In politically turbulent times, big cities are hotbeds of revolution'.[43]

As several of the Germans mentioned above stated explicitly, the primary danger in the present arose from the urban surge of Social Democracy. The

Social Democratic Party, founded in 1875, had survived a dozen years of anti-socialist legislation between 1878 and 1890, emerging in national elections held at the end of that period with nearly one-fifth of the vote, a total greater than that of any other party. Shortly after the turn of the century, a conservative historian, Dietrich Schäfer, buttressed his contention that the inhabitants of big cities manifested 'a special inclination toward extreme views, particularly radical ones', by pointing out that in the elections of 1898 twenty-six out of the forty-three Reichstag constituencies in the *Grossstädte* had been won by socialists. In the rest of the nation, the socialists had won only twenty seats out of a total of 354. (Their share of the overall vote had climbed to over 27 percent, but because the boundaries of the electoral districts had remained unchanged since 1871, the cities were under-represented and the party's strength in the Reichstag lagged behind its support among voters.) A few years later, a Protestant pastor, Friedrich Schlegelmilch, pointed out anxiously that the Social Democratic vote in Berlin had risen between 1903 and 1907 from 50 percent to 52 percent of the total. These statistics, in his view, reflected the fact that it took only a short time for the unspoiled migrant from the countryside to sink to the level of the 'big-city proletarian', who threatened the future stability of the whole nation.[44]

Paul Beusch, a young economist who saw many advantages in cities, provided quite detailed statistics during the First World War that thoroughly documented what was in his opinion the highly dangerous forward march of socialism in Germany's urban centers. In the elections of 1912, the socialists had received close to 35 percent of all valid votes: only 19 percent in the countryside, but 49.3 percent in towns of 10,000 or more inhabitants. In all of the five largest cities, its share had exceeded 54 percent, reaching the astonishingly high levels of 62.3 percent in Hamburg and 75.6 percent in Berlin. As Germany continued to urbanize, the chances of holding socialism at bay looked decidedly dim.[45]

The fear of Social Democracy was paralleled by political anxieties that stemmed less from ideological considerations than from ethnic ones. Urbanization seemed to constitute a threat to national solidarity not only because it strengthened the left but also because it increased the numbers and enhanced the influence of alien elements in the German Empire. These elements, it was feared, might well work to undo Otto von Bismarck's great territorial achievement in the interests of their own national aspirations, and their growing presence would in any case diminish the internal cohesiveness of the polity he had forged. This sort of argument depended heavily on the demographic analyses that projected a long-term need for migrants from the countryside to replenish urban populations that would never succeed in sustaining themselves without external assistance. Having exhausted the rural reservoirs in Germany, it was argued, the cities would be forced to keep up their numbers by attracting more and more foreigners. As one writer put it, 'When there is no more German migration, then there are Poles, Czechs, gypsies, and Mongols.... In this way, men restlessly build a Tower of Babel, so that one day linguistic chaos will reign'. Walther Classen warned that the growing urban presence of Italians and especially of Poles confronted Germany with the danger of further racial degeneration. Borée, noting the large number of foreigners in German cities, regarded 'this international, this cosmopolitan element' as a dire threat to the security of the nation. Like others who pursued this line of attack, he believed that such dangers could only be counteracted through vigorous efforts to stem the tide of urban expansion.[46]

American critics, like continental Europeans, had a somewhat stronger sense than Englishmen of the politically disruptive potentialities that inhered in urban populations, although the relative unimportance of right-wing ideology in the American political constellation meant that their views lacked the strongly reactionary flavor evident in the writing of Le Bon and many of his German contemporaries. Especially clear pronouncements regarding the perils of urban politics came from two clergymen, Josiah Strong and Samuel Loomis. In addition to all the other 'perils' that the city exacerbated, Strong pointed anxiously to socialism. 'Socialism', he wrote, 'centers in the city, and the materials of its growth are multiplied with the growth of the city'. Nourished both by the presence of foreign immigrants and by the stark 'contrast between opulence and penury', it revealed 'the volcanic fires of a deep discontent'. If its influence remained unchecked, it would lead to 'anarchy and destruction', thus helping to substantiate Tocqueville's opinion that '"the size of certain American cities, and especially the nature of their population"' threatened '"the security of the democratic republics of the New World"'. Strong ended by prophesying,

> When our urban population has been multiplied several fold, and our Cincinnatis have become Chicagos, our Chicagos New Yorks, and our New Yorks Londons; when class antipathies are deepened; when socialistic organizations, armed and drilled, are in every city, and the ignorant and vicious power of crowded populations has fully found itself ... THEN will come the real test of our institutions, then will appear whether we are capable of self-government.[47]

Loomis wrote in a similar if less colorful vein. He carefully delineated the differences and the conflicts between the cities' upper and middle classes on the one hand and their working classes on the other. 'The contrast between the condition of the two classes', he warned, 'is every day becoming greater and harder for the workingman to bear'. Like Masterman, he pointed out that 'the breach between rich and poor' was being widened not only by the growing belief among the latter that they had been cheated by the former but also by changes in patterns of residence. The flight of the well-to-do to the suburbs added a spatial and physical dimension to the process of social separation. In conjunction with differences of race, language, and religion, it

15   The Haymarket Bombing in Chicago. This engraving depicts one of the most famous of all the outbreaks of violent protest in the late nineteenth century (source: *Harper's Weekly*, May 15, 1886).

was actually, Loomis argued, producing an even greater gulf between the workers and those above them than the one that existed in England, France, and Germany. The result of this split was 'the new gospel for workingmen', characterized by socialist doctrines that led directly to anarchism. This was the social and political legacy of urbanization: 'fever-sores' that became 'redder and more angry' as they grew in size. It did not require an extraordinarily sensitive ear to detect in such passages echoes of the Haymarket bombing in Chicago, which had occurred only a year before Loomis' book was published.[48]

The political problems posed by American cities stemmed not only from the danger of revolutionary upheaval at some point in the indefinite future but, more immediately, from disorder of another sort that stood out in marked and painful contrast to the urban experience in Europe. American as well as European students of municipal government around 1890 agreed almost universally that cities in the United States were run abominably by greedy and corrupt 'bosses', who manipulated the lower classes in general and immigrants in particular for their own benefit and to the detriment of the community as a whole.[49]

The phenomena of urban bossism and corruption were by no means novel at this time, either in fact or in consciousness. During the early 1870s, Thomas Nast had memorably pilloried the fraudulent William Marcy Tweed, the leader of Tammany Hall in New York, in *Harper's Weekly*. Other cartoonists elsewhere in the country had helped during the same decade to develop a stereotypical image of bosses in general as men who almost always had Irish facial features, had their hands in the public till, and were surrounded by dirty, grinning, and tough-looking cronies.

Later, as the numbers of immigrants swelled, as growing governmental expenditure meant that the bosses had more money at their disposal to use illegally, and as the forces of reformist progressivism gathered strength across the nation, the outcry against abuses of the public trust by urban politicians became noticeably louder and more articulate. Strong and Loomis both expressed alarm about the men who ran the cities, the one stating that 'our largest cities are the worst governed', the other observing that 'the governments of most of our important cities have for a long time been more or less rotten, and in some cases little more than gigantic systems of fraud'. Andrew Dickson White, the first president of Cornell University, wrote in 1890, 'Without the slightest exaggeration we may assert that, with very few exceptions, the city governments of the United States are the worst in Christendom — the most expensive, the most inefficient, and the most corrupt'. White, along with many others, looked with dismay at the moral as well as the technical defects of American municipalities in comparison with their counterparts in Europe, especially in Germany, where honest and efficient administrators safeguarded the public interest in ways that were not at all customary in the United States. European observers at the time helped to confirm the sense of American inferiority with regard to municipal morals. Lord Bryce, the most eminent interpreter of American institutions from abroad since the days of Tocqueville, asserted that city government was the one area in which Americans had conspicuously failed. A few years later, in more sharply biting prose, Rudyard Kipling referred to the government of New York as 'the shiftless outcome of squalid barbarism and reckless extravagance'. Few Americans who wrote about municipal affairs at the time would have disagreed with either of these Englishmen.[50]

No man did more to enlighten Americans about urban corruption in high places than Lincoln Steffens, the left-leaning journalist whose articles of 1902-03 in the muckraking *McClure's Magazine* appeared in 1904 as a book under the title *The Shame of the Cities*. He obtained his evidence not through original detective work but rather by finding out and publicizing what was generally common knowledge in the cities about which he wrote. Much of what he had to report came from men who were directly implicated in the sort of wrongdoing he was investigating. As he told an interviewer, 'I got corruption from corruptionists, bribery from those who bribed and were bribed. I interviewed successfully political bosses, politicians and business men.... From political bosses I got a great deal of help. None of these men are loth to tell something of what they know. As a matter of fact, they have a strange pride in what they do'.[51]

Steffens produced a pioneering text in urban politics. He showed precisely how municipal institutions really operated, using a wealth of unpleasantly revealing details of a sort that had seldom been included in the writings of most earlier critics. The functioning system he depicted certainly bore little resemblance to what his readers might have expected on the basis of constitutions, city charters, or courses in civics. Focusing on St. Louis, Minneapolis, Pittsburgh, Philadelphia, Chicago, and New York, Steffens named the givers and takers of bribes, and he disclosed the exact sums that had changed hands and the places and times at which the illicit payments had taken place. He revealed that in one city nearly half of the police force had been fired when a corrupt boss came to power, and he gave the name of a specific burglary that some of the policemen who remained had planned and executed. He showed that in another city the firm of the city's boss had received paving contracts worth $3,517,731, whereas only $33,400 had gone to other companies. In Philadelphia, which he regarded as the most corrupt city in the country, newly appointed teachers had to pay $120 out of their first $141 of salary to 'the ring'. Everywhere Steffens looked, similar practices betrayed the lack of moral standards in civic life.[52]

The radicalism of Steffens' work emerged most clearly from his introductory assertions to the effect that municipal malfeasance resulted not from the greed of the patently wicked few nor from the venality of swarthy newcomers but rather from the values and the actions of the great bulk of the urban population. '... No one class is at fault, nor any one breed, nor any particular interest or group of interests', he wrote. 'The misgovernment of the American people is misgovernment by the American people'. Unlike many progressives, Steffens had little faith in businessmen. Admiration for such men in combination with disparagement of politicians displayed a 'conceit of our egotism'. The typical businessman was 'a bad citizen', not because he was politically passive but rather because he was 'busy with politics, oh, very busy and very businesslike ... buying boodlers ... defending grafters ... originating corruption ... sharing with bosses ... deploring reform ... and beating good government with corruption funds'. Dishonest government reflected 'the commercial spirit', which was 'the spirit of profit, not patriotism; of credit, not honor; of individual gain, not national prosperity; of trade and dickering, not principle'. It arose naturally among people who, even if they felt shocked by official wrongdoing, had no qualms about using 'pull' for their own questionable ends. 'The spirit of graft and lawlessness', he wrote in summary, 'is the American spirit'. At this point, Steffens' indictment clearly reached beyond not only the bosses and the immigrants but also the city itself. Corruption seemed not typically urban but typically American.[53]

Nonetheless, the roots of Steffens' thinking lay in the widespread tendency around the turn of the century to view the city as a place where weak and selfish men found tempting opportunities to perpetrate dishonest and wicked deeds. The civic corruption that Steffens revealed could easily be regarded as part and parcel of the general pattern of urban disorder and urban immorality that emerged from the writing of many of Steffens' contemporaries, both in America and in Europe. Though written by a man whose views were far from conservative, *The Shame of the Cities* fitted in with and helped to confirm the widespread view that the big city was populated by bad citizens and that it was the scene if not the cause of political behavior that endangered the well-being of the nation.[54]

Cultural aversions to the crowd

The belief that trends in the cities militated against valuable traditions and that they pointed toward chaos and disorder — a recurrent sentiment in much of the writing about urban morals and urban politics — was paralleled by many men's apprehensions with regard to urban culture. The critique of the nineteenth-century city included the expression of powerful aversions to its physical deficiencies on aesthetic grounds and to the ways in which city dwellers supposedly perceived and thought about the world in which they lived. Novelists, poets, literary essayists, and increasing numbers of architects and city planners, among others, were deeply offended by the visual ugliness, monotony, and mediocrity that seemed to surround them, not only in the townscapes of the newer industrial cities but also in the refurbished centers of many administrative cities. Moreover, there was a widespread belief that the big city diminished men's basic intellectual and artistic capacities, sapping the wellsprings of genius and creativity and also rendering them unfit to appreciate the cultural achievements of the past. In this view, ugly cities were producing dull people, men and women whose cultural narrowness and insensitivity exacerbated the spiritual impoverishment, the rootlessness, and the instability of the societies in which they lived.

Visions of the sort conveyed by Charles Dickens and John Ruskin, who had penned memorable denunciations of urban ugliness during the century's third quarter, reappeared later in the century in the writings of several other Englishmen, of whom the best known was undoubtedly William Morris. The noted poet, artist, and socialist, who proclaimed that his 'leading passion' was 'hatred of modern civilization', had expressed his distaste for the modern city unmistakably in 'The Earthly Paradise' (1870), which began:

> Forget six counties overhung with smoke,
> Forget the snorting steam and piston stroke,
> Forget the spreading of the hideous town;
> Think rather of the pack-horse on the down,
> And dream of London, small, and white, and clean.

In his lecture on 'Art and Socialism' (1884), Morris referred to London as a 'spreading sore ... swallowing up with its loathsomeness field and wood and heath without mercy and without hope, mocking our feeble efforts to deal even with its minor evils of smoke-laden sky and befouled river'. About the same time, in another lecture, he labeled London and the other large towns of Britain 'mere masses of sordidness, filth and squalor, embroidered with patches of pompous and vulgar hideousness'. The manufacturing districts were marked by 'black horror and reckless squalor'.[55]

Although Morris repeatedly voiced his outrage at the economic injustice and social callousness he saw in contemporary civilization, his socialist sympathies were motivated in large part by his belief that the urban-commercial-industrial environment of his day militated against men's finer feelings and subtler pleasures as well as the health of their bodies. His most extensive treatment of urban life, his utopian novel *News from Nowhere* (1891), makes this point implicitly but forcefully by portraying an aesthetically pleasing as well as socially just London of the future — a London in many ways reminiscent of the Middle Ages — as the welcome successor to the real London that Morris and his readers could see around them.

Other novelists helped to propagate criticisms of the sort expressed by Morris in works that dealt more specifically with the city of the late nineteenth century. Walter Besant observed in his *All Sorts and Conditions of Men* (1882) that in the eastern parts of the metropolis there were 'no public buildings of any importance, no municipality, no gentry, no carriages, no soldiers, no picture-galleries, no theatres, no opera'. What one encountered instead of any of these amenities and diversions was 'mile upon mile of streets with houses — small, mean, and monotonous houses; the people living the same mean and monotonous lives, all after the same model'. As one of his central characters, who denied that extreme poverty was the real problem for most inhabitants of the area put it, 'What we want here is a little more of the pleasure and graces of life'. Arthur Morrison expressed much the same view a little over a decade later in his *Tales of Mean Streets* (1894). Denying that want and misery existed on a spectacular scale even in East London, he too emphasized that the greatest defect in the lives of its inhabitants was unrelenting monotony, symbolized by the multitude of streets that all in effect became a single thoroughfare. 'This street', he wrote, 'is hundreds of miles long. That it is planned in short lengths is true, but there is no other way in the world that can more properly be called a single street, because of its dismal lack of accent, its sordid uniformity, its utter remoteness from delight'.[56]

Early in the twentieth century, partly owing to the influence of Ruskin and Morris but also in part because of influences emanating from Central Europe, similar criticisms began to find more systematic expression in works written by architects. The outstanding representative of aesthetic tendencies in British town planning of the period, Raymond Unwin, published an influential text in which he emphasized the need for improved urban design by reminding his readers of the visual defects of most cities as they existed at that time. Despite improvements in sanitation, many problems remained, and some seemed to be getting worse. '... There are growing up around all our big towns vast districts', he lamented, 'which for dreariness and sheer ugliness it is difficult to match anywhere, and compared with which many of the old unhealthy slums are, from the point of view of picturesqueness and beauty, infinitely more attractive'. When, however, he denounced the 'endless rows of brick boxes, looking out upon dreary streets and squalid backyards' that seemed to dominate the contemporary townscape, what he had in mind by way of contrast was not so much the early nineteenth-century slum as the truly pleasing town of the Middle Ages, with its informal beauty that arose from asymmetrical design and unending variety. Urban ugliness was characteristically modern. It had developed and spread during the preceding century of industrialization under the impact of 'the passion for individual gain', which undermined all civic art that might express and enhance 'a full civic life' and 'a joy and pride in the city' of the sort that had joined men together in the communities of earlier centuries.[57]

A few years later, Charles R. Ashbee struck a similar note. He denounced the industrial cities of the nineteenth century as 'formless things of mighty power and dreadful horror'. Instead of the beautiful orderliness manifest in the remains of earlier towns, what they displayed was a physical profile that revealed 'a monotonous and commonplace life, uncultured, uncivilized'. Such statements summarized a strongly felt attitude toward modern cities that pervaded the thinking of many other artists and architects, especially those connected with the 'arts and crafts' movement. Their attachment to what they saw as the rich legacies from earlier centuries reflected deep disaffection with the barrenness and rootlessness of the cities they saw around them.[58]

Meanwhile, the sense of physical monotony articulated by imaginative writers and by architects was paralleled in the thinking of other intellectuals by criticisms of urban people for their drab uniformity and their lack of creativity. The historian Charles Pearson feared that the future 'city type' would be not so much 'that of the mobile, critical, originative Athenian ... as of the Manchester ... operative ... with an horizon narrowed to parochial limits, with no interests except those of the factory or the Trades-Union; with the faith of the Salvation Army, that finds expression in antics and buffoonery'. Men who wanted to do great work, he felt, already found city life uncongenial, in large part because the inhabitant of a large town was becoming 'a very small part of a very vast machine, with narrow horizons and little originality'. Geniuses could not expect to be recognized and to thrive in such an environment, and they went elsewhere.[59]

Charles Masterman, the most articulate British critic of the period with regard to urban mentalities as well as to so many other aspects of city life, developed this line of attack at much greater length in several of his books and essays. Although he feared the turbulence and upheaval that might result from continuing deprivation and the decline of social control, he wrote eloquently about a quite different but equally dismal possibility: the danger that men and women would succumb to a drab, dull, colorless uniformity, learning to adjust all too easily to lives that lacked opportunities for either idealism or individuality. He suspected that one result of metropolitan living would be 'the elimination of the highest and lowest elements of human nature'. In the city, man was 'rubbing his social angles down'. In the future, everything would be 'ordered, smooth, clean, similar'. The typical urbanite would be 'a sort of polished, whitewashed variety of man, with life reduced to its simplest dimensions', who would 'pass from the great deep to the great deep, industrious, vacant, cheerful, untroubled by envy, aspiration or desire'. In a still more pessimistic and misanthropic vein, the cultured liberal expressed his apprehensions regarding the qualities of men in the urban milieu as follows:

> It is in the city Crowd, where the traits of individual distinction have become merged in the aggregate, and the impression (from a distance) is of little white blobs of faces borne upon little black twisted or misshapen bodies, that the scorn of the philosopher for the mob, the cynic for humanity, becomes for the first time intelligible.

Like Pearson, Masterman displayed a tendency to regard modern city dwellers as faceless and undifferentiated beings, whose lack of individuality reflected the pervasive sameness of large parts of the towns in which many of them lived.[60]

In Germany, the same combination of concerns was still more readily apparent, manifesting itself in the writings of a large number of architects and cultural critics. Disaffection with urban culture was not only widespread and vociferous but also saturated even more fully than comparable British thinking with a socially and political conservative longing for earlier times and older ways. Such nostalgia appeared clearly in the works of architects and city planners, many of whom deeply disliked the modern city as a physical artifact. They regarded their predecessors — e.g., Reinhard Baumeister in Germany and Baron Haussmann in France — as having been obsessed with hygienic problems and the flow of traffic in the streets. As a result, they complained, historically and aesthetically valuable sections of cities that dated from the Middle Ages had been destroyed in order to make way for new buildings and thoroughfares that were as spiritually deadening as they were monotonous and ugly.

German city planners and other aesthetic critics of big cities drew much of their inspiration from a path-breaking book by an Austrian architect, Camillo Sitte. His *Der Städte-Bau nach seinen künstlerischen Grundsätzen* (1889) deplored broad, straight avenues such as the Ludwigsstrasse in Munich, the gridiron layouts of streets in many of the newer urban areas, and public squares open to traffic on all sides. His own sympathies lay with the city planners of earlier centuries. Their achievements, Sitte believed, were characterized by greater individuality and by a more humane scale than the cities that had developed in the nineteenth century.[61]

Sitte attracted a devoted following among city planners, architects, and art historians in Germany. Early evidence of sympathy for his views appeared during the 1890s in the work of Karl Henrici. Henrici's prize-winning plans for the cities of Dessau and Munich, as well as his more general writings, revealed the deep impression left by Sitte's ideas. But in certain ways Henrici went beyond Sitte, linking his views about planning to larger cultural and social concerns. In a lecture delivered in 1894, Henrici quoted favorably Riehl's derogatory remarks four decades earlier about the Ludwigsstrasse as a symbol of the modern spirit of conformity and materialism and then went on to lament that contemporary city planning lacked any links to the traditions of the past. One observed a 'bleak desert' when walking through any modern city. 'In all cities and localities that have grown up in this century', he wrote, one could detect 'the leveling influence of crass, calculating materialism, which recognizes no fatherland and takes account only of what can be numerically calculated and recorded'. Whereas Germany's medieval cities displayed 'national individualism', their modern counterparts betrayed 'a cosmopolitan lack of character'.[62]

After the turn of the century, other men with professional interests in urban planning added their voices to this current of criticism. Theodor Fischer, a professor of architecture as well as a city planner, deplored the decline of aesthetic considerations relative to materialistic and scientific ones. Nowhere was 'the unnaturalness and perversity of [modern] culture' so evident as in urban design and housing. In the modern city, everything resembled everything else, like the products of a factory. Cornelius Gurlitt, an art historian, denounced modern city planning as an outgrowth of French imperial pomposity during the Second Empire and also as an expression of democratic intolerance for individual freedom and diversity. In addition, there were numerous articles favorable to Sitte's ideas in a new periodical, *Der Städtebau*, edited by Sitte and by Theodor Goecke, and in a series of publications sponsored by the Seminar for City Planning at the Royal Technical Institute in Berlin.[63]

Although the belief that the modern city was to be detested for its geometric uniformity and monotony found its most vigorous exponents among the writers discussed above, they were by no means alone. Critical attitudes articulated by professional experts appeared frequently in writings aimed at a broader public. Karl von Mangoldt, the general secretary of the German Society for Housing Reform, denounced modern urban design in general, tracing its defects to materialistic greed and to the loss of contact with traditional models of architectural beauty as a result of the uprooting of migrants from their native localities. Hans Rost, focusing on the aesthetic deficiencies of gigantic apartment houses, saw the deleterious consequences of 'an almost totally predominant political and economic liberalism, with its basic principle of letting things take their own course'. In a similar vein, Eugen Kalkschmidt bemoaned the role played in modern urban design by engineers and technicians, whose reliance on strictly geometric forms led to undifferentiated physical surroundings in which no one could feel truly at home.[64]

Contemporary observers also pointed to what they regarded as links between city planning and national integrity. The art critic Karl Scheffler regarded the layout of the newer parts of Berlin as a symbol of the sacrifice of 'centuries-old national cultural values' in favor of the 'international civiliza- tion' most clearly evident in the cities of North America. Modern Germans, with their tendency to impose highly schematic and geometric designs upon new urban areas, were not only failing to display 'creative fantasy and artistic organization' but also championing a 'colorless modernity' that in his view bore no relationship whatsoever to the best traditions and values of the German people. The economist Adolf Weber subscribed to Field Marshal Helmuth von Moltke's view that straight streets displayed 'less patriotism' than crooked ones. He expressed his deep regret that in the modern city there was so little evidence of 'historic and aesthetic feeling for the homeland' of the sort that could be sensed immediately by anyone who walked through the old streets of truly German towns such as Heidelberg, Hildesheim, and Nuremberg.[65]

For all these writers, as for many of the professional city planners, aesthetic defects in urban design were of far greater than purely aesthetic significance. They were consequences, indicators, and also causes of mal- functioning within urban society and of a weakening of national character. Urban ugliness and monotony reinforced the other trends in city life that already imposed a far too heavy burden on the individual urbanite and on the structure of the nation in which he lived.

Just as the architectural critique of the city manifested itself even more strongly in Germany than it did in Britain, so too did disaffection with other aspects of urban culture. Many more Germans than Englishmen — some university teachers, others freelance men of letters — expressed the sort of misgivings about city dwellers evinced by Pearson and Masterman. Like the architectural critics, they framed their arguments in such a way as to strengthen not only cultural fears but also social and political ones. At the same time that they denounced the metropolis for its supposedly harmful impact both on the creative powers of thinkers and artists and on the aesthetic sensibilities of more ordinary city dwellers, they sought to heighten alarm regarding the broader implications of this development for German society and the German nation. Many of these men lived and worked in urban environments, but their dependence on the stimuli and the resources provided by big-city life did not prevent them from ventilating deep antipathies toward urban centers whose cultural influence on them and their fellow citizens seemed to be exceedingly pernicious for a whole host of reasons.

Several academics who criticized the quality of thought and feeling in big cities in general during the first decade of the twentieth century came to strikingly similar conclusions. Theodor Petermann, an educator who wrote on a variety of subjects, gave a lecture in connection with the Dresden City Exhibition of 1903 in which he treated the big city's role in the life of the intellect from antiquity to the present. He argued that the book trade, newspapers, universities, and theaters — all of which had become heavily dependent upon densely populated areas of settlement — had induced 'an excess of intelligence' to crowd into the big cities. As a result, individuals who might have made a worthy contribution to the culture of small towns or the countryside were overwhelmed by their competitors and their talents were wasted. The urban milieu did help some men to develop their intellectual capacities, but in many more cases it tended to reduce men to a common level of mediocrity. Although the metropolis was a 'sounding board' that facilitated the dissemination of ideas, it was 'more an enemy than a friend of great originality'.[66]

Others said the same sort of thing, but with a still stronger emphasis on the city's defects and less recognition of its compensatory advantages. Georg Steinhausen, in the first edition of his influential history of German culture, referred to the big cities as 'great boils on the body of the nation'. Their growth both reflected and aided the rise of the proletariat and the democratization not only of politics but also of education and art, which had led to 'a leveling of the inner human being'. At the same time, urbanization had also undermined the viability of traditional costumes and customs, thereby weakening the foundations of German *Volkstum*. Kurt Breysig, an eminent historian and philosopher of history, made an especially strong statement of the general case against urban culture from an explicitly conservative standpoint. He asserted that the big city had failed utterly to produce 'culture'. Instead, it had produced 'civilization'. Generally in Germany around this time, the contrast between *Kultur* and *Zivilisation* complemented and reinforced the one between *Gemeinschaft* and *Gesellschaft*. In each case, the first term signified something that was both traditional and spontaneous, whereas the second implied mechanical and unfeeling modernity. Breysig's terminology bore clear witness to his stereotypical understanding of urban 'civilization'. In his view, the big city entailed 'pulverizing, the piling up of masses, quantitative development'. The urban proletariat, having been cut off from the beneficial influence of nature, had lost 'the old, simple joys of songs and customs' and had received instead 'the filthy humor of the big city and the monotonous claptrap of socialist speeches'. Moreover, the flattening of individual personalities extended in Breysig's view far beyond the lower classes. Many members of the middle and upper classes had also become 'smooth pebbles', devoid of any 'distinguishing profile'. In this view, which clearly echoed Masterman's, one of the big city's worst flaws was that its inhabitants lacked colorful and interesting personalities.[67]

One city stood out in the thinking of many critics as the primary locus of the most dangerous cultural trends of the day. That city was Berlin, which attracted a kind of vituperative commentary for which there was little if any equivalent in the case of London. The best-known critic of the culture of the imperial capital was a leading anti-modernist intellectual, Julius Langbehn. In his enormously influential *Rembrandt als Erzieher*, which went through forty-nine printings between 1890 and 1909, Langbehn fastened on the German capital as a symbol of much of what he found most abhorrent in the modern world. Berlin, Langbehn charged, had always been 'an abode of rationalism ... an enemy of creative education'. The city's inhabitants suffered from 'spiritual emptiness' as a consequence of their restless preoccupation with business and pleasure, both of which led them away from aesthetic concerns. To be sure, Berlin had its museums, but these had arisen, Langbehn suggested, from 'cultural pillage'. Berlin might serve as a depot for works of art, but it did not stimulate creativity. Artists went there to continue their work and gain a reputation but only after developing their capacities in the countryside.[68]

Friedrich Lienhard, one of Langbehn's devoted disciples, a prolific poet, playwright, and essayist, and a leading figure in the movement to promote *Heimatkunst* (native art), presented a much lengthier and more detailed indictment of the culture of the capital a decade later. Instead of simply bemoaning the lack of artistic creation, he turned his attention to some of the literature that Berlin *had* produced, and he subjected it to a scathing critique. Much of what had been written in the metropolis recently — in particular the works of the literary naturalists — lacked 'soul and warmth' and revealed all too many symptoms of 'that contemporary sickness of negativism'. Modern realism, whose advance in Germany had been powerfully assisted by the rise of Berlin and the growing tyranny of the trend-setters in that city over the cultural standards of the country as a whole, bore witness to the triumph of democracy and liberalism in the republic of letters and of the search for novelty at the expense of German tradition. The literary culture that predominated in Berlin displayed a deadening attachment to traditions imported from abroad. Its exponents sought to emulate the examples of men such as Zola and Ibsen instead of their German forebears, thus cutting themselves off from the culture of their own country.[69]

Ludwig Fulda, a poet and playwright who himself participated in literary naturalism during the 1890s, helped to reinforce the view that Berlin was out of step with the national traditions of the people for whom it functioned as a political capital. Unlike London, Paris, and Rome, it possessed no long-standing relationship to the nation as a whole. In fact, Fulda regarded it as 'an American city': American not only because of its rapid growth but also because of its 'uninhibited modernity' and its 'lack of old culture, of a monumental past, of a splendid tradition, and established taste'. Moreover, the critical spirit and unfeeling rationalism that emanated from Berlin threatened to destroy German creativity both within the city and throughout the rest of the country. One of Germany's great glories in Fulda's view was its cultural heterogeneity, and a metropolis that sought to impose its standards on the rest of the nation threatened the very foundations of the national character.[70]

Neither in France nor in the United States was there anything like as much cultural antipathy to the city as appeared in Britain and especially in Germany. In the French case, the comparatively low profile of the industrial agglomerations and the absence of anything in Paris comparable to the vast monotony of East London were of crucial importance. So too, quite obviously, was the widely acknowledged role of the French capital as both a gathering place and a source of inspiration for French artists and men of letters. On the other hand, the relative newness of all American cities compared to European ones meant that even as cities grew explosively in the nineteenth century the sense of aesthetic and cultural decline was not especially acute, except among romantics and agrarians who regretted the loss of 'natural' beauty. For most men with highly cultivated sensibilities who disliked some or all of what they saw on the urban scene, the real trouble lay not in the newness of the modern city but rather in the rawness and rootlessness of the whole nation. Still, two American writers of great stature — in their own time and in ours — did focus critically on their country's culture with particular attention to the urban milieu. They denounced the contemporary city not because it lacked unspoiled rivers and fields but because it and its inhabitants failed to measure up to their standards of taste and refinement, standards that had been deeply influenced by exposure to the urban culture of traditional Europe.

Henry Adams, the patrician philosopher of history, was certainly no pastoralist. A highly urbane man of letters, he disliked much of what he saw in American cities of the Gilded Age precisely because it fell far short of his conception of the best that civilization should and could offer. Adams' disaffection with the modern city could already be detected in the 1870s, while he was teaching medieval history at Harvard. He wrote then to a friend that in Boston there was 'no society worth the name, no wit, no intellectual energy or competition, no clash of minds or schools, no interests, no masculine self-assertion or ambition'. His cultural discontent grew in the 1890s as he shifted away from his early optimism and faith in science toward a deeply pessimistic view of the modern world, according to which the second law of thermodynamics dictated the gradual slowing down and the eventual death of civilization. In his autobiographical *Education*, begun around 1902, he was especially harsh on contemporary New York. Here, he felt, industry and Jewry had triumphed over not only agriculture but also craftsmanship and learning. At the end of the book, he recorded his impressions upon returning to New York from Europe in 1904.

> The outline of the city became frantic in its effort to explain something that defied meaning. Power seemed to have outgrown its servitude and to have asserted its freedom. The cylinder had exploded and thrown great masses of stone and steam against the sky.... Prosperity never before imagined, power never yet wielded by man, speed never reached by anything but a meteor, had made the world irritable, nervous, querulous, unreasonable and afraid.

In such passages, Adams stated clearly his deepening conviction that the pursuit of material gain by urban men had wreaked havoc both with the appearance of the city and with the life of the mind.[71]

Henry James, the most distinguished novelist writing in the English language in any country around the turn of the century, felt an even deeper sense of estrangement from the cities of his native land, which led him to spend most of his life after 1876 in England and to become a British subject in 1915. Much enchanted by the 'aesthetic presence of the past' in the cities of Europe and gratified by the warm reception he had received in literary London, he recoiled from America's cities as places marked by ugliness and chaos and wholly lacking the compensatory advantages of history and culture. Like Adams, he too expressed his disdain for America's greatest city most clearly in the context of an account of a return to his native shores from abroad. In *The American Scene*, written on the basis of his observations in 1904-05, James devoted far more of his attention to New York than to any other city, and he made it quite clear that he detested much if not most of what he had seen. James was revolted by 'the look, the tramp, the whole quality and allure, the consummate monotonous commonness, of the pushing male crowd, moving in its dense mass — with the confusion carried to chaos for any intelligence, any perception'. Both the materialism and the restless impermanence endemic in American society were symbolized for James by a New York skyline that reminded him of 'extravagant pins in a cushion already overplanted, and stuck in as in the dark, anywhere and anyhow'. The skyscrapers of Manhattan were 'crowned not only with no history, but with no credible possibility of time for history, and consecrated by no uses save the commercial at any cost'. James wrote, 'We defy you even to aspire to venerate shapes so grossly constructed as the arrangement in fifty floors', and he regarded their growing presence as the perfect indicators of a civilization in which the taste for durable beauty had been sacrificed to the appetite for transitory wealth.[72]

Adams and James did not represent a movement that comprised large numbers of other American thinkers. Their view of the big city enjoyed far less acceptance in the United States than it did in England and Germany. Moreover, they themselves were much less virulently anti-urban than either William Morris or Julius Langbehn, to name only two of their European contemporaries who attacked the city much more harshly. Nonetheless, they shared much in common with these and other European critics of big-city culture. Like many others who placed a premium on what they regarded as cultivated refinement, these intellectual aristocrats viewed the contemporary city as an environment that impoverished men's minds and their sensibilities and intensified the chaos endemic in urban society in general. Theirs was a fundamentally conservative rejection of much of what they saw in the artistic and intellectual life of their country in their time, and it marked them clearly as leading representatives of an attitude toward the culture of the modern city that appeared on both sides of the Atlantic, although less pervasively in America than in Europe.

A wide range of men and women denounced urban anomie, turmoil, and mediocrity, as well as poverty and poor health, during the four decades that spanned the turn of the century. Comparing these years with the earlier period, one is inevitably struck not only by the greatly increased importance of Germans and Americans in an intellectual effort that was by now quite clearly international but also by the extent to which critical ideas emanated from many different groups within any given country. Conservatives, radicals, and reform-minded liberals, physicians and clergymen, philosophers and social scientists, and architects and city planners, together with journalists and novelists, articulated a much louder and more broadly based critique of city life than the one that could be heard half a century earlier. The opinions and the evidence pertaining to the realms of personal morality, of politics, and of culture which they presented added great emotional and intellectual depth to the criticisms that focused on material deprivation and on physiological decline. An unmistakable impression left by the totality of what they had to say was that urban conditions threatened not only the economic wealth and physical health of the countries in which they lived but also their moral purity and and national integrity. Another conclusion that might be drawn was that national well-being necessitated opposition to the big city *per se*. That, however, was only one conclusion among several.

Part Three

Positive Views of City Life, *1880–1918*

8

Urban Values and the Promise of Modernity

Although the criticisms we have examined in the last three chapters served as potential bases for and sometimes led directly to anti-urbanism and rejection of the big city, they also led in quite different directions. Many writers believed that the only sensible way of coping with the problems the large towns presented was to seek solutions for them within the urban milieu itself. Growing numbers of moderate conservatives, 'new' liberals, and socialists called for a wide range of measures designed to improve the city so that its component parts would operate properly and its inhabitants could live happily. This response was nourished not only by a somewhat fatalistic feeling that whether one liked them or not big cities had come to stay but also by genuine affection for urban life, pride in urban accomplishment, and confidence in urban progress. Throughout the nineteenth century and well into the twentieth, cities continued to enjoy the respect and admiration of men with progressive views and liberal sympathies. Their contributions to material well-being, to cultural vitality, and to both freedom and morality were widely recognized and highly valued. Every point in the critical indictments of the city was rebutted or at least countered by numerous writers who regarded town life as a perfectly natural and ultimately — if not immediately — beneficial experience both for the individual and for society. It is to the pro-urban sentiments and convictions of these men and women that we now turn, beginning with the general views according to which urban civilization, for all its admitted defects, was eminently worth saving and improving.

The city as a natural artifact

Empirical students of society — especially economists, economic historians, and statisticians — displayed a basically favorable attitude toward the cities of their time. They regarded them as quite natural results of inevitable and fundamentally beneficial trends in the realms of agriculture, commerce, and industry. Many either denied the critics' contention that the big cities suffered from unacceptably acute impoverishment or simply turned a blind eye to the deprivation experienced by the urban lower classes, preferring instead to celebrate the continuing advance of the urban economy. Some took specific issue with the arguments of the anti-urban demographers to the effect that urban populations were doomed to degeneration and extinction. The city's defenders did not necessarily welcome all the consequences of urban growth. But the unpleasant side-effects of the rise of the large town seemed to them to be at worst the temporary price men had to pay in order to enjoy an enormous change for the better that had enriched the lives of most urbanites both economically and in a whole host of other ways as well. They calculated that primarily because of material progress the benefits from urban growth outweighed the costs, and they concluded that the rise of the city was therefore to be welcomed as a force for good in the modern world.

Economic perspectives on the city that provided both explanations of and justifications for the process of urban growth appeared quite clearly in substantial works by two Frenchmen, both of which were published during the 1890s. The better known of these authors was Emile Levasseur, an economist, geographer, and statistician who held a number of prestigious posts in the French academic world. In a long study of the French population, Levasseur devoted considerable attention to the rise of the city and the city's functions in modern society. He began his treatment of the urban sector by summarizing some of the salient statistics pertaining to urbanization not only in France but also in other countries. He thereby emphasized the international dimensions of this trend and in so doing implicitly conferred upon it an aura of legitimacy or at least inevitability that it might have appeared to lack had it been presented within the more limited context of the experience of a single nation. He went on to explain that men had left the countryside primarily because new machinery had rendered their labor in the fields superfluous and that they had taken jobs in the towns in order to earn the money they needed to purchase not only the bread they had formerly helped to produce but also other foodstuffs and manufactured goods. 'This is', he wrote, 'a spectacle that should bring joy to the philosopher and the statesman'. Although it admittedly entailed some drawbacks, urbanization contributed to 'an augmentation of productive energy', and that counted for much more than anything else.[1]

Levasseur focused in particular on the spectacular growth of Paris, whose inhabitants, he pointed out, had more than quadrupled in number between 1801 and 1886. The absorption by the capital of an ever larger percentage of the French population, which had been growing quite slowly for some time, provided an excellent illustration of a law of nature that obtained in human affairs just as it did in the world described by the physicists: '... the force of attraction of human groups, like that of matter, is in general proportional to mass'. Levasseur went on to identify a number of specific factors that lay behind the attractiveness of the French metropolis: its centuries-old status as the national capital; the educational institutions and the recreational opportunities associated with the presence of literature, the sciences, and the arts; and above all the economic developments that had made the city a 'hive' of light industry and drawn much heavy industry as well, caused it to become the center of the national network of railroads, and made it 'the principal warehouse of French commerce'. As we saw earlier, he recognized that Paris suffered from marked deficiencies with regard to birth rates and death rates, and he drew attention to its social and political problems too. Nonetheless, he concluded his analysis in the same vein in which he had begun it. He insisted that Paris was not 'a monstrous wart that had sprouted accidentally on the face of France' but rather 'an essential organ of the nation', comparable to a head or a heart, whose prosperity was intimately linked to that of the whole country. Like other large cities, it was to be viewed not as a necessary evil but instead as a partially defective force for good.[2]

In Levasseur's eyes, if one considered a nation as a 'living organism', many urban ills could be seen in a perspective that seemed to render them almost harmless. Levasseur observed that 'the countryside produces more human beings than it can use ... [and] the cities absorb and consume a part of the excess and return to the nation in exchange considerable value in wealth and civilization'. In this view, Paris and other urban centers not only contributed to economic progress but also helped maintain a social equilibrium. They functioned in the overall scheme of things in such a way as to enhance national wealth and, by providing employment for surplus countrymen, to promote the stability of society.[3]

The urban themes that Levasseur treated within the context of demographic history in general received much fuller consideration a few years later in a major work of synthesis written by one of his students. In a doctoral thesis, dedicated to Levasseur, Paul Meuriot sought to elucidate the expansion of 'urban agglomerations' as a European-wide phenomenon. Observing that this change had proceeded in the nineteenth century with 'a degree of intensity and universality' unparalleled in earlier times, he provided copious statistics on the urban development of numerous countries in addition to his own. Like his teacher, he explained the far-reaching redistribution of Europe's inhabitants by placing primary emphasis on technological and economic variables. Coal, steam, industry, commerce, and new means of transportation had all wrought 'this economic revolution, which explain[ed] above all the formation of the large urban agglomerations'. In more detail than Levasseur, Meuriot pointed out the demographic and social penalties that resulted from the rise of the city in general and from the rise of the metropolis in particular. But at the same time that he documented all of these ills and dangers, he insisted strongly on the basic benefits that could be seen to have accrued from the whole process of urbanization when everything was taken into account. Returning to the area of economics, he pointed not simply to high urban productivity but also to the stimulating effects of urban demand for food on agricultural output, on the salaries of rural workers, and on the prices of land suitable for cultivation. In his view, the cities certainly did not impoverish the countryside; on the contrary, the urban economy spread wealth among urbanites and countrymen alike.[4]

Another point made by Meuriot, not apparent in Levasseur's work, deserves special emphasis. Meuriot argued that, far from contributing to general depopulation, the growth of cities helped to maintain the number of people living in the nation as a whole by providing an alternative for migrants from the countryside to leaving the state altogether. 'Indeed', he wrote, 'these internal migrations do not represent depopulation but rather a transformation of the manner in which a country is inhabited; the essential thing for a state is to conserve and augment its human capital, whether this capital … lives more or less in the countryside or in the city'. For this reason, as well as for reasons having to do with political prestige and national culture, urban decline would be an unmistakable 'symptom of stagnation or retrogression of civilization in general'. Again, we encounter an interpretation of urban growth as a natural process that reflected the legitimate desires of the men and women who were participating in it and contributed to the overall well-being of the countries in which it was taking place.[5]

Two years after the appearance of Meuriot's work, a young American economist and statistician, Adna Ferrin Weber, published a comparable dissertation, which still stands as one of the most informative and incisive books ever written on the whole subject of modern cities. His *The Growth of Cities in the Nineteenth Century: A Study in Statistics* (1899) is best known and most frequently cited for its systematic survey of changes in city size, country by country, throughout the world.[6] But Weber accomplished far more than just the careful compilation of basic data regarding the rates and the extent of urban development, heroic though that labor was in and of itself. He also took up a wide range of questions that pertained both to the causes and the consequences of the townward trend, a trend he warmly welcomed largely on the basis of considerations that lent themselves fully to the quantitative reasoning that was his forte.

At great length, Weber argued that urban growth had resulted from the need for a shifting of population that would accord with 'the constant striving to maintain as many people as possible upon a given area'. The rise of the city reflected the need 'so to distribute and organize the masses of men that they can render such services as favor the maintenance of the nation and thereby accomplish their own preservation'. As a result of increased productivity on the farm, the quickened tempo of trade, and the rise of the factory, the city exerted a magnetic pull as 'the superior field for ambition'. Every young man who wanted to rise in the world had to go to a great city to make his mark. Weber admitted that the cities housed hopeless poverty as well as enormous wealth and that among some workers high rents might more than offset high wages, but he still insisted that society as a whole — not just the ambitious few — clearly gained from urban growth. 'Did it not result in the production of greater wealth', he observed, 'it would soon cease'. Higher density meant increased specialization and the optimal use of strength and skill, and consequently 'preeminent talent' came to the fore. Weber recognized the hypothetical possibility that increased production might, owing to inequitable distribution, fail to benefit the workers, but he quickly added that in point of fact the city fostered trade unionism, thus helping to ensure that most if not all city dwellers would enjoy the fruits of urban prosperity.[7]

In a more combative vein, Weber took issue directly with the theorists of demographic decline and degeneration. Like Levasseur and Meuriot, he sought to deflect the arguments of the city's most hostile critics with respect both to the quantity and the quality of the urban population, but his strategy was more complex than either of theirs. While he admitted that 'the concentration of population produces an enormous drain on the vitality of a people', he hastened to add that there was 'no inherent and eternal reason why men should die faster in large communities than in small hamlets'. The extremely low death rate of 17.14 per thousand in the densely populated tenth ward of New York in 1894 showed that through rigid adherence to sanitary laws (the inhabitants of the ward being largely Jewish) men and women could effectively neutralize the worst physical effects of urban crowding. Weber found additional cause for hope in the enormous reductions in urban death rates that a number of countries had experienced during the preceding several decades. However bad the ratio of mortality in the town to mortality on the land might be now, he argued, it was much less unfavorable around the time he was writing than it had been in the past. In England, Weber showed, the ratio of urban to rural death rates had dropped from 124:100 in 1850-61 to 116:100 in 1893. In Prussia, whereas the rural death rate had decreased from 24.6 in 1880 to 23.4 in 1890, the death rate in big cities had dropped from 27.5 to 22.8.[8]

On the basis of calculations such as these and many others too intricate to be discussed here, Weber systematically criticized one of the chief authorities on demographic questions among the anti-urbanists, the German Georg Hansen. In Weber's view, big cities were inimical neither to the perpetuation of humanity in general nor to the survival of the middle class. They admittedly worked to eliminate some individuals while favoring others, but far from damaging a nation's biological resources through their class-specific impact on births and deaths they served as 'instruments of natural selection ... weeding out the incapable and inefficient, while advancing the more capable members of society'. In short, although Weber saw more cause for concern in the health of the urban population than he did in the structure of the urban economy, he remained fundamentally hopeful on both counts with regard to the city's future. Both from an economic and from a physiological and a demographic standpoint, the growth of the town appeared to be quite consistent with the enhanced well-being of the nation.[9]

Imperial Germany did not produce any one study of urban growth comparable in its range or detail to the works of Meuriot and Weber, but it compensated for this lack with a large number of men who incorporated economic variables into briefer studies of the topic, both by way of explanation and by way of justification. Living in a country which was successfully challenging Britain for industrial leadership in Europe, they were inevitably sensitive to the close links between the creation of wealth and the rise of the town.

Among professional social scientists, Karl Bücher, a professor of economics at the University of Leipzig, stood out clearly. An incisive observer of the urban scene during the late nineteenth and early twentieth centuries, he reached a broad audience and was frequently cited by others. He pointed out in several public lectures that in many respects urban growth was highly beneficial, both for the individuals who experienced it and for the nation as a whole. He admitted freely that rapid urbanization was accompanied by 'unpleasant side-effects', but he regarded these as remediable, and in any case they did not outweigh the basic gains that resulted from the rise of the city. The fact that modern towns conferred tangible advantages upon their inhabitants was strikingly demonstrated by the manner in which they had grown and were continuing to grow. Unlike the administrative centers established in earlier centuries, they had not arisen as a result of princely decrees but rather owing to free choices by men and women who had migrated to them voluntarily. 'As a result of a purely social development', he wrote, 'they have grown up on a foundation of civil freedom, and their claim to carry the flag in the victory march of modern culture is based not on a piece of parchment but on the facts of social selection, through which they bring together the most dynamic intellectual and economic forces of the nation'. Bücher asserted that the 'marvelous power of attraction' displayed by the big city stemmed from the fact that as 'a place of struggle' it offered 'to every outstanding talent the highest reward'. Moreover, he insisted that the growing national division of labor facilitated by the urbanization process would enable men not only to maximize their separate economic interests but also to enhance the collective welfare of the whole country. Almost everyone would ultimately benefit from the great transformation.[10]

Other social scientists supported Bücher's general line of argument, demonstrating a similar awareness of the basic advantages of urban growth. In highly civilized countries, asserted Gustav Rümelin, cities constituted 'the integrating skeleton of the social organism'. The establishment of towns marked the entrance of a people 'into the higher realms of economic as well as intellectual development'. Alexander Wirminghaus described migration to the towns as 'both a natural and a necessary process'. Movement by the rural

population into the cities had been stimulated by fundamental changes in modes of production and levels of monetary compensation in both the agrarian and the commercial-industrial sectors. Men who sought to improve their economic and social status inevitably went to the city because they rightly perceived it as a place of opportunity. Franz Oppenheimer explained that urban growth had vastly concentrated the demand for all kinds of manufactured goods, leading to much higher levels of industrial specialization and in turn to far greater productivity. Adolf Weber observed in the first of his series of lectures on urban life,

> The big cities are the consequence of our economic development, which is intimately bound up with the immense quantitative and qualitative augmentation of material forces — on the one hand, with a population increase unknown to earlier centuries, and on the other, with the marvelous skill these newly gathered masses of men have shown during the last century in subordinating nature to their own purposes.

He added, 'The big city ... helps mightily to sustain economic life through the part it plays in the magnificent increase of wealth that is taking place nowadays'. Awareness of these facts dictated basic acceptance of the idea of the city, even though the city in its present form still left a great deal to be desired.[11]

This version of the reasons for urban growth and of the impact of such growth on the people who experienced it found expression in the writings of many men in addition to economists and other social scientists. Julius Beloch, a distinguished historian of classical antiquity, asserted that the quickest way to gauge the level of economic development in any country was to determine its level of urbanization. 'Rapid growth of cities', he wrote, 'is always a sure sign of economic advance, whereas, if the urban population remains stationary or declines the economy stagnates or decays'. Heinrich Boos, the historian of Worms and other cities in the Rhineland, also regarded modern urban development as 'an entirely natural process'. Most migrants to the city were motivated not by the desire for pleasure or adventure but rather by the necessity of discovering a place where they could enjoy more favourable conditions of working and living. 'Even the diet is generally better in the city than on the land', he added, 'and it brings about a more rapid physical and intellectual development'.[12]

Publicists and other non-academic authors praised the material benefits that were sought in and conferred by the modern city still more effusively. Eugen Kalkschmidt, an art critic who wrote about many aspects of contemporary life, welcomed the city because it offered the individual 'thousands of chances to make the most of his life through competition with like-minded men'. In the *Grossstadt*, men and women were on their own, and their need to

16 A shopping street in Berlin. The illustration celebrates bourgeois prosperity in the capital of the recently established German Empire (source: Max Ring, *Die deutsche Kaiserstadt Berlin und ihre Umgebung*, I [Leipzig, 1884], 105).

assert themselves in order to achieve success strengthened the larger collectivities of the nation and the state. Free enterprise had thrust Germany into a
leading position as an economic power, and it needed to be borne in mind
that without the economic assistance provided by the big city the innovative-
ness of the entrepreneur would be like 'a child without its mother's breast'.
Felix Linke, writing for a popular magazine, contrasted modern cities with
their ancient predecessors by emphasizing that they were centers of production, not just consumption. Unlike ancient Rome, they did not live at the
expense of the countryside. They were 'the headquarters of labor', on which
all modern progress depended. Another writer, Heinrich Lee, buttressed
these views in a series of descriptive sketches of sixty individual towns, many
of which first appeared in the *Berliner Tageblatt*. He found evidence of
economic dynamism in almost all of the larger cities about which he wrote,
especially in the great commercial and industrial centers of the Ruhr Valley.
He marveled at Düsseldorf as a place in which all sorts of economic
organizations were located, including the German Steel Association and two
stock exchanges, 'one for mining and metallurgy, the other for the highly
developed trade in groceries'. He celebrated Essen as 'the greatest armorer in
the world', the seat of the gigantic Krupp iron and steel works, without
which the spectacular growth of the city during the preceding half century
would have been unthinkable, and he gave many other cities comparable
accolades.[13]

Numerous other authors paid their respects to the restless energy and
enormous productivity displayed by the imperial capital. The spirit that
pervaded them was neatly summarized by a thoroughly obscure author, one
Max Eyth, who wrote a poem for a festive gathering of German engineers in
which he proclaimed that the greatest among Berlin's several claims to fame
and high repute was the hard labor performed by its inhabitants. In his
concluding stanza, he exulted, 'Arrogant sloth is no longer in!/The sons of
labor greet you, Berlin!/Productive city, brimming with power,/City of work,
moving each hour'. In a similar vein, the mayor of the city during the First
World War, Adolf Wermuth, wrote an essay for an art magazine in which he
proudly asserted,

> Work is the basis of this young metropolitan giant. He feels content in it, sensing
> the steady growth of his powers.... The hallmark of Berlin remains its labor....
> Here the threads of the great enterprises run together; commerce and industry,
> science and technology have procured for themselves in Berlin vital centers,
> from which they incessantly exert their influence throughout the whole world.

In such passages the economic justification for the modern *Grossstadt* reached
its zenith.[14]

Some Germans — though admittedly not many — also sought to bolster
the image of the city by disputing or otherwise counteracting the medical and
demographic arguments of the theorists of urban degeneration. They shared
the view of Levasseur, Meuriot, and Weber that such theories either

distorted the truth or missed the point. Albert Moll, a Berlin-based psychiatrist, denied that big-city life as such caused disproportionate rates of mental illness. Some statistics seemed to suggest such a conclusion, but it had to be remembered that urbanites found it relatively easy to visit psychiatrists; moreover, white-collar workers, who were at greater risk of becoming mentally ill than manual laborers, were over-represented in the towns. In any case, Moll saw the big city as 'a necessary product of modern development', and he contended that each part of society, like each part of a physical organism, contributed to 'the well-being of the whole'. Hans Fehlinger, who wrote about a variety of scientific as well as social questions, also sought to deflect charges that the city harmed its inhabitants, either mentally or physically. High urban death rates, he argued, affected primarily those who had migrated from the land, not those who had spent their lives in the city. What the urban milieu did, through the struggle for survival, was to weed out people with hereditary defects, many of whom would have survived and passed their infirmities on to a large number of descendants had they stayed in the countryside. This was a clearly Darwinian justification of the city. Its emphasis on a favorable process of biological selection nicely complemented Bücher's arguments with regard to the prerequisites for success in the urban economy. Again, the city appeared as a natural and self-regulating system, which turned apparent loss into real profit.[15]

Somewhat surprisingly, Britain contributed less during the period than any of the other countries to the general line of defense we have been considering so far in this chapter. One can only speculate whether the reason for this deficiency in a country where economic factors had been so very prominent in pro-urban thought earlier in the century lay in a feeling that there was no need to belabor the obvious or in Britain's gradual loss of industrial dynamism and leadership. In any event, no Englishmen made scholarly apologias comparable to those of Levasseur, Meuriot, and Weber, nor did very many of them articulate at any length views comparable to those expressed by Bücher and the other Germans whose ideas we have just encountered.

One of the few who spoke up in a general way was the little known Everard Digby, who, in an article critical of James Cantlie that appeared in the *Contemporary Review*, asserted,

> The disappearance of the city from modern life would be neither healthy nor satisfactory.... The city is not a disease, but a necessary organic center of civilised life. It is in the city that the saving of individual time produces the highest efficiency in the individual.... It is in the city that particular talent has a greater — sometimes the only — opportunity of exercising itself, owing to the larger mass of townspeople and the variety of their requirements.... The great city may be compared to the furnace of a steam engine which supplies energy to all its numerous activities.... The active energetic countryman enters the town and his descendants burn away within two generations, supplying in the

meanwhile all the physical and mental energy which keeps the interminable wheels of civilisation a-spinning.[16]

Like Levasseur, Digby viewed the ostensible inability of the big city to maintain itself demographically as a perfectly acceptable phenomenon in the overall scheme of national development.

Other writers expressed their urban sympathies with regard to particular towns. A useful compendium of their views was a multivolume work edited by Edwin Hodder and published under the title *Cities of the World: Their Origin, Progress, and Present Aspect* (1886-89). To give examples pertaining to only two of the nearly four-score cities in Britain and elsewhere that qualified for consideration, one author praised Glasgow by writing, 'The peculiarity of this city is its tenacious grip of business, its amazing power of adjusting itself to new conditions of commerce, its invaluable gift of finding compensation in some new industry when an old staple trade fails'. Another author remarked of Newcastle that a visitor to the city would be 'most impressed by the everywhere visible signs of industrial energy, prosperous commerce, and accumulated wealth.... Its ships are on all seas; its machinery may be found in all civilized lands; its trade has put a girdle round the earth; and its present fame far eclipses the glory of its antiquity'. An anonymous contributor to *The Spectator* reflected in the same year on conditions of life in the metropolis in a way that subtly echoed these paeans to urban energy and productivity. He denied that London exhausted its inhabitants. The city gave the very force it required from those who lived and worked there. 'Laziness is of the country, not London', he wrote, 'because it is in London that work, owing to a strength imperceptibly derived from the vivid life around, is least distressing'.[17]

All of these men admired cities for their dynamic energy and their productive output. Like many of the earlier urbanites, they welcomed large towns as places in which men were strengthening the material foundations of their societies in ways that benefited both the individual and the group. They recognized that material hardships still beset some city dwellers and that the profit and loss columns in the areas of birth rates and death rates still looked less favorable for the city than for the country, but they adhered to the view that demographic deficits were an acceptable price to pay in view of the other surpluses generated by urban growth.

Like some urban critics, many of these men used biological reasoning in order to strengthen their case. Instead of focusing on evidence of physical degeneration, they employed Darwinian models of social development as a way of making life in the city appear both useful and desirable from the standpoint of the species. The widespread popularity of social Darwinism throughout the Western world during the years when they were writing made it seem entirely plausible to portray the sufferings of some individuals in the big cities not just as a regrettable misfortune but also as an essential prerequisite for the advancement of society as a whole. The city did not offer an easy life, but these men valued it in large part precisely because they regarded strenuous competition as the surest path to social progress. The city, they asserted, brought out the best in men by bestowing abundant rewards upon those who seized the new opportunities that it offered to the resourceful. The city served as a selective sieve, in which some elements of the population found themselves blocked so that others could realize their capacities and pass them on to their descendants, thus enhancing instead of diminishing national strength.

In any case, quite apart from intellectual efforts such as these to rationalize the pain and suffering experienced by urban society's losers, it must be remembered that there was an enormous body of writing by city boosters in all countries about the growing prosperity of particular places. The books and articles of men such as Heinrich Lee and Edwin Hodder represented the tip of an iceberg, the lower portions of which can be readily examined in the local history sections of many urban libraries. There, in countless works by authors whose names have long since passed into oblivion, the continuing pride in the urban economy felt by many of those who had profited from it still shines forth even today.

The city as a cultural stimulus

The city functioned in the eyes of many of its defenders as a source not only of material progress but also of mental and aesthetic progress. The economy and intellect were of course intimately linked, inasmuch as economic advances depended heavily on the discoveries of inventors and the acuity of entrepreneurs, and many commentators referred to both sorts of progress in the same breath. But numerous men valued the benefits that cities conferred in the realms of intellect and art for reasons that had little or nothing to do with the considerations we have been discussing up to this point. They regarded the big city as a bundle of cultural stimuli that were to be prized quite independently of any economic calculations, for the ways in which they enriched men's minds and their sensibilities. They responded positively to the urban world not just because it exuded commercial and industrial dynamism but also because it energized them and others mentally and artistically by providing a wealth of opportunities for study, for writing, and for creativity.

One way of justifying urban growth in terms of cultural progress was to focus on the favorable impact of the demands for intellectual and artistic production that emanated from urban society, on the cultural advances made possible by the division of labor, and on the cultural institutions to which some if not all city dwellers had access. Lorenz von Stein, one of the founding fathers of German sociology, put culture in a clearly economic perspective when he observed, 'At first it is only the city that makes intellectual work as such economically remunerative, and therefore anyone who regards himself as intellectually productive in an economic sense goes to the city and finds a niche that is seldom found elsewhere'. The economist Heinrich Waentig pointed out that the big city was 'the source of the most advanced culture' and 'the most important producer of intellectual goods'. In fact, as heavy industry moved away from city centers to outlying areas, the inhabitants of the *Grossstadt* were turning more and more toward culturally oriented sectors of the economy such as printing, the book trade, newspaper publishing, architecture, and 'learned and artistic occupations of every sort'. Eugen Kalkschmidt believed that 'the heightening of nervous life' in the city caused not only neurasthenia — a typical urban illness — but also greater sensitivity of a sort that led to praiseworthy productivity in the realm of 'cultural labor'. He asserted that everywhere one looked one could see 'the stream of stimuli and new ideas originating in the big city'. The ideas themselves, he admitted, had not necessarily been formulated in an urban setting, but in order to have any practical effect they needed an audience, and the big city provided just that. 'With compelling force', he wrote, 'the concentrated big-city public draws scattered ideas to itself in the same way that a magnet attracts iron filings; here, they are melted down and fused together'.[18]

In the United States, the progressive reformer Frederic C. Howe summarized matters in more prosaic fashion, and he gave more explicit attention to the cultural impact of urban institutions upon the great mass of the urban population. He wrote gratefully,

> ... The city has given the world culture, enlightenment, and education along with industry and commercial opportunity. The advance in recent years in this regard has been tremendous.... To-day, to an ever-increasing mass of the population, opportunities are crowding one upon another. Not only is education generously adapted to the needs of all, but night schools, art exhibitions, popular lectures and concerts, college settlements, the parks, playgrounds, a cheap press, labor organizations, the church, all these are bringing enlightenment at a pace never before dreamed of.

In Howe's view, the big city was facilitating the dissemination and consumption of culture more and more effectively with every passing decade.[19]

Let us again descend from the general to the particular. Many writers who addressed ordinary middle-class readers looked admiringly at the cultural life of numerous large towns, each of which, it was felt, could take pride in its own cultural peculiarities while at the same time boasting of its participation in a general movement that improved the minds of city dwellers everywhere. In England, during the 1880s, the positivist historian and sociologist, Frederic Harrison, celebrated London for the richness of its history and the memories of earlier cultural attainment its buildings helped to keep alive in the present. 'What a world of associations', he exclaimed, 'cling to the very stones, and names, and sites of it still! Can any city show so great an array of buildings and scenes identified with poetry and literature, with the memories of poets and thinkers, of so high an order?' John Morley, in comparing modern London with ancient Rome, emphasized not only its economic and political but also its intellectual centrality in a vast empire in which the English language and English literature reigned supreme.[20]

Although London epitomized the rich possibilities for cultural development offered by the urban milieu, other English cities received comparable accolades too. Thomas Escott, a thoughtful journalist who surveyed all of English society, praised the commercial and industrial towns of the north and the Midlands for having expended their energies not only on the pursuit of wealth but also on the refinement of intellect. The populations of the large manufacturing centers might appear to live only for material success, but they were also 'stirred by higher thoughts'. Escott wrote,

> The teaching of art and letters is not wanting to the members of these communities. Science has attractions independently of the power over Nature with which she invests man. The workers may appear as wholly absorbed in the pecuniary successes of their tasks as the artificers of Dido with the walls of rising Carthage. But there are the instruments of culture as well as the greed of gain; and if Manchester is to England all that and more than Carthage was to Africa, the graces and ornaments of Athens are not quite forgotten.

In Manchester and Liverpool, well-attended musical productions and lectures on science, history, and literature, antique stores, and schools and colleges all indicated the desire of businessmen to use their wealth for ideal as well as material ends. In Manchester and Birmingham, this desire had borne fruit in free libraries and art galleries. In short, the largest of the provincial towns could take much pride in their contributions to culture as well as to commerce.[21]

No metropolis enjoyed as many devoted admirers as Paris, and the numerous works that described this city and recounted its past were almost wholly laudatory. Among the many qualities that won the favor of observers of the French capital, none seemed more impressive than its contributions not only to national but also to world civilization. As Charles Delon put it in 1888, a year before the great exhibition that marked the centennial of the French Revolution, 'Whoever loves France loves Paris. Whoever does not know Paris is ignorant of France. Why? Because Paris is France'. Paris had forged the national spirit and the national language, and it had thought as well as fought for the French nation. But the influence of the city extended far beyond France's borders. Offering in rich abundance 'the noble pleasures of the mind', Paris served as 'a salon, a museum, so to speak, a school, and the foremost in the world'. It was 'the great universal workshop of intellectual labor'. For Charles Simond, Paris was 'a factory of ideas, which never goes on strike, working day and night'. Men's minds fermented there incessantly, and their sensibilities always remained sharp. As he looked toward the future, Simond predicted, 'Modern life will become cosmopolitan

17 Parisian artists on parade. The action takes place the morning after the artists' annual festival. The picture, by Edouard Cucuel, suggests some of the colorful vibrancy of cultural life in the French capital and a certain rapport between artists and non-artists in the Parisian population (source: W. C. Morrow, *Bohemian Paris of To-day*, 3rd ed. [Philadelphia and London, 1900], 105).

in the twentieth century, but Paris will remain the hearth of this cosmopolitanism, and all attention, all dreams, and all desires for approval will converge on this home of light and englightenment'.[22]

German authors bestowed special praise on two of their big cities. Berlin stood out for its excellence on many counts. In a series of books titled *Stätten der Kultur*, the art historian Wolfgang von Oettingen denied strenuously that the growth of the Prussian-German capital stemmed solely from industrial and political developments. The Berliners' labor had been devoted not only to the acquisition of wealth and power but also to the 'the pursuit of higher intellectual culture, whose power to bind and unite men redounded to the benefit of the community'. Religious, scholarly, and artistic movements had all helped to make the city great. A history of Berlin that appeared in 1900 asserted proudly that during the preceding several decades scholarship and the arts had blossomed under the benevolent patronage of the Prussian monarchs. The spectacular growth in the size of the university and the high repute of its faculty, which included distinguished scholars in many fields, provided the most notable but by no means the only evidence of cultural progress in the vibrant *Hauptstadt*. The establishment of professional associations for medical doctors and natural scientists, the founding of new secondary and primary schools, and the provision of continuing education for adults all bore witness to the march of intellect. In the realms of theater, opera, music, painting, and architecture, Berlin had also made great strides forward.[23]

No German city enjoyed a higher reputation as a mecca for writers and artists than Munich, where the Wittelsbachs had long been active as collectors and patrons *par excellence*. The journalist Theodor Goering pointed out that whereas energy and intelligence predominated in the north, Germany's 'spiritual side' (*Gemütsseite*) emerged more clearly in the south. In the Bavarian capital, this quality revealed itself in the liveliness of the drama and especially in the influence of Richard Wagner, who had been summoned there by Ludwig II, as well as in the presence of a large number of outstanding painters. 'And it is', wrote the cultural essayist Max Haushofer, 'these artistic elements that bestow upon the life of Munich its greatest zest. The labor and the leisure of Munich's artistic community infuse characteristic traits into the existence of all other groups, especially a certain contempt for sober philistinism'.[24]

The life of the mind attracted less attention from commentators on American cities than from their counterparts in Europe, but it still found a secure place in almost every survey of a large metropolis. Consider, for example, the case of New York. Despite a persistent tendency to view New York as an uncultured place whose denizens thought first and foremost of getting rich, there was a growing awareness of its rapidly burgeoning array of institutions devoted to the advancement of art and intellect. Several works of popular history published during the 1890s all made much the same point. Almost half of the concluding volume of a collaborative work edited by James G. Wilson consisted of essays on authors, libraries, newspapers and magazines, music, monuments and statues, the fine arts, the sciences, the theater, and schools and colleges. Martha J. Lamb and Mrs. Burton Harrison ended their survey by touching on many of the same topics. Developments in education and in theatrical and musical life and the rapid expansion of art collections and libraries all testified to a growing appreciation of cultural artifacts, wherever they might have been produced. Theodore Roosevelt, writing for the British *Historic Towns* series just before becoming head of the New York City police board, expressed his pride in institutions such as the Metropolitan Museum of Art, the American Museum of Natural History, and Columbia University. The recent history of these places pointed to 'a development which tends to make the city more and more attractive to people of culture'. The growth of literary and dramatic associations and the establishment of high-quality magazines such as the *Century*, *Scribner's*, and *Harper's* also bore witness to the cultural vitality of the great metropolis.[25]

Martha Lamb and Theodore Roosevelt, like Thomas Escott, Charles Simond, and Wolfgang von Oettingen, articulated a view of the urban scene that, like the celebrations of urban wealth, found expression in numerous works of description and history written for a large popular audience. These books possessed little inherent merit, either intellectual or literary. But they testified clearly and persistently to a widespread belief among middle-class townsmen everywhere that life in the city offered a broad range of opportunities for mental as well as material enrichment. Intellectual aristocrats might condemn the city as an agent of either chaos or homogenization, and urban workers would doubtless have found it difficult to feel much enthusiasm for the museums and the many other institutions of high culture from which they were still largely excluded. But large numbers of educated burghers saw images of places they recognized and liked in the many books that effusively praised the cultural life of the towns in which they lived.

Another way of celebrating the city in a cultural perspective was not to focus on supply and demand, on patrons and institutions, or on the mere presence and influence of thinkers, writers, and artists but instead to point out the ways in which the urban milieu provided a stimulating spectacle for sensitive observers who lived there. In this view, the city itself deserved and received artistic attention, thereby strengthening certain currents in the cultural stream, simply by virtue of its own peculiar attractiveness as an object of contemplation and reflection. As Lisbeth Stern, a socialist cultural critic in Germany, wrote in 1903, 'Poetically and pictorially, the big city is equally fruitful, as a few names, such as those of Zola, Baudelaire, Steinlen, and Menzel, suffice to show'. She argued that in the *Grossstadt* a great wealth of visual images imprinted themselves on men's imaginative faculties. 'The countless voices of the big city, which blend into a powerful roar', she added, 'speak a more meaningful language to the modern artist than nature does'.[26]

Writers who shared and helped to provide evidence for this belief did not necessarily regard the big city as a thing of beauty. Some did welcome the railroad, the factory, and the skyscraper as aesthetically admirable phenomena, referring approvingly to 'the beauty of technology' and 'a technological and aesthetic spectacle',[27] but in their opinion valuable art — whether verbal or pictorial — did not require a pleasing subject. What the cultural yea-sayers liked most about the cities in which they lived was the sheer variety of the urban scene. Hermann Platz wrote in Germany that in the big city 'the vision of the poet ... could fathom all the depths of humanity but also admire all the heights, which would give him the material for a modern *Divine Comedy*'. In a similar vein, George Sims introduced a popular work about London that consisted of scores of essays by almost as many authors by asserting that it presented 'a great human drama ... a complete and comprehensive survey of the myriad human atoms which make up this ever-changing kaleidoscope'.[28]

Three authors, all of whom wrote about cities during the first decade of the twentieth century, manifested this sensibility in an especially clear fashion and at much greater length than did any of the writers mentioned so far. August Endell, a leading practitioner of *Jugendstil* architecture and an art critic who lived in Berlin, displayed it lyrically and unreservedly in a long essay on 'the beauty of the big city'. Endell rejected the romantic paean to the beauties of nature and the charms of the past. He admitted that urban life suffered from all sorts of drawbacks, but he still insisted that the *Grossstadt* was a beautiful and joyful place in which to live.

> ... The big city, despite all the ugly buildings, despite the noise, despite everything in it that one can criticize, is a marvel of beauty and poetry to anyone who is willing to look, a fairy tale, brighter, more colorful, more diverse than anything ever invented by a poet, a home, a mother, who daily bestows new happiness in great abundance upon her children.

Urban beauty appeared first and foremost in the realm of labor — in workshops and factories, in tools and machines, all of which displayed 'a wealth of imaginative power'. Moreover, the institutions that directed and regulated men's labor also had their charms. Writing about big businesses, Endell compared them to 'crystalline forms' because of what he regarded as their clear and streamlined organizational structure. Outside the workplace, in city streets, the great variety of sounds and sights, which continually changed in appearance depending upon whether they were viewed in the bright sun, through fog and mist, or after dark, all provided a fascinating feast. So too did the brilliant panorama of different types of human beings whom one might encounter on a street car, even — indeed especially — when some of their faces were marked by sickness and despair. 'How fine the sick complexions of big-city children are', he enthused, 'and see how often their features take on a marvelously severe beauty precisely as a result of need and deprivation'. In passages such as these, Endell clearly echoed Charles Baudelaire and the *fin de siècle* decadents, as he transmuted the social hardship of the many into the aesthetic pleasure of the few.[29]

In England, the novelist Ford Madox Hueffer (later known as Ford Madox Ford) expressed somewhat similar views in a sensitive interpretation of life in London. He displayed no traces of aesthetic decadence, but he clearly took great pleasure in the spectacle offered by the people and places he observed in the metropolis. He valued London most for its great diversity, which provided enormous freedom of choice and splendid entertainment.

> ... London, perhaps because of its utter lack of unity, of plan ... is the final expression of the Present Stage. It owes its being to no one race, to no two, to no three. It is, as it were, the meeting place of all Occidentals and of such of the Easterns as can come, however remotely, into touch with the Western spirit.... In it may be found, as it were 'on show', the best of all music. And it has at odd

moments 'on show' the best products of the cook, of the painter, of the flower-gardener, of the engineer, of the religious and of the scientists.

Hueffer denied the existence of a 'London type'. London was 'a meeting place of all sorts of incongruous types'. He referred to 'the great swarm of tiny men and women', but he did not subsume them beneath the general rubric of 'the crowd'. Each person possessed 'his own soul, his own hopes, his own passions, his own individuality'. Moreover, despite the efforts by builders to create box-like houses indistinguishable from one another, each dwelling had its own peculiar characteristics. 'Here a door has been painted green, here a handle has been polished till it shines like gold, here the curtains are clean, here a window has been broken and replaced with gummed paper. So that from each of those houses a soul seems to peep forth, differing from each other soul'. All of these aspects of modern London contributed mightily to the pleasure Hueffer experienced in observing and writing about it.[30]

In America, aesthetic appreciation of the big city manifested itself most forcefully in the often lyrical sketches of life in New York written by Theodore Dreiser between 1900 and 1915 and subsequently published under the title *The Color of a Great City*. As we saw earlier, both in his novels and in many of these sketches, Dreiser laid bare the material and moral hardship that afflicted the urban poor. But despite his strongly naturalist tendency to focus on urban suffering, he also expressed an almost romantic love of the city. His metropolitan sympathies came most clearly to the fore in his essay 'On Being Poor'. Writing at a time when he himself was struggling to survive, Dreiser insisted that although he had very little money he did not feel poor. Unable to afford the price of a theater ticket, he could nonetheless avail himself of numerous museums, exhibitions, and libraries that opened their doors to the public free of charge.[31]

Dreiser derived still more satisfaction from 'the beauty of life itself ... a shifting, lovely, changeful thing ever'. Many of the beauties to which Dreiser referred included natural phenomena, but he added a paean to 'the tortuous, tideful rivers that twist among great forests of masts and under many graceful bridges' and to 'the crowding, surging ways of seeking men'. It was, as he made clear in other sketches, the enormous variety of human beings that riveted his attention most closely to the urban scene. The city's physical artifacts — its railroad yards and its docks as well as its tall buildings — all possessed their picturesque charm, but nothing fascinated him as much as the great panorama of humanity. Encompassing the whole gamut of society, from the wealthy few to the impoverished many, the different sorts of human beings made the big city endlessly absorbing. As Dreiser put it in his essay on 'Characters',

> The glory of the city is its variety. The drama of it lies in its extremes. I have been thinking to-day of all the interesting characters that have passed before me in times past on the streets of this city: generals, statesmen, artists, politicians, a most interesting company, and then of another company by no means so

distinguished or so comfortable — the creatures at the other end of the ladder who, far from having brains, or executive ability, or wealth, or fame, have nothing save a weird astonishing individuality, which would serve to give pause to almost the dullest.

In Dreiser's view, as in Endell's, misery as well as joy contributed to the aesthetic appeal that emanated from the urban milieu.[32]

Endell, Hueffer, and Dreiser displayed aesthetic sensibilities that recalled those of Dickens as well as Baudelaire. They approached the city not so much with an eye for beauty of any conventional description as with a taste for strangeness, variety, and dissonance. All of these authors shared the belief that both the sharp contrasts and the kaleidoscopic changes everywhere evident on the urban stage made the city an endlessly stimulating and fascinating spectacle for the reflective and creative observer. Such sentiments did not manifest themselves nearly as often as the more prosaic views expressed by the men who celebrated the march of urban intellect and the flowering of urban culture. But they pointed clearly to a growing awareness of the fruitfulness of urban themes that was to become one of the central tenets of literary and artistic modernism in years to come.

The moral defenses of urban society

Advocates of urban life buttressed their case on a variety of moral as well as material and cultural grounds. Not content simply to celebrate the wealth, the comfort, and the intellectual and aesthetic benefits that accrued from the rise of towns, they insisted on presenting the personal conduct of urban men and women and the broad social and political consequences of urban growth in as favorable a light as possible too. Although they realized that they could not refute all of the charges that anti-urbanists and other social critics had leveled against modern urbanites, they sought to soften their impact by showing that many of them were greatly exaggerated. They also argued that the censorious tone of the harshest critics failed to do justice to the wide range of moral virtues nourished by city life and displayed by city dwellers. Whatever might be the city's moral defects, in their reckoning signs of personal probity and contributions to public well-being in the broadest sense finally outweighed the evidence of wickedness and the portents of chaos and decline. This line of defense was not articulated as explicitly and fully as either the moral indictment of the critics or the justifications of the city on economic and cultural grounds. Its true force became apparent only in the specific contexts treated in the next chapter. Nonetheless, it recurs repeatedly in the general literature of urban advocacy, and it needs to be considered now in conjunction with the other major reasons for welcoming the rise of an urban civilization.

There were some occasions when pro-urban writers took close looks at putative evidence of the city dweller's propensity for wrongdoing and announced that they found it far from fully persuasive. They cared most about the charges that pertained to sexual misconduct and to crime, charges that Adna Weber sought to counteract not only with the statistical skills that were his stock-in-trade but also by means of non-quantitative arguments too. Weber examined various statistics on illegitimacy — some of which he drew from the work of Emile Levasseur — and came to the conclusion that although childbirth outside wedlock occurred about twice as frequently in the town as it did in the country, the case against urban sexual morality was not nearly as strong as it appeared at first glance. The presence of maternity hospitals in the cities, he pointed out, attracted young women from the countryside who would otherwise have given birth in the rural areas where they had become pregnant. In Paris, nearly half of the illegitimate births resulted from liaisons among men and women from the lower classes that were generally regarded as a form of marriage by those who had entered into them. Weber also pointed out that the population at risk in the cities was high to start with owing to the relatively large numbers of women who were both young and single. The fact that in Prussia in 1890-91 there had been 2.5 illegitimate births per 100 single or widowed women between the ages of 16 and 50 on the land compared with only 2.4 per 100 in the towns seemed to provide strong support for Weber's case. Weber conceded that prostitution was 'certainly a city institution', but he quickly referred to 'the large proportion of prostitutes who were first corrupted in country homes' and then went on to observe that 'sociologists who know the facts declare that a very large part of the Parisian vice is supported by travelers and foreign sojourners'. In any case, it was a great mistake to regard the entire population of Paris or any other city as immoral. Although the big cities did have a great deal of vice, it was 'the property of a distinct class of the population', not a distinguishing characteristic of whole communities.[33]

Weber wrote in a similar vein about urban crime more generally. Referring to British statistics, he admitted that the frequency of offenses against the law was at least twice as high in urban areas as in rural ones, but he then pointed out that within the cities crime did not seem to be increasing as fast as population. Statistics for France showed that whereas, between 1841-45 and 1881-85, the urban sector had expanded from 23 percent to 35 percent, the percentage of those charged with indictable offenses who inhabited that sector had risen from 38 percent to 46 percent. Apparently, the rural-urban gap was narrowing. Weber also argued that only a limited segment of the urban population actually engaged in crime. 'The fact is', he wrote, 'that in the city the crime is localized; it is confined to particular classes and the remaining classes are so much the cleaner. There are perhaps relatively more offenses committed in the city than in the village, but not so many more offenders'. Once again, quantitative reasoning upheld the moral reputation of the modern town against its detractors.[34]

No one else sifted the evidence of sexual and criminal deviance with an eye to blunting the attacks by the city's critics as carefully and systematically as did Weber, but numerous other writers supported one or another of the points he had made. In France, the social scientist Jean Guillou clearly echoed Weber when he explained not only high rates of illegitimacy but also high rates of crime in large part by reference to disproportionate numbers of single, young adults. Moreover, he showed that France's city dwellers continued to account for less of an increase in the nation's criminality than urban growth by itself would have led one to expect. The cities still suffered from a slight moral deficit, but the rural-urban gap seemed to be shrinking. In Germany, the cultural publicist Eugen Kalkschmidt conceded that crime might be more frequent in the cities than elsewhere, but he sought to soften the force of this concession by pointing out that 'where there is bacon, mice are near by' and that 'criminals gladly come to the big city in search of money and valuable goods'. The countryside bred its fair share of parasites and malefactors too, but because they were geographically dispersed such people made much less of an impression there than they did in large towns. Kalkschmidt concluded his discussion of urban morals by warning his readers to be wary of all attempts to saddle the big city with responsibility for the ills of society and to portray 'this organism' as 'a gruesome and horrifying Moloch'.[35]

As Kalkschmidt and many others indicated, big cities seemed admirable not primarily because they suffered from fewer defects than the critics charged or because the defects they did display stemmed from mitigating circumstances that lessened their guilt but instead because they both permitted and encouraged good things to prosper. Cities were widely regarded by their friends and their foes alike as focal points of change, as places that represented the cutting edge of modernity in all its moral and social as well as economic and cultural dimensions. For men of forward-looking tendencies, the ongoing transformation of inherited attitudes and institutions was essential for a good society, and they welcomed the big cities as both the locations and the agents of many changes that they subsumed favorably under the general rubric of 'progress'. Adna Weber expressed this view forcefully when he wrote,

> Socially, the influence of the cities is ... exerted in favor of liberal and progressive thought. The variety of occupation, interests and opinions in the city produces an intellectual friction, which leads to a broader and freer judgment and a great inclination to and appreciation of new thoughts, manners, and ideals.... The rural population is not merely conservative; it is full of error and prejudice; it receives what enlightenment it possesses from the city.[36]

A still louder and more emphatic paean to a particular city as a force for progress appeared in Emile Zola's novel *Paris* (1897). Throughout the book, Zola gave his readers abundant evidence not only of poverty but also of selfishness and corruption in the French capital. Nonetheless, he repeatedly evoked memories of the city's role as an agent of praiseworthy changes in the past and depicted Paris in the present by means of images that aroused hopes of more such changes in the future. He regarded Paris as 'a huge vat in which the wine of the future was fermenting'. Paris was a place where evil as well as goodness contributed to the accomplishment of a better tomorrow. He wrote that 'all boiled in the huge vat of Paris; the desires, the deeds of violence, the strivings of one and another man's will, the whole nameless medley of the bitterest ferments, whence, in all purity, the wine of the future would at last flow'. In conclusion, Zola changed his metaphor, comparing the city as it sparkled in the light of a setting sun to a vast field of golden corn.

> It now seemed as if one and the same crop had sprung up on every side, imparting harmony to everything, and making the entire expanse one sole, boundless field, rich with the same fruitfulness.... And Paris flared — Paris, which the divine sun had sown with light, and where in glory waved the great future harvest of Truth and of Justice.

Here, Zola affirmed the city unequivocally as a place and an agent of human betterment.[37]

Among the progressive developments that Weber, Zola, and many other admirers of urban civilization welcomed most warmly were the enlargement of individual liberty and the advancement of equality before the law. Cities gained favor in their eyes by virtue of their signal contributions to both sorts of modern change. These writers implicitly accepted the conservative view that urbanization militated against the traditional restraints upon personal conduct and social mobility that had been and to some extent still were operative on farms and in villages. They chose, however, to regard this process not just as something destructive but also as a positive development that enabled those who experienced it to lead richer and ultimately more moral lives. In any event, liberty and equality were valuable enough in their own right to count among the greatest goods bestowed upon city dwellers by city life.

In England, the liberal M.P. Joseph Cowen linked cities and liberty quite clearly in his speech on 'The Rise and Strength of Great Towns', which he delivered in 1881 at the celebration of the jubilee of the manufacturing city of Middlesbrough. He praised that community as 'an epitome of modern times — of that irresistible and victorious civilization which has for its foundation, industry and freedom'. He asserted that the history of Middlesbrough and of other towns like it marked the rise of the nation from feudal oppression to modern liberty. 'The boroughs built by ... doughty traders', he wrote, 'were the citadels of freedom, the mansion-houses of liberty.... The noise of the workshops rose ... over the embattled towers, the bastions, and the barbicans of the steel-clad chiefs, and proclaimed the dawn of the day when trade asserted its independence, and industry claimed its rights'. This was not primarily an economic encomium but instead a moral justification that focused on men's enhanced power to shape their own lives.[38]

L. Lynn Linton, writing a dozen years later, stated the case for urban living in a more contemporary context in an article for the progressive *New Review* on the familiar theme of 'town or country'. Linton chafed under the impediments to free thought that weighed upon him continually among the 'dwellers in Sleepy Hollow'. He resented 'the ruthless closure with which outraged orthodoxy, entrenched and dominant, cuts short free speech', the prying curiosity of his rural neighbors, and their unwillingness to tolerate 'any appearance of "reforming" customs, usages, conditions'. Life in London, on the other hand, was propelled by 'the energising principle, creating now good and now evil', but providing in any case the freedom to think and act without which the greatest goodness could never be attained.[39]

In Germany, although urbanization had failed to bring about all the reforms anticipated earlier by pre-Bismarckian liberals, there was a strong residual attachment to the belief that the growth of the city and the growth of freedom went hand in hand. Werner Sombart, the noted economist and economic historian, wrote about the emancipatory function of the big city in words that far transcended the realms of trade and production. He argued that what attracted the migrant to the metropolis even more than the prospect of material advantage was the possibility of leading his whole life as he pleased. 'The freedom that earlier resided on the mountains', he wrote, 'has today moved into the cities, and the masses follow after it.... It is above all the freedom of personality in the broadest sense that appears to be attractive; negatively expressed, liberation from the bonds of clan, of neighborhood, and of class domination'. Heinrich Waentig, another economist, wrote that the medieval saying that 'city air makes free' (*Stadtluft macht frei*) still applied to the big city of modern times. Men and women had come there, Waentig asserted in language almost identical to Sombart's, not just because of economic motives but also because of a longing for individual liberty, for discovery of their own personalities, and for 'independence from clan, neighborhood, and authority'. They had found these desiderata and more, including a large measure of equality. To be sure, the city still suffered from sharp conflicts among classes, but 'the old rural differences among social estates' were disappearing under the influence of the large town. 'Large numbers suppress them', he wrote, 'and imperceptibly the new mobile elites of intellect, money, and labor supersede the old aristocracy of birth'.[40]

Johannes Tews, a progressive pedagogue, came to quite similar conclusions a few years later from a rather different standpoint, via an extensive discussion of urban education. Unlike other commentators on the problems of big-city youth, such as Reginald Bray in Britain and Jane Addams in America, Tews accentuated the benefits rather than the harm that flowed from the urban environment. Among the ways in which the city helped make young urbanites better people, he emphasized the impulses it generated in the direction of freedom and equality. 'The big city', he asserted, 'gives the capable personality the freedom that is theoretically granted to the individual everywhere but in reality denied to the socially disadvantaged in the village and the small town'. Moreover, the city street inculcated the values of democracy. 'Here', Tews observed, 'the child learns to recognize equal rights.... He himself steps on to the pavement as a full-fledged member of the great community of pedestrians'. Elegantly dressed men and women whom he might pass on this stage counted for no more in his eyes than ordinary workers in their blue shirts, and the deference toward one's supposed betters that characterized most residents of small communities had little chance to take root. From their very early years, in Tews' view, urban children were continually taught that they lived in a much more open and fluid world than the one their parents had left behind.[41]

American authors, living in a country where the grip of the past had never been as tight and the separate rungs on the social ladder had never been as clearly defined as in Europe, had less reason than others to praise the city as a stimulus to liberalism and democracy. For many of them, the emancipatory role the city seemed to have played in the old world had been taken over in the new one by the frontier. Nonetheless, American progressives still looked back warmly at the urban past, commending the cities for their part on the great stage of world history. After surveying the political impact of town growth in Europe since the Middle Ages, the liberal journalist (and former mayor of Toledo) Brand Whitlock wrote, 'Thus the cities have ever been in advance. In them the great battles of liberty on the intellectual and political, the social and industrial field have been fought. In them the fierce mobs have poured forth, and flung up the barricade to shelter liberty'. Implicitly comparing the possibilities of urban life in the present with those now available in the countryside, he added, 'It [the city] is the expression of man's determination to free himself from the slavery of obdurate isolation, and from the thralldom of primitive fears, the symbol of his Titanic effort to conquer nature, to rise above the merely physical, and to release the spirit to higher flights'. In Whitlock's view, urbanization reflected 'the irresistible urge of democracy', and all attempts to throttle it were rightly doomed to fail.[42]

Whitlock, like Zola, Cowen and Sombart, advocated a classically liberal view of urban civilization as a force that liberated men from bondage — bondage to the past and bondage to other men. In a manner reminiscent of the arguments employed by such earlier liberals as Robert Vaughan and Carl Welcker, they welcomed the city as their ally in the struggle to weaken the bastions of tradition and privilege. Much of what the conservatives regarded as proof of social fragmentation was exalted by these urban progressives as evidence of individual fulfillment. The city, it seemed, offered the prospect of personal freedom and personal dignity to all those who wished to pursue it. Liberal individualism admittedly exerted less influence during these years than it had in the 1840s, but it remained very much alive, and its exponents still found much to praise in the modern city.

The city's champions, ever mindful of the charge by anti-urbanists that freedom to be oneself could quickly degenerate into license to live selfishly and wickedly, hastened to add that the urban milieu nourished not only liberty but also the true spirit of community. Life in towns, they argued, did not simply produce isolated individuals. Instead, it brought people into contact with one another. It also generated voluntary cooperation in the pursuit of objectives that benefited both the individual and the collectivity. The hallmark of urban society was not only personal freedom but also free association. Many of the defenders deeply believed that free men and women, living in areas where the division of labor compelled them to cooperate in their work, had built and would continue to build a complex network of new social and political as well as economic structures. These structures seemed in many ways, moreover, to foster far stronger bonds and to provide far greater advantages than the ones that had supposedly been left behind in the beloved *Gemeinschaft* of the agrarians and other traditionalists.

In England, one William Harris articulated this outlook in a lecture delivered in Birmingham in the early 1880s, when memories of the exemplary strides forward during the preceding decade under the bold leadership of Joseph Chamberlain were still fresh in men's minds. In Harris' view, the rise of cities not only conferred benefits on individuals but also imposed duties, duties that city dwellers had recognized and at least partially fulfilled ever since the first cities had been founded. The effect of city life from the outset had been 'to broaden the bases of morality — merging the idea of kinship into the wider and less personal one of citizenship', and it had 'almost infinitely increased the occasions on which self had to be subordinated, and the claims and the rights of others had to be recognised.'[43]

S. A. Barnett, widely known as the first warden of Toynbee Hall in East London, voiced a quite exalted view of the city as a potential if not an actual community in his pamphlet *The Ideal City*, which he published shortly after becoming Canon of Bristol Cathedral in 1893. He rejected the pessimism of the anti-urbanists. 'They forget', he wrote, 'that the highest possible life for men may be a city life'. Justifying the city in religious as well as secular terms, he asserted confidently,

> We are on the line of progress as we gather in from the country districts, and by common action build up a common home. The activities of the street, of the shop, and of the town meeting, are for many characters the best preparation for life in the City of God. We have as our neighbours in a city, not the trees and the beasts, but fellow human beings. We can from them learn greater lessons, and with them do greater deeds. We can become more human.

In Barnett's view, although the city of the present was still plagued by many ills, it bore the seeds of cooperation, which augured exceedingly well for the future of urban society.[44]

Many Germans expressed such views, indicating an especially vivid sense in their country of the city dweller as a real or potential participant in and beneficiary of communal endeavor. Although Protestant clergymen frequently voiced deep misgivings about the city, some praised it, primarily for its tendency to encourage cooperation. Reinhold Seeberg, a professor of theology in Berlin, welcomed not only the urban movement away from small-minded arrogance and groveling servility but also the 'educational awareness of being a member of a large community ... of togetherness and unity'. Residents of big cities, he argued, were inclined 'to make common cause with others, to establish associations and pursue their goals by organizing their energies'. Georg Koch, another clergyman, compared the urban worker with the farm laborer, much to the detriment of the latter. The typical inhabitants of towns were more idealistic, more progressive, and more generous than their counterparts in the country. 'Here [in the city]', he asserted, 'brother-hood, the capacity for devotion and for great sacrifice, and "solidarity" therefore flourish'. Koch recognized that all of this helped to foster socialism, on which he looked askance, but in and of itself the feeling of solidarity with one's fellow man was still to be welcomed as a basic benefit that stemmed from urban living. The pedagogical writer, Johannes Tews, observed that 'those who live close to one another become more aware than those who live alone of the blessings conferred by the community'. The big city educated men to be 'conscious supporters of the common good', nourishing in their minds 'the thought of general well-being'. Otto Karstädt, another education-ist, wrote that 'the big city embodies to a quite different degree than do the small city and the village the tendency toward subordination beneath the general will.... Self-centered egoism ... is nowhere so quickly and so permanently suppressed as in the urban milieu'.[45]

One can detect similar sentiments in some poetry. The naturalist Karl Bröger praised the city lyrically in his poem 'Unsere Heimat', which began and ended as follows:

> We all call you mother, O city,
> You who have raised us up since birth.
>   ...
> You give us no peace, you wear us down,
> And yet you make us free and strong.
> Because you point us toward each other,
> You nourish in all a common bond.
> You raise us to a higher level
> And create among us brotherhood.
> And thus we love you, our great city,
> You who have raised us up since birth.

While Bröger by no means overlooked the city's destructiveness, he emphatically celebrated the communal bonds that grew in strength as a result of the interdependence that forced urbanites inexorably to work and live with one another.[46]

Analysts and advocates of urban society in America depicted the city in much the same light. For them, as for their counterparts in Britain and in Germany, the city served not only to concentrate large numbers of men and women but also to unite many if not all of them in the pursuit of order and justice, fostering all sorts of social solidarity among the individuals who inhabited it. Adna Weber emphasized that city life offered numerous opportunities for virtue as well as vice. 'Every day', he wrote, 'the city witnesses the performance not merely of acts of generosity and self-denial, but of heroic self-sacrifice'. Policemen, firemen, and contributors to charitable organizations all worked selflessly to advance the common welfare, and many of the nameless poor did their part by performing 'the thousand and one generous acts of service ... for the relief of the unfortunate in their midst'. Precisely because the cities displayed the worst abuses that had resulted from industrialization, they also summoned forth the best in the way of humanitarianism. 'Men cannot live long in close contact', he observed, 'without acquiring a painful sense of the separateness of individual interests, of the absurdity of identifying the individual's interest with the interest of society and the consequent policy of *laissez-faire*'. In short, the city made it both easy and necessary for men to help one another.[47]

A young urban sociologist, Howard B. Woolston, made much the same point a decade and a half later in an interpretive essay on 'the urban habit of mind'. Woolston regarded the city as a primary agent in the whole process of socialization in the modern world. It was the city that best fitted men to live and work together. Woolston emphasized the ennobling sublimity of the experience that urban men underwent as they mixed and interacted.

> Merely mingling with the crowd that passes along the thoroughfares gives a man a different idea of his personality. He feels both less and greater than when alone — less, in so far as his individual powers are overshadowed by the throng about him — greater, in that he derives a sense of strength from the presence and co-operation of his fellows.... He has caught a glimpse of a larger self realized in the activities of those about him. He recognizes the city as more than a place, a corporation, or a political unit. To him it is a spiritual unity, a unity not yet complete, but growing, enlarging, and striving for the realization of an adjusted order in which all men may share.

Woolston focused here on the quality of consciousness — on the ways in which individuals perceived themselves in relation to a larger totality. But, he suggested, their sentiments in the aggregate constituted a moral fact of great weight. They testified and contributed to powerful bonds that united all urbanites who felt their force.[48]

Affirmation of the city as an agent and an exemplar of both individual and collective rectitude marked the highest level of enthusiasm for urban life. Social morality was the goal toward which urban commerce, industry, intellect, and even art were all leading in the eyes of the city's strongest defenders. To be sure, hard work in and of itself was a virtue, and heightened consciousness possessed real value in its own right. But it was only when men's efforts and their desires could be seen as contributing not only to freedom but also to cooperative pursuit of the common good that the case for the defense was conceptually complete. To assert, however, that it was complete in this sense is not to assert that the urban advocates had no more to say. The general belief that town life fostered cooperation was paralleled and substantiated in a whole host of writings in which evidence of urban progress as a result of common endeavor was proudly hailed by men and women who had studied it in great detail — and in some cases had helped to make it happen. We turn to their views in the next chapter.

9

The Sense of Communal Achievement

Many observers of the urban scene around the turn of the century derived deep satisfaction from and took personal pride in what they regarded as an impressive and heartening record of urban improvement. They were struck not only by problems but also by progress. The affirmative attitude toward city life that was voiced in general terms by the defenders of the urban economy, of urban culture, and of urban morals found concrete expression in increasingly confident as well as numerous celebrations of communal achievement at the local level. The feeling that in some if not all respects the quality of urban life had changed and would continue to change for the better as a result of the purposeful mobilization of urban resources was voiced repeatedly and loudly by men and women who believed fervently in the virtues and the benefits of big cities. They warmly welcomed the efforts of those who sought to ameliorate the cities' drawbacks, and they frequently asserted that such strivings were making more and more headway in their own time. It was the identification and the recounting of such advances — occasionally lyrical but more often both precise and sober — that constituted the most widespread and effective counterweight to the chorus of anti-urban criticism.

Many of the writers who articulated this view most fully and forcefully had participated in some if not all of the developments about which they wrote. Others were employed in some capacity by the institutions whose achievements they were celebrating. This body of writing clearly contained a large element of self-congratulation by progressive urban reformers and administrators. But similar sentiments also appeared in many writings by men and women who had no direct stake in the public reputation of the efforts and achievements they saw fit to celebrate. Their comments indicated a quite broadly based — though by no means universal — sense that urban ills were indeed being effectively combated.

In so far as they tried to bring about further change, these men and women necessarily called their readers' attention to persisting urban troubles, but their outlook was fundamentally hopeful. Many — some of whom we encountered above in Part Two — were quite appalled by the threats to bodily and moral health and to social and political stability that seemed to emanate from the urban environment. Their awareness of these dangers was, however, coupled with a strong belief in the existing as well as the potential advantages of city life. They increasingly exuded a spirit of self-assured optimism. In their view, countervailing forces already at work within the urban centers had done and would continue to do an enormous amount to redeem the cities to whose further betterment they were deeply committed.

They tended to focus in great detail on particular places and corporate groups in whose histories urban communalism seemed to have manifested itself most clearly and most beneficently. Far more readily apparent in Britain, Germany, and the United States than in France, this form of urban pride came to the surface with particular reference to London and Glasgow, Berlin and Frankfurt, and New York and Chicago — and a host of lesser cities as well — rather than to the city as a general type. Two sorts of institutions bulked largest in the consciousness of these urbanites: those that had originated from voluntary cooperation and those that operated under the aegis of municipal governments. Each type of urban endeavor will be considered in turn, primarily through the eyes of those contemporary observers who held it up for public scrutiny and admiration.

New forms of urban voluntarism and their champions

The belief in the reality and the efficacy of urban voluntarism had roots that reached well back into the earlier part of the nineteenth century. Robert Vaughan, writing in the 1840s, had commended the inhabitants of large towns for sustaining 'those voluntary combinations of the virtuous in the cause of purity, humanity, and general improvement, which hold so conspicuous a place in our social history'. But the evidence of such sentiments became noticeably more widespread after about 1890, and it remained highly visible throughout the years leading up to the First World War. By this time, enough efforts to combat urban poverty and social pathology were under way so that many urban critics as well as others could point with considerable satisfaction to a great deal of good work of the sort Vaughan had had in mind more than half a century earlier. Urban voluntarism figured much more prominently in the thinking of Englishmen and Americans than it did in the perceptions of continental Europeans. The traditions of religious pluralism and political liberalism produced in Britain and the United States a milieu that was far more conducive to private charity than the one that existed in Germany and France.[1] Numerous observers in the Anglo-Saxon world therefore had good reason to laud heartily the private attempts by groups of concerned individuals to improve the lives of their fellow urbanites, focusing their attention primarily on the charitable efforts of churchmen and other social workers to spread salvation and to build social settlements in urban slums.

One sort of voluntary effort to remedy urban ills that attracted much attention was the Salvation Army. Begun in 1865 by William Booth, a Methodist minister, as the East London Revival Society and shortly thereafter renamed the Christian Mission, the movement received its present name in 1878. By the mid-1890s, there were sixteen 'corps', or congregations, in the slums of London and a dozen more in other English cities. Having crossed the Atlantic in 1880, the movement spread still more rapidly in the United States, where, by 1900, there were over 700 corps, staffed by 3,000 urban missionaries and other 'officers'. Booth and the members of his brigades waged their war against the forces of urban darkness at the lowest levels of the social hierarchy. They sought to rescue a multitude of individuals whom Booth saw as comparable in their spiritual and social degradation to the stunted and dwarfish denizens of an African jungle. Offering soup, shelter, and songs as well as the lure of a uniform and the hope of salvation, the Army directed its appeal with growing success at the poorest of the poor and the lowest of the low. Its soldiers sought to effect moral rehabilitation within a stable institutional environment, ministering both to the physical and to the spiritual needs of the many thousands of destitute and fallen urbanites whom they attracted to their banner.[2]

The founding father's daughter-in-law, having emigrated with her husband in 1886 to take charge of the Army's work in the United States, defined the Army's self-image succinctly for a rather wider audience than the one reached by its official organ, *The War Cry*. In an article written for *Scribner's Magazine* in 1894, Maud Ballington Booth pointed proudly to the hundreds of thousands of 'street loungers, drunkards, wife-beaters, wild, reckless youths, and fallen women' who had flocked to the Army's halls both in England and in America. The members of the Army's Slum Brigades had successfully reached out to the urban poor — well before the founding of Toynbee Hall and other college settlements — 'with the neighborly interest and affection that can only be acceptable when given by those who breathe the same atmosphere and live in the same surroundings'. Through the performance of 'kindly offices', such as caring for children, nursing the sick, and stepping in as peace-makers in drunken brawls, they had won the trust and devotion of numerous slum dwellers who had been totally ignored by respectable society. Booth referred glowingly to the 'brave heroism and love' displayed by the Army's soldiers through their toil and suffering, and she concluded on the following note of confident hope: 'As the gnarled and ungainly oyster-shells from the mud and ooze of the sea-bottom are forced to yield up to the earnest seeker their precious pearls, so from the midst of the darkness and degradation of the slums purified and precious gems will be gathered, and those who toiled and found shall be among the "blessed" and the rich of heaven'. The Army's soldiers were to receive a heavenly reward for the good work they had done on earth in redeeming the city of man from the forces of darkness, acting as exemplars of neighborly helpfulness and as models for their fellow citizens. In the meantime, they clearly deserved the admiration and gratitude of all right-thinking people.[3]

The manifest self-righteousness that was essential to the Army's crusading fervor made the organization an inviting target for satiric barbs of the sort directed against it by George Bernard Shaw in his play *Major Barbara* (first performed in 1905), but Shaw's distrust hardly typified the views of most middle-class reformers. Many of them voiced a growing measure of admiration for what the Army was doing, frequently pairing it with the settlement movement as one of the two most significant attempts then under way to apply the principles of Christianity to the problems of the big city. For Walter Besant, a prolific novelist and popular historian, the Army was one of 'two forces now acting upon the mass of the people which seem to promise the most powerful influence upon the future'. It was not so much what the Army had done in the way of religious work that impressed Besant as its contribution in the area of social work. Numerous representatives from the 'lower levels' of the East London population had benefited enormously from conditions in the Army's efficiently run lodging houses and workshops and in its agricultural colony outside the city limits. Enabling men and women who had sunk into despair to feel pride and self-respect, hope and a new sense of purpose, was 'a great and noble work', which elevated the giver of aid as well as its recipient. As Besant put it, 'The twopenny doss-house, the refuge, the home, the rescue, the colony — do they not also raise and rescue and strengthen the people who administer and direct them?' H. Rider Haggard was another Englishman whose many novels and other books reached an even larger audience and whose views of the Army were just as sympathetic. In a book titled *Regeneration*, he recounted the good works being performed by Booth and his followers in London, Liverpool, Manchester, and Glasgow. In his view, other charities also deserved commendation, but the Army's colossal scale made it unique. 'Its fertilizing stream', he wrote, 'flows on steadily from land to land, till it bids fair to irrigate the whole earth'.[4]

American clergymen lauded the Army in much the same way. Charles Stelzle, the superintendent of the labor department in the national Board of Home Missions of the Presbyterian Church in the United States, emphasized the Army officers' keen understanding of human nature, their fearlessness, and their sympathy for men and women who suffered privations that many of the officers had experienced directly in their own lives. It was the way in which the Army made use of 'waste bits of humanity' as well as of industrial

18   A Salvation Army shelter in East London. Joseph Pennell's drawing depicts a place where members of the urban under-class could obtain cheap food and lodging and free advice and encouragement (source: Walter Besant, *East London* [New York, 1901], 232).

wastes, turning 'the driftwood of the city slums' into social servants, that most impressed Charles Sears, general secretary of the New York City Baptist Mission Society. In his view, elevating the poor to a point where they could participate actively in the elevation of others was a markedly more impressive achievement than simply making use of idealistic graduates from colleges and universities.[5]

Although none of these men participated directly in the Army's affairs, they all expressed deep admiration for what they regarded as an inspiring and highly successful effort to gather the poor beneath a communal banner of respectability as a way of helping them to escape from rootlessness and degradation. In their eyes, the Army's hundreds of corps unquestionably augmented in a most impressive manner 'the forces in the redemption of the city' that were working to overcome urban anomie and disorder. We still have very little in the way of substantial scholarship by disinterested historians that would enable us to judge the validity of this view fairly, but it is clear from the comments of numerous contemporaries that the Army was making a sizable effort to help at least some of the urban lower classes.

Frequently paired with the Army, the settlement house enjoyed much more popularity among members of the educated middle classes. The settlement house ideal originated and first bore fruit in England, in large measure as an outgrowth of Christian and Ruskinian socialism. Revulsion from the class conflicts, the squalor, and the moral ugliness endemic in industrial cities had led Frederick Denison Maurice, a Unitarian turned Anglican theologian, to open a Working Men's College in London in 1854. He and John Ruskin, among others, sought there to combat urban degradation by means of popular education. Ruskin later exerted a powerful influence on two young men from prosperous families, Edward Denison and Arnold Toynbee. Both subsequently took up residence in East London in order to live among, learn about, and provide assistance to the denizens of that area. Both died at an early age, in part as a result of health problems that were exacerbated by the slum environments in which they had chosen to live. The striving for close personal contact with the poor that characterized the brief lives of Denison and Toynbee served as an example and an inspiration to Samuel Augustus Barnett, an Anglican clergyman who knew Toynbee well. Shortly after marrying Henrietta Rowland, a co-worker with Octavia Hill in the Charity Organization Society, Barnett had, in 1873, become the vicar of St. Jude's, Whitechapel. Here, in a parish labeled by its bishop 'the worst in the diocese, inhabited mainly by a criminal population', Barnett considerably deepened his own familiarity with the plight of the East London poor. Beginning in 1875, he paid periodic visits to Oxford, where Toynbee introduced him to an idealistic group of undergraduates who wanted to advance the cause of social reform.[6]

Barnett's efforts entered a new phase in the 1880s. Shortly after Toynbee's death, in the same year that witnessed the appearance of Andrew Mearns' *Bitter Cry of Outcast London*, Barnett gave talks at Cambridge as well as Oxford in which he urged his listeners to live and work with him among the urban poor. He offered a vision of a new mode of reformist activism that would go beyond both 'scientific charity' and the work of a 'college mission'. The settlement, as Barnett expressed it, was to provide 'common ground for all classes', offering a place where 'at the weekly receptions of "all sorts and conditions of men" the residents would mingle freely with the crowd'. Both by helping to spread culture among those who lacked it and by learning for themselves at first hand about the neediest of their fellow citizens, representatives from the upper classes would work directly to overcome 'the division of classes' and 'poverty in its true sense, including poverty of the knowledge of God and man'.[7] Late in 1884, more than a dozen young men moved into a new building in Whitechapel, constructed with money raised through charitable donations. Named Toynbee Hall and administered by the Barnetts, it marked the start of a settlement movement that was to become increasingly conspicuous in urban slums on both sides of the Atlantic during the next three decades.

By the mid-1890s, Barnett and others who had lent their support to his efforts through their own contributions to settlement work were looking back with quiet pride at the good they had done and forward with unmistakable confidence to further progress in the future. In 'A Retrospect of Toynbee Hall', published in *The Nineteenth Century*, Barnett celebrated his own settlement and more than a dozen others founded by kindred spirits elsewhere in London, in Glasgow, in Bristol, in Manchester, and in Edinburgh, as heartening evidence of the 'growth of the human spirit'. Men and women active in such institutions had risen above 'old forms of benevolence ... patronising in character' in order 'to assert their fellowship with the poor'. Visitors to Toynbee Hall could see classrooms that served over 1,000 adult students, who took evening courses in English and foreign literature, science, and economics, among numerous other subjects. The lectures and discussions they attended aimed 'at adding joy to life rather than ... pence to wages'. Beyond serving as a center of intellectual advancement, Toynbee Hall had served as a neighborhood club house and as a home base for individual residents who participated in various civic undertakings in the larger community around them. 'The men live their own life in Whitechapel instead of in West London', Barnett wrote, 'and do — what is required of every citizen — a citizen's duty in their own neighbourhood'. Their participatory energies strengthened by their association with one another, the men who lived at Toynbee Hall had looked and continued to look outward rather than inward, forging close ties to those below them as well as to their university-trained peers.[8]

Among Toynbee Hall's greatest virtues, in Barnett's view, was that such efforts on the part of its inhabitants had tended to mitigate suspicion and conflict between social classes.

At first men have met their neighbours as members of a committee; they have, perhaps, taken part in the administration of relief, or joined in a game at a club, or spoken in a debate. They have made acquaintance naturally on an equal footing, and in some cases acquaintance has ripened into friendship. Two men born in different circumstances, educated by different means, occupied in different work, have in such meeting felt themselves akin. They have become friends and sharers in each other's strength.... Poor men have seen that rich are not what they are pictured by orators, and the rich have found that the poor have virtues not always expressed by their language.

Barnett acknowledged the absurdity of expecting twenty men to make much of a mark on the opinions of the great mass of the East London population, but he remained convinced that their settlement had brought about 'an increase of good-will' worthy of note if only because it augured well for the prospects of others who might choose to follow their example.[9]

Barnett's philanthropic and educational efforts in East London and those of his fellow settlement workers there and elsewhere received enthusiastic accolades from numerous Englishmen who viewed the existing city critically but saw places such as Toynbee Hall as clear evidence of an incipient civic revival. Sir John Gorst, a Tory M.P. of liberal persuasion who had known the Barnetts for some time and was later to reside with them during sessions of Parliament, gave a rectorial address at the University of Glasgow in 1894 in which he praised settlements on several counts. At one level, he saw the men and women who lived and worked there as combatants against the danger of social and political upheaval. 'The instinct of self-preservation should', he wrote, 'make society grateful to anybody who will spend his life in gaining the confidence of the masses and guiding their ideas into channels in which the common good of all is the prevailing influence'. But the essential motive that he discerned was religious: 'the revival, as a real force for the guidance of human life, of the doctrines taught by Jesus Christ and practised by the Christians of the first century'. In any event, Gorst regarded the cultivation of friendly relations with urban workers as far and away the best method for the privileged few to study urban poverty and to devise remedies for overcoming it.[10]

Others in Britain reiterated such views in later years. Walter Besant, whose *All Sorts and Conditions of Men* (1882) had rendered in fiction a Palace of Delight that served many of the functions later to be performed by university settlements, gave such places his unstinting praise shortly before the turn of the century. Settlement workers helped to spread 'the life of culture' among urban workers through personal example as well as by teaching. Among the most valuable examples they set was that of participating in local government. Accustomed by life in the settlement itself to 'the surrender of self-will and of will worship' (a phrase Besant borrowed from Barnett), they served quietly but effectively as Poor Law guardians and as vestrymen, as members of school boards and as school visitors. In so doing, they inspired every branch of local government with 'the sense of duty and of principle' and simultaneously taught this duty to their fellow citizens. When one considered in addition that the settlements reduced class suspicion and provided wholesome recreation, they appeared all the more clearly as 'lamps in a dark place', which spread their light throughout the gloom by which they were surrounded. Victor Branford, a sociologist and a disciple of Patrick Geddes, waxed equally eloquent a decade and a half later when he described settlements as an expression of 'the common sense of fellowship between student and citizen'. They represented in his view an effort to awaken a sense of urban community reminiscent of medieval cities, and they betokened 'widespread recognition of the policy and possibility of civic revival implicit in their personal and humane adventure'. For all of these men, the movement symbolized by Toynbee Hall had vastly improved the quality of life in the neighborhoods where it had taken root, and it held out the promise of continuing betterment in the future.[11]

The force of Barnett's example reached far beyond Great Britain. Already during the late 1880s, Toynbee Hall had attracted the attention of many reformers in the United States, several of whom visited Barnett in order to profit from his experience and to prepare their own plans for establishing similar settlements at home. Stanton Coit, an idealistic graduate of Amherst College with a Ph.D. from the University of Berlin, spent three months at Toynbee Hall in 1886 and then organized the Neighborhood Guild on the Lower East Side of New York City shortly after returning to his native country. Here, he hoped to lay the foundations for a civic renaissance that would spread throughout America. Coit, together with other intellectuals and idealists of diverse backgrounds and outlooks, quickly began to make a perceptible mark on the cultural life of the area in which he took up residence, but after he moved to England in 1887 it soon became apparent that the Neighborhood Guild would not fulfill its founder's grandiose expectations. Nonetheless, the settlement idea rapidly took hold among men and women elsewhere in New York and in many other cities as well. By 1900, America had produced over 100 settlement houses, and by 1910 their number was to exceed 400, nearly ten times as many as existed at that point in Britain. A movement that had originated in the slums of East London flourished across the Atlantic on a far more impressive scale than it ever attained in the country where it began, and consequently it generated much more in the way of proud reflection and laudatory comment.[12]

Far and away the most influential of the exponents of the settlement house idea in the United States was Jane Addams, the daughter of a prosperous manufacturer and landowner in northern Illinois. Having already decided that she wished to do something to improve the lot of the poor, she visited Toynbee Hall in 1888. After returning to Illinois, she and a college class-mate, Ellen Gates Starr, moved in 1889 — only a few days after a group of women from Smith College had established the College Settlement near the Neighborhood Guild in New York — into a mansion in Chicago. The settlement they began, later known as Hull House, was to become famous among social reformers everywhere in the English-speaking world during years to come. Addams' stature as an effective friend of the urban poor fully equaled Barnett's, and the name of the place in which her efforts had begun became an internationally known byword for ameliorative action by educated men and women in deprived and depressed neighborhoods.[13]

Addams inspired many other women to join her in her efforts not only through personal example and contact but also through her publications, writing several books on social problems and on the ways in which settlement work could help to solve them. She wrote with great sensitivity about the threats to social well-being that abounded in the cities she knew — especially among immigrants and among young people.[14] No other American surpassed either her intensity or her insight as a critic of certain aspects of city life. But there was another, much more positive side to her perception of the urban scene: a forward-looking belief in the efficacy of organized goodwill of the sort displayed at her own settlement. This conviction found its classic expression in her best and most popular book, *Twenty Years at Hull House* (1910).

Addams portrayed the settlement movement as in part an outgrowth of a 'subjective necessity' felt by large numbers of cultivated young people who lacked a sense of meaningful purpose in their own lives — a need to do something socially useful in a world that suffered from obviously painful maladjustments. Addams put her finger on a source of social activism that was especially compelling for members of her own sex, many of whom felt an obligation to demonstrate through good deeds for other human beings that their college education had served a socially useful purpose. This personal motivation had been reinforced, in Addams' view, by broader currents of changing opinion in society at large: by a growing desire to extend the principle of democracy and by newer tendencies in the area of Christian social ethics. 'The Settlement movement', she observed, 'is only one manifestation of that wider humanitarian movement which throughout Christendom, but preeminently in England, is endeavoring to embody itself, not in a sect, but in society'.[15]

The object of Hull House had been 'to provide a center for a higher civic and social life, to institute and maintain educational and philanthropic enterprises, and to investigate and improve the conditions in the industrial districts of Chicago'.[16] Addams and her fellow workers had sought to develop the existing social life of their neighborhood, focusing it and giving it form and bringing to bear upon it 'the results of cultivation and training'. Toward these ends, they had undertaken a whole host of projects within or near Hull House itself. Beginning with young children, they had organized a kindergarten, but they had insisted equally on the importance of providing opportunities for education and fellowship to grown people too, ministering to 'the deep-seated craving for social intercourse that all men feel'. They had performed such humble tasks as washing new-born babies, preparing the dead for burial, and nursing the sick in order to establish links with battered and oppressed as well as with more comfortable members of Chicago's working class. The adults who came within their sphere of influence had benefited not only from such kindly services but also from enlightenment about other urban institutions with which they had to deal (Addams described the settlement at one point as 'an information and interpretation bureau') and from classes in home-making and the various trades. In addition to such instruction, there were the college extension courses taught by faculty members from the University of Chicago and the literary, dramatic, and debating clubs. All of these, she believed, reflected and nourished a powerful desire for intellectual self-improvement among working men and women. Other clubs to which Hull House had given a home had pursued philanthropic objectives, while still others had been primarily social and recreational, but in Addams' view they had all worked effectively against urban disorganization and anomie. These and other activities with which Hull House had been associated led Addams to conclude hopefully that it now seemed 'impossible to set any bounds to the moral capabilities which might unfold under ideal civic and educational conditions'. Pride in the history of Hull House clearly strengthened Addams' confidence in the future of the city in which it had evolved and in the future of other cities as well.[17]

As in England, settlements held a special appeal for socially conscious Protestant clergymen, one of whom, William Jewett Tucker of Andover Theological Seminary, sent a young social worker by the name of Robert Woods to Britain to observe a variety of social movements in 1890. Woods spent six months at Toynbee Hall, making several short visits afterwards to other cities in England and Scotland. Having collected enough material for a book on what he had seen, which naturally included a laudatory chapter on university settlements, he returned to become head of Andover House in Boston, which Tucker founded in 1891. Renamed South End House in 1895, it remained under Woods' direction until his death in 1925. A center of clubs for boys and of various educational activities for adults from the outset, it became one of the most fruitful centers of social study anywhere in the United States, and the men associated with it helped Woods to become a significant contributor to sociological research. South End House was also a laboratory for experimentation in the area of social work — a place where, as at Hull House, representatives from the educated middle classes came to live among urban workers with a view to devising new and better ways of helping them to cope effectively with the burdens imposed by the urban environment.[18]

Woods tirelessly championed the settlement idea, both in Boston and more generally in the United States, not only through his organizational efforts but also through his numerous lectures, articles, and books. As a lecturer in social ethics, first at Andover Theological Seminary between 1890 and 1895 and then at the nearby Episcopal Theological School between 1896 and 1914, and also as the organizer of the National Federation of Settlements (established in 1911), he was well placed to propagate both specific and general perceptions of what the movement was doing.[19] The pioneering collaborative study which he edited in 1898, *The City Wilderness*, included not only several contributions that emphasized the bleakness suggested by the book's title but also an essay by Woods himself on 'Social Recovery'. Here, Woods pointed to South End House, Denison House (for women), and several other Boston settlements as places that were successfully developing 'simple neighborly relations with people'. Woods placed much more weight than did Addams on serving the needs of rather small populations living in the immediate vicinity of the settlements themselves — in the case of South End House, a territory covering no more than about ten city blocks. In his view, the real use of settlements in the contemporary world was 'to reestablish on a natural basis those social relations which modern city life has thrown into confusion, and to develop such new forms of cooperation and public action as the changed situation may demand'. Toward this end, the settlement workers sought not only to strengthen family ties but also 'to rehabilitate neighborhood life and give it some of that healthy corporate vitality which a well-ordered village has'.[20]

Subsequently, Woods reiterated and amplified this view again and again, with a deepening conviction that the objectives he sought were indeed being achieved. As he was to write in the early 1920s, progress had admittedly been slow, but if one calculated in terms of decades rather than of years the positive results attributable to South End House were clear and undeniable. Early in the settlement's third decade, clubs and classes had grown in number, a separate music school had opened its doors, and resident visitors had helped to collect savings, to organize summer vacations, and to strengthen the ties between homes and schools. During the war, settlement workers had performed a whole host of additional civic duties as well. Both in Boston and in many other American cities, the settlement, 'the most distinctive new social institution in an age of unparalleled discovery and invention', had pointed the way, through a growing circle of neighborhoods, toward 'the moral unity of mankind' and toward 'the millennium of the City of God'.[21]

American outsiders to the movement who looked with favor upon the settlement workers' strivings and achievements included socially conscious clergymen such as Charles Stelzle. In a survey of the forces then at work for urban betterment, he recalled the ideals of Maurice, Denison, and Barnett and the establishment of the Neighborhood Guild, the College Settlement, and Hull House. His survey included the following laudatory description of the spirit at work in the minds of these men and in the activities at these places, which he drew almost word for word (though without attribution) from *Twenty Years at Hull House*: 'It aims in a measure to lead whatever of social life its neighborhood may afford, to focus and give form to that life, to bring to bear upon it the results of cultivation and training; but it receives in exchange for the music of isolated voices the volume and strength of the chorus'. Charles Hatch Sears wrote in a similar vein a few years later. In his view, the settlement rested 'upon faith that the good is as communicable as the evil; that God has made lives responsive to each other; that heart responds to heart as chord to chord in a musical instrument; that there is a spiritual reciprocity growing out of contact of class with class, which produces mutual confidence and respect, and provides for the exchange of the best that the heart affords'.[22]

Men and women who inhabited and observed the settlements, like supporters of the Salvation Army, demonstrated and celebrated the efficacy of voluntary groups as vehicles for rectifying urban ills, thus maintaining a clear line of continuity with earlier nineteenth-century liberalism. The adequacy of this approach to the solution of social problems in general was increasingly open to question around the turn of the century, and nowadays we inevitably look somewhat askance at the claims made then by the leaders of voluntary movements and their sympathizers. How much of an impact on urban poverty and on the urban poor did the settlement workers really make? Did the leaders have a grossly inflated sense of their own importance, or did they articulate a feeling of achievement that was not only widespread but also legitimate? As in the case of the Army, one of the obstacles to answering these questions is that so much of what we think we know about the settlements comes to us from the accounts of settlement workers, the major exception being Allen Davis' work on the United States. Another difficulty, again as in the case of the Army, has to do with a certain ambiguity about just whose uplift was really intended and how it was to be effected. If the purpose was to provide direct benefits to urban workers, then in the overall scheme of things the movement's success was quite limited, especially in England. But in so far as it was to sensitize potentially influential members of the middle classes who lived in the settlements to the needs of their fellow urbanites — including needs that could not be met by the settlements themselves as well as those that could — they succeeded quite impressively.

Both in England and in America, life in the settlement houses stimulated men and women to advocate vigorous action by the institutions of government. Settlement workers devoted much of their energy to campaigns aimed at inducing elected authorities to shoulder a larger share of the urban burden, and much of their self-satisfaction stemmed from a well-founded belief that they had agitated to good effect. Jane Addams wrote proudly about having helped to improve the collection of refuse by becoming a garbage inspector and having seen to it that certain streets were properly paved for the first time, as well as about many other aspects of her involvement in civic affairs. 'So far', she wrote, 'as a Settlement can discern and bring to local consciousness neighborhood needs which are common needs, and can give vigorous help to the municipal measures through which such needs shall be met, it fulfills its most valuable function'. Woods had less to say about his own impact in the area of urban public policy and administration, but he clearly welcomed the expansion of municipal responsibility, recalling with quiet pride that residents at South End House had helped to bring about the establishment of their city's first public baths. Jacob Riis, a friendly and influential outsider, expressed his admiration for the tangible gains won by settlement workers in New York who had acted jointly for the public weal with their fellow citizens on the Lower East Side. Their support for civic reform had contributed to cleaner streets, more parks and playgrounds, and better housing, and he expressed his deep gratitude to 'these "crusaders" who came to help and ... wrought so well'. To use Allen Davis' phrase, all of these writers saw the settlements quite rightly as 'spearheads for reform', which were prodding public officials as well as setting an example for private individuals, and they enthusiastically welcomed any evidence of increased governmental responsiveness to such pressures.[23]

The record of municipal advance in Britain

The late nineteenth and early twentieth centuries witnessed a vast outpouring of books, pamphlets, and articles about matters pertaining to city government. These writings discussed the work that ought to be and was being undertaken by city governments in order to safeguard and enhance the well-being of their citizens. The subject of municipal reformism as a constellation of often conflicting proposals for new beginnings and further changes and of competing agendas for as yet unrealized improvements lies outside the scope of this study. It belongs more properly to historians of public policy, planning, and administration. What merits our attention in the present context is the way in which positive change at the local level was increasingly perceived by many observers as an undeniable fact of life in the experience of the big city. Whatever their misgivings with regard to the city's continuing problems and difficulties, numerous well informed and articulate men of affairs, in addition to social scientists and historians, were proudly proclaiming to their readers that town life had recently undergone a vast improvement. Especially in Britain, Germany, and the United States, where municipal services became much more highly developed than in France, they attributed this change for the better in no small measure to the achievements of local officials — men who had effectively used their political and administrative authority to pursue the common good in the places where they were employed. These men were seen as having made contributions to communal betterment that paralleled the ones made by groups such as the Salvation Army and the settlement workers but also extended far beyond them, leading to urban amelioration on a truly impressive scale for millions of other city dwellers. It was in celebrations of the good works emanating from the town hall, the city hall, and the *Rathaus* that the belief in urban progress through organization and cooperation found its clearest and most triumphant expression.

These writings were part and parcel of a larger movement of opinion in favor of positive steps by public authorities at every level to deal aggressively with social and economic problems that had formerly been left to individuals and to voluntary associations. They reflected not only the ongoing redefinition of liberalism at the hands of men such as T. H. Green and Leonard T. Hobhouse but also, in Germany, the updating of bureaucratic traditions inherited from an authoritarian past. Municipal reformers participated in a broadly based effort to make government more truly responsive to the social and economic needs of the governed. At the same time, many of them asserted during these years that in their cities this effort had already borne an abundance of impressive results.

In Britain, where the achievements of several municipalities had already received a good deal of favorable publicity in the 1850s, 1860s, and 1870s — one thinks above all of Manchester and Liverpool, of Leeds and Bradford, and especially of Birmingham — civic pride became ever more widespread as time went on. The conviction that town governments were demonstrating their ability to cope successfully with the urban challenge asserted itself more and more forcefully with each passing decade. Joseph Chamberlain, the mayor of Birmingham during its great period of civic transformation in the early 1870s, commented two decades later as a national politician that the growing importance of municipal institutions had been among the most remarkable features of British public life throughout the preceding half century. Seizing the opportunity offered by the Municipal Corporations Act of 1835, town councils had steadily enlarged their spheres of influence, granting new rights, imposing new duties, and assuming new obligations. 'The municipal corporation of one of our large towns today', he wrote, 'is in large measure responsible for the lives, the health, the education, the comfort and the happiness of the whole community'. City governments controlled the police and fire departments, managed drainage, sewage, and lighting, took care of streets, and in many cases regulated the construction of housing, established hospitals, provided baths, maintained libraries, museums, and schools, and supplied gas, water, and electricity. These activities revealed 'an intense sentiment of corporate energy and enterprise ... of the responsibility of citizenship', and they led Chamberlain to exclaim that 'the modern corporations bid fair to rival the fame of the medieval cities of Italy and Germany'.[24]

Writing at about the same point in time, a much less well known individual by the name of Frederick Dolman commented on recent developments at the level of local government in much the same spirit. In his *Municipalities at Work* (1895) — the very title of which clearly conveyed his sense of purposeful dynamism — he pointed to the recent achievements of town councils and the agencies over which they exercised supervisory authority as powerful illustrations of the Emersonian doctrine of 'compensation'. To be sure, migration from the country to the city did lead to dirt, disease, overcrowding, and crime, but the cause of such evils also worked to produce their cure. 'If the concentration of many people on a small area causes the conduct of everyone to be of concern to the whole', he observed, 'it also enables collective control to be exercised over the individual with little difficulty or expense'. It was the duty of the municipal authority 'to make the most of the power which the concentration of numbers places in its hands, in order that the evil arising from this concentration of numbers may be counterbalanced — and more than counterbalanced — by the good', and in Dolman's view this duty was being successfully performed by more and more public servants. Having begun in the 1830s and 1840s by focusing their attention on such elementary matters as the organization of police departments and the paving and lighting of streets, the newly formed municipal bodies had gone on to regulate sanitation and housing, to gain control of gas and water works, to provide baths and parks, and finally to establish libraries and art galleries. In short, town governments now cared just as much about culture as about cleanliness, and the pace at which they were moving forward suggested that in the future their efforts could well result in the elimination of all the worst ills that currently beset their inhabitants.[25]

Throughout this period, it was still the governments of Britain's northern cities that aroused the most enthusiasm among commentators on municipal affairs. There, as the perceptive journalist Thomas Escott put it, active citizenship had developed to a much higher degree than in the gigantic and amorphous capital. Free from the oppressive burden of vastness and possessing a keener sense than Londoners of the potential efficacy of their civic efforts, the inhabitants of the 'provincial capitals' displayed a participatory zeal that put the metropolis to shame.[26]

Among the large towns located in England, Birmingham continued to enjoy a quite special reputation. Manchester, Liverpool, Bradford, and Leeds each received a chapter at the hands of Frederick Dolman, and each was examined in more detail by others,[27] but the place that was now known as 'the Midland metropolis' still seemed to many observers around 1890 to be 'the best governed city in the world'. Charles Hibbs saw it as the quintessential community in which individual energies were 'leavened' with the civic pride that led men to work for the well-being of all and thereby to speed the progress of the nation. Dolman wrote admiringly, 'Municipal reformers look to Birmingham as the eyes of the faithful are turned to Mecca.... Birmingham was the first to initiate, in a broad and comprehensive spirit, the new regime of municipal socialism on which our hopes of improvement in the condition of large towns now so greatly depend'. Well over a decade later, a lecturer at the city university continued in the same vein, asserting that since Chamberlain's mayoralty the town's government had been maintained 'at a level of

19 A bird's eye view of Birmingham. The civic buildings come strongly to the fore against a background of busy industry (source: Edwin Hodder, *Cities of the World*, IV [ca. 1889], 41).

excellence which cannot be disputed'. The zeal, the ability, and the integrity of the men who ran the municipal administration reflected, he believed, a persistent spirit of unselfish devotion to the common good among many of Birmingham's most prominent citizens.[28]

Although the government of Birmingham continued to enjoy a high reputation both within and outside the city, it gradually ceded its pre-eminent position as the leader among progressive municipalities to Glasgow. Long known as 'the second city of the Empire' by virtue of the fact that its population was surpassed only by that of London, the Scottish metropolis emerged clearly in the late nineteenth century as the most important place to watch anywhere in Britain for those who cared about large-scale efforts at the local level to improve urban life. Whereas historians of Glasgow writing around 1880 had, when dealing with social progress, placed most of their emphasis on charitable activities, at the end of the decade another observer focused much of his attention on the 'innumerable proofs of its [the council's] high civic capacity'. These, he insisted, had earned the municipality 'great fame all over the English-speaking world for its strength, foresight, and courage'.[29]

In the mid-1890s, Garrett Fisher described Glasgow in the pages of the

20 The new municipal buildings in Glasgow. These buildings made manifest a high level of civic energy in the second largest city in Britain (source: Edwin Hodder, *Cities of the World*, 139).

influential *Fortnightly Review* as 'a model municipality'. Like Dolman, who depicted the city at about the same time in much the same way, Fisher regarded Glasgow as an exemplary center of municipal progress. He argued that it deserved in several respects to be regarded not as the second but instead as the first city of the British Empire. The Corporation of Glasgow had begun to emerge as a leader among city governments as early as the middle of the century, and it continued to play a pace-setting role in the present. The Corporation had been guided for several decades by an awareness of three basic duties: to administer the city's finances economically, to improve public health both physically and morally, and 'to give brightness and the possibility of happiness to civic life'. It had begun to pursue these ends vigorously as early as the mid-1850s by municipalizing the water supply, a step followed in 1869 by the takeover of two private gas companies. In 1894, Glasgow had established the first city-owned tram company, a move that resulted in better service, lower fares, and more income for the city government. Such enterprises had provided monetary resources that enabled the Corporation at the same time to lower the rates of local taxation and to improve city services in a wide range of areas beyond the realm of public utilities. Seven model lodging houses for the former inhabitants of slum dwellings that had been demolished under the auspices of the City Improvement Trust and the provision of a small number of working men's tenements demonstrated in Fisher's view at least an incipient commitment to the pursuit of better housing. A whole host of other measures, beginning with the establishment of the Glasgow Sanitary Department in 1863 and including the recruitment of an energetic army of health inspectors, the efficient management of sewage, and the building of five public baths in the most densely populated districts of the city, all showed that Glasgow was moving steadily to improve its citizenry's physical well-being. Moreover, the municipality had endowed the city with half a dozen parks, a fine art gallery, and several other museums, and it was constructing a People's Palace in order to encourage still further progress in the use of leisure time and thereby 'the brightening of civic life'.[30]

As in many other cities, the most exhaustive and the most adulatory celebrations of municipal activity in Glasgow were written by men who had participated actively in it. James Bell, a former Lord Provost, co-authored a survey of the Corporation in which he praised the work of its 10,000 officials and employees department by department. Owing to their endeavors, modern Glasgow had become 'a marvel of ingenious and bold engineering, a highly finished and complex machine'. The men who kept this machine in proper working order and labored to improve it displayed 'constant watchfulness and untiring zeal', and, in the case of the unpaid town councillors, a good deal of self-sacrifice as well. Two decades later, Bell's successor introduced another hefty volume of the same sort with a paean of praise to a developing 'civic spirit' that supposedly permeated all sections of the population. Ordinary citizens, he asserted, were 'proud of the greatness of their city' and strenuously supportive of those town councillors who advocated 'large and generous schemes of amelioration and increase of public amenity'.[31]

London around the turn of the century still lagged far behind the large towns of the north in the provision of public services, and the great bulk of writings about the capital focused on problems rather than progress, but at the same time there was some recognition that here too change for the better had been taking place. The positivist philosopher and publicist, Frederic Harrison, wrote approvingly that the passage of the Local Government Act of 1888 had given a powerful impulse to the movement toward 'organic unity' within the city's numerous boroughs. He pointed to a recent upsurge of 'local municipal patriotism' in boroughs such as Battersea, Chelsea, and St. George's in the East and voiced a confident expectation that eventually, as in northern towns, there would emerge throughout the whole city 'the spirit of pride and attachment which the great cities of the Middle Ages bred in their citizens of old'. Despite continuing reluctance by the recently established County Council to impose new financial burdens on ratepayers, the metropo-

lis had already done much to earn such affection — opening parks, building
fire stations, and combating disease, among other worthy endeavors — and
the prospects for the future seemed decidedly bright. 'The civic patriotism of
London has lain dormant for centuries, but in our generation it is reviving',
he wrote. 'And we may hope that ere the twentieth century is far advanced, it
may create a new London worthy of its past history and its vast
opportunities'.[32]

Two decades later, Laurence Gomme, a former clerk of the London
County Council, asserted confidently that in the metropolis as elsewhere the
functions of city government were on the way to being greatly extended in
order to keep pace with the expansion of the city itself. Gomme foresaw the
continuation of a great upsurge of 'municipal ideals and aspirations', leading
to a higher stage of civilization. In this process, London was destined to play
a central role, 'endowed with powers of self-government within the empire to
which she belongs' and working alongside other cities at home and abroad in
the search for effective solutions to common problems.[33]

No Briton took a broader view of urban progress toward the end of this
period than Patrick Geddes. A native of Scotland who held a professorship of
botany at University College in Dundee between 1889 and 1914, Geddes had
begun to demonstrate a growing interest in cities during the mid-1890s by
setting up a Civic and Regional Museum at Outlook Tower in Edinburgh.[34]
Subsequently becoming a zealous advocate of measures designed to heighten
'civic consciousness' elsewhere as well,[35] he also became active as a practicing
city planner, producing an influential plan for the Scottish city of Dunferm-
line shortly after the turn of the century[36] and then organizing a Cities and
Town Planning Exhibition that toured Britain, the European continent, and
India.

Geddes' most important book, *Cities in Evolution* (1915), drew the lessons
that were implicit in much of his exhibition. While highly critical of what had
happened in and to the 'paleotechnic' cities of the nineteenth century, with
their 'mean streets' and their pervasive slums, Geddes took heart from what
he regarded as a movement of urban renewal that had already made great
strides forward and promised many more benefits in the future. 'The civic
awakening and the constructive effort are fully beginning', he wrote, 'in
healthy upgrowth, capable not only of survival but of fuller cultivation also,
towards varied flower and fruit — flower in regional and civic literature and
history, art, and science; fruit in social renewal of towns and cities, small and
great'. Among the developments occurring in Britain that gave him grounds
for both satisfaction and hope, Geddes emphasized a growing sense of
responsibility among town councillors, who had become 'more awake to
public and civic interests, to the condition of the people, and their need of
improved housing'. He also drew attention to the beneficial effects of the
Housing and Town Planning Act that had been passed by Parliament in
1909, a piece of legislation that permitted municipalities to set up Town

Planning Committees for the purpose of controlling land use in formerly undeveloped areas outside the city centers. Although most reformers regarded this particular legislation as ineffectual, Geddes saw it as part of a larger pattern of urban improvement. This progress was leading inexorably in his view toward a new age in which 'discords of parties' and harmful competition would give way to cooperation and 'the promotion of the common weal'. Through an enhanced sense of municipal responsibility and the extension of town planning, cities were becoming exemplars of a new social harmony that would surely outlast the unfortunate conflict among nations which had begun in 1914.[37]

The example of Germany

The country in which Geddes and many others discerned far and away the most impressive municipal advances anywhere in the world during the early twentieth century was Imperial Germany. Geddes repeatedly praised the innovative and beneficial plans that had been put into practice in the rapidly growing cities of Britain's chief rival. He emphasized strongly that urban efficiency provided a vital source of national strength and that Germany had managed to pursue this objective while at the same time giving due regard to urban aesthetics. He did not advocate emulating German cities in every respect, but he still left no doubt that British cities could gain greatly from close attention to what had been accomplished by the administrators of their burgeoning counterparts across the Channel.[38]

Geddes' admiration for German city government reflected a widespread sentiment in Britain among supporters of interventionist reform in the urban sector, who used the German example of municipal progress as a way of prodding their countrymen to make further improvements in their own towns. During the new century's first decade, Thomas Horsfall, Henry Lunn, and R. H. Tawney all published laudatory studies of German local government in which their own country appeared in a quite unfavorable light by comparison. A few years later, William Harbutt Dawson praised German cities at great length, stressing the enormous powers and responsibilities of their governments — especially in the areas of planning, land acquisition, trading (gas, water, electricity, etc.), social welfare, and culture — and the professional expertise of the men who ran them. For all of these writers, Germans clearly pointed the way toward the next stage of city development via the route they had traveled themselves as they moved to impose municipal order on urban chaos.[39]

The men who received the major share of credit for the achievements that Dawson and other students of urban Germany esteemed most highly were the numerous administrators who staffed the offices of dozens of big-city governments. The most powerful and the best known of these officials were the *Oberbürgermeister* — men such as Max Forckenbeck in Berlin, Erich Zweigert in Essen, and Franz Adickes in Frankfurt — who had usually received extensive training in public law and finance and continued to receive substantial salaries during terms of office that usually lasted for at least twelve years if not for life. Below them, there existed large armies of trained bureaucrats who occupied subaltern positions in the local administrative structure, including a multitude of housing and medical inspectors, welfare workers, museum directors, educators, and planner-architects. Collectively, these civil servants constituted a powerful force for urban betterment that was quite superior to the bureaucratic institutions that had come into being anywhere else.[40]

Such men, together with other civic-minded members of the *Bürgertum* who served without pay on town councils and scholarly specialists in the academic disciplines in which the top administrators had been trained, proudly proclaimed their consciousness of themselves as leading participants in a great movement of urban rebirth and renewal. Their ethos and their sense of success became plainly evident shortly after the turn of the century. In 1903, a German City Exhibition was held in Dresden, the capital of Saxony and one of the great showplaces of Baroque art and architecture. Representing 128 city governments as well as more than 400 manufacturers and occupying two dozen buildings, including a central hall with eighty rooms, it comprised a vast array of models, pictures, and charts. The municipal exhibits were arranged under eight main headings, which may be summarized as follows: (1) transport, lighting, street-building, and drainage; (2) city expansion, building inspection, and housing; (3) civic art and architecture; (4) health, welfare, and police; (5) schooling and education; (6) care for the poor and the sick and various charitable institutions; (7) financial institutions; and (8) record-keeping. The exhibits clearly conveyed to over 400,000 paying visitors the administrators' view of the *Grossstadt* as an increasingly attractive place in which to live. Together with the commentaries and reflections they stimulated, almost all of them evinced a triumphant sense of self-confidence and optimism that arose from the steadily widening range of useful services city governments were in the process of providing.[41]

The great panoply of materials that had been made available for inspection and comparison led the *Oberbürgermeister* of Dresden, Ernst Beutler, to exclaim in his opening speech on May 20, 'We may well assert without conceit concerning the German cities that they have generally shown

21 Housing for municipal employees in Frankfurt am Main. This picture, like the one below, was shown at the German City exhibition in Dresden in 1903 (source: Robert Wuttke, *Die Deutschen Städte*, II [Leipzig, 1904], 59).

22 A power plant for public transport in Berlin. Both this picture and the one above strongly assert German pride in the municipal progress for which German cities were justly famous (source: Wuttke, *Die Deutschen Städte*, II, 190).

themselves to be fit for the large and diverse responsibilities that have devolved upon them during the last several decades'. Robert Wuttke, a professor at the Dresden Technical Institute, commented shortly after the exhibit had closed,

> The City Exhibition ... proved that with the passage of time we have become independent. We have learned abroad, but foreign countries are no longer our teachers. If one compares what has been achieved in hospital construction, in subway and sewer construction, in park-building, and so on in Germany and elsewhere, one can easily assert without exaggeration that we, in these as in many other areas, have risen to the top.

In a similar vein, a town councillor from Erfurt was moved to write that once again, as in the Middle Ages and the first part of the early modern period, German cities had attained 'the first place on the world scene'. These men and many others had no doubt about at least one major lesson taught by the Dresden exhibition: German city governments were leading the way toward a better urban future in which all German patriots ought to take a considerable measure of national pride.[42]

During the decade just after the Dresden exhibition, the evidence of municipal self-confidence became ever more widespread. The reformist Verein für Sozialpolitik published over a dozen volumes on urban government, including an exhaustive collection of articles by statisticians and other experts that treated German municipal trading in the areas of water, gas, electricity, transport, slaughtering, foodstuffs, storage, and publishing. Otto Most, a statistician who taught at an academy in Düsseldorf that prepared men to work in local government and served there as a town councillor, published a lengthy survey of 'the German city and its administration'. He dealt with finances and taxation, art and education, economic and social policies, city extensions and city planning, street construction and other public works, and the measures taken to safeguard the citizenry's health. His survey served to reinforce a basic view of German cities as the leading centers of 'the economic, intellectual, and artistic life of the nation'. He admitted that serious problems still beset urban populations, particularly in the areas of public health and morals, but he much preferred to point out the enormous progress the cities had recently experienced and to anticipate the further advances of which they were clearly capable. German cities were 'the standard-bearers of intellectual, economic, and social progress, to the advantage of the whole fatherland', and German urban development ought to elicit both 'patriotic pride' and heartfelt gratitude toward the men who had made it possible for this transformation to proceed so smoothly. The author of an article on cities that appeared in a standard encyclopedia of political science used identical language with regard to 'standard-bearing' and then went on to add that through their institutional arrangements they had earned 'the admiration of the entire civilized world'. Paul Fuss, the *Oberbürgermeister* of Kiel, held up much the same sort of municipal activity for inspection and approval. His view of big-city growth as a natural and normal process of development went hand in hand with a confident belief that city administrators were providing their fellow citizens with the essential prerequisites for 'surviving and progressing in the struggle for existence'.[43]

Around the time when these expressions of municipal enthusiasm were finding their way into print, there occurred in Düsseldorf in 1912 a large-scale gathering of urban experts. More than 900 individuals, most of whom were professionally involved in city government, came together for five days to instruct and congratulate one another on their various successes as managers and solvers of urban problems. Organized by local authorities as a 'congress for urban studies', the program for the conference provided for tours to an exhibition on planning and progress in Düsseldorf and to nearby utilities, hospitals, and schools. In addition, the conferees could choose from among ninety-four lectures by specialists from all over the nation who were well prepared to expound the state of the art in city planning, in the management of municipal enterprises, and in 'the cultivation of learning, art, and welfare'. The welcoming speech by the *Oberbürgermeister*, Dr. Oehler, made explicit the message that was implicit in the conference as a whole. Despite some drawbacks, German urbanization had been basically 'satisfying and healthy', owing largely to the power, the energy, and the knowledge possessed by a steadily growing army of trained civil servants — not just men with legal training, but also medical doctors, engineers, architects, economists, and educators. Another local official, a town councillor and building inspector by the name of Carl Geusen, drove home the point in a speech that marked the end of the formal proceedings. 'The progress of culture', he exclaimed, 'has always been closely linked with the flourishing of cities.... Through cooperation, we have striven to attain the very best for our cities. We have achieved much and will achieve much more'.[44]

This general attitude toward the modern *Grossstadt* was both anticipated and echoed in a large number of books and articles that either focused exclusively or contained substantial chapters on the work done in particular cities by their governments. No one German city stood out as clearly as Birmingham during the 1870s or Glasgow around the turn of the century. Among the large provincial towns, Stettin in the east, Chemnitz, Dresden, Leipzig, and Magdeburg in central Germany, Nuremberg in the south, and Düsseldorf, Cologne, Mannheim, and Frankfurt in the west all served as subjects for laudatory works of local history during the first decade and a half of the century.[45] In addition, nine volumes of descriptive studies were published between 1912 and 1914 in a new series that appeared under the title *Monographien deutscher Städte*. In the words of Erwin Stein, a writer who specialized in urban economics and served as the series editor, the contributors depicted individual cities and 'their work in the economy, finance, hygiene, social policy, and technology'. The authors were local officials, who wrote not only for their colleagues but also for businessmen and other citizens who wished to familiarize themselves either with the administrative institutions of their own cities or with the most successful techniques and innovations that had been introduced elsewhere. What they wrote conveyed a strong sense that German towns were forging ahead.[46]

If any one city occupied a pre-eminent position as a putative center of municipal energy, it was the *Hauptstadt*. Imperial Berlin possessed special significance for admirers of urban progress just as it did for critics of urban disorder. The capital was the subject of much favorable commentary by publicists and other writers as well as by officials and scholars, all of whom regarded its leading administrators as men who were setting an excellent example for their counterparts elsewhere in and outside the Reich. Already in the mid-1890s, the popular writer Paul Lindenberg saw fit to introduce a book of anecdotes and pictures by calling his readers' attention not only to new museums but also to new educational establishments, hospitals, parks, markets, slaughterhouses, and sewage and water works, most of which had been constructed by municipal authorities. These structures made manifest an enormous amount of civic energy, quite unlike anything to be discerned in contemporary London or Paris. The inhabitants of the capital — especially, it seemed, the men who administered it — gave abundant evidence of a 'buoyant spirit of enterprise' and a 'restless striving upward, ever more conscious of the goal, more independent, more deserving of respect'. Subsequently, Leo Fernbach updated a lengthy work of popular history by adding several concluding chapters in which he traced Berlin's recent evolution under the guidance of its governors in considerably greater detail, ending with the assertion that during the 1890s the city had steadily advanced on all fronts. As a result, it had become 'more and more a worthy focal point of the united German Empire'. Paul Goldschmidt conveyed much the same image a decade later in a chapter centering on recent municipal activity that appeared under the title 'The Development of a World City'.[47]

The authors of more than two dozen articles that were published in 1914 in a volume on Berlin in Erwin Stein's series of municipal monographs raised their voices in a similarly favorable refrain. Ernst Kaeber, the city archivist, summarized the main thrust of these contributions to the self-understanding of the capital when he looked back proudly on the vast array of new responsibilities undertaken by the city government since the middle of the nineteenth century. He pointed in particular to the growth of public education, to the establishment of public gas and water works, and to the building of public tramways, slaughterhouses, and hospitals, all of which demonstrated exemplary municipal enterprise. For Kaeber, as for many others, the officials who managed the local affairs of the capital were compiling a record of achievement in which Germans everywhere ought to take a large measure of patriotic pride.[48]

After 1914, the *Grossstadt* continued to elicit great enthusiasm from students of and participants in municipal government. The themes of power politics and national pride that had frequently appeared in much earlier writing now came clearly to the fore. In the eyes of many urban partisans, the big city played an indispensable role in the German war effort, providing the nation as a whole with vital strength that was essential for ultimate victory over its foreign antagonists. Emil Stutzer, a publicist and popular historian whose eyes were fully open to a wide range of urban defects, pointed with unmistakable approval to the new responsibilities that city governments had taken on since the outbreak of hostilities. He mentioned in particular the provision of higher levels of support for the families of soldiers than were required by national law and the accumulation and distribution of foodstuffs. The willingness of local officials to raise taxes in order to conduct these and other wartime activities gave striking proof of the indispensability of urban self-government for the well-being of the nation, 'especially in times of danger'. Dr. Wilms, the *Oberbürgermeister* of Posen, approached the end of his survey of German cities for a popular weekly magazine by referring not only to the management of food supplies and support for soldiers' families but also to exemplary care for servicemen who had been wounded. He concluded,

> Established in peace and strengthened from decade to decade, self-government has far exceeded its peacetime achievements during the war, and the German cities may look back proudly on everything their citizens have accomplished in war and peace for the common good not only of their local areas but also of the larger totalities, the state and the Empire, the *Volk* and the fatherland.

For these men, city administrators were refuting daily through their deeds the charges by anti-urbanists that the growth of towns weakened the nation. Far from undermining German power, the modern city enhanced it mightily, in large part by means of its highly effective apparatus of public administration.[49]

The men who expressed these laudatory views of urban government during the first two decades of the twentieth century were members of the upper middle classes whose political sympathies could best be described as National Liberal, and their opinions were not universally shared. They applauded their municipalities as institutions that were moving in a generally progressive direction with regard to technological, economic, and social matters while remaining under the firm control of the educated and propertied *Bürgertum* — a situation that resulted from unequal voting rights at the local level which very few of them showed any interest in changing.[50] The political spokesmen for the bulk of the urban workers saw the situation somewhat differently. Social Democrats displayed markedly less enthusiasm for what was emerging in the way of reform from city halls in which they enjoyed far less power than their strength in the urban population as a whole seemed to warrant. According to Hugo Lindemann, the leading socialist expert on communal problems, 'class egoism' still prevailed in urban government, and every progressive innovation required a hard fight. Two socialist commentators on the Dresden exhibition struck the same note. One wrote that modern city planning had almost exclusively benefited the owners of property. 'For the mass of the laboring population', he added, 'the big old blocks with back courtyards ... and high tenements must still suffice'. In general, the exhibition was essentially a middle-class 'smokescreen', which by no means provided an accurate picture of urban social welfare. According to these men, urban administrators and legislators deserved nowhere near as much credit for their achievements as they seemed to think they ought to receive.[51]

Although they frequently scoffed at the inflated claims made by middle-class bureaucrats and their spokesmen, German socialists could not deny that urban government was making a tangible difference in the quality of urban life. All around them, they saw irrefutable evidence that the cities in which they lived were moving in the right direction — not as quickly or willingly as they ought to but steadily and surely nonetheless — and more and more they sought a major share of the credit for what was happening. One anonymous commentator in the pages of the Social Democratic *Kommunale Praxis* on the development of Essen commended the city for its healthy residential areas, which the municipality had helped to make possible through the extensive acquisition of parcels of land. Another coupled his criticisms of an exhibition on the history of Cologne with grudging recognition of the enormous advances that had in fact occurred during recent decades. Twenty years earlier, there had been little if any awareness of the social responsibilities incumbent upon the government of a big city, but since then the dissemination of socialist thought had helped to bring about a remarkable change. The exhibition provided abundant proof of 'the permeation of city administrations by the basic ideas of socialism'.[52]

Paul Hirsch, a socialist member of the Berlin city council, and other socialists struck the same note. Hirsch recalled a quarter of a century of administrative evolution in the German capital in which he and other members of his party had played a more and more important part. He provided specific support for the revisionist moderation of the likes of Eduard Bernstein by documenting in great detail the variety of benefits that Social Democratic politicians had helped to win for their followers through hard work and give-and-take within the framework of existing institutions. Despite the disadvantages imposed upon them by the discriminatory three-class suffrage, they had succeeded in 'infusing the administration with a social spirit and in helping to gain recognition for the ideal of municipal socialism'. During the war, a Social Democratic Reichstag member and journalist, Edmund Fischer, wrote a book on 'the evolution of socialism' in which he paid special attention to 'the communal economy'. Developments in this sector marked the most pronounced social progress that had occurred anywhere during the last several decades, and they pointed the way to further advances that would surely be made in the future after the last barriers to democracy had been eliminated.[53]

German municipalities enjoyed just as high a reputation in the United States as they did in Britain. American specialists in urban government, like their English contemporaries, looked with undisguised admiration and envy around the turn of the century at the exemplary advances that were occurring in the obviously well-run cities of Central Europe. Albert Shaw, a prominent progressive who wrote extensively about political institutions at home and abroad, asserted in the mid-1890s that 'municipal housekeeping' was being attended to 'in a more systematic, thorough, and businesslike way' there than anywhere else in the world. The Germans had, he wrote, displayed locally 'more of the scientific method than any other people', applying highly disciplined intelligence to the practical realization of a lofty moral ideal: a conception of the city as a 'social organism' in which government bore the responsibility to promote both its own welfare and that of its citizens in every way it could. Two decades later, Frederic C. Howe, another prominent reformer about whom we shall have more to say shortly, wrote about German municipalities in much the same vein: 'The German city is governed by experts. This and its many socialistic activities is what most distinguishes the German city from other cities of the world'. Like William Harbutt Dawson in England, Shaw, Howe, and many other experts on municipal affairs in the United States regarded the German record of administrative progress at the local level as both a marvel to behold and a reproach to ponder.[54]

Hope and pride among American progressives

American analysts of urban government remained acutely aware throughout most of this period that cities in their own country left a great deal to be desired. Dissatisfaction with the state of urban affairs at home, which was clearly implicit if not explicit in the writings of men who praised the example set by Imperial Germany, remained one of the major motivating forces for progressive reformers long after it had received classic expression in Lord Bryce's *The American Commonwealth* (1889) and in Lincoln Steffens' famous exposé, *The Shame of the Cities* (1904).[55] As Delos Franklin Wilcox wrote in 1910, three years after becoming chief of the bureau of franchises of the public service commission in New York City, 'American cities as units of government [still] have a bad name. When the roll of civic honor is called, there are few to respond, except the neophytes that boast of having been virtuous for a few months past'. In his view and in the eyes of numerous others who carefully scrutinized what was happening in American city halls, multitudinous sins of omission and commission posed a continuing challenge to the conscience and the competence of the good citizen. The all too frequent and successful pursuit of private gain and the failure to make sufficient provision for the common weal marked American municipalities as decidedly inferior to most all of their European — not just their German — counterparts.[56]

Despite the reformers' continuing unease over the manifold defects that still marked the institutions by which they and their fellow Americans were governed at the local level, many of them struck another note that sounded very different indeed. They manifested a growing measure of well deserved pride in the ways they and others were helping to ameliorate the conditions they found so deplorable — in part through their own criticisms, in part through the elaboration and the implementation of positive solutions to the problems they had brought to light. In their opinion, the very fact that so many men and women like themselves had turned their attention to urban ills boded quite well for the cities' future well-being. The fact that reformed city governments were taking an ever larger view of their responsibilities to those who elected them and that they were actually adopting many of the proposals set forth by their erstwhile critics gave even greater reason to believe that urban America had turned a difficult corner and that it was moving steadily in the right direction.

Richard T. Ely, an influential economist who studied in Germany before teaching at Johns Hopkins and the University of Wisconsin and contributed powerfully to a whole host of reforms pertaining to monopolies, child labor, and trade unions, voiced this emerging confidence in 1902 in a long lecture on 'The Coming City'. He began by observing that the title he had formerly used for some of the remarks he was about to deliver — 'Neglected Aspects of Municipal Reform' — would no longer do. The considerations he wished to set forth were finally attracting the attention they had long deserved. 'When I think about this remarkable change in the quantity, and still more in the quality, of thought on ... municipal reform', he wrote, 'I cannot repress a certain feeling of elation. My soul is warmed with gentle optimism for the future'. More exuberantly, he exclaimed, 'We rejoice in the revival of civic patriotism, believing that it will grow still broader and deeper'. He concluded joyfully on a note of secularized reverence. He asserted that he and his compatriots were learning, in the modified language of the Psalmist, to say, 'If I forget thee, O Chicago, O New York, O St. Louis, let my right hand forget her cunning. If I do not remember thee, let my tongue cleave to the roof of my mouth; if I prefer thee not above my chief joy'.[57]

A few years before Ely spoke, reformers had launched a new periodical, *Municipal Affairs* (1897-1903), and within a decade after his remarks appeared in print they established two more of the same sort: *The American City* (1909-75) and the *National Municipal Review* (1912-69). Each of these later publications strongly supported the belief that Ely's expectations were indeed coming to fruition. Avowedly designed as 'a clearing-house for the experience of cities and organizations' that were seeking 'to rebuild our American cities along better lines', *The American City* opened with a confident assertion by its editor that the urban centers of the United States were 'awakening to self-consciousness and to a sense of their larger responsibilities'. They were outgrowing their earlier 'childishness' and 'coming of age'. The *National Municipal Review*, established as the organ of the National Municipal League (a good government group that had come into existence in 1894), led off three years later with a long article by its editor in which the same basic sentiment was expressed in considerably greater detail. Clinton Rodgers Woodruff lauded 'a new spirit' that was already producing desirable results. 'After all is said', he asserted, 'the most notable tendency in American municipal life is toward hopefulness. The men who bewail existing conditions and close their eyes to the work that is being done to improve them, are diminishing in number'. In conclusion, he invoked as a corroborating witness James Bryce. He quoted at length from a speech given before the New York City Club in 1911 in which the distinguished Englishman had heartily commended his audience for the steps they had taken in recent decades to rectify their earlier shortcomings.

> Your administration is becoming more and more of a business administration, certainly in this city, than ever before, and that is generally true of cities all over the Union.... In nearly all the cities the sky is brighter, the light is stronger. A new spirit is rising. The progress you may expect to see in the elevation and purification of your city government within the next twenty or thirty years may well prove to be greater and more enduring than even that which the last forty years have seen.

This was sweet music indeed, coming as it did from a man who had long been regarded as one of municipal America's harshest and most accurate critics.[58]

During a period of about a decade and half that roughly spanned the first appearance of these two journals in 1909 and 1912, at least ten books by more than half a dozen experts on municipal affairs provided systematic surveys of the state of the art in urban politics and administration. Some of these works contained more than others in the way of proposals and recommendations, emphasizing what ought to be done rather than what had been done, but all of them provided extensive, coherent, and basically optimistic accounts of American city government. D. F. Wilcox, Charles Beard (the noted political scientist and historian), Charles Zueblin (a professor of sociology), Horatio Pollock and William Morgan (statisticians employed by the state of New York), Morris L. Cooke (the former director of public works for Philadelphia), and Frederic C. Howe (a writer and public servant) all surveyed the municipal scene nationwide and came to the same basic conclusion.[59]

In their view, while American city government was still far from perfect it had become and was becoming far more efficient in its operations and equitable in its effects than ever before. These men all believed in and took satisfaction from structural changes in the institutions of city government designed to facilitate the enhanced honesty and competence referred to by Woodruff and Bryce. Like other progressive reformers, they advocated simpler methods of nomination and election, the centralization of power in the hands of mayors, the reduction of political patronage, the establishment of independent comptrollers, and increased power for the electorate to express its will through referenda and the recall of elected officials. They saw such reforms as crucial elements of the growing effort by informed citizens to liberate their cities from the clutches of corrupt machines and their bosses. But they had a vision of civic progress that went well beyond structural reforms such as these, encompassing a wide range of innovations of the sort that the editor of *The American City* had in mind when he referred approvingly to 'larger responsibilities'. They looked for and found increasing evidence not only of honest competence and efficient virtue but also of vigorous regard for the social well-being of the average city dweller. In their eyes, limited government, no matter how free from the taint of corruption, could no longer pretend to be good government when measured against the best practice in the leading cities of early twentieth-century America.

Two of these authors, Howe and Zueblin, made especially notable contributions to the literature of municipal reform and civic pride, both of them emphasizing the growing intervention by urban government in the urban economy and in urban society. Howe had studied under Shaw, Ely, and Woodrow Wilson at Johns Hopkins in the 1890s, had worked as a lawyer, and had served for several years as a city councilman in Cleveland under Mayor Tom Johnson before writing his best-known book, *The City: The Hope of Democracy* (1905).[60] Howe thrilled to the city as a place where 'the game of life' was to be played to the hilt, where 'opportunity and fortune' were to be found in abundance, and where life was 'full and human', but most of all he sang its praises as a place where the hope for a more just society was already in the process of realization. The city had given rise to 'a new conception of municipal purpose'. Private philanthropy had sparked beneficent innovations such as kindergartens, playgrounds, lodging houses, and hospitals, but these institutions were now passing under public control; moreover, other responsibilities too were being taken on continually by city administrations. 'The humanizing forces of today', Howe wrote, 'are almost all proceeding from the city. They are creating a new moral sense, a new conception of the obligations of political life, obligations which, in earlier conditions of society, did not and could not exist'.[61]

A decade later, after serving as a state senator in Ohio, a member of the Cleveland Tax Commission, and Commissioner of Immigration of the Port of New York, Howe took another wide-ranging look at what city governments had accomplished abroad and at home, and he made it quite clear that he liked what he saw. American municipalities merited special commendation for their well-run fire departments, their free public libraries, their generously financed public schools, and their extensive parks and playgrounds. In all of these departments, the cities of the United States now ranked as high as if not higher than their European counterparts. Howe found the situation in the area of public utilities far less satisfactory. In contrast to the public authorities in the cities of both England and Germany, American municipalities still enjoyed rather little in the way of direct control over these operations. Municipal ownership, Howe observed, was largely limited in the United States to water works and to electric-lighting plants, but in a few cities there were now public gas works and garbage plants, in others there were municipal docks, and in one, San Francisco, the municipality held title to its own street railway system. Howe displayed similar ambivalence with regard to American city planning, his country's 'most costly failure'. The predominance of a *laissez-faire* philosophy had retarded efforts to impose functional and aesthetic order on the city's physical structure, but here too signs of change were everywhere to be seen. Starting with the World's Fair of 1893 in Chicago, with its famous model city designed by Daniel Burnham, there had been a great upsurge of urban planning, in Washington, in Cleveland, in Chicago, and in over one hundred other cities across the land, leading Howe to conclude that this tendency gave promise of being 'the most hopeful municipal movement in the country'. In every way he could think of, Howe viewed American city governments as increasingly potent forces for good in the lives of American city dwellers.[62]

Charles Zueblin, though much less well known than Howe, stands out equally in the present context, owing to the particularly meticulous way in which he recorded civic improvement between 1902 and 1916. Having established the Northwestern University Settlement House in 1891, Zueblin taught in the sociology department at the University of Chicago between 1892 and 1908, thereafter devoting himself to research and writing. The first edition of his *Municipal Progress*, published in a series of popular works on economics, politics, and sociology under the editorship of Richard T. Ely, was still somewhat tentative. Though basically optimistic, it displayed little of the zestful enthusiasm that was to characterize Howe's work from the outset. But by the time the second edition (dedicated to Clinton Rogers Woodruff) made its appearance almost a decade and a half later, Zueblin's exuberance asserted itself loudly and clearly on the opening page. 'American municipal progress', he wrote, 'is spectacularly evident to any doubting Thomas from achievements of the twentieth century that could not be recorded in the first edition of this book'. He summarized that progress in its economic and social aspects as follows:

> Already this century has witnessed the first municipalized street railways and telephone in American cities; a national epidemic of street paving and cleaning; the quadrupling of electric lighting service and the national appropriation of street lighting; a successful crusade against dirt of all kinds ... and the diffusion of constructive provisions for health like baths, laundries ... school nurses and open air schools; fire prevention; the humanizing of the police and the advent of the policewoman; the transforming of some municipal courts into institutions for the prevention of crime and the cure of offenders; the elaboration of the school curriculum to give every child a complete education from the kindergarten to the vocational course in school or university or shop; municipal reference libraries; the completion of park systems in most large cities and the acceptance of the principle that the smallest city without a park and playground is not quite civilized; the modern playground movement giving organized and directed play

to young and old; the social center; the democratic art museum; municipal theaters ... a greater advance than the whole nineteenth century compassed.

Thereafter, Zueblin substantiated this view relentlessly via nearly 500 pages of text, appendixes, and bibliography, concluding with the confident assertion that 'the progressive satisfaction of the wants of all the people has ceased to be a utopian ideal; it is the only reasonable municipal program'.[63]

Among the particular cities that Howe, Zueblin, and other commentators on municipal life in general regarded most favorably, two may usefully be singled out for special attention, primarily through the eyes of men who worked in and for them. The versions of progress articulated by leaders in these cities provided especially clear parallels in American urban consciousness to the sense of communal achievement generated in Europe by the histories of such municipalities as Birmingham, Glasgow, Frankfurt, and Berlin. As in Europe, the celebration of specific places by men who could legitimately claim a major share of the credit for the ways in which those places had changed for the better in recent years helped mightily both to produce and to substantiate the more general reflections of other urban enthusiasts.

At the end of the nineteenth century, leading Bostonians took great pride not only in their distant but also in their recent past. Robert Woods, the dominant figure in the local settlement house movement, wrote in 1898 that in Boston a chief executive with 'rare administrative genius' was inducing the city government to devote more and more attention to 'the great common interests of the people'. He was putting into practice 'this principle that the administration of modern cities must more and more be socialized'. The man to whom he referred, Josiah Quincy, served as mayor between 1895 and 1899. Shortly after finishing his term of office, Quincy looked back proudly on the changes his city had experienced under his enlightened leadership, cataloguing a whole host of expanded municipal responsibilities and functions. He devoted most of his attention to the establishment of free public baths, but he also discussed the erection of free public gymnasiums, the use of schoolyards as summer playgrounds, and the provision of free concerts, as well as the use of public-spirited (and unpaid) commissioners for purposes of administrative supervision. Very much a patrician by breeding and temperament, Quincy saw urban improvement in large measure as a successful effort by men rather different from the sort who ordinarily ran for elective office to spread cleanliness, culture, and contentment among the urban masses.[64]

In several midwestern cities — most notably Detroit during the 1890s and Cleveland, Toledo, and Milwaukee between 1901 and 1920 — reforming mayors gained enviable reputations as prime movers in the effort to make urban government more responsive to the economic and social needs and the express desires of the average city dweller. Among these men, two mayors of Howe's Cleveland, Tom L. Johnson (1901-10) and Newton D. Baker (1912-16), deserve special consideration. Johnson, who had made a fortune in

23 The subway entrance at the Boston Public Library. This photograph neatly conveys a widespread feeling that American municipalities were making dramatic advances both in the realm of technology and in the realm of culture (source: Charles Zueblin, *American Municipal Progress* [New York, 1917], 34).

urban transport, received Howe's praise and support — and the adulation of the common people in his city — for his vigorous efforts to improve the life of the ordinary citizen in a number of ways that went well beyond the goals pursued by Josiah Quincy and other reformers whose basic thinking primarily reflected the values of the upper middle classes. Like Quincy, Johnson had worked effectively to develop facilities for public recreation, including baths, parks, and playgrounds. He had also seen to it that the streets were properly cleaned and lit, and he had encouraged the adoption of a comprehensive plan for five new public buildings around a spacious mall. Most notably, however, he had taken on the special interests that clung to profitable monopolies granted by venal city councils at the expense of their constituents, forcing down the price of gas and attempting to establish a municipally owned street railway. Although ultimately defeated in the latter of these two campaigns (succeeding only in bringing about a reduction of the fares), Johnson had fought the good fight, and both he and Howe remained convinced that further progress in the direction of the goals they sought was only a matter of time. As Johnson wrote in his autobiography, 'Agitation for the right, once set in motion, cannot be stopped. Truth can never lose its power. It presses forward, gaining victories, suffering defeats, but losing nothing of momentum, augmenting its strength though seeming to expend it'.[65]

Baker, a Johnson protégé, was less controversial but no less able, and his administration won praise not only from Howe but also from the more conservative *National Municipal Review*. In the words of one author, 'Schooled by his association with Tom Johnson, Newton Baker has gone on and beyond it'. As another author observed several years later, by the end of his two terms in office Baker had completed the new city hall, brought about further improvements in the street railway service, built a municipal lighting plant, and worked effectively to improve public health by developing a network of treatment centers for sufferers from tuberculosis. In Cleveland, 'the prevalent municipalism' revealed a growing awareness of 'the increasing interdependence of community life' and the concomitant need to provide a wide range of public services, under the control either of carefully regulated corporations or of the municipality itself.[66]

The hope and the satisfaction that pervaded all of these detailed accounts of the tasks being performed in great American cities were articulated in summary fashion by Walter Weyl. A former settlement worker who had long been active as a progressive reformer and more recently had helped to found the liberal *New Republic*, Weyl wrote glowingly in 1915 about the many attractions offered by city life. He insisted unequivocally 'that in a moral as well as a physical sense the city advances more rapidly than does the country, and that it is precisely in the city, with its errors and its carelessness and its ruthlessness, that the foundations are discovered upon which is to be reared a great moral democratic American civilization'. While agrarian anti-urbanists urged in vain that men return to the land, 'a new social civic ideal' was arising amidst the admitted evils that beset urban life. 'Everywhere in America', he asserted, 'city problems are being envisaged and attacked. City poverty, city crime, city carelessness, city misgovernment, are being studied, analyzed, and combated'. City dwellers displayed cooperation and solidarity at every level of urban experience, from the neighborhood school to the city hall. In so doing, they were not only giving the lie to the aspersions cast upon them by their narrow-minded detractors but also helping to form — and to improve — the character of the entire American nation. In Weyl's vision, which was widely shared by other reformers of his day, the collectivist tendencies evident in the big city occupied a central place among the most promising forces for change in the whole country in which they were developing. Organized urban communities pointed the way toward a better social order for all men and women, urban and non-urban alike.[67]

An enormous amount of extravagant enthusiasm appeared in Britain, in Germany, and in America in a voluminous body of literature on the recent development of municipal institutions. Germany served to some extent as an example for and a reproach to municipal leaders in the other two countries, but numerous observers in all three nations displayed a strong sense that urban government was moving rapidly in the right direction. They believed fervently that the public authorities in the big cities were making consistent and substantial contributions to the health and the happiness of their citizens and that as a result of these efforts city life would become better and better in the future.

To be sure, there were conflicting currents of opinion. Some conservatives looked askance at further growth in the social and economic powers of government at any level. Others contended that, no matter what reforms might be attempted from within, big cities would remain as sores on the social organism and the body politic. At the other end of the ideological spectrum, many on the left believed that the municipal enthusiasts took too much pride in too little achievement and that they seriously underestimated the extent and severity of the remaining problems that afflicted the urban lower classes. Among middle-class liberals, there was also a growing recognition that the defects in urban society would require intervention at the state as well as the local level — intervention of the sort undertaken in Germany during the 1880s, in Britain between 1905 and 1911, and in the United States roughly between 1901 and 1917.[68] All of this might suggest that municipal pride ought to be viewed as merely a self-serving defense of the *status quo* by people who already enjoyed wealth and power in capitalist societies.

But despite a certain amount of inflated rhetoric, the men who expressed this pride knew what they were talking about. In large part as a result not only of progressive institutional developments but also of new technologies that had made it much easier than ever before to provide things such as water, energy, and transportation, city life really was improving for the great majority of the population.[69] At the same time, it must be remembered that most of the municipal enthusiasts did not want to rest on their laurels. They recognized that the achievements they were celebrating constituted at best a substantial start. The highest compliment they could pay the cities of the present was to assert that they contained within themselves the seeds of further improvements that would occur in years to come — seeds their writings were to help cultivate.

Part Four
Conclusions

10

Continuities and New Concerns between the Wars

During the interwar years, national differences in the perception of cities became much more pronounced than they had been since roughly the middle of the nineteenth century. To be sure, many of the parallels and similarities that marked the period 1880-1918 persisted. Moreover, new concerns too — in particular a growing awareness of the special problems posed by the metropolises — manifested themselves across national boundaries.[1] But the amount and the intensity of intellectual grappling with urban phenomena varied widely from one country to another, as did the specific configurations of urban thought and the implications derived from them. Not only France but also Britain receded into the background during these decades as centers of concern with specifically urban questions, whereas Germany and the United States came to the fore. German and American commentators on urban life clearly usurped the central position enjoyed by their English forebears a century or so earlier.

There were other national differences too. Whereas the British and to some extent the French seem to have become somewhat more negative, especially in the 1930s, the Germans displayed a great deal more than ever before in the way of an exceedingly gloomy anti-urbanism — a sentiment that was closely bound up with the rise and the self-justification of National Socialism. Americans, on the other hand, retained a considerable degree of optimism. This shone through in, among other writings, much of the work that came from a characteristically American group of thinkers, the urban sociologists. It is on these distinctions that we shall focus as we examine the ways in which inherited modes of perceiving the urban scene were brought to bear in a changing climate of political and social opinion on a changing urban world.

Pessimism, planning, and pride in Britain and France

During the 1920s and 1930s, the British evinced relatively low levels of interest in and of concern about the specifically urban aspects of their society.

There was certainly far less writing on these themes addressed to the general public than there had been during the 1880s and 1890s.[2] Britain had become so heavily urbanized that the problems of the city were almost coextensive with the problems of society as a whole. Cities no longer stood out in the same way they had formerly as peculiar places that needed to be scrutinized and evaluated separately from the rest of the nation, and they seldom elicited the same intensity of feeling that had been so readily apparent in earlier years.

Much of the commentary on cities that did appear betrayed an unmistakable grimness. Many of the criticisms of British towns that had been made during the nineteenth century were reiterated at both ends of the political spectrum, indicating an increasingly pervasive disenchantment with the urban legacy that remained from the age of industrialization.

Books and essays written during the 1920s by several men of generally conservative persuasion illustrate continuing awareness of the terrible penalties that urbanization had inflicted on Britain in modern times and a growing sense that far too little had been done to ameliorate its disruptive and depressing after-effects. William Ralph Inge, the dean of St. Paul's and the best-known conservative of the twentieth century among clergymen of the established Church, wrote a popular survey of contemporary England in which he voiced a wide range of traditional misgivings with regard to the 'sudden transplantation of the countryman ... into the unnatural surroundings of the large town'. He deplored 'the wretched physique of the slum-dwellers' and the 'rebellious class consciousness' prevalent among those who had been 'uprooted from the soil'. He also expressed great anxiety over the prospects of avoiding political and social revolution of the sort that had occurred in Russia in a Britain that now had practically no peasantry whatsoever. Moreover, he indicated his aesthetic disapproval, repeating the by now familiar charge that 'at no time or place had the hand of man erected anything so squalid or hideous as the new towns of England'.[3]

David Lindsay, Earl of Crawford and Balcarres and chancellor of the University of Manchester, wrote concerning British cities, 'Their rapid growth in the last few generations connotes a rural depopulation which is not wholesome'. He was worried not only by economic and social problems but also by 'the noise and bustle, the speed and breathlessness of modern life' and, to an even greater degree, by the lack of variety and individuality among towns that seemed to distinguish the British cityscape so sharply from the urban world of continental Europe. Pleading for a revival of civic spirit that would aim at something more than mere civic efficiency, he bemoaned the 'deadly uniformity', the 'monotony', and the lack of amenities that in his view made town life far less vital and interesting in Britain than in Germany, Italy, and France.[4]

A. Williams-Ellis, writing on 'our squalid towns' for *The Spectator*, made much the same point. He asked, 'Who would, or anyway who does, spend so much as a day's leisure in Manchester or Leeds, Crewe, or St. Helen's,

Wolverhampton, or even in the comparatively "town proud" cities of Leicester or Bristol?' The obvious answer to this rhetorical question was to be explained by the fact that 'smoky and dreary, they provide as a rule no facilities except for sleep and work' and that they suffered from 'an absence of gaiety and charm'. Turning in more detail to industrial Sheffield, he pointed out that towns like this one could no longer boast that they were conferring the basic economic benefits upon their inhabitants that had once provided both justification and compensation for all their social and cultural shortcomings. Disheartened by the high levels of unemployment that had beset Britain as a whole and the north in particular since shortly after the end of the war, he lamented, 'Now the warmth of the ferment has failed — the muck has stayed, the money has gone. Population grows, and the industries of our time apparently now do not produce enough money to build the workers shelter, let alone to make their towns homes for them'.[5]

Many of these discontents surfaced again, albeit from different sources and with different purposes in mind, during the 1930s in writings by various authors on the socialist left. A broad range of misgivings with regard to the modern city found expression in a book on *The Town and a Changing Civilisation* (1935). Written by David Glass, a young sociologist who believed in socialism and was later to gain distinction as a demographer, it constituted the only effort by anyone in Britain to provide a general overview of urban society of the sort that numerous academics in America were producing during these years. Intended to present a scholarly and balanced view of its subject, the book nonetheless conveyed a strong sense of disenchantment with the quality of urban life as it existed at that time. Glass called attention to, among other ills, low birth rates, crime, selfish individualism, the threat of revolution, monotonous work, and the decline of the family. 'The big city', he argued, 'no longer retains its special advantages of efficiency in production and distribution, while on the costs side it shows a balance of disadvantages'. Glass regarded the big city of the 1930s with considerable unease, and many others on the left as well as the right certainly shared his feelings.[6]

J. B. Priestley, a novelist, playwright, and essayist who sympathized with Labour throughout his life, undertook a tour of England in 1933, and he recorded his impressions in a work of social description whose scope and format invite comparison with books written almost a century earlier by authors such as George Head and William Cooke Taylor. Priestley's sentiments, however, were far less buoyant than those of his predecessors. As soon as he found himself outside the central core of Birmingham, all he could see in and around the city was 'a parade of mean dinginess ... ugliness,

24 An industrial town in Britain during the great depression. This picture and the book in which it appeared describe working-class life in northern towns that depended too heavily on factories for whose products there was too little demand (source: J. B. Priestley, *English Journey* [New York and London, 1934], frontispiece).

squalor ... vulgarity'. Bradford, 'a large dirty town that might almost be anywhere and mostly built of sooty bricks', had worsened markedly in Priestley's eyes since the days when he had known it as a young man before 1914. The city had lost many of its earlier cultural attractions, in part because of the decline of the wool trade and in part because the richer merchants and manufacturers no longer lived within the city limits. In Lancashire, the evidence of deterioration under the impact of economic hard times was still more depressing. Here Priestley saw a multitude of 'towns meant to work in and not to live in and even robbed of their work'. In almost all the cities he visited, Priestley was struck by the general meanness of everyday life and the lack of hope for a better future.[7]

Several years later, George Orwell, an unorthodox socialist, made a more limited journey of the same sort, visiting similar places in the Midlands and the industrial north. Having accepted a commission from Victor Gollancz, the publisher for the Left Book Club, to report on conditions among the unemployed, he conveyed his experiences and his findings in his widely read *Road to Wigan Pier* (1937). Monotonous squalor was omnipresent according to Orwell's blunt and incisive book. Industrial England, he wrote, was 'one enormous town', its physiognomy relieved by only occasional 'patches of cleanness and decency' in the relatively unspoiled areas between one city and the next. After twenty minutes or so of riding by train trough the country-side, one came to 'villa-civilization ... and then the outer slums, and then the slag-heaps, belching chimneys, blast-furnaces, canals and gasometers of another industrial town'. He continued in the same vein with respect to the impressions he gained while touring by foot: 'As you walk through the industrial towns you lose yourself in labyrinths of little brick houses blackened by smoke, festering in planless chaos round miry alleys and little cindered yards where there are stinking dustbins and lines of grimy washing and half-ruinous w.c's.' In view of the extreme shortage of decent housing, the money spent by some municipalities on ostentatious public buildings, such as the new town hall in Barnsley, struck him as 'mysterious' if not outrageous. As for the public housing that was being built, Orwell remarked that although clearly desirable from one standpoint it suffered nonetheless from an 'almost prison-like atmosphere' and that it was 'ruthless and soulless'. In any event, both in the slums and in the newer corporation estates, an intolerably large portion of the working-class population con-tinued to suffer from the prolonged and debilitating joblessness that afflicted almost all of the urban-industrial north.[8]

The persistence and the exacerbation of urban dreariness in the Midlands, in Lancashire, and in Yorkshire during decades of economic depression was by no means the only or even the most prominent theme in the thinking of urban critics at this time. An equally and increasingly serious set of urban problems arose from the ceaseless growth of Greater London — that vast agglomeration whose inhabitants, in the words of G. D. H. Cole, now numbered 'one-fifth of the nation'. Much less severely affected by the general economic downturn than the older industries of the north, the newer branches of the economy that were developing in the metropolis attracted more and more newcomers, whose arrival in what was already the largest city in the world induced in many observers an acute sense of anti-metropolitan anxiety. Apprehension over the quality of life in the British capital became increasingly noticeable starting around 1930. E. W. Shanahan, an economic geographer, pointed out that very big cities, such as London, New York, Paris, and Berlin, confronted enormous difficulties with respect to supplies of water and food, to traffic, and to 'nervous wear and tear on the active inhabitants and the resulting impairment of their efficiency'. He recognized that generally speaking urbanization fostered economic development, but he believed that this correlation held good only up to a point — a point that, in his view, London had clearly passed by the time he was writing.[9]

Victor Branford, a sociologist and disciple of Patrick Geddes, criticized great capitals such as London not for their economic inefficiency but instead for the ways in which their growth was intertwined with heightened levels of harmful conflict, not only within polities but also between them. A pessimistic view of metropolitan society in a Darwinian perspective emerged quite clearly from passages of his such as the following:

> In the great capitals more especially, does the intensity of struggle for individual survival, and for group or class dominance, compound with rivalries, intercivic and international; and thus to generate, in metropolitan populations, two characteristic habits of mind. One is a chronic habituation to a mood of fear, mitigated, yet in the long run intensified, by periodic rebound into extravagance of hope; and the other, an impulse to exploit every situation of peril, real or imaginary. Both tendencies react to sharpen the edge of competitive traffic at home, and warlike rivalries abroad.[10]

As the 1930s wore on and as the military threat posed by Nazi Germany became more and more ominous, other writers made critical connections of another sort between international warfare and metropolitan growth. A popular author by the name of Cicely Hamilton wrote in a chapter on 'the menace of London' that one among many reasons to fear the enormous expansion of that city's population arose from 'the character with which the power of the air has invested the outsize city'. London found itself in an especially vulnerable situation, 'having more noncombatants to be terrorized and panicked' than the capital of any other country with which Britain was likely to be engaged in military hostilities. Sidney Vere Pearson, a medical doctor with an interest in population studies, made essentially the same point in a book published in 1939 that indicted the growth of the metropolis for a whole host of reasons. Among them, he noted 'the drawbacks of thickly populated areas ... in times of war or rumours of war when thoughts are turned to air raids and difficulties of food transport'. Militarily, London was 'the weakest place on earth ... the Achilles heel of Britain, and of the British

Empire'. These dangers, together with the persistent evidence of disease, dirt, and various forms of social pathology and the increasingly uniform vulgarity of 'mob amusements', made London seem more threatening than ever to a growing number of social critics during these years.[11]

Such considerations with regard to the metropolis, together with a more general concern about the whole range of penalties that might result elsewhere too from the overgrowth of the large cities, underlay a good deal of the literature produced during these years by town planners. A town planning profession developed quite rapidly in Britain during the decades after the passage of the Town and Country Planning Act in 1909. Between the wars, the architects and other experts who were devoting their energies to this new field of activity played an increasingly important part in helping to shape public consciousness of urban issues. Their specific proposals pointed more and more insistently toward decentralization of industry and population, thus indicating their general agreement with misgivings of the sort referred to above. Frederic Osborn, an amateur planner and publicist who functioned as one of the chief spokesmen for Ebenezer Howard's garden city movement, made his contributions in works such as *New Towns after the War* (1918) and *Transport, Town Development and Territorial Planning of Industry* (1934). Raymond Unwin and other specialists pursued these themes in a symposium titled *Decentralisation of Population and Industry* (edited by Herbert Warren and W. R. Davidge; 1930). In 1937, a Royal Commission on Distribution of the Industrial Population began to meet under the chairmanship of Sir Montague Barlow. The report of the Barlow Commission, issued in 1939-40, pointed out once again the need to reduce congestion in the major urban centers. A more even distribution of industry and the creation of satellite towns, among other measures, were to combat the urban overdevelopment that was still occurring, especially in the Greater London area. Several years later, Patrick Abercrombie, a professor of town planning at University College, London, took this thinking one step further in his influential Greater London Plan (1945), which was prepared for the London County Council with a view to implementing decentralization during the postwar years.[12]

Not everyone viewed Britain's existing cities as gloomily as did most of the interwar observers whom we have encountered up to this point. Books in which London received the praise it deserved for the great wealth of experience it offered to those who wished to sample its many and varied delights continued to make their appearance, recalling Samuel Johnson's sentiments nearly two centuries earlier. Paul Cohen-Portheim, an urban émigré from Germany, described it favorably as 'the most complex city in the world'. Its diversity endowed it with a unique and unending attractiveness unequaled by any other city he knew. He wrote enthusiastically,

> Paris with the addition of Marseilles, Berlin with that of Hamburg, New York with that of Washington would yet not attain its completeness; but London

resembles none of them, and is like nothing in the world except itself.... In a
world growing more uniform every day ... its fascination will grow on you; you
will never tire of it, because you will never feel you really know it; it is too vast
for that, and too complex.

Here we see once again the traditional affirmation of London as a place in
which the sensitive individual could refresh and enhance his own *joie de
vivre*.[13]

Less lyrically, other students of metropolitan society who approached the
city not as men of letters but as empirical social scientists conveyed a basically
positive view of the everyday life of the ordinary Londoner. A balanced view
of the urban scene, devoid of smugness but still marked by a pervasive sense
of progressive change for the better, found its way into print between 1930
and 1935 in a nine-volume work titled *The New Survey of London Life and
Labour*. Based on a vast investigation begun in 1928 at the London School of
Economics that was designed as a sequel to the work of Charles Booth, it
conveyed a strong feeling that conditions had improved greatly in the interval
between the two surveys. Hubert Llewellyn Smith, one of Booth's erstwhile
assistants, summarized his and his collaborators' most important findings.
He reported that according to the new survey the percentage of the
population living in poverty (adjusting Booth's standards only for inflation)
had fallen by between two-thirds and three-quarters, that crime rates and
death rates had declined, and that there had been a vast improvement in the
quality as well as the quantity of leisure. As he wrote in conclusion, 'Of all the
manifold impressions left upon my mind by the Survey, the deepest and most
abiding is not the gravity and multiplicity of the still unsolved problems of
London life and labour, but the energy and vitality of the human response to
each new need as it has arisen. And so far there is no sign that the sources of
this vital energy are running dry'.[14]

While Smith focused on metropolitan society, other academics — and
some men of affairs — voiced parallel satisfaction with regard to developments in the area of local government, devoting most of their attention to
cities other than London. The centenary of the Municipal Corporations Act
provided the perfect occasion for an extensive exercise in self-congratulation
by men who took a special interest in local administration. It led to the
publication in 1935 of *A Century of Municipal Progress*, under the editorship,
among others, of Harold J. Laski, who like Smith taught at the London
School of Economics. Laski, Elie Halevy, J. L. Hammond, and over a dozen
other authors produced their retrospective account under the auspices of the
National Association of Local Government Officers, which sought guidance
for the future in the light of the past. The book's message came through loud
and clear in chapters on topics such as the town council and the committee
system, sanitation and housing, and libraries and museums. English city
dwellers, it was asserted, enjoyed far better city services than ever before, and
they could look forward confidently, under the progressive leadership of their

local officials, to steady progress in years to come. As William A. Robson, another L.S.E. faculty member, wrote in conclusion, 'There are plenty of causes for pessimism in the world; but the outlook in English local government is not amongst them. An unlimited vista of future usefulness and expansion stretches before us. We can look forward to the coming century in the most cheerful sense of the term'.[15]

Arthur Redford, an economic historian at the University of Manchester, chimed in a few years later with a massive account of the evolution of local government in the city where he worked. Published in connection with the hundredth anniversary of that town's incorporation as a chartered borough, it too emphasized progress since the first half of the nineteenth century, offering much detail on the perfecting of administrative machinery and on the provision of economic, social, and cultural services. Regarding the years between 1918 and 1935, Redford wrote,

> ... The City Council ... had done very good work in extraordinarily difficult circumstances. It had built about 25,000 houses, many new schools, a magnificent new library and a still more magnificent extension to the Town Hall. It had constructed two great roads, and cleared large areas of slum dwellings. It had provided food in some years for nearly ten thousand children, and relief for the workless on an exceptionally generous scale at a time of grievous unemployment, when the prosperity of the city was at its lowest ebb. It had not only completed the great Thirlmere Waterworks, begun nearly half a century earlier, but it had made considerable progress with the execution of the still more ambitious Haweswater scheme. All this had been achieved in a spirit of sturdy local independence, often without adequate national support, and sometimes in the teeth of strong opposition.

Since then, the city council had done its best to meet the town's growing needs within the limits imposed by the persistence of financial stringency, showing that Manchester was indeed a city that 'could face lean times with a stout spirit'.[16]

Writers such as Smith, Robson, and Redford proudly sustained and updated the kind of urban commentary propagated earlier by the admirers of Birmingham and Glasgow and to some extent by Patrick Geddes. They reminded their readers that for all the terrible problems British towns were experiencing during the depression, the average city dweller was still far better off in almost every respect than his or her parents and grandparents had been several decades earlier. Nonetheless, most expressions of this view sounded far less enthusiastic than the celebrations of municipal progress around the turn of the century, and they seemed to carry measurably less

25   The new city library and the town hall extension in Manchester. This picture and the book in which it appeared show that admiration for municipal achievements still came to the surface in England during the 1930s despite the generally somber mood of the times (source: Arthur Redford, *The History of Local Government in Manchester*, III [1940], 386).

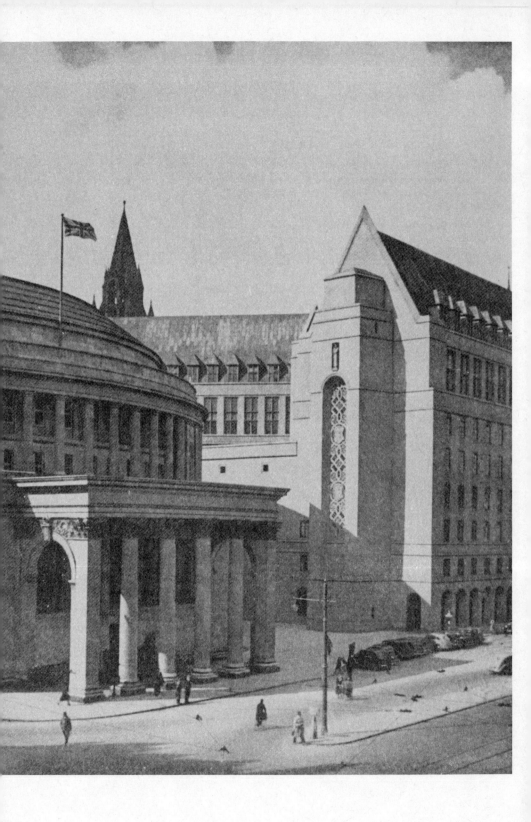

weight in the overall realm of articulate opinion than the views of men like Inge, Orwell, and Osborn.

The French, never in the forefront among those concerned with the urban variable, had still less to say about the city during these years than in earlier ones, perhaps in part because of the slowing pace of urban growth. The element of continuity in their thinking can be seen most clearly during approximately the first half of the period in the reaffirmation of Paris for a whole host of reasons by non-specialist authors who wrote for a popular audience. Pierre Albin, a popular historian, defended the city as a productive workplace, whose great size was fully justified by its economic functions and benefits. He also rejected the notion that Paris was a 'modern Babylon', asserting that Parisian morals were just as good as if not better than those of the rest of the country. Other writers, reflecting heightened awareness of the new importance outside as well as inside France that Paris had gained in the aftermath of the First World War, celebrated the city as a focal point not only for the nation but also for the world. Paris, to which large numbers of writers and artists kept coming during the decade after the peace conference of 1919, appeared to the publicist Gustave Rodrigues to be 'not the capital of a nation but the chief city of the universe'. It was 'Athens ... but an enlarged, international Athens'. Quoting the nineteenth-century German poet, Heinrich Heine, he suggested that it was 'the capital of the entire civilized world ... the meeting place of the intellectual notables'. In a similar vein, André Warnod described it as 'the spiritual capital of the civilized world ... the crucible where the civilization and the arts of the entire world have been blended'.[17]

As in England, about 1930 there seems to have been a change in the climate of opinion. The French capital's glories and its charm were extolled less frequently and exuberantly, and misgivings about metropolises and their prospects were heard more often. Blanche Maurel, another popular historian, wrote about the need to decentralize Paris by using the transportation network in order to facilitate the dispersion of hospitals, schools, and markets in the *banlieue* outside the city limits. But she did not want to see Paris develop in such a way that it simply filled up the department of the Seine. 'Its present growth', she wrote, 'borrowed from the rest of the nation, has impoverished it [France]; such a monstrous city is a social and political danger'.[18]

Similar sentiments became apparent in much greater and more influential measure in the thought of Charles-Edouard Jeanneret, known to the world simply as Le Corbusier. This brilliant representative of the modern movement in architecture had already, in the mid-1920s, started referring to 'the sickness of great cities', asserting that 'city centers are fatally ill, while their outskirts are being gnawed away as if by vermin'. He spoke of 'the cancer of Paris', thus recalling William Cobbett's references a century earlier to

London as 'the great wen', and he called attention to 'symptoms ... of breakdowns in people's health, and of [undesirable] economic, social, and religious changes'. He wrote, 'Paris is pitiless; there, a battle is fought with no quarter asked or given. It is a venue for championship fights or gladiatorial contests. We face up to one another and kill one another. Paris is paved with corpses'.[19]

Throughout the 1920s, Le Corbusier's disgust with the crowding and the chaos that had resulted from nineteenth-century urbanization was coupled with a basically affirmative attitude toward the big city as such, which he wished to redesign rather than to limit or to eliminate. Both in his plan of 1922 for a Contemporary City for Three Million Inhabitants and in the plan for a Radiant City (exhibited in 1930), he accepted the great metropolis as the most desirable form of human settlement for modern man. The urban landscape was to be freed from the burdens imposed by the recent past not through the resettlement of its inhabitants outside the city but instead through the careful combination of vertical density in high-rise apartments and office buildings with increased amounts of open space within the city itself.

After the Radiant City exhibit, Le Corbusier displayed growing doubts about the advantages of really large agglomerations. He seems to have come to the conclusion, as a result of the great depression, that the big cities' social attractions had led to increases in the numbers of their inhabitants far greater than those justified by economic considerations alone, thus exacerbating unemployment and poverty. By early 1931, he no longer accepted the figure of 3,000,000 inhabitants as a desirable population for Paris, and in 1934 he suggested that a figure of 1,000,000 was the optimum. Subsequently, he turned more and more toward regional planning as a means of reversing the concentration of his countrymen in the French metropolis. Like many observers of London during the same decade, Le Corbusier believed that Paris had become far too vast and that something had to be done in order to reduce its overwhelming size.

The triumph of ideology in Germany

During the interwar years, the amount of writing about cities and their problems produced by Germans far exceeded the output of the British and the French combined. Already having begun to demonstrate an acute interest in the modern *Grossstadt* shortly before the turn of the century, German thinkers continued to grapple with the issues it raised and the challenges it posed throughout the 1920s and the 1930s. They developed and expressed their thoughts until 1933 within a political and an intellectual milieu that was marked by increasingly bitter controversy and conflict regarding the whole development of modern civilization, a civilization symbolized perfectly for many of them by the big city. Differences of opinion about the urban scene therefore tended to reflect more basic ideological differences as well. The big city certainly had its champions during the Weimar period, but as the death of democracy drew near more and more critics raised their voices in order to warn their countrymen of the dangers to which urban growth exposed them. Subsequently, anti-urbanism of an especially virulent sort became one of the central components of the official *Weltanschauung*, or world view, espoused by the chief apologists for the Third Reich.

To speak of Weimar Germany inevitably brings to mind an especially rich period in the history of urban culture. Between the end of 1918 and early 1933, major artistic and intellectual movements emanating from or clustering in big cities contributed mightily to an image of Germany as a country in which not only urban life styles but also an urban mentality had gained the upper hand. A wide range of developments in literature, in the theater, in the pictorial arts, in architecture, in the cinema, and in the academic disciplines gave Berlin, Frankfurt, and other *Grossstädte* well deserved reputations for innovative vitality.[20]

Many thinkers and writers who adhered to modern and progressive values displayed great receptivity to some or all of these developments, seeing in them both the triumph of individual creativity and an overdue expansion of opportunity for the ordinary citizen. An urban historian by the name of Paul Sander, after asserting that 'the high points in cultural evolution [had] coincide[d] entirely with the high points in urban life' throughout past centuries, went on to argue that this correlation remained equally valid in the present. Despite the advent of newspapers and telegraphs, of railroads and automobiles, all of which now enabled villagers to swim in the cultural mainstream, cities had lost none of their old cultural significance. They were 'the focal points of intellectual life' just as much as or even more than they had been in the past. The role of really large urban centers was especially important, leading Sander to conclude, 'What we today call modern culture is essentially the culture of the big city'.[21]

Agnes Waldstein, an art historian and critic writing for a progressive Protestant journal in 1929, focused more specifically on the present. Rejecting the anti-urban charge that the big city exercised a generally 'degenerative' influence, she pointed hopefully to 'new forms of life ... which ... enjoy the same validity and the same possibilities as earlier ones'. In contrast to the rigid discipline imposed by the rhythms of labor in urban workplaces, greater and greater opportunities for stimulating play were opening up during the city dweller's leisure time, with the result that several branches of popular culture displayed great vitality. The desire felt by many urbanites to possess useless objects such as blown-glass figurines and artificial flowers ('toys for adults') and a growing taste for attractive clothing among all classes bore witness to 'a quite new delight in what is visible'. This cultural tendency manifested itself still more clearly in the rise of the movies, which constituted the most effective response yet to the widespread yearning among the masses for visual play. Another new tendency on the urban scene was the rise of modern architecture. Office buildings, stores, schools, and apartment houses, with their severely functional simplicity, all testified to the triumph of a new urban style that not only enlivened the city's appearance but also benefited the city's inhabitants.[22]

Another art historian and publicist, Max Osborn, wrote in the same year and in the same vein about Berlin, celebrating it as a cosmopolitan *Weltstadt* in which all sorts of cultural developments were enhancing the quality of urban life. He too saw 'the new beauty of the technical age' in contemporary architecture, especially in the newer department stores. Moreover, he praised the achievements of musical conductors such as Wilhelm Furtwängler and Bruno Walter, of theatrical producers such as Max Reinhardt and Erwin Piscator, and of the numerous artists who came to the capital because it offered far and away the best avenues anywhere for developing their talents and finding a public. Institutions of higher learning — the university, the technical institute, and various other *Hochschulen* established for special purposes — manifested the same power of attraction, drawing huge numbers of students to their rapidly expanding facilities. For all these reasons, as well as for others, Osborn regarded Berlin enthusiastically as 'the city of unlimited possibilities'.[23]

Other and much more frequently articulated reasons for thinking well of the big city during the Weimar period harked back to the great pride felt by many Germans in their municipalities before the First World War. Praise for the work done by city governments continued to be heard throughout the 1920s. Now dependent for their legitimacy on electorates that were no longer subdivided into different voting groups according to wealth, and in many cases entrusted with responsibility for much larger territories as a result of postwar amalgamations, local officials added constantly to the list of tasks they regularly performed. The satisfaction felt by many of them as a result of the job they were doing found expression again and again.

At a fairly general level, this pride can be seen in an essay by Paul Mitzlaff, an *Oberbürgermeister* in Bamberg and an officer of an intercity organization known as the German *Städtetag*.[24] Writing early in the decade, he asserted in a spirit of exhortation that city governments were fully capable of meeting the enormous challenges that had arisen to confront them in the aftermath of war and revolution. He called for 'pride and confidence in the not yet exhausted energy of the cities *vis-à-vis* the most difficult problems'. The reasons for this confidence were clear enough. 'Through tedious and detailed work ... they [the cities] are struggling both for their own development and for the reconstruction of the Reich'. Oskar Mulert, a man trained in financial administration who served as president of the *Städtetag*, called attention half a decade after the worst postwar difficulties had been surmounted to the recent accomplishments for which German cities could now claim credit.

Since the stabilization of the currency in 1924, the cities had moved aggressively to heal the wounds caused by war and inflation. They were not only continuing to perform their pre-war tasks but also enlarging their sphere of action to include more in the way of vocational education and of social welfare activities. The latter included care for crippled veterans and for the survivors of those killed in wartime hostilities, as well as for others who were aged, young, poor, or sick. 'Whoever surveys the whole sphere of responsibility belonging to the German cities', he concluded, 'will find the basic *Leitmotiv* of many-sided ... municipal activity, that is to say, the preservation and the advancement of the efficiency of the German people, which is the prerequisite for the recovery of our fatherland'.[25]

As always, such sentiments were expressed most concretely in assessments of conditions in particular cities. In Berlin, the archivist Ernst Kaeber spoke for many of his fellow officials when he wrote in a collaborative volume on the 'city of four million' that the *Weltstadt* was once again becoming a home town, or *Heimat*, for its ordinary inhabitants. As a result of its government having become both more democratic and more powerful in recent years, it could lay claim with growing justification to their loyal devotion. While the major expansion of governmental responsibility mentioned by Kaeber pertained to the creation of Greater Berlin in 1920, *Oberbürgermeister* Gustav Böss pointed to more specific accomplishments in areas other than the structure of the municipality itself. He emphasized 'the first parts of a large rapid transit network, the extension of the Berlin harbor, the great halls at the fairgrounds ... the energy works ... the new people's parks, athletic fields, and playgrounds, the free baths ... the airport, the city opera, and the planetarium', all of which gave a foretaste of still greater achievements to be expected in years to come. Subsequently, a book published under Böss' name outlined the full range of the city government's growing responsibilities in systematic detail. It started with *Sozialpolitik* (e.g., care for the unemployed and public health measures), touched on many other topics along the way, and ended with planning, housing, construction, and education.[26]

Berliners were especially eager to publicize the progress of their city, but they were by no means alone. Cologne, which enjoyed the able leadership of Konrad Adenauer between 1917 and 1933, received similar treatment from Valmar Cramer, the chief of the city's press department. Proudly recalling a spirit of harmonious cooperation between the executive branch and the popular forces that had greatly increased their political power in 1918, he celebrated a whole host of successes during the postwar years. The green belt, a sports stadium, new housing, industrial parks, the new university, and other recently established cultural institutions all presaged an increasingly happy future for the ancient city on the Rhine. Among other big cities, Dortmund, Essen, Stettin, Barmen, and Nuremberg all benefited from highly favorable accounts of the recent changes brought about and the work currently being done by their elected and their appointed officials. For the contributors to such works, most of whom were themselves public servants at the local level, the urban prospect seemed very bright indeed.[27]

Despite the continued expression of such sentiments by some, the overall picture of the big city during the Weimar years was gloomy, and it became darker and darker as time went on. Discontent with the quality of urban life manifested itself in many quarters during these decades, chiefly though by no means exclusively among the enemies of the Republic, especially those on the far right who were fundamentally opposed to political and social democracy.

Let us begin on the left, where numerous poets and artists active during the 1920s laid bare what they saw as the sordid corruption, the widespread suffering, and the general malaise endemic in a nation of cities that had not yet experienced a true social revolution. Max Barthel, one of a number of working-class poets, described the city starting in the early 1920s as a 'prison', 'a heap of stone and hunger', and 'a furious monster, wildly seeking the flesh of hearts', whose evils would be eliminated only after a great popular uprising. The much better known Bertolt Brecht, who was to explicitly accept Marxism in the late 1920s, wrote one poem titled 'The Crushing Weight of the Cities' (1925) and another titled 'Concerning the Cities' (1926) that read as follows: 'Under them there are sewers./There is nothing in them, and above them there is smoke./We were inside them./We have enjoyed nothing./We died quickly./And slowly they are wasting away too'.[28]

George Grosz and Otto Dix, the leading artists in the postexpressionist movement known as the *Neue Sachlichkeit*, both felt extreme antipathy toward bourgeois society, and they displayed it venomously in their depictions of the *Grossstadt*. Grosz's satirical attacks on wartime Berlin were followed during the postwar years by other portrayals of urban street scenes that featured fat capitalists, vicious militarists, war cripples, and naked women. All of these figures, situated with regard to one another in ways that suggested both alienation and chaos, pointed up the unsavory and corrupt qualities of the big city in Grosz's eyes. A similar view asserted itself in Dix's *Big-City Triptych* of 1927-28. In the central panel, which represents high society, featureless men in tuxedos and painted women dance frenetically but joylessly to jazz music, while in the side panels war cripples vye for attention unsuccessfully with prostitutes who appear quite similar to the ladies at the dance.[29] Grosz and Dix, like Barthel, Brecht, and many others who sympathized with revolutionary ideas, throve in an urban environment. Without it, they would have been much the poorer as creative individuals. But the fruit of their labors must have tasted bitter indeed to anyone who held the city as a whole in genuinely high esteem.

Among more moderate men closer to the ideological center, misgivings about many aspects of the big city became increasingly apparent, leading to pleas for the reduction of urban density. Karl Scheffler, an art and architectural critic who had already expressed grave concerns about the

culture of Berlin and other aspects of urban society before the First World War, voiced a much greater degree of anxiety in the mid-1920s. He observed that since the war whatever had existed earlier in the way of optimism concerning the cities' future prospects had largely given way to skepticism. Housing shortages, strikes by public utility workers, and traffic congestion as a result of increasing numbers of automobiles had all made clear 'the fundamental failings of the big city'. Scheffler did not fully share 'the pessimism and the despair over the big city' that he perceived all around him. But he certainly recognized the very real problems from which they arose, and he made it clear that the only way to deal with them was to spread industry and population more evenly throughout the countryside.[30]

Karl von Mangoldt, a political liberal who had served since 1899 as general secretary of the German Society for Housing Reform, wrote in 1928 that 'the naive delight in the impressive growth of the big cities' had given way to 'gloomy dread'. The question of 'whether it was not necessary instead to divert this whole development as much as possible in a new direction' had to be faced. After summing up all the increasing costs as well as the remaining benefits of life in the *Grossstadt*, he concluded his overall assessment by asserting,

> ... The current extent and mode of our big-city development clearly threaten the roots of our whole existence in four ways: biologically through the enormous decline in birth rates, especially in the big cities; politically through the negation of the bases of a healthy democracy, on which we now depend; militarily through the obvious and particularly great vulnerability of big cities in wartime; and morally through the enormous obstacles that the contemporary big city places in the way of the necessary moral regeneration of our nation.

This liberal defender of political democracy thus proposed agricultural colonization, industrial relocation, and general decentralization, as well as various efforts to reform the big city from within.[31]

Franz Oppenheimer, a progressive sociologist at the University of Frankfurt, expressed sentiments that sounded quite similar. 'Man', he wrote, 'needs a bit of unspoiled land in order to thrive. He cannot strike roots in the paved streets, and the results are the restlessness and nervousness of the urban population, its political radicalism both on the right and on the left, alcoholism, and its evil companions, prostitution and crime'. In order to combat these ills, he called for the redistribution of land and the establishment of agricultural colonies, which would hopefully stop if not reverse the mass migration to the already overcrowded cities.[32]

These criticisms by leftists, liberals, and moderates bore witness to a pervasive sense of unease over the modern city that was incorporated to much more devastating effect in the thinking of the radical right. According to the

26 'Friedrichstrasse': a view of Berlin by George Grosz. This engraving, executed in 1918, graphically expresses the artist's view of post-World War One Berlin as a center of violence and corruption (source: George Grosz, *Ecce Homo* [1923], 1).

'conservative revolutionaries', the words *Grossstadt* and *Weltstadt* implied
fear, revulsion, and contempt. For many of these men, the big city made
manifest fundamental flaws in modern civilization as a whole that necessitated a thorough restructuring of the German state if the German people were
to survive and prosper as a united nation.[33]

No one did more to propagate pessimism about the role of the metropolis
in the life of the modern world than Oswald Spengler, one of the chief gurus
among the neoconservative enemies of the Weimar Republic. Having worked
for several years as a teacher in German secondary schools, he resigned from
his position in Hamburg and moved to Munich in 1911 in order to devote
himself to a lonely exploration of the basic forces at work in the course of
world history. The first volume of his magnum opus, titled *Der Untergang des
Abendlandes*, was largely finished by 1914, but it was not published until
1918, when its counsels of despair quickly found a receptive audience in a
country that had just experienced a shattering defeat. The volume was strewn
with gloomy remarks on cities that echoed the conservative anti-urbanism of
the pre-war decades. But it was not until the appearance in 1922 of the
eagerly awaited second volume, which contained a long chapter on 'The Soul
of the City', that Spengler's views about the metropolis were expressed in
more or less systematic fashion. The phrase 'more or less' is appropriate here,
because Spengler was never a rigorous thinker. Having decided that he would
not permit his search for large-scale insights to be hindered by adherence to
the canons of academic respectability, he wrote intuitively and often con-
fusingly. Nonetheless, the main thrust of what he had to say was unmistakable. Bringing together almost every element in the criticisms of the city by
his conservative predecessors and combining them in colorful and powerful
prose that greatly heightened their intensity, he portrayed the metropolis as
the supreme symbol and the final cause of the decay of culture and the death
of civilization.[34]

In Spengler's view, the growth of cities was intimately linked with the
cycles of development and decline in world history. 'World history', he
wrote, 'is the history of civic man. Peoples, states, politics, religion, all arts,
and all sciences rest upon one prime phenomenon of human being, the town'.
Such a statement seemed to suggest a positive recognition of some of the
city's virtues, but Spengler quickly changed his tone. As cities grew larger
and larger, ultimately becoming giant *Weltstädte*, their inhabitants lost their
sense of national identity. 'Today', he wrote, 'a Brandenburg peasant is
closer to a Sicilian peasant than he is to a Berliner'. Modern cities conformed
to 'a more and more uniform type', which cut across national boundaries. It
was only 'the small number of genuine megalopolitans at the top' who were
'at home wherever their spiritual postulates [were] satisfied', but these
'spiritual postulates' were becoming more and widespread in the thinking of
metropolitan man in general. 'Man', he asserted, 'becomes intellect, "free"
like the nomads, whom he comes to resemble, but narrower and colder than

they'. The cold, unfeeling rationality of the modern urbanite was, for Spengler, as different from the mentality of the peasant as water was from blood. It found expression in the abstractions of political democracy and a money-based economy, in chess-board layouts of streets, and in reluctance to have children, as well as in the realm of high culture. The world cities themselves, with their 'deep, long gorges between high, stony houses filled with coloured dust and strange uproar', were becoming more and more remote from unspoiled nature.[35]

Spengler believed that these consequences of urban growth presaged an inevitably grim future. In the end, 'the stone Colossus' would turn the man whose culture had been formed in the countryside 'into its creature, its executive organ, and finally its victim'. The *Weltstadt*, 'insatiably and incessantly demanding and devouring fresh streams of men', would 'suck the country dry' until it grew weary and died 'in the midst of an almost uninhabited waste'. After sacrificing 'the blood and soul of its creators to the needs of its majestic evolution and then the last flower of that growth to the spirit of Civilization', the giant city of the future, like the giant cities of the past, would bring about its own destruction and thereby the downfall of civilization itself. This was the unavoidable destiny of metropolitan societies, the inescapable fate of men who were 'committed to stone and to intellectualism'. Biological sterility and spiritual petrifaction would bring the cycle of historical development back to the point at which it had begun, and no reforms could forestall this outcome.[36]

The Spenglerian view of the *Weltstadt* pervaded a great deal of the writing about cities that appeared during the late 1920s and the early 1930s. Among earlier critics, only Wilhelm Heinrich Riehl had exerted a measure of influence at all comparable to that enjoyed by this deeply pessimistic man. Spengler's fatalistic belief that the death of an urban civilization was inevitable — that nothing could be done to forestall the eventual completion of the cyclical process — did not find many adherents. But his gloomy forebodings helped to crystallize the anti-urban animosities of a large number of his contemporaries in ways that led toward advocacy or acceptance of the same revolutionary conservatism to which their philosophical mentor had already lent his support. Karl Weidel, an educational philosopher, neatly summarized Spengler's message in a brief essay aimed at primary school teachers. In contrast to the peasant, he argued, the urbanite was enamored of intellect and skeptical of authority. He was a 'nomad' both physically and emotionally, and his character suffered from 'superficiality and inner emptiness'. The inhabitants of cities did not constitute a true 'community of fate' but only a mass of 'loosely related atoms'. To forestall the disaster he foresaw if the cities continued to eat away at the nation's healthy core, its remaining peasantry, he advocated strenuous efforts by rural teachers to keep their pupils on the land.[37]

Others who wrote under the influence of Spengler's prophecies expressed their views with a still greater sense of alarm and clearer indications of where they stood politically as well as socially. Viktor Grimm, a medical doctor, wrote a book on 'the struggle between the peasantry and the big city' in which he too acknowledged his debt to Spengler. He went into much more detail than either Spengler or Weidel with regard to the specific pathologies that afflicted urban society. He indicted the city as a prison that was full of people who suffered from both physical and emotional infirmities. He portrayed it as a place in which domestic morality was disintegrating and national strength was disappearing. Like Weidel, he too sought to defend the rural sector against further assaults from without. But rather than relying on mere persuasion, he called for 'a dictator ... a man of great importance, a national hero', who would have the will and the power to implement a far-reaching program of agricultural redevelopment.[38]

Richard Korherr, one of whose earlier works had been introduced by Spengler, was a professional statistician who wrote broadly about the whole range of threats that he saw emanating from the capital. His long essay of 1930 on Berlin, unlike the works of Weidel and Grimm, was just as pessimistic as Spengler's. Without in any way suggesting that the German peasantry offered the hope of salvation, Korherr applied the Spenglerian perspective at great length to their nation's world city. Asserting forthrightly at the outset that he had always hated Berlin, he proceeded to buttress his argument that its growth spelled ruin for Germany by drawing parallels between it and earlier cities. 'Half barbarian, soulless, international — a world city on a grand scale. With its masses of men, masses of art, masses of intellect, with its poison, a final flash before extinction. A single point, which attracts and consumes all life, like ancient Rome'. He then elaborated on all of the capital's weaknesses and its sins. He made it quite clear that he was especially dismayed by the great influence of 'the mob or crowd' and by the power exercised by Social Democratic politicians, who threatened to dominate all of Germany from this politically strategic place. Such dire warnings made Korherr's right-wing animosity toward the Weimar Republic impossible to ignore. He, like Spengler and Grimm, belonged without a doubt to the camp of the conservative revolutionaries.[39]

Operating within an intellectual and political milieu that had become saturated with a kind of free-floating anxiety as well as specific fears concerning the big city, many men who wrote under the influence of National Socialism displayed extreme antipathy toward the urban world. As in the Weimar period, toward the end of the 1930s a more positive attitude began to assert itself here and there. But on the whole the *Grossstadt* enjoyed an abysmally poor reputation, both among avowed proponents of Nazi ideology before and after 1933 and among others who were in a position to propagate their ideas within the Third Reich. The Nazis certainly did not invent anti-urbanism, whose roots in Germany can be traced, as we have seen, at least as far back as the middle of the nineteenth century. What they did was to appropriate an ideological tradition that had gained greatly in intensity and in popularity during the postwar years of political and economic crisis. They then exploited that tradition with a high degree of shrewdness, first for the purpose of gaining power and then for the purpose of legitimating their newly established regime.[40]

For a capsule statement of Nazi hostility to the big city, one can do no better than to turn to Alfred Rosenberg's *Myth of the Twentieth Century*. First published in 1930 and subsequently reprinted *ad nauseam*, this characteristically vague but nonetheless authoritative exposition of the National Socialist world view by the party's chief ideologist included a harsh denunciation of existing *Gross-* and *Weltstädte*. Many of the familiar complaints reappeared, with a strong admixture of Nazi hostility to non-Aryans, to Marxists, to pacifists, and to liberals.

> We see today the racially destructive migration from the land and the provinces to the big cities. The cities swell in size, enervating the nation, attracting adventurers and schemers of all colors, and thereby furthering racial chaos. The city, which used to be a center of culture and morality, has, through the world cities, become a network of advance positions for the Bolshevik onslaught.

After strengthening his assault with additional warnings of biological decline and Marxist revolution, Rosenberg also expressed fears that arose from the vulnerability of the big city under conditions of modern warfare. In order to survive the coming struggle for existence among nations that would inevitably and rightly involve entire populations in armed conflict, Germany could ill afford its present degree of urban concentration. Rosenberg rejected Spengler's fatalistic view that nothing could be done to avert the growth of the world city, a view he regarded as evidence of the 'cowardly intellectuality' that was yet another characteristically urban defect. But he did admit that continued urbanization was inevitable in a situation in which individuals retained complete freedom to live where they chose. The hypnotic effect of movies, department stores, and nightclubs, as well as of the stock exchange, was simply irresistible. Urbanization, which was not only nourished by the hopes of revolutionary Marxists but also permitted by the basic values of democratic liberals, provided compelling evidence in Rosenberg's eyes of the need to eliminate the basic system of individual rights that were guaranteed by the constitution of the Weimar Republic.[41]

Hans F. K. Günther, the party's leading academic authority in the area of *Rassenkunde*, or 'racial science', propagated similar views at much greater length in a later work dedicated to Rosenberg that dealt with urbanization's 'dangers for the nation and the state'. This tract was supposedly based on 'research into life and social science', and it did incorporate a good deal of material drawn from the work of other scholars, including social scientists in England and America. But Günther's basic intentions were clearly political. Using his considerable prestige as the first Nazi academic to gain a university professorship, Günther pilloried the big city in large part as a way of validating the seizure of power by Adolf Hitler that had taken place during the year before his book first appeared.[42]

Much of Günther's indictment had long constituted the stock-in-trade of anti-urban ideologists. He reiterated the customary charges having to do with declining birth rates and the declining quality of the German population, charges that fully retained their earlier significance with regard both to the nation's biological health and to its military strength. The big city was in his view a place in which 'the hereditarily inferior ones' and Jews managed to adapt and to survive, while the most worthy elements of the German *Volk* were destroyed. At the same time, Günther denounced the 'mass soul', 'the hatred of all cultivation', and the 'new barbarism' that either prevailed or threatened to prevail among big-city populations.[43]

These warnings were combined with less familiar arguments that served to buttress Günther's defense of the new regime. Günther recalled Thomas Jefferson's observation over a century earlier that city dwellers lacked the capacity for responsible self-government. 'Germanic democracy' of the sort supposedly prized by Jefferson required a primarily rural population, consisting in large measure of independent freeholders. The virtual elimination of this class in a country such as Germany meant that any sort of democracy was, at least for the time being, no longer viable. The 'mass rule' that had come about as a result of urbanization could not endure. It had to give way either to a Marxist dictatorship or to a dictatorship that accorded with the traditions of the German people. As Günther put it,

> Statesmen and professors of constitutional law in the nineteenth century believed that one could govern and administer all the more 'progressively' to the extent that the population was more urban and therefore more 'enlightened'. The contrary is true. The less agricultural and aristocratic a people of Germanic stamp ... the more dictatorially it must be ruled. The more a people is dominated by mass feeling, the less fitted it is for Germanic freedom and equality.

However much or little in the way of true autonomy for ordinary citizens may have been implied by the clearly hierarchical concept of 'Germanic freedom', it was quite evident according to Günther that even this limited liberty could not be permitted in an urban Germany.[44]

Friedrich Burgdörfer, who had become director of the Reich Statistical Bureau in 1929 and continued to hold that position under the Nazis, repeatedly sang the anti-urban refrain in ways that reflected his particular expertise in the study of population trends. He formulated a more specific indictment of the *Grossstadt* in the light of empirical data than either

27   Anti-urban demography for the ordinary reader in the Third Reich. The heading reads, 'How would the population of Berlin develop over a period of 150 years without migration from outside?' The pictures and the numbers beside them foretell the same story of demographic decline, stemming from low urban birth rates (source: 'Die Grossstadt als Massengrab des Volkes', *Deutchlands Erneuerung*, 17 [1933], 559).

Wie würde sich Berlins Bevölkerung ohne Zuzug von außen im Laufe von 150 Jahren entwickeln?

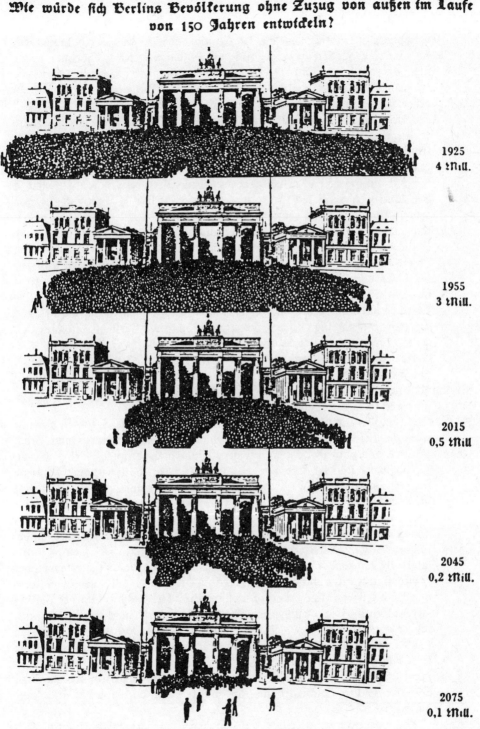

1925
4 Mill.

1955
3 Mill.

2015
0,5 Mill

2045
0,2 Mill.

2075
0,1 Mill.

Rosenberg or Günther, but his demographic analysis was closely linked to a broader view of current society and politics that was clearly congenial to the men who employed him. Deeply worried by the sharp drop in the overall German birth rate since the First World War, Burgdörfer pointed to an especially severe problem in the big cities. From 1926 through 1933 they had produced slightly under three-fifths of the children necessary to maintain their populations at constant levels over the long run without replenishment from a countryside that was now reproducing itself with only a narrow margin of safety. Clearly the danger that the *Volk* as a whole would eventually begin to disappear had to be taken much more seriously now than when it had first been predicted in the writings of men like Hansen and Ammon around the turn of the century. In the medium run, the population deficit that manifested itself in the cities heightened the likelihood that Germany would have to import growing numbers of foreign workers in order to keep up the size of a declining labor force. All too likely to have migrated from the Slavic East, these workers would undermine the biological integrity of the German *Volk*, thereby hastening its decline and fall.[45] Burgdörfer, like Günther and other leading city haters among the National Socialists, attacked the growth of the big city as a force that diminished German autonomy and strength in other ways as well. The First World War had shown that Germany could not afford to depend on foreign markets for its food, and the development of aerial bombardment demonstrated the folly of high urban densities from a purely military standpoint. Once again, the need to be prepared for armed conflict came to the fore.[46]

A complementary set of rather different concerns emerged from a major work on the city written by two architects, Werner Lindner and Erich Böckler, and published late in the decade under the auspices of the German Labor Front. Böckler, like many of his predecessors both within and outside the planning profession, excoriated the modern city in large part on account of its aesthetic failings. Behind the pompous facades that lined the major streets one could see 'a maze of narrow and dark courtyards, residential areas mixed with small businesses, planned haphazardly and without order, billboards with oversized and tattered advertisements, dirty factory walls, [and] oily garages'. Böckler, again like many earlier critics of the urban scene, regarded this environment as a breeding ground for all sorts of cultural degeneracy beyond the realm of architecture. The 'swampy soil' of the big city had given rise to 'cubist painting, cinema kitsch, [and] jazz music with nigger dancing', all of which now threatened to pollute the taste and the morals of non-urbanites as well as their city cousins. In this view, the *Grossstadt* once again appeared as a place where visual ugliness went hand in hand with a more general decline of traditional standards of the sort that Günther had undoubtedly had in mind when he wrote of the 'new barbarism'.[47]

The most prominent critics of urban society in Germany during the Nazi period were on the whole much less interested in reforming the city than in escaping from it. They rejected the very idea of large agglomerations as suitable places of residence for German men and women. Instead, they fervently advocated the retention and the re-establishment of patterns of settlement that harked back to the centuries preceding the industrial revolution. Their sentiments were truly anti-urban, or at least opposed to the big city if not to all cities, and the solutions they proposed reeked of that ostensibly conservative nostalgia which was one of the main sources of the Nazis' deeply emotional appeal to large numbers of their followers.

One of the most prominent threads in the Nazis' ideological banner was the theme of *Blut und Boden*, or 'blood and soil'. Idealization of the supposedly unspoiled peasant and all that he represented functioned as a *Leitmotiv* in official pronouncements concerning the positive values for which the Nazis were fighting. The peasant stood for everything that the denizens of the big cities were either losing or destroying: physical health, racial purity, large and stable families, religious faith, adherence to folk culture, and acceptance of authority. The already well-established tradition of what Klaus Bergmann aptly calls 'agrarian romanticism' flourished under the careful cultivation of Nazi ideologues.

The most influential representative of this outlook by far was Richard Walther Darré, the party's leading expert on agriculture. Having relentlessly sung the praises of the peasantry and condemned the weakness and wickedness of the urban masses before 1933 in works such as *The Peasantry as the Wellspring of the Nordic Race* (1929) and *A New Nobility of Blood and Soil* (1930), Darré continued to propagandize fervently in favor of the agrarian sector after the seizure of power. First as Reich Peasant Leader and then as Minister of Food and Agriculture, he advocated a view of a good Germany as a country in which the great bulk of the population would once again be living on the land. Darré was a muddle-headed philosopher rather than a practical planner, and most men who wrote about urban problems in any detail did not go nearly as far as he did in simply wishing the cities out of existence. Nonetheless, he voiced a basic attitude, an agrarian myth, that enjoyed widespread (if necessarily modified) support among his fellow critics of the modern city. Both Günther and Burgdörfer, for instance, indicated a strong desire to stem and reverse the tide of rural to urban migration, as did numerous other writers throughout the 1930s. Their critiques of the big city pointed quite clearly in the general direction advocated by the blood and soil agrarians.[48]

Another counter-image to that of the *Grossstadt* seemed to offer rather more hope to most men who thought about the city in any detail than the notion of turning urbanites back into farmers. This was the idea of the city of small to medium size. A powerful mystique continued to surround the *Kleinstadt*, the sort of settlement founded and maintained in a spirit of supposedly idyllic harmony during the Middle Ages. Repeatedly evoked with nostalgic affection by conservative critics starting in the nineteenth century, its high repute had also helped to inspire reformers such as the advocates of garden cities before being used by the Nazis for their own purposes in the 1930s.[49]

Rosenberg, rejecting calls for abolition of the city as such, pleaded instead for the founding of new cities as soon as the population of existing ones approached the 100,000 mark. He envisaged a network of such towns spread all over Germany, with only a few centers as large as 500,000. 'In place of perhaps a hundred great centers that contaminate their inhabitants', he wrote (apparently referring to an area a good deal larger than Germany), 'there can eventually be ten thousand that nourish culture, if strong-willed men rather than Marxism and liberalism determine our fate'.[50]

Many other writers called in much more detail for cities of modest size, whose maintenance or establishment would have depended similarly on the authoritarian rule of which Rosenberg and other Nazis were thoroughly enamored. Böckler urged that the big cities not be permitted to grow any larger. The development of existing small cities should be encouraged instead. 'Endeavor for the German *Kleinstadt*', he wrote, 'is endeavor for the German people'. Gottfried Feder, an engineer and amateur economist who had been one of the party's founding fathers and had served as head of the Reich Homestead Office of the Labor Front in 1934-35, wrote at still greater length in another official work on city planning about the need to revitalize existing small towns and to create new ones. Desirable though it might be simply to keep the children of farmers on the land, it was 'of still more political value ... to transplant hereditarily sound working-class families out of the suffocating air of the *Gross-* and *Weltstädte* into the rural and natural sphere of newly established cities with populations of about 20,000'. This view elicited a great deal of sympathy in Nazi Germany, at least in print.[51]

Other currents of opinion and other hopes were more in accord with the actual course of economic and social development during the Third Reich, which did not in fact move in the directions indicated by anti-urban ideology.[52] As the agricultural sector continued to shrink and the urban centers continued to grow, a not insignificant number of Germans expressed much more positive attitudes toward the *Grossstadt* than the officially sanctioned one. Without in any way challenging the central tenets of National Socialist political ideology, they indicated at least acceptance of and in some cases real enthusiasm for the big city — if not in its present form, then in the form they expected it to take under Hitler's continuing leadership.

At one level, there were those who sought to restore some balance to the overall picture of urban life. They reminded their readers in eminently sensible fashion that the big cities and their inhabitants were not all bad and that for better or worse they could not be eliminated. While frequently admitting that the large urban centers did indeed suffer from appalling defects, they hastened to add that anti-urban criticism had to be tempered by recognition of the city's legitimate attractions and its real benefits. As one author, an art critic, put it,

> Millions of human beings live in the cities, which mean more to them than simply material opportunities.... False romanticism must not induce us to ignore the city dwellers in favor of the landed element.... It is nonsense to arrive at a National Socialism that does not acknowledge the city, just as it is wrong to regard technology as the gravedigger of culture.[53]

Willy Hellpach, a Weimar democrat, a medical doctor, and a professor of ethnology at the University of Heidelberg, developed similar views at much greater length. His *Mensch und Volk der Grossstadt* (1939) was the only work published in Germany during the interwar years that stands comparison as a scholarly overview of the urban scene with the numerous urban sociology texts that appeared in the United States. He began it with an effort to put some distance between himself and the likes of Hans F. K. Günther. After emphasizing that he carried no brief for the *Grossstadt*, he nonetheless reminded his readers that it existed for a wide range of reasons: economic, cultural, and political. In order to combat the ills of the big cities effectively, one had to understand 'their achievements, their positive values, and their current indispensability'.[54]

Another strategy, which became increasingly apparent toward the end of the decade, was to indicate recent improvements in the quality of urban life that seemed to reflect credit on the National Socialist regime. After all, it was one thing to rail in 1933 or 1934 against an urban world that had been inherited from the pre-Nazi period and something else to persist in casti-gating mercilessly places that had enjoyed half a decade of Nazi rule. F. Linke, a professor of meteorology and geophysics at the University of Frankfurt, summed up matters as follows at the conclusion of a scholarly volume on urban health written by two dozen scientific specialists:

> That the big city acts unfavorably on many organisms, especially human beings, is undeniable. But the frequently expressed pessimism of recent decades is exaggerated. There is no reason to condemn the big city outright as a living space for men. Everywhere there is successful striving by state and municipal authorities to combat the real misgivings about the city through city-planning, hygienic, and organizational measures. Behind many of these efforts stands the new Germany, with its new knowledge and policies.[55]

Local officials were especially optimistic. A city councillor in Berlin pointed out that the local birth rate was on the rise, having climbed to 14.9 per thousand in 1937 and to 15.6 in 1938. In clear contrast to the years 1926-33, when deaths in the capital had exceeded births by 70,000, the city was now producing a surplus, which was growing from year to year. Another Berlin city councillor sang the praises of the resurgent *Grossstadt* more generally. 'Can the big city be a home?' he asked, a question he clearly answered in the affirmative. Under the guidance of the new regime, the spirit of communal solidarity was reasserting itself at every level of the state and society, including the metropolis. A whole host of measures were, he suggested, helping to improve the lot of ordinary urbanites and to strengthen their sense of belonging to the places in which they lived. His remarks were necessarily brief. Reforms designed to benefit the urban masses did not stand very high on the Nazis' list of priorities, and most improvements in the quality of urban life during these years resulted primarily from the general improvement of the economy. But it is not surprising that a servant of the new Germany who worked for it at the local level would try to salvage some sense of urban pride in a way that was thoroughly consistent with his overriding loyalty to the national government.[56]

Looking toward the future expansion of German influence outside Germany as well as at the rise of National Socialism within Germany, some men explicitly recognized the importance of the big city from the standpoint of political and military power, a theme that had last asserted itself during the First World War. Hellpach expressed this view when he wrote, 'The collection of a large following is only possible within the walls of vast agglomerations.... We cannot imagine Mussolini without Milan and Rome or Hitler without Vienna and Munich.... Big cities are like national military camps, without which no commander can fight battles and direct his campaigns.... Population density is essential for effectiveness'. Florian Wallenstein, a Viennese engineer, argued against any effort to recapture the rural past. He asserted, 'Only if Central Europeans of the future are not merely farmers and artisans but also a technological *Volk* will they ... be materially rich and spiritually of high quality, a dominant people, peace-loving but also capable of war'. The way to avoid the dismal future prophesied by Spengler in the coming age of international conflict was not to abandon the city but instead to exploit its modernizing possibilities for the purposes of national preparedness. A city councillor in Essen celebrated his city in much the same vein. He reminded his readers not only that the Nazis had found many supporters there before 1933 but also that in recent years it had once again become 'the armorer of the German Reich'.[57]

A favorable view of a certain kind of modern city reappeared, again with strong emphasis on dictatorial control inside the state and intimations of power outside it, in the thinking of Adolf Hitler and the architect Albert Speer. Both of these men envisaged a series of mammoth building projects. Hitler announced on January 30, 1937 that the planned redevelopment of Berlin and several other cities was to serve as a visible sign of the resurrection of the German people. The plans he and Speer developed were characterized by the pursuit of heroic monumentality, which they viewed as the architectural antidote within an urban framework to the urban chaos produced by nineteenth-century liberalism. Following the lead of earlier planners such as Baron Haussmann in France and Daniel Burnham in America, they designed city centers that were intended to be intimidating in their grandiosity. Broad avenues, vast squares, and huge public structures were to express not only

28 The Berlin of Adolf Hitler and Albert Speer. The viewer proceeds visually from the Victory Column along a monumental boulevard that had been expanded under Speer's direction. The view leads to the Brandenburg Gate and other structures from earlier centuries in the background. It clearly conveys a powerful sense of pride in the capital of Nazi Germany (source: Albert Speer and Rudolf Walters, *Neue deutsche Baukunst* [1941], 56).

order and unity at home but also the leading position in Europe and the world enjoyed by Germany and its *Führer*. As Speer pointed out in 1939, these plans depended for their realization on the dictatorial control they were supposed to represent. What he did not point out, although it became self-evident later, was that because of their enormous scale and great cost they also presupposed military conquest of non-German peoples. Only the direct exploitation of foreigners that was to be facilitated by the existing cities would have made it possible to bring Hitler's vision of an urban future to fruition.[58]

Despite the recognition by practical men that cities were not all bad and that they had vital functions to perform in a nation that aspired to world power, and despite Hitler's grandiose dreams, it is necessary to emphasize that the prevailing tone of articulate sentiment in Nazi Germany remained deeply hostile to the modern city. The *Grossstadt* in general and more particularly the big cities inherited from the period before the seizure of power continued to serve as potent symbols of the modern malaise the Nazis were supposedly working to overcome. In so far as it seemed to dictate a return to the countryside, and consequently the acquisition of more *Lebensraum* in the east, anti-urbanism clearly contributed to the policy of imperialist expansion for whose success an urban-industrial economy was essential but not sufficient.[59] Toward the end of the Third Reich, as the final result of that policy, the anti-urbanists were to witness the almost total destruction of many of the cities they had so bitterly reviled. It was only thereafter, when they were forced to rebuild them, that Germans truly rediscovered how essential their cities had always been to their well-being as a nation and as individuals.[60]

From ideology to sociology in the United States

Like Germany, America witnessed a great deal more in the way of reflection on and debate about cities and their prospects during the interwar years than either Britain or France. Having already experienced a wide range of urban phenomena in steadily growing measure during the decades leading up to the First World War, America was to cross the rural-urban divide during the 1920s. The sense of living in a nation in which the urban sector was securing for itself a clearly dominant position *vis-à-vis* the countryside and the small town stimulated an enormous outpouring of books and articles about urban affairs. As in Europe, much of the debate about the quality of city life took place within the familiar framework of pre-war categories and attitudes. But, again as in Europe, there was also a steadily growing recognition that the very large city, the metropolis, posed special challenges rather different from the ones that arose in other urban centers. Another new feature of the intellectual landscape in America, far more evident than in Europe, was urban sociology. Its many practitioners created a field of academic study that marked the culmination — and in certain respects constituted a synthesis — of many of the intellectual traditions that have been treated in this book.

Traditional anti-urbanism can be discerned most readily in the writings of men who sought to defend the agricultural way of life. Writers who had been born and raised in the South, still the most heavily rural and staunchly conservative area in the nation, played an especially notable part in this effort. Twelve such authors, led by four poets known as the Fugitives who had clustered around Vanderbilt University in Nashville, undertook around the middle of this period to justify a pre-urban social and cultural order in a famous manifesto, *I'll Take My Stand: The South and the Agrarian Tradition* (1930). John Crowe Ransom, Allen Tate, Robert Penn Warren, Donald Davidson, and their eight fellow essayists supported 'a Southern way of life against ... the American or prevailing way', and they all agreed that the basic distinctions they had in mind could be reduced to the phrase 'Agrarian versus Industrial'. The main targets against which they hurled their critical barbs were the values and the life styles associated in their minds with a certain mode of production, and they had little to say about the city as such. Their basic anti-urbanism was, however, unmistakable, and at various points they clearly identified urban centers as the geographic focal points for those tendencies they most abhorred.[61]

As Ransom observed in his 'Reconstructed but Unregenerate', the greatest threats to inherited southern values emanated from the growing southern cities.

> There is one powerful voice in the South which, tired of a long status of disrepute, would see the South made at once into a section second to none in wealth, as that is statistically reckoned, and in progressiveness, as that might be estimated by the rapidity of the industrial turnover. This desire offends those who would still like to regard the South as, in the old sense, a home; but its expression is loud and insistent. The urban South, with its heavy importation of regular American ways and regular American citizens, has nearly capitulated to these novelties. It is the village South and the rural South which supply the resistance, and it is lucky for them that they represent a vast quantity of inertia.

In Ransom's view, places like Atlanta, Birmingham, and Memphis were the outposts of an alien and a destructive materialism that ran completely counter to southern gentility.[62]

Davidson, in his 'Mirror for Artists', identified the big cities more specifically as places inimical to the aesthetic as well as the spiritual virtues present in southern culture. 'Our megalopolitan agglomerations, which make great ado about art, are actually sterile on the creative side; they patronize art, they merchandise it, but do not produce it'. City dwellers lacked the 'nearness to nature' that was essential for artistic creativity, while they were all too close to 'the commercial fury', the intrigues, and the jockeying for position that afflicted 'the merchandising centers'.[63]

In these and other essays, we encounter an attitude toward the industrial-urban world that recalls the social romanticism of the nineteenth-century 'sages' in England (e.g., Arnold and Ruskin) as well as the anti-urbanism of conservatives such as Julius Langbehn in Germany. These southern men of letters situated themselves self-consciously in a regional milieu. But the way in which they did so indicated a world view for which cultural critics of modernity on the far side of the Atlantic had already supplied numerous antecedents.[64]

While conservative southerners expressed nostalgic affection for the countryside and the past, other writers criticized rural society's present-day antithesis much more explicitly and with quite different ends in view. Many of the thinkers who focused most clearly and intensely on what they regarded as the overgrowth of big cities were men whose political sympathies lay well to the left of center. These men did not reject urban society *per se*. But they did evince grave anxiety over the conditions of life in the great metropolises, and many of them voiced a fervent hope that metropolitan concentration would gradually give way to regional decentralization.

An almost Spenglerian pessimism asserted itself in 1922 in a general assessment of New York that appeared in *The Nation*, one of the chief organs for the expression of left-liberal opinion during the interwar years. Written by Ernest H. Gruening, a journalist who was later to become a Democratic governor of and then senator from Alaska, it described that city as 'the culmination of twentieth-century civilization ... a great synthetic monolith of steel and cement and stone, an ordered macrocosm to house man and his works'. As it 'tunneled through rock, buried rods beneath the surface [of] the rebelling springs and streams it could not annihilate, flattening every undulation, straightening every variation, squeezing itself into endless rows of rectangles, as impersonal as pig iron', the city had 'forecast the regimentation that is America'. In Gruening's view, this regimentation was both physical and spiritual. As a result of densely crowded living conditions, there was 'limitation not only for the eye, but for every sense', and men's souls became the prisoners of their environment. 'New York', he wrote, 'is hard, cynical, ruthless, even beyond other cities. From their early repression, its children emerge sophisticated, both stunted and overdeveloped, perverted, premature, forced by the artificiality of their environment'. Consequently, 'love, friendship, and human contacts' were 'harassed and trammeled', and men ceased to become neighbors. And finally, evoking the Spenglerian sense of the metropolis as a consumer of men and women, he referred to the city as a 'Moloch [that] demands and gets its victims. Countless moths and butterflies are singed at its flame, countless brave swimmers dragged down into its maelstrom, sunk without a trace'. In such passages, Gruening condemned New York not because of the ways in which it had separated men from tradition but instead because of the manner in which it was depriving them of their autonomy and their humanity. Although not without a certain aesthetic element, his critique went well beyond that of the conservatives, indicating a broader awareness of the heavy price that urban life exacted from the great mass of those who experienced it.[65]

The young John Dos Passos, who was to emerge during these decades as one of America's leading novelists, expressed his radical disaffection with postwar society in his sharply negative *Manhattan Transfer* (1925). The sense of doom and foreboding conveyed by Gruening via the journalistic essay found expression here at the level of experimental art. The book's title foretold its style. Dos Passos quickly jumps back and forth from scene to scene and from character to character, with no transitions whatsoever. With its emphasis on discontinuity and fragmentation, the style of the novel goes hand and hand with its theme. Form and content are all of a piece. Dos Passos depicts New York as a place where men and women live stunted and pointless lives, marked by a pronounced lack of interpersonal love or personal development. The main characters all experience one or another form of the disorder that is endemic in the urban milieu around them: economic, political, or moral. Some suffer from exploitation, others become corrupt, while others descend into drunkenness, infidelity, or some other sort of destructive irresponsibility. The themes of social disintegration and impending catastrophe that underlie the book as a whole are enunciated explicitly with regard to the city in its entirety in the ranting of a crazy tramp that appears in the final chapter.

> Do you know how long God took to destroy the tower of Babel, folks? Seven minutes. Do you know how long the Lord took to destroy Babylon and Nineveh? Seven minutes. There's more wickedness in one block of New York City than there was in a square mile of Nineveh, and how long do you think the Lord God of Sabboath will take to destroy New York City an Brooklyn an the Bronx? Seven seconds. Seven Seconds.

The novel does not end on an apocalyptic note, but it is clear as Jimmy Herf abandons the city in a mood of alienation and loneliness that New York is simply not to be endured by those who require humane fellowship with other human beings.[66]

Other writers active during the 1920s and 1930s, none of whom was as radical as Dos Passos but several of whom clearly belonged to the left-liberal intelligentsia, treated the problems posed by the growth of the large agglomerations from the standpoint of city and regional planning. Many of these men were members of the Regional Planning Association of America, a loosely structured organization with a diverse membership that came into existence in 1923 in order to promote decentralized urban development.[67] Clarence Stein, an architect-planner who was one of the Association's founders, expressed feelings of apprehension and anxiety over the expansion of what he called 'dinosaur cities'. He admitted that in the metropolis the few received much, but he asserted that the millions received less and less. 'In spite of sanitary codes, tenement house laws, and various other urban reforms, the prospects for decent human living have become distinctly worse in New York during the last generation'. Stein's misgivings arose primarily from physical and technological concerns. Severe traffic congestion and inadequate water and sewage systems as well as overcrowded housing were all contributing to a general decline in the quality of metropolitan life. In Stein's view, the ills that beset ordinary New Yorkers in their daily lives could not be

29 A bird's eye view of Chicago. This photograph conveys a sense of the giant city as a place that had become amorphous and deadening as a result of too much growth for its own good (source: Clarence S. Stein, 'Dinosaur cities', *Survey*, LIV [1925], 134).

solved within the big city. Their severity showed that 'the great city, as a place to live and work in, breaks down miserably; that it is perpetually breaking down; and that it will continue to do so as long as the pressure of population within a limited area remains'.[68]

Stuart Chase, a member of the Association who was an economist and a regular contributor to the liberal *New Republic*, prophesied an equally bleak future for metropolitan man. He was just as sensitive as Stein to the dangers of technological breakdown inherent in metropolitan vastness, interdependence, and complexity. In addition, he expressed a more acute awareness of the psychic damage the great city did to the human beings who inhabited it.

There are more painful than pleasurable sensations in one's contact with a huge American city of the present day.... Pain is found in noise, dust, smell, crowding, the pressure of the clock, in negotiating traffic, in great stretches of bleak and dour ugliness, in looking always up instead of out, in a continual battering sense of inferiority.... Megalopolis is not a pleasant home for many of its citizens, awake or asleep.... Look at the faces in the street. The machine has gathered us up and dumped us by the millions into these roaring canyons. Year by year more millions are harvested, the canyon shadows deepen, the roar grows louder. No man, no group of men, knows where this conglomeration of steel and glass and stone, with the most highly complicated nervous system ever heard of — a giant with a weak digestion — is headed.

Chase's best guess was that ultimately the giant would collapse, as its inhabitants finally decided to abandon it, an eventuality he clearly welcomed.[69]

Lewis Mumford, another of the leading intellectuals on the liberal left, emerged during these years as the Regional Planning Association's most effective spokesman and as one of a handful of the most searching students of urban life in America or anywhere else. A prolific cultural historian and cultural critic, who ranged widely in his studies through time and space, Mumford brought to the analysis of urban trends a wealth of learning and an intensity of feeling stimulated by his early association with Patrick Geddes and unsurpassed by any other observer of the city in the modern period. It would be a mistake to portray Mumford as an anti-urbanist *tout court*. Throughout his distinguished career, he evinced warm affection for certain kinds of urban settlements: the Greek polis, the medieval city, the New England town, and modern Amsterdam, all of which in his view helped their inhabitants to realize their potentialities as individuals and as members of communities. But his approval for places such as these went hand in hand with deep antipathy toward the cities that have tended to predominate since roughly the seventeenth century: the Baroque capitals, the 'insensate industrial town', and above all the giant 'megalopolis'.[70]

Much of what Mumford had to say about metropolitan life, especially in his classic *The Culture of Cities* (1938), summarized and reworked accusations that had frequently been leveled against big cities in general as well as metropolises in particular by others before him. Like many another critic of urban society, he saw the metropolis as the chief enemy of the natural environment. 'Nature', he wrote, 'except in a surviving landscape park, is scarcely to be found near the metropolis; if at all, one must look overhead, at the clouds, the sun, the moon, when they appear through the jutting towers and building blocks'. Similarly, he indicted the metropolis on biological grounds. 'For all its boasted medical research, for all its real triumphs in lessening the incidence of disease and prolonging life, the very big city must bow to the countryside in the essentials of health: almost universally the expectation of life is greater in the latter, and the effect of deteriorative disease is less'. Marked by 'sprawl and shapelessness as an inevitable by-product of its physical immensity', the metropolis was deficient in social as well as physical cohesion. Social control based on effective association was sorely lacking in places where the density of settlement was so great that men remained strangers even to their immediate neighbors. As a result, the metropolis offered 'positive encouragement to a-social or anti-social actions', including crime as well as vice.[71]

The great force of Mumford's attack, however, stemmed from a much more intensive analysis of the relations between metropolitanism and threats to individual liberty than appeared in any of the works we have discussed so far. Mumford was not alone in expressing greater fear of regimentation than of the loss of social control. We have already seen indications of such an outlook in some of what Ernest Gruening had to say about New York. Indeed, Paul Boyer has argued that during the 1920s and 1930s, after a century in which American social thinkers had repeatedly denounced the city as a cause of social disintegration, there was a growing tendency to view it as 'the dwelling place of millions of conformists'.[72] The idea that the metropolis acted as a powerful leveler was thus already in the air well before Mumford adopted it, but it received far fuller treatment in his work than in anyone else's.

In order to push along the process of metropolitan concentration and thus to reap the profits that accrued to them from the metropolitan economy, Mumford argued, monopoly capitalists worked to establish a monopoly of opinion. By means of advertising, news reporting, and periodical literature, they sought 'to give the stamp of authenticity and value to the style of life that emanates from the metropolis'. The effect of such efforts was to drain outlying areas not only of many of their inhabitants but also of much of their peculiar character and identity. Even people who stayed at home succumbed to the homogenizing influence of metropolitan civilization. 'Though the physical radius of the metropolis may be only twenty or thirty miles, its effective radius is much greater: its blight is carried in the air, like spores of mold. The outcome is a world whose immense potential variety ... has been sacrificed to a low metropolitan standardization'.[73]

Maintaining the grip of the metropolis on the life of the country implied other necessities as well: a powerful political bureaucracy and a war machine that would protect the lifelines between the giant city and the markets it exploited, both at home and abroad. The bureaucrats and the soldiers sought to strengthen their own positions by fomenting 'the demented cult "patriotism": coercive group unanimity: blind support of the rulers of the state: maudlin national egoism: an imbecile willingness to commit collective atrocities for the sake of "national glory"'. They used the physical structure of the city itself as a means toward these ends. 'The buildings of the imperial metropolis', wrote Mumford, 'serve as an appropriate background for these war-ceremonies and reinforce these pretensions'. Not only Tokyo, Berlin, and Rome, but also Washington provided 'a monotonous reflection of the military-bureaucratic mind'. The end result of the action of these forces, which Mumford sketched in a section of his book titled 'A Brief Outline of Hell', was 'the paralysis of all the higher activities of society: truth shorn or defaced to fit the needs of propaganda: the organs of cooperation stiffened into a reflex system of obedience: the order of the drill sergeant and the bureaucrat ... a regime ... deeply antagonistic to every valuable manifestation of life'. In a manner reminiscent of the forebodings of another of Geddes' disciples, Victor Branford, Mumford thus linked megalopolitan concentration to preparations for the impending conflict among nations. What Albert Speer and some other National Socialists found good and necessary in cities — authority, uniformity, and power — were precisely the qualities that caused Mumford to feel the greatest despair as he contemplated the urban scene on the eve of the Second World War.[74]

Mumford, like the overwhelming majority of American intellectuals, was nowhere near as gloomy as Spengler about the prospects of modern civilization as a whole. Although he was certainly influenced by his German predecessor, he offered an alternative to the processes of further metropolitan concentration and encroachment upon the life of the hinterlands. Conscious planning and construction of much smaller regional cities — containing about 50,000 inhabitants — was not only a theoretical possibility but also a real one, indicated, among other tendencies, by the garden city movement.[75] But like Stein and Chase, he left little doubt that the metropolis itself was doomed. The basic question regarding its future was not whether it would survive and prosper but whether its ultimate disappearance would occur in conjunction with a renewal of more humane forms of urban life or in an orgy of destruction.

The eloquent hostility toward giant cities such as New York expressed by Lewis Mumford fitted into a broader pattern of anti-metropolitanism that was evident on both sides of the Atlantic, especially during the 1930s, but it would be a great mistake to let Mumford have the last word. To a markedly greater extent in America than in Europe, the whole interwar period witnessed the persistence and the elaboration of powerful alternatives to city-centered fear and anxiety.[76] By the end of the 1920s, as the historian George Mowry has written, the United States had become a truly urban nation — not only in a statistical sense but also in 'its cast of mind, in its ideals, and in its folk ways'.[77] Americans became much more familiar with and used to their urban civilization than ever before. As a result, old stereotypes that emphasized the city's wickedness and its dangers, although still cherished by the supporters of prohibition and the opponents of Al Smith, receded into the background. They gave way, both among men writing for a popular audience and among many academics, to a much more balanced and positive view of city life than was to be found in Britain, in France, or certainly in Germany.

The urban sentiment continually reasserted itself in a wide range of popular writings, which included enthusiastic celebrations of giants such as New York and Chicago as well as of many smaller but rapidly growing cities across the land. In 1924, Charles Beard, an historian and political scientist with a reputation for radicalism, offered the general reader an eloquent encomium to metropolises in general and to New York in particular.

> The huge urban agglomeration . . . may be linked to Fujiyama, rising in the social plain and dominating the social landscape with imperious majesty. To take it away would be to destroy spirit and power as well as people and structures. The modern city is yet something more. In an age of steam and steel and wireless its economic forces and its intellectual influence are interlaced by a million flashing shuttles with the fabric of world civilization. What a garment is being woven ... upon the roaring loom of time.

In Beard's view, New York's vast array of municipal services, its fashionable stores and busy factories, its complex system of transportation, its diverse cultural institutions, and its towering architecture made manifest an awesome degree of variety and energy that stimulated interest and commanded respect.[78]

One of the period's outstanding essayists and cultural critics, H. L. Mencken, praised New York for the nourishment it provided the creative imagination, a theme that had appeared before the war in the paeans of August Endell, Ford Madox Ford, and Theodore Dreiser. Mencken's praise was ironic, but it was still praise. He observed that New York was rife with 'frauds and scoundrels ... quacks and cony-catchers ... suckers and visionaries'. None of these characters was admirable, but they were all fascinating. New York had 'passed beyond all fear of Hell or hope of Heaven', but nobody could accuse it of being dull. 'The gorgeous, voluptuous color of this greatest of world capitals' meant that, 'if only as spectacle', the city was 'superb', and Mencken argued that 'this spectacle, lush and barbaric in its every detail, offer[ed] the material for a great imaginative literature'. He made it quite clear that he felt little love for New York. '... I see nothing in it to inspire the fragile and shy thing called affection.... But ... the spectacle of New York remains — infinitely grand and gorgeous, stimulating like the best that comes out of goblets, and none the worse for its sinister smack. It is immensely trashy — but it remains immense'.[79]

Such ecstatic delight in the colorful dynamism of New York tended to abate after the onset of the great depression,[80] but comparable sentiments could still be detected in the writings of less well known authors who extolled the virtues of Chicago. Mary Borden, a novelist who had been born there and had later moved to England, returned to her native habitat for a visit in 1930. In her account of her trip, she described Chicago as 'the city of magic'.

> Genii had risen out of the lake and ogres out of the prairie land. They had woven monstrous spells above this spot where I stood, and the earth had opened, and towers of steel had spurted into the air like geysers, like fountains, and great

30   Lower Manhattan seen from beneath Brooklyn Bridge. Brightly lit skyscrapers strongly suggested metropolitan vitality (source: *New York City Guide: A Comprehensive Guide to the Five Boroughs of the Metropolis ... Prepared by the Federal Writers Project of the Works Progress Administration in New York City* [New York, 1939], 76).

blocks of marble had gone hurtling through space and had been planted in stone
gardens and clustered, tapering groves of stone, and a great energy had poured
through the bodies of these stones, galvanizing them into life.

In this view, in contrast to Spengler's, Gruening's, and Mumford's, stone
was not a harbinger of death but a manifestation of vitality. Morris Markey, a
journalist and travel writer, referred approvingly to a 'deep personal belief in
the magnificence of their town' among the Chicagoans he had met. This civic
pride arose quite legitimately from the city's 'new and quite exciting beauty',
its 'elemental quality of bulk and stature', and the 'breathless outpouring of
energy' that overwhelmed the visiting observer. Bessie Pierce, an historian of
Chicago who wrote to commemorate the city's centennial in 1933, drew
together these and other themes with less lyricism but no less enthusiasm.
She shared the view that Chicago was 'a city of infinite possibilities', and she
supported that view with plenty of facts. She heartily felt a full measure of the
civic enthusiasm that Markey had noted the year before.[81]

Buoyant enthusiasm was equally apparent in the comments of other
popular writers who turned their attention to urban development in somewhat smaller cities in the South and the West as well as in larger ones in the
North and the Midwest. Shaw Desmond, writing about 'America's city
civilization', pointed to the upsurge of big cities all over the country, each
working for its own glory, as evidence of America's 'individualist genius' and
its 'loosely knit ... decentralized soul'. Freeman Tilden asserted in the same
vein that every city had its 'soul', which lived independently from its physical
structure, and that the typical citizen of Dallas or Birmingham as well as of
Boston embodied this spirit. 'He believes in his city; and how can he help it if
he believes in himself? He knows it will be bigger, and he tells himself it will
be better'. In Kansas City, in Salt Lake City, and in San Francisco, men were
also 'nursing an infant idea that, full grown, will give a new impetus to life in
that city'. These authors recorded and in large measure shared a straightfor-
wardly affirmative attitude that pervaded the thinking of city boosters
throughout the nation.[82]

The waning of progressivism during the 1920s and the financial constraints
on local government that stemmed from economic hard times in the 1930s
undercut municipal innovation of the sort that had earlier given rise to the
pride and optimism of men like Frederic C. Howe and Charles Zueblin. As a
result, the interwar years no longer saw celebrations of municipal progress
comparable in scope and format to the ones that had appeared in great
profusion between 1902 and 1917.

Nonetheless, this theme remained an important element in the positive
image of city life, especially in the thinking of men who had cultivated a
professional interest in city government. Charles Beard, a long-time member
of the National Municipal League, addressed a joint meeting of that group
and others like it in 1928. In his remarks, he insisted that with regard both to
sanitation and to virtue the cities no longer had any reason to fear comparison

with the countryside. City government was, in his view, no longer 'the most conspicuous failure of American democracy'. Instead, it was using modern technology to make the city itself a steadily more congenial place in which to live. Similar sentiments emerged half a decade later from typical articles in *The American City*. The editor used the twenty-fifth anniversary of the journal's founding as an occasion for looking back both at what the journal had done and at what cities had done during the preceding quarter-century. He made it quite clear that he liked what he saw as he contemplated the changes that had been wrought by men of the sort for whom *The American City* had been published. 'Solid municipal and civic progress' could be discerned in a wide range of areas, such as planning and zoning, the treatment of garbage and sewage, the organization of police and fire departments, and the establishment of public playgrounds. Admittedly, the depression had militated against municipal activism. But on the whole it seemed that city governments still had a right to take real pride in their various achievements and that they could look forward to the future with hope and confidence as they worked to master the problems that still confronted them.[83]

Among all the works dealing with cities that appeared in America between the wars, the most substantial and significant as a group were the studies produced by the urban sociologists. Their writings constituted a distinctively American contribution to thinking men's awareness of the modern urban world. No other country witnessed a comparable efflorescence of sociological efforts to understand specifically urban phenomena and processes. The urban sociologists' purposes were scholarly, not polemical. They did not view themselves as opponents of urban growth, or advocates of social reform, or champions of municipal progress. Through their activities as urban researchers and as teachers, they generated and synthesized an enormous amount of data pertaining to almost every aspect of city life. The facts they collected and the analyses they produced indicated a great deal of ambivalence about the subject of their study. Much of what they had to say referred to the cities' darker sides. But at the same time many of them clearly reveled in the urban milieu, and they indicated fundamental acceptance of the urban society in which they lived.

As an academic subdiscipline that operated within a clearly defined institutional framework, urban sociology developed first at the University of Chicago. The founding father of what came to be known as 'the Chicago school' and the doyen of the new field of study was Robert Park. Born on a small farm in 1864, he began his career as a social investigator informally by working for a big-city newspaper, subsequently did graduate study in psychology and philosophy at Harvard, attended the lectures of Georg Simmel at Berlin and took a Ph.D. in philosophy at Heidelberg, worked for several years with Booker T. Washington at Tuskegee Institute in Alabama, and finally, in 1913, became a university teacher. At Chicago, he belonged to the nation's first academic department of sociology (established in 1892), and he enjoyed both a congenial setting in which to work and a strategic place from which to exert a broad influence on men who were already located or were later to go elsewhere. Park began to establish his intellectual reputation via a highly influential essay titled 'The City: Suggestions for the Investigation of Human Behavior in the Urban Environment', which first appeared in the *American Journal of Sociology* in 1915. Park's essay set forth not only an agenda for research but also a systematic set of generalizations for others to test. Subsequently, he and Ernest Burgess developed a dynamic program of instruction and research that involved large numbers of colleagues and students in local studies, many of which represented efforts to follow through on one or another of his seminal suggestions.[84]

A grant from the newly established Social Science Research Council in 1923 facilitated a large number of publications by the University of Chicago Press. These included two symposia — *The City* (1925), edited by Park and Burgess, and Burgess' *The Urban Community* (1926) — and a host of monographs, most of which focused on conditions within Chicago itself. Among the specialized works, books such as the following were especially noteworthy: Nels Anderson, *The Hobo* (1923); Frederick M. Thrasher, *The Gang* (1927); Harvey W. Zorbaugh, *The Gold Coast and the Slum* (1929); Walter C. Reckless, *Vice in Chicago* (1933); Norman S. Hayner, *Hotel Life* (1936); and Robert E.L. Faris and H. Warren Dunham, *Mental Disorders in Urban Areas* (1939).[85]

Urban sociology developed rapidly at many universities outside Chicago. Numerous scholars trained by Park and his colleagues and many others who had received their training elsewhere propagated the new field of study at institutions of higher learning across the land. Men from Chicago built up sociology departments at Cornell, Vanderbilt, Ohio State, Michigan, Indiana, the University of Washington, and Hawaii.[86] Among the universities which had sociologists unconnected with Chicago who were active in urban studies, one can point to Harvard, Yale, Columbia, Kansas, and Minnesota. Scholars who taught at these and other schools produced a substantial corpus of general surveys of urban society as well as a host of more specialized publications in which urban variables figured prominently.[87]

The urban sociologists regarded the city as an ideal place in which to observe not only collective behavior but also many other aspects of human life. The city functioned for these academics as a testing ground for all sorts of hypotheses pertaining to modern man and the society he inhabited. Urban sociology seemed to provide a set of lenses that enabled its practitioners to focus on the problems and possibilities of contemporary society more generally with an exceptional degree of precision and clarity. As Park put it in his most famous essay,

> Because of the opportunity it offers, particularly to the exceptional and abnormal
> types of man, a great city tends to spread out and lay bare to the public view in a

massive manner all the human characters and traits which are ordinarily obscured and suppressed in smaller communities. The city, in short, shows the good and evil in human nature in excess. It is this fact, perhaps, more than any other, which justifies the view that would make of the city a laboratory or clinic in which human nature and social processes may be conveniently and profitably studied.

T. V. Smith, another Chicagoan, articulated a similar outlook when he wrote, 'In the modern city more perhaps than anywhere else on earth ..., is present in condensed, rapid, observable form the social mobility that makes fruitful research possible'. He went on in a more lyrical vein to depict study of the city as an enterprise that yielded a kind of aesthetic delight, comparable to 'the fascination that captivates the onlooker at a horse race or a partisan at a football game as the senses feast upon the colors and scents and expectancies fused into a complex whole'. Whether they said so explicitly or not, many other sociologists doubtless shared these sentiments.[88]

Most members of the Chicago school, as the titles of the monographs listed above indicate, concentrated heavily on social disorganization, deviance, and pathology, and many other sociologists evinced a similar awareness of the big city's morally problematic features. They were fully aware of urban society's many and ugly blemishes. In Park's words, the big city produced an 'increase of vice and crime'. The migrant to the city, 'no longer backed by the collective wisdom of the peasant community', was far freer than ever before, and his situation typified that of city dwellers in general. 'Everyone is more or less on his own in a city. The consequence is that man, translated to the city, has become a problem to himself and to society in a way and to an extent that he never was before'.[89] Emory S. Bogardus emphasized the prevalence of 'the lack of fellow-feeling and understanding which characterizes social distance ... everywhere ... in cities'. Louis Wirth, in his classic essay on 'Urbanism as a Way of Life', argued that the mode of existence typical of big cities led to 'anomie', 'mutual exploitation', 'loneliness', 'the acceptance of instability and insecurity in the world at large as a norm', and 'personal disorganization, mental breakdown, suicide, delinquency, crime, corruption, and disorder'. One could go on almost endlessly, quoting language from the writings of these and other sociologists that would have been quite congenial to Mumford and Spengler.[90]

The Chicago sociologists and those whom they influenced, unlike many of their German forebears, were not content to analyze the various aspects of urban life in such a way that the city would appear to be a uniform entity, cut from whole cloth. While they believed strongly in the existence of regularities among cities, they also pointed repeatedly to varieties within cities, and the models they used in order to conceptualize internal variation and heterogeneity contributed powerfully to their understanding of the mechanisms that produced urban disorganization. Although, to be sure, it was possible to discern certain characteristics that attached to big cities as such, it was ultimately more important in their eyes to specify the ways in which these and other attributes were distributed geographically among the city's 'natural areas'. As Park put it, 'Natural areas are the habitats of natural groups. Every typical urban area is likely to contain a characteristic selection of the population as a whole. In great cities the divergence in manners, in standards of living, and in general outlook on life in different urban areas is often astonishing'. Burgess developed this idea by using charts that schematically divided the city into five concentric zones that theoretically took shape everywhere in the course of urban expansion: a central business district (named 'The Loop' after the downtown area of Chicago), a transitional zone of older housing that was being invaded by business and light industry, a more stable zone of working men's homes, a residential zone characterized by high-class apartments and single-family homes, and a suburban commuters' zone. Numerous other authors made use of this ecological model in their specialized studies of social pathology, showing how disorganization and vice arose from the instability that was most clearly evident in the transitional zone adjacent to the urban core. This was the place where the city's problems were most severe.[91]

In the sociological perspective, although the big city suffered from severe problems it certainly did not deserve condemnation. Seeking to understand their subject rather than to mete out either praise or blame, the urban sociologists made a conscious effort to provide a balanced picture of the urban scene. This effort frequently led them to accentuate the positive as a way of counterbalancing the anti-urban prejudices of many who lacked their expert knowledge of the city's multifaceted complexity. Even Louis Wirth took pains to emphasize that for all their social and moral deficiencies cities were the 'dwelling-place and the workshop of modern man' and the centers where 'the fulfilling and meaningful life' was most readily available. Wirth never romanticized rural life, nor did he bemoan rural to urban migration, and in this respect he typified the attitudes of most of his fellow sociologists.[92]

The bases for acceptance of the city — not just as a fateful necessity but also as a mode of settlement and association that offered real benefits not to be taken lightly — were set forth quite clearly by Park. One point that emerged from his thinking with particular force was that urban conditions permitted an exceptional degree of individual freedom. The 'breaking down of local attachments' and the 'weakening of the restraints and inhibitions of the primary group' made possible a great variety of differing life styles and accomplishments, which Park warmly welcomed. The city attracted people in large part because it possessed 'an element of chance and adventure'. Whoever stayed was sure to find 'somewhere among the varied manifestations of city life the sort of environment in which he expands and feels at ease … the moral climate in which his peculiar nature obtains the stimulations that bring his innate dispositions to full and free expression'. Park believed that 'the big, booming confusion and excitement of city life' opened the doors of opportunity to the eccentric and the genius, offering them rewards they could never obtain in the small town. Here was a powerful restatement of the nineteenth-century liberal view, according to which the big city was to be highly prized because of its contributions to the liberty of the able and the ambitious, to diversity, and to innovation.[93]

Park and other sociologists were equally attentive to the multiplicity of 'secondary' relationships that had sprung up in the urban milieu in place of the 'primary' relationships that were being steadily drained of their emotional vitality and their moral force. Far from welcoming the city simply because it enhanced men's powers to control their separate destinies, they insisted that the urban world manifested a great wealth of associations that tended to promote collective order and direction. Park pointed to the functions performed by neighborhood institutions such as the public schools, the churches, and the settlement houses, by trade unions and other occupational groups, and by the press as evidence that the city was by no means inimical to social cohesion *per se*. Nels Anderson and Eduard C. Lindeman, obviously doubtful that urban morals were really inferior in any fundamental way to rural morals, pointed to the city as a place where 'new forms of social organization come into existence, and new social and moral values arise'. They too employed the distinction between primary and secondary controls, the latter being enforced in their view most clearly by municipal government. Howard Woolston, who had already celebrated the city as a seedbed of associative energy before the First World War, did so again with undiminished enthusiasm a quarter of a century later. He found the multiplicity of combinations that linked townsmen to one another to be amazing. 'Hundreds of organizations twist and tie them into a social fabric, as threads are woven on a Jacquard loom'. Numerous agencies operated in towns to promote health, to relieve want, and to prevent crime, all indicating a strong desire to alleviate urban problems and, along with much else, bearing witness to 'a social or civic consciousness'.[94]

At the very end of the period, a political scientist at Chicago who had worked closely with the Chicago sociologists summarized succinctly the element of optimism that permeated many of their general surveys of city life. Charles E. Merriam concluded a talk given in late 1939 to commemorate the tenth anniversary of the University of Chicago's Social Science Research Building and published in the *American Journal of Sociology* on a note of clearly hopeful expectation. The faults of modern cities, he argued, were 'not those of decay and impending decline but of exuberant vitality crowding its way forward under tremendous pressure'. The assets of an urban-industrial civilization — 'highly specialized activities ... the advantages of association ... the vast expansion of productive power ... the growth of centers of science, medicine, education, invention, religion ... high levels of attainment in artistic and cultural achievement' — were very real and very great. The municipal history of the past generation, together with much other evidence of urban advance, foretold 'a day of hope', when still better 'patterns of community structure' would lead to 'wiser plans and programs of action, and

higher levels of material and spiritual prosperity'.[95] Merriam's confidence that
city life would continue to improve and that one day all city dwellers would
thrive pointed in a very different direction from the pessimism of a Lewis
Mumford. At the same time, it represented a view of the city — both
reformist and positive — that found a good deal more support during the
1930s in the United States than it did anywhere in Europe.

11

Perceptions of Cities in Retrospect

First in Britain during the 1820s and 1830s and subsequently in France, Germany, and the United States, big cities became primary objects of concern and stimuli to reflection and debate for large numbers of articulate men and women. Commentators on contemporary society inevitably gravitated toward urban themes. The history of the perception of cities between the early nineteenth century and the mid-twentieth century encompasses writers of many sorts, both familiar and obscure. In this study, we have encountered major novelists and men of letters — such as Charles Dickens, John Ruskin, Victor Hugo, and Theodore Dreiser — and some much less impressive but equally relevant authors of pulp fiction and popular poetry. Well-known social theorists and sociologists — Friedrich Engels, Ferdinand Tönnies, Charles Booth, Lewis Mumford, and Robert Park, to name only a few — have also figured prominently, as have numerous other social scientists of markedly smaller repute in our day (though not always in their own). The names of Thomas Macaulay and Oswald Spengler are the most familiar on the list of historians, but there were hundreds of lesser lights who sought to make sense of the course of urban development in particular cities and towns. Protestant clergymen, medical doctors and sanitary experts, municipal administrators and local reformers, architects and planners, and a host of essayists and journalists who wrote for weekly and monthly magazines also played their parts in helping to awaken and shape public consciousness of urban life. Only a few of the names of these individuals — e.g., Edwin Chadwick, Jane Addams, Le Corbusier, and H. L. Mencken — evoke much recognition today, but numerous others commanded attention among their contemporaries.

The big cities — rapidly growing concentrations of flesh, blood, stone, and glass, of men and machines, of people and power — seemed to encapsulate within their boundaries a vast range of crucially important processes and trends that went hand in hand with urbanization. Cities have always possessed a high degree of symbolic significance, and in the nineteenth and the first half of the twentieth centuries they served especially well for the purpose of bringing general changes in the structure of society and the quality of life into sharp and specific focus. By and large, the city stood for modernity and the future, whereas tradition and the past were represented by the small town and the countryside. More particularly, it stood for industry, for centralization, and for rationality, to name only a few of the phenomena whose secular rise has done so much to shape the world in which we live today. To the extent that these and related developments were controversial, the places in which they seemed to be occurring most intensively generated an especially high degree of interest and emotion.[1]

Throughout the period treated in this book, big cities provided a great many inviting targets for critics of modern society. These writers focused on problems and difficulties which, though by no means peculiar to urban centers, were certainly most obvious in such places. Much of the sharpest criticism had to do with the material and physical hardships that stemmed from the clearly excessive crowding of too many people into too little space in the areas inhabited by ordinary city dwellers. The seeming inability of many urban men and women not only to live reasonably long and healthy lives of their own but also to raise adequate numbers of offspring was a basic source of deep anxiety for urban critics during almost all of the period. Fears that pertained to sanitation, housing, death rates, and birth rates were closely linked to the belief that the big cities undermined the bases of religion and morality, that they militated against stable families and other forms of primary social control, and that they manifested far more than their fair share of vice, crime, and the propensity to revolt. A less pervasive but nonetheless quite powerfully expressed worry was that the cities — if only because of the sheer ugliness that seemed to disfigure so many of them — were producing a race of men and women who possessed a woefully underdeveloped sensitivity to beauty and an equally deficient capacity for creative originality of any sort.

Each of these sets of concerns was matched by a corresponding cluster of much more affirmative attitudes toward the various changes that had already occurred in the urban milieu and toward the possibilities for further progress that seemed to be opening up as a result of ongoing urban developments. Awareness of the poverty and poor health that afflicted some urbanites was countered and tempered by frequent reminders that the economic growth of modern society as a whole depended heavily on a division of labor that was unthinkable without the geographic concentration of productive forces. Only the city, it was pointed out, made this possible. In the same vein, it was emphasized again and again that urbanization was taking place as a result of voluntary migration that presumably stemmed from accurate perceptions by most individuals of their own best interests. The urban sentiment thus reflected deeply felt convictions that the loosening of traditional restraints on personal liberty was to be welcomed rather than deplored. But pro-urbanists did not rest their moral defense of city life on this belief alone. More and more — especially for several decades after about 1890 — they insisted also on the role that cities played in generating and supporting communal efforts to deal effectively with their own worst problems. As for cultural concerns, there was repeated recognition not only that the big cities facilitated intellectual as well as other modes of productive labor but also that they provided a great wealth of sights and sensations that could greatly enrich the works of creative artists — including those artists who chose to portray what they saw around them in an essentially negative light.

This summary may suggest that it makes sense to divide the writers who dealt with urban themes into two groups, the anti-urbanists and the pro-urbanists, but that has not been my intention. Such an an enterprise would necessitate an artificial and bootless effort to label men and women as exponents of either one attitude toward the city or another. To be sure, at one extreme, there were bitterly hostile critics of the big city as such. These writers — most notably men such as Wilhelm Heinrich Riehl and Oswald Spengler — seemingly loathed the very idea of large agglomerations. Others, such as John Ruskin, Charles Masterman, and Lewis Mumford, had few if any kind words for the big city as it existed during most of the period when they were writing. At the other extreme, there were those who celebrated either the big city in general or particular big cities almost unreservedly — e.g., Robert Vaughan, Walt Whitman, and the countless admirers of the splendors of Paris. But in a great many if not in most cases the conflicting perspectives and attitudes referred to above divided observers within themselves as well as from other observers with whom they disagreed. As a recent student of the city in literature has put it,

> Indeed, the image of the city stands as the great reification of ambivalence, embodying a complex of contradictory forces in both the individual and the collective Western minds. The idea of the city seems to trigger conflicting impulses, positive and negative ... mixed feelings of pride, guilt, love, fear, and hate toward the city.[2]

The majority of those who wrote about urban phenomena can be classified neither as city haters nor as city lovers. They saw the urban world as a complex mixture of both good and evil, a realm marked by sharp contrasts that suggested a superabundance of both dangers and opportunities. The writings of Charles Dickens and Charles Kingsley, Emile Zola and Emile Levasseur, Georg Simmel and Adolf Weber, and Jane Addams and Robert Park all evince this dual sensibility.

It is also important to bear in mind that criticism of cities led in many different directions. Men and women might express common concerns with regard to poor housing, an unfavorable ratio of births to deaths, or juvenile delinquency, and then proceed to offer sharply contrasting prescriptions for setting matters right. The advocacy of high protective tariffs on grain or of efforts to immunize rural schoolchildren against the lure of city lights obviously evinced a strong anti-urban bias. So too did a good deal of the support for the garden city movement begun by Ebenezer Howard. On the other hand, the numerous nineteenth-century critics of existing cities who sought sanitary reform and extended municipal services or worked to build up settlement houses can hardly be accused of wanting to turn back the clock in the area of urban development. Nor can one make this charge with regard to those twentieth-century architects and planners — including not only Le Corbusier during the 1920s but also Walter Gropius, Mies van der Rohe, and many others associated with the modern movement — who sought to reduce residential density by combining multistorey housing with open space on the cities' outskirts.[3] In all these cases, discontent with one or another facet of the big city of the present went hand in hand with acceptance of the big city as such and a determination to make the best of it.

Even though I have not been considering one camp in conflict with another and even though some degree of ambivalence toward the big city has characterized most commentators' reflections on it, one may still ask legitimate questions about the relative strengths of the various currents of thought and feeling with which I have been concerned. Which intellectual and emotional responses to city life were predominant? Which enjoyed not only the best informed and the most intense but also the most widespread support among articulate observers of the urban scene? It was in order to be able to speak to such questions — to identify not only originality but also typicality — that I conducted the research for this study broadly. Any effort to weigh precisely the representativeness or the influence of competing ideas and opinions on a large scale remains fraught with pitfalls and difficulties with which most cultural and intellectual historians are already quite familiar. While useful evidence abounds, most of it is not readily susceptible to quantitative treatment, and conclusive proof regarding the thought patterns of even the small minority of any society that appears in print is exceedingly elusive at best. But some kinds of generalizations are easier to arrive at than others, and it is sensible to begin our final assessment of urban thinking in those areas where the problems of judgement are least difficult.

Some of the most obvious links and patterns emerge when we consider the attitudes toward cities that have appeared in particular genres of writing and in the thinking of men and women who can be classified under different occupational headings. In so far as the major novelists, poets, and all-purpose cultural philosophers have focused on urban themes, they have generally dwelt on pain and suffering rather than on pleasure and profit. To be sure, Dickens was deeply attracted to London, Gaskell evinced pride as well as anxiety with regard to Manchester, and Balzac, Hugo, and Zola all thrilled to the grandeur and vitality of Paris. But all of these writers devoted just as much if not more attention to urban ills and urban sorrows as they did to the more joyful aspects of urban life. Moreover, when numerous other authors — such as Carlyle, Gissing, and Orwell; Baudelaire, Raabe, and Rilke; and Howells, Dreiser, and Dos Passos — are added to the mix, the preponderance of critical sentiment among literary artists becomes unmistakable. Medical doctors and clergymen, who, like the novelists, played an especially crucial role in defining urban consciousness during the nineteenth century, also stressed urban shortcomings. This was entirely natural for the physicians. They dealt as a matter of course with sickness rather than with health, and they found an abundance of environmentally conditioned disease in the big cities. Clergymen tended to excoriate the city dwellers' moral defects not only because they were always on the lookout for evidence of human sinfulness but also because of their awareness that the urban milieu posed a special threat to many forms of organized Christianity. In this connection, it is important to bear in mind that the most notable exception to this generalization, Robert Vaughan, belonged to one of the Dissenting denominations that was doing rather well in the cities at the expense of the established Church of England.

On the other hand, there were the professional groups whose members' attitudes can be described as balanced to positive. Numerous social scientists, especially economists and economic historians, subscribed to a view of the big city as an indispensable component of a social order that facilitated material progress for the great bulk of society's members. Emile Levasseur, Karl Bücher, and Adna Weber all took this position during the late nineteenth century and justified urban growth on other grounds as well in careful analyses that were widely cited by other social scientists. Among representatives of the newer discipline of sociology, there was admittedly a great deal of concern with the problem of urban poverty — one thinks in this connection first and foremost of Charles Booth — and more generally with the various forms of social pathology studied by members of the Chicago school in the United States. But Robert Park and his followers never condemned the big city out of hand, regarding it instead as a place that presented enormous possibilities for good as well as for evil. Architects and planners, in so far as they commented explicitly on the existing city, usually expressed their sense of its physical and aesthetic defects. But aside from the men associated with the garden city movement and Frank Lloyd Wright very few of them can be described as really hostile to the big city.[4] They might wish to redesign and rebuild it, but they seldom rejected it. Camillo Sitte and his followers desired a return to medieval complexity, and Le Corbusier called for modern verticality, but all of them and many others regarded the big city as a place that was amenable to rational control and aesthetic betterment. A parallel attitude appears in the writings of urban administrators and other men employed by city governments. They certainly recognized that they had their hands full with enormous difficulties, but again and again they proclaimed their belief that they were well on the way toward resolving them. Joseph Chamberlain, Frederic C. Howe, and the many speakers at the German City Exhibition of 1903 in Dresden all expressed a positive viewpoint that enjoyed a great deal of support among other men whose job it was to make cities work. That view was also supported by countless amateur as well as professional historians and by just as many publicists and journalists who sought to describe the evolution or the present condition of particular urban communities, including not only London, Paris, and Berlin but also such cities as Birmingham, Lyons, Frankfurt, and Cleveland. These writers almost always displayed an intense civic pride.

Another set of correlations pertains to the links between attitudes toward cities and men's general ideological persuasions. Social, political, and cultural conservatives tended to evince a relatively high degree of anti-urban hostility. Men who felt nostalgic sympathy for bygone or threatened traditions, especially those of the Middle Ages, often depicted the big city as the evil antithesis of all they longed for and held dear. From the writings of Robert Southey to those of William Morris, one encounters a powerful aversion toward modern urbanism among the cultural aristocrats of Victorian England. This sentiment found more extreme expression in Germany in the works of men like Wilhelm Heinrich Riehl, Otto Ammon, Julius Langbehn, and Oswald Spengler, to name only a few of the many German anti-urbanists who helped to strengthen the forces of the political right. The link between conservatism and anti-urbanism also appears in the United States. Consider, for example, the fears expressed by Josiah Strong, the aversion to the American city displayed by Henry James, and the manifestoes of more recent southern agrarians like Donald Davidson. On the left, the critics of capitalism probed more deeply into the hard lot of the urban lower classes, producing mounds of evidence that all too many city dwellers were suffering both physically and morally from an inequitable distribution of economic and social goods that had seemingly reached its apex in the urban world. Eugène Buret and Friedrich Engels in the nineteenth century and George Orwell, George Grosz, and John Dos Passos in the twentieth all articulated this conviction in one way or another, as did numerous other socialists and communists who criticized particular aspects of urban society.

Acceptance of the city was most pronounced among men and women closer to the ideological center. The nineteenth-century belief that spontaneous urban growth was a good thing precisely because it stemmed from free choices by autonomous individuals and because it constituted a vital part of a self-regulating process of change for the better reflected the basic presuppositions of classical liberalism. Thomas Macaulay, Robert Vaughan, Carl Welcker, and Horatio Alger all affirmed urban life in the light of shared liberal values. Early in the twentieth century, moderate reformers who sought to remedy urban defects in order both to achieve social justice and to maintain social stability — men such as William Harbutt Dawson, Karl Bücher, and Frederic C. Howe and women such as Jane Addams and Lillian Wald — also affirmed the modern city. It was, after all, the place that had given birth to the progressive movements they admired and represented.

It is somewhat more difficult but still feasible to make certain generalizations about particular countries and particular periods. Although I have constantly sought to demonstrate the pervasiveness of shared concerns that united men and women along occupational and ideological lines which cut across national borders, I have also pointed to national differences. What can be said about these differences by way of conclusion? Whatever may have been the overall balance between criticism and affirmation within any one country, it is clear that the constellation of thoughts and feelings varied significantly from one country to another. Without question, Germany produced the most extreme polarization of opinion. It was also the country in which anti-urban hatreds were most pervasive. For reasons that have to do primarily with the tenacious grip of pre-modern attitudes and values among powerfully entrenched social groups whose members felt increasingly threatened by an extremely rapid process of industrialization, the big city attracted markedly more animosity in Germany than anywhere else. In Britain, where urbanization began earlier and took place somewhat more gradually, it met with a greater degree of acceptance, which reflected both an awareness of its inevitability and a more moderate level of social and political debate in general. To be sure, there were critics aplenty of London, Manchester, and other large towns, but one looks in vain for any who even approached Riehl or Spengler in the intensity of their opposition to the big city as such. The French, who were never forced to think about urbanization as a general phenomenon on anything like the scale dictated by developments in Britain and Germany, regarded cities still more favorably. The fact that Paris seemed to outweigh all the other *grandes villes* put together in the eyes of French urban thinkers no doubt contributed a great deal to their urban sympathies. American thinkers were the most pro-urban of all. From the mid-nineteenth century through the 1930s, supporters of cities responded to the critics and the conditions they criticized with a degree of assertive self-confidence that surpassed markedly the support expressed by Europeans. In this connection, the absence of an old regime, the relatively favorable conditions in the cities themselves, and the exuberant optimism of the American people all played their parts.

Finally, one can point to certain rhythmic alternations of sentiment as one moves chronologically through time from one end of the period to the other, alternations that roughly correspond to cyclical changes in the economy that had obvious and far-reaching effects on urban life. During the years between about 1820 and 1850, critics of cities set the prevailing tone of urban consciousness. Englishmen writing about their own cities during the decades when the maladjustments to sudden growth were most painfully evident, Frenchmen and Germans who visited England in large part because it was becoming the first urban society, and Frenchmen who wrote about Paris before the revolution of 1848 tended on the whole to be more negative than positive, as did the early and influential Ralph Waldo Emerson in the United States. Then, for several decades after 1850, a more benign view seemed to be in the ascendant. In Britain, France, and America, many observers began to sense that some of the worst problems stemming from the early phases of the urbanization process were being effectively combated. But toward the end of the nineteenth century, first in Britain during the early 1880s and subsequently in the other three countries as well, liberal satisfaction with the urban present and confidence in the urban future were challenged strongly by the revelations of a new generation of social investigators. Their concerns and those of many other critics continued to find highly vocal expression for several decades. Increasingly after around 1900, however, the element of optimism came to the fore, as progressive reformers and administrators and their admirers pointed with growing satisfaction to a wide range of tangible improvements in the quality of urban life that were traceable to private organizations such as settlement houses and to the various agencies of municipal government. A more somber mood became apparent once again during the interwar years. The belief grew that the very big cities, the metropolises, posed quite special challenges, which made them appear to be especially problematic modes of human settlement. This awareness, coupled with the widespread pessimism about life in general that characterized a period beset by the aftermath of a world war and by the continuing presence of a great depression, helped to create a climate of opinion about cities that was much less buoyant than before in Europe, although the change was less pronounced in America.

The general point that seems to me most worth emphasizing by way of conclusion is that during the period when Europe and America were urbanizing most rapidly their big cities enjoyed a broad base of intellectual support. As millions of men and women flocked to the growing urban centers from the small towns and the countryside during the nineteenth and early twentieth centuries, numerous observers of societies in transition were attracted intellectually and emotionally to urban ways of life. This is not to deny that there were powerful currents of anti-urbanism throughout the period treated in this book and that toward the end of it, especially in the 1930s, the urban world elicited rather little in the way of joy or hope. Nor is it to deny that many of the city's defenders were painfully aware of urban problems. But it is to deny that anti-urban fear, loathing, and gloom were predominant among articulate men and women in general. Particularly when one dips below the higher levels of intellectual sophistication, examining the sentiments of more ordinary writers of the second and third rank, one encounters a widespread belief during most of the period that the cities were places of promise and opportunity. This sense of hope was fueled in large part by many intellectuals' realization that the urban milieu, with its great freedom and its many stimuli, was indispensable for the life of the mind in general and more particularly for the dissemination of whatever they had to say. But it also emerged from a well-founded perception that many of their criticisms were in fact helping to make the cities they inhabited better places in which to live.

Notes

A note on the notes and the bibliography: if no place of publication is indicated for a book, it should be assumed that a book in English was published in London, one in French in Paris and one in German in Berlin.

Chapter 1

1   See the pages in the works by Mitchell and Still cited under Table III.

2   See Köllmann (cited under Table I) and Charles N. Glaab and A. Theodore Brown, *A History of Urban America* (2nd ed., New York and London, 1976), 79.

3   Still, 79, 210–11.

4   Jacques Ellul, *The Meaning of the City*, trans. D. Pardee (Grand Rapids, Michigan, 1970), 1–5, 10–21, 94–101, 113–14; James Dougherty, *The Fivesquare City: The City in the Religious Imagination* (Notre Dame and London, 1980), 8.

5   Ellul, 113–14; Dougherty, 15–16, 23–43.

6   Raymond Williams, *The Country and the City* (New York, 1973), 14–19, 46–8.

7   Thucydides, *The Peloponnesian War*, Crawley translation (Modern Library, 1951), 102–9; Mazzolani, *The Idea of the City in Roman Thought: From Walled City to Spiritual Commonwealth*, trans. S. O'Donnell (Bloomington and London, 1970), 11, 173–6.

8   Schorske, 'The idea of the city in European thought: Voltaire to Spengler', in Oscar Handlin and John Burchard, eds., *The Historian and the City* (Cambridge, Mass., 1963), 96–9

9   Max Byrd, *London Transformed: Images of the City in the Eighteenth Century* (New Haven and London, 1978), 92–3, 97, 100–1, 109–11, 115.

10   Elisabeth Pfeil, *Grossstadtforschung* (2nd ed., Hannover, 1972), 10–11, 27–9; Robert Minder, 'Paris in der französischen Literatur (1760–1960)', in *Dichter in der Gesellschaft* (Frankfurt am Main, 1966), 291–5; Morton and Lucia White, *The Intellectual versus the City: From Thomas Jefferson to Frank Lloyd Wright. (Cambridge, Mass., 1962), 13–14.*

11   Byrd, 16–39, 51, 71, 82–3, 86–91, 124–8, 150, 158.

12   See M. J. Cullen, *The Statistical Movement in Early Victorian Britain* (New York, 1975) and Statistisches Amt der Stadt Dresden, *Die deutsche Städtestatistik am Beginne des Jchres 1903* (a supplement to the *Allgemeines statistisches Archiv*, VI [Tübingen, 1903]; see also Pfeil, 32ff.

13   Thomas Chalmers, *The Christian and Civic Economy of Large Towns* (3 vols, Glasgow, 1821–6).

14   Minder, 298.

15   Three examples from among many that could be cited: the socialist

313

Kommunale Praxis (1901–22), the liberal *Stadtverordnete* (begun in 1906), and the Catholic *Kommunalpolitische Blätter* (begun in 1910). See H. Lindemann and O. Most, 'Literatur, allgemeine kommunalpolitische', in Josef Brix *et al.*, eds., *Handwörterbuch der Kommunalwissenschaften*, III (Jena, 1923), 286–304.

16   E.g., *Municipal Affairs* (1897–1903), *American Municipalities* (1898–1946), *The American City* (1909–1975), and the *National Municipal Review* (1912–1969).

Chapter 2

1   Cobbett, *Rural Rides* (Everyman Library, 1966; first edition in 1830), I, 123–4, and II, 184.

2   M.W. Flinn, 'Introduction' to Edwin Chadwick, *Report on the Sanitary Condition of the Labouring Population of Gt. Britain* (Edinburgh, 1965), 18–26. I have relied heavily on Flinn, 18–73, at many points in what follows.

3   Michel Foucault, *The Birth of the Clinic: An Archaeology of Medical Perception* (1974), 136, cited and elaborated upon by Graeme Davison in 'The city as a natural system: theories of urban society in early nineteenth-century Britain', in Derek Fraser and Anthony Sutcliffe, eds., *The Pursuit of Urban History* (1983), 358–9.

4   Thackrah, *The Effects of the Principal Arts, Trades, and Professions, and of Civic States and Habits of Living, on Health and Longevity: With a Particular Reference to the Trades and Manufactures of Leeds* (1831), 3–5, 37 ff., 84–5, 113–14.

5   See also John Hogg, *London as It Is: Being a Series of Observations on the Health, Habits, and Amusements of the People* (1838), 39–42, 133–4, 343.

6   James Phillips Kay, *The Moral and Physical Condition of the Working Classes Employed in the Cotton Manufacture in Manchester* (2nd ed., 1832), 5–6, 21–4, 27, 42.

7   *Ibid.*, 77–9, 106.

8   M. J. Cullen, *The Statistical Movement in Early Victorian Britain* (New York, 1975), *passim;* William Farr, *Vital Statistics*, ed. N. A. Humphreys (1885), 146–78.

9   Davison, 360–3.

10   On Chadwick and the public health movement, see not only Flinn but also S. E. Finer, *The Life and Times of Sir Edwin Chadwick* (1952), 209 ff.

11   Chadwick, *Report*, 78.

12   *Ibid.*, 80, 87, 108.

13   *Ibid.*, 104.

14   *Ibid.*, 243.

15   *Ibid.*, 219 ff., 234.

16   F. B. Head (anon.), review of Chadwick, *Quarterly Review*, LXXI (1843), 452–3.

17   Seeley (anon.), *The Perils of the Nation: An Appeal to the Legislature, the Clergy and the Higher and Middle Classes* (3rd ed., 1844), xxi, 143.

18   On Slaney's role, see P. Richards, 'R. A. Slaney, the industrial town, and early Victorian social policy', *Social History*, IV (1979), 85–101.

19   For a summary of the law, see Leonardo Benevolo, *The Origins of Modern Town Planning*, trans. J. Landry (Cambridge, Mass., 1971), 94–7.

20   Farr, 160. At 'healthy district rates', the figure for children 0–5 would have been 135,470. The actual number of deaths was 338,990.

21   Morgan's lecture was published in 1866. See 18, 39–40. Foster's was published in London and Birmingham in 1875. See 10–11.

22   See Brian H. Harrison, *Drink and the Victorians: The Temperance Question in England, 1815–1872* (1971).

23   Kay, 57–72.

24   Chadwick, 198, 200.

25   Gaskell's first book, *The Manufacturing Population of England*, appeared in

1833. A revised and expanded version appeared in 1836 under the title *Artisans and Machinery: The Moral and Physical Condition of the Manufacturing Population*. Engels relied on the earlier version.

26   *Ibid.*, 12, 14, 19.

27   *Ibid.*, 103, 124, 133–4, 253, 256 ff., 361–2.

28   Shaw, *Travels in England: A Ramble with the City and Town Missionaries* (1861), 105.

29   *Dictionary of National Biography*, III, 1358–63.

30   Chalmers, *The Christian and Civic Economy of Large Towns* (3 vols, Glasgow, 1821–6), I, 24–7.

31   *Ibid.*, 27–9; see also I, 59, 66, 79, 127, and II, 40–1.

32   R. A. Soloway, *Prelates and People: Ecclesiastical Social Thought in England, 1783–1852* (London and Toronto, 1969), 280, 282, 298–9, 306–15, 435–8.

33   Boone, *The Need of Christianity to Cities* (1844), 10.

34   *Ibid.*, 13, 14–15.

35   *Ibid.*, 18–22.

36   Soloway, 193–4, 200–5, 209, 219, 222–31; see also E. R. Norman, *Church and Society in England: A Historical Study* (Oxford, 1976), 122 ff.

37   Nunns, *A Letter to the Right Hon. Lord Ashley, on the Condition of the Working Classes in Birmingham, Considered in Reference to Improvement in the Condition of the Same Classes in Manufacturing Districts, and Large Towns Generally* (Birmingham, 1842), 5, 7, 9–16, 22–7, 33–52.

38   Kingsley, 'Great cities and their influence for good and evil', in *Sanitary and Social Lectures and Essays* (London and New York, 1880), 190–220. For other writings of the period by clergymen about cities that call attention to urban ills, see John Garwood, *The Million-Peopled City: Or, One-Half of the People of London Made Known to the Other Half* (1853); Thomas Guthrie, *The City: Its Sins and Sorrows* (Glasgow, 1859); and G. R. Gleig (anon.), 'Spiritual destitution in the metropolis', *Quarterly Review*, CIX (1861), 414–63. Slightly later, see John Cumming, *The Cities of the Nations Fell* (1871). Guthrie and Cumming were both Scottish.

39   Alison, *The Principles of Population and Their Connection with Human Happiness* (2 vols, Edinburgh and London, 1841), II, 76, 80, 96–7; Alison, *History of Europe from the Fall of Napoleon in MDCCCXV to the Accession of Louis Napoleon in MDCCCLII* (8 vols, Edinburgh and London, 1854–9), I, 66, II, 14–15, 566, and III, 570–82.

40   Shaw, *Manufacturing Districts: Replies ... to Lord Ashley, M. P., Regarding the Education, and Moral and Physical Condition of the Labouring Classes* (1843), 7, 25, 43, 47.

41   Slaney, *State of the Poorer Classes in Great Towns* (1840), 14–15, 27, and *A Plea to Power and Parliament, for the Working Classes* (1847), 39.

42   Mudie, *London* (2nd ed., 1836), II, 111, 208–11, 296 ff.

43   Grant: *The Great Metropolis, First Series* (3rd ed., 1838), I, 13, 17–18, 294–5; *Travels in Town* (1839), I, 7; *Lights and Shadows of London Life* (1842), I, 156–7, 279. For a comparable outlook with regard to British towns in general, but still with special emphasis on London, see William Johnston, *England as It Is: Political, Social and Industrial in the Middle of the Nineteenth Century* (1851), I, 64–117, 153–4, and II, 301–25.

44   See the introduction by A. D. King to the reprinted edition of *Town Swamps* (Leicester, 1972).

45   See the introductions by E. Yeo and E. P. Thompson to *The Unknown Mayhew* (New York, 1971) and G. Himmelfarb, 'The culture of poverty', in H. J. Dyos and M. Wolff, eds., *The Victorian City: Images and Realities* (London and Boston, 1973), II, 707–36. For the reviewer's assessment see *Meliora: A Quarterly Review of*

Social Science in Its Ethical, Economical, Political, and Ameliorative Aspects, IV (1862), 297.

46   Avoidance is emphasized in all of the following: E. D. H. Johnson, 'Victorian artists and the urban milieu'; G. R. Stange, 'The frightened poets'; G. Levine, 'From "Know-not-Where" to "Nowhere"'; and U. C. Knoepflmacher, 'The novel between city and country' (all in Dyos and Wolff, Vol. II). For general interpretations of some of the writers I shall be discussing, see the classic treatment by Raymond Williams, *Culture and Society* (1958), and Martin J. Wiener, *English Culture and the Decline of the Industrial Spirit, 1850–1980* (Cambridge, Eng., 1981), 31–40.

47   Southey, *Sir Thomas More* (2nd ed., 1831), I, 59–60, 108–15, 170–1.

48   On Carlyle, see Levine, 499–501. *Sartor Resartus* first appeared in *Fraser's Magazine* in 1833–4. It was first published in book form in Boston in 1836. Quotations are from the Everyman edition, 14, 16.

49   Gaskell, *Mary Barton* (Everyman's Library), 78; see Coral Lansbury, *Elizabeth Gaskell: The Novel of Social Crisis* (1975), 22–50.

50   P. Collins, 'Dickens and London', in Dyos and Wolff, II, 539, 537; F. S. Schwarzbach, *Dickens and the City* (1979), 114.

51   Arnold, *Culture and Anarchy*, ed. R. H. Super (Ann Arbor, 1965), 103–4, 105–6.

52   Ruskin, *The Crown of Wild Olive* (1866), in *Works*, ed. E. T. Cook and A. Wedderburn, XVIII (1905), 448, 406.

53   James Clark Sherburne, *John Ruskin, or the Ambiguities of Abundance: A Study in Social and Economic Criticism* (Cambridge, Mass., 1972), 272–3.

54   Macaulay, *Critical and Historical Essays* (Everyman's Library), II, 196–7.

55   Porter, *The Progress of the Nation, in Its Various Social and Economical Relations, from the Beginning of the Nineteenth Century* (2nd ed., 1847), 26–7, 627.

56   John Blackner, *The History of Nottingham, Embracing Its Antiquities, Trade, and Manufactures from the Earliest Authentic Records to the Present Period* (Nottingham, 1815), 8, 194–5; Henry Smithers, *Liverpool, Its Commerce and Institutions, with a History of the Cotton Trade* (Liverpool, 1825), 78–9, 198–201.

57   Head, *A Home Tour through the Manufacturing Districts of England in the Summer of 1835* (1836), 20–1, 179–81, 183–5, 187.

58   For biography, see *Dictionary of National Biography*, XIX, 478–9, and the introduction by W. H. Chaloner to the 1968 reprint of Taylor, *Notes of a Tour in the Manufacturing Districts of Lancashire* (2nd ed., 1842).

59   Taylor, 'Moral economy of large towns', *Bentley's Miscellany*, VI (1839), 476–82, 575–83; VII (1840), 131–6, 470–8, 596–604; VIII (1840), 355–64, 558–68.

60   Taylor, *Notes*, 3, 6, 14; see also 163–5.

61   *Ibid.*, 15, 110, 269, 302–3.

62   *Ibid.*, 26, 63–4, 140–1.

63   *Ibid.*, 7–8, 10, 136, 260, 291–3.

64   Baines, *The Social, Educational, and Religious State of the Manufacturing Districts* ... (1843); for biography, see *Dictionary of National Biography*, XXII, 100–1.

65   Baines, 5–6.

66   *Ibid.*, 9–10, 13–26, 29, 58–62.

67   See *Dictionary of National Biography*, XX, 174–6, and Davison, 355–6.

68   Vaughan, 11, 101–2.

69   *Ibid.*, 108, 112, 116–17, 130–1, 134, 136–41.

70   *Ibid.*, 146 ff., 152.

71   *Ibid.*, 221–34, 250–1, 253, 225.

72   *Ibid.*, 296–7.

73   'Improvement of towns and their population', *The Penny Magazine of the*

Society for the Diffusion of Useful Knowledge, X (1841), 92; Knight, ed., *London*, I (1841), ii-iii.

74   T. Spring-Rice (anon.), 'Distress of the manufacturing districts — causes and remedies', *Edinburgh Review*, LXXVII (1843), 197–219; 'Great cities, their decline and fall', *Fraser's Magazine*, XXIX (1844), 211.

75   The phrase was coined by W. L. Burn in *The Age of Equipoise: A Study of the Mid-Victorian Generation* (1964).

76   Martineau, *The History of England during the Thirty Years' Peace, 1816–1846*, II (1850), 234–45; Kingsley, 190, 195.

77   Knight, *The Popular History of England*, VIII (1862), 391–4, 399 ff., 403; J[ohn] M. Ludlow and Lloyd Jones, *Progress of the Working Classes, 1832–1867* (1867), 1–7, 26–84, 101–80, 199–244, 299–304.

78   Gaskell, *North and South* (Everyman's Library), 296; Lansbury, 95–127.

79   Lamb: 'The manufacturing poor' (anon.), *Fraser's Magazine*, XXXVII (1848), 1–16; 'Manchester, by a Manchester man' (anon.), *Fraser's Magazine*, XLVII (1853), 611–26; and 'Our manufacturing districts and operative classes' (anon.), *Fraser's Magazine*, LXVI (1862), 363–82.

80   Fordyce, *History of the City of Manchester, Past and Present, and of the Borough of Salford* (Manchester, 1862), 9 (publisher's comment on the back of the first part).

81   Baines: *History of the Commerce and Town of Liverpool, and of the Rise of Manufacturing Industry in the Adjoining Counties* (London and Liverpool, 1852), 676–7; and *Liverpool in 1859* (1859), I, 8, 115.

82   John James, *Continuation and Additions to the History of Bradford and Its Parish* (London and Bradford, 1866), 139; Baines, *Yorkshire, Past and Present*, II, pt. 1 (1871), 299 ff., 314, 315 ff., 335.

83   *Ibid.*, 155, 218

84   Joseph Hunter and Alfred Gatty, *Hallamshire: The History and Topography of the Parish of Sheffield* (rev. ed., 1869), 197, 224. See also Asa Briggs, *Victorian Cities* (New York and Evanston, 1965), 137–83.

85   Doran, *Memories of Our Great Towns, with Anecdotic Gleanings Concerning Their Worthies and Their Oddities* (1878), 96–7, 100, 106.

86   Briggs, *History of Birmingham*, II (1952), 55 ff., 61, 66; Langford, *Modern Birmingham and Its Institutions: A Chronicle of Local Events, from 1841 to 1871*, I (Birmingham and London, 1873), 69 ff.; see also 'Great towns and their public influence: Birmingham' (anon.), *The Gentleman's Magazine*, N. S., XIII (1874), 50–3.

87   Briggs, *History of Birmingham*, 68 ff.; *Mr. Chamberlain's Speeches*, ed. C. W. Boyd (1914), 42; see also E. P. Hennock, *Fit and Proper Persons: Ideal and Reality in Nineteenth-Century Urban Government* (1973), 61–176.

88   Bunce, *History of the Corporation of Birmingham* (Vols I-II, Birmingham, 1879-85), I, 354–6, and II, xliv-xlv.

89   Robert Dent, *Old and New Birmingham: A History of the Town and Its People* (Birmingham, 1880), 620.

90   George R. Emerson, *London: How the Great City Grew* (1862), 1, 3, 4; Sala, *Twice Round the Clock, or the Hours of the Day and Night in London* (1859), 9, 10 (biographical information in the introduction by P. Collins to a 1971 reprint by Leicester University Press).

91   Thornbury, *Haunted London*, ed. E. Walford (1880), v, 3; also, Thornbury, *Old and New London* (6 vols, New York and London, 1872-8). For a good recent overview of the city during this period, see Francis Sheppard, *London, 1808-1870: The Infernal Wen* (1971).

Chapter 3

1   Crapelet (anon.), *Souvenirs de Londres en 1814 et 1816* (1817), 251–4; d'Haussez, *Great Britain in 1833* (1833), 14–15, 19; Barrie M. Ratcliffe and W. H. Chaloner, eds., *A French Sociologist Looks at Britain: Gustave d'Eichtal and British Society in 1828* (Manchester, 1977), 13, 23–4, 33, 41.

2   Montulé, *Voyage en Angleterre et en Russie pendant les années 1821, 1822 et 1823*, I (1825), 126, 128–9; Blanqui, *Voyage d'un jeune Français en Angleterre et en Écosse pendant l'automne de 1823* (1824), 97–120 (esp. 117).

3   Von Raumer, *England in 1835: Being a Series of Letters Written to Friends in Germany*, trans. S. Austin and H. E. Lloyd (Philadelphia, 1836), 29–30; Fontane, *Journeys to England in Victoria's Early Days, 1844–1859*, trans. D. Harrison (1939), 19–22.

4   Tristan, *Promenades dans Londres, ou l'aristocratie et les prolétaires Anglais*, ed. F. Bedarida (1978; based on the edition of 1842), 68–70.

5   Faucher, *Études sur l'Angleterre* (1845), I, 195, xxx, 49–52.

6   Jäger, *Neuestes Gemälde von London* (Hamburg, 1839), I, 97, 99, 141, 254.

7   Tocqueville, *Journeys to England and Ireland*, ed. J. P. Mayer (Garden City, 1968), 82, 93–6.

8   Raumer, 467–8, 472–4.

9   Faucher, I, 195–296 (Liverpool), 297–470 (Manchester); II, 1–120 (Leeds), 131–91 (Birmingham); for Faucher on Manchester, see the translation, *Manchester in 1844: Its Present Condition and Future Prospects* (London and Manchester, 1844), 15, 16, 21, 24–5, 34–64, 74, 85, 90–3.

10   Buret, *De la misère des classes laborieuses en Angleterre et en France* (1840), I, 9, 17, 68–9, 136, 315–40.

11   Kohl, *England and Wales*, trans. T. Roscoe (1844), 8–9, 103, 13, 112–14, 117, 126.

12   Venedey, *England* (Leipzig, 1845), III, 154, 170, 175–7, 248 ff., 663–4.

13   W. O. Henderson, *The Life of Friedrich Engels* (1976), I, 2–3, 12–26, 43–8. The first German edition bore the title *Die Lage der arbeitenden Klasse in England, nach eigener Anschauung und authentischen Quellen* (Leipzig, 1845). The first English translation, by F. K. Wischnewetsky, appeared in the United States in 1887 and in England in 1892. A new translation by W. O. Henderson and W. H. Chaloner, with a highly critical introduction and copious notes that provide a running commentary on the text, was published in Britain in 1958 (by Basil Blackwell in Oxford) and in the United States in 1968 (Stanford University Press). Page references are to their edition.

14   Henderson, 50, 72; see also Steven Marcus, *Engels, Manchester, and the Working Class* (New York, 1974), 145.

15   Engels, 31, 34, 54–5.

16   *Ibid.*, 57, 61, 75; see esp. 'Results of Industrialization', 108–49, for evidence of social degradation.

17   *Ibid.*, 137; see also Engels' later statement along the same lines, in his study of the housing question, a series of articles titled 'Zur Wohnungsfrage' that appeared in 1872 in the Leipzig *Volksstaat*: 'Only the proletariat created by modern large-scale industry, liberated from all inherited fetters including those which chained it to the land, and herded together in the big cities, is in a position to accomplish the great social transformation which will put an end to all class exploitation and all class rule' (Karl Marx and Frederick Engels, *Selected Works*, I [Moscow, 1951], 511).

18   Henderson, 61–5.

19   Ledru-Rollin, *De la décadence de l'Angleterre* (2 vols, Brussels, 1850); Huber, *Reisebriefe aus Belgien, Frankreich, u. England im Sommer 1854* (2 vols, Hamburg, 1855); Taine, *Notes on England*, trans. W. F. Rae (New York, 1872).

20   On Lachaise, see Louis Chevalier, *Laboring Classes and Dangerous Classes in*

Paris During the First Half of the Nineteenth Century, trans. F. Jellinek (New York, 1973), 150–1. Villermé's most important article on Paris in these years was 'De la mortalité dans les divers quartiers de la ville de Paris, et des causes qui la rendent très différente dans plusieurs d'entre eux, ainsi que dans les divers quartiers de beaucoup de grandes villes', published in the *Annales* in 1830; on Villermé, see B.-P. Lecuyer, 'Médecins et observateurs sociaux: les Annales d'hygiène publique et de médecine légale (1820-1850)', in François Bedarida *et al.*, *Pour une histoire de la statistique*, I (1977), 451–2, and William Coleman, *Death Is a Social Disease: Public Health and Political Economy in Early Industrial France* (Madison, 1982), 4–14, 241–76. On Parent-Duchâtelet, see the introduction by F. Leuret to the work cited below in n. 21.

21   Parent-Duchâtelet, *De la prostitution dans la ville de Paris, considérée sous le rapport de l'hygiène publique, de la morale et de l'administration* (1837), I, 7, 569–86, and II, 528.

22   Frégier, *Des classes dangereuses de la population dans les grandes villes et des moyens de les rendre meilleures* (Brussels, 1840), 11–16; see also Chevalier, 141–2.

23   On Villermé and also on Buret, see Hilde Rigaudias-Weiss, *Les enquêtes ouvrières en France entre 1830 et 1848* (1936), 25–112.

24   Villermé, *Tableau de l'état physique et moral des ouvriers employés dans les manufactures de coton, de laine et de soie* (1840), I, 82–3, 445–6.

25   Buret, I, 237–8.

26   *Ibid.,* 255, 256, 259–60, 342, 343–9. Note the critical thrust conveyed by the subtitle of the work: *De la nature de la misère, de son existence, de ses effets, de ses causes, et de l'insuffisance des remèdes qu'on lui a opposés jusqu'ici; avec l'indication des moyens propres à en affranchir les sociétés.* For his proposed solutions, see II, 175–469.

27   Chevalier, 50–1, 152, 154–7.

28   Fanger, *Dostoevsky and Romantic Realism: A Study of Dostoevsky in Relation to Balzac, Dickens, and Gogol* (Cambridge, Mass., 1965), 21; Chevalier, 41.

29   Fanger, 28–64; Chevalier, 70–9.

30   On Sue, especially in relation to Hugo, see Volker Klotz, *Die erzählte Stadt: Ein Sujet als Herausforderung des Romans von Lesage bis Döblin* (Munich, 1969), 125–31.

31   Hugo, *Les misérables*, Modern Library edition, trans. C. E. Wilbour, 397, 628.

32   *Ibid.*, 1058.

33   Pierre Citron, *La poésie de Paris dans la littérature française de Rousseau à Baudelaire* (1961), II, 190, 202, 222, 226.

34   Hugo, 378, 499, 500, 502.

35   Citron, I, 258–9, 264–78.

36   Citron, II, 238–66.

37   Esquiros, *Paris, ou les sciences, les institutions et les moeurs au XIXe siècle* (1847), I, 1, 24–5. A more straightforward statement of the view that French cities in general had facilitated the progress of political liberty from the Middle Ages up to the present appears in Aristide Guilbert *et al.*, *Histoire des villes de France*, I (1844), xx, xxii.

38   Theodore Barrau, *La Patrie: description et histoire de la France* (1860), 55–9; Legoyt, *Du progrès des agglomérations urbaines et de l'émigration rurale en Europe et particulièrement en France* (Marseilles, 1867), 263–6. The bulk of Legoyt's book provided basic information about urban growth and offered an evenhanded assessment of its good and bad consequences. In general Legoyt viewed the city as a necessity, with which men would have to cope one way or another. Compare his views with those of Levasseur and Meuriot, treated in ch. 8 below.

39   Du Camp, *Paris: ses organes, ses fonctions et sa vie dans la seconde moitié du 19e siècle* (6th ed., 1875), I, 5, 8, 26. Few of the books about French cities other than Paris begin to approach the level of general interest achieved by numerous nineteenth-century works on British towns other than London. Most remain at the levels of

topographical description or mere chronicle. Significantly, one of the few exceptions treated Lyons, which experienced the most extensive rebuilding program of any city other than the capital. See Jean Baptiste Monfalcon, *Histoire monumentale de la ville de Lyon* (9 vols, Paris and Lyons, 1866–9), esp. Vol. IV.

40 Baudelaire, *The Flowers of Evil*, ed. M. and J. Mathews (rev. ed., New York, 1963), 113, and *Petits poèmes en prose*, ed. M. Zimmerman (Manchester, 1968), 91. For commentary, see A. E. Carter, *Charles Baudelaire* (Boston, 1977), 92–7, 109–14.

41 For the social as well as intellectual contexts within which social change was perceived at the time, see especially Theodore S. Hamerow, *Restoration, Revolution, Reaction: Economics and Politics in Germany, 1815–1871* (Princeton, 1958) and *The Social Foundations of German Unification, 1858–1871*, Vol. I: *Ideas and Institutions* (Princeton, 1969).

42 On Riehl's social thought more generally, see George Mosse, *The Crisis of German Ideology: Intellectual Origins of the Third Reich* (New York, 1964), 19–22, and Andrew Lees, *Revolution and Reflection: Intellectual Change in Germany during the 1850's* (The Hague, 1974), 147–53.

43 Riehl, *Die Naturgeschichte des Volkes als Grundlage einer deutschen Social-Politik*, I (Stuttgart and Augsburg, 1854), 75, 78.

44 *Ibid.*, 75–6, 47, 78, and III (1855), 223–4.

45 *Ibid.*, I, 76–8, and II (1854), 96, 305–41.

46 *Ibid.*, III, 185–6, and I, 79–82. Other men who shared Riehl's attachments to the countryside and the small town, which functioned in his thought as the positive antitheses to the big city, have been treated in two fine books: John G. Gagliardo, *From Pariah to Patriot: The Changing Image of the German Peasant, 1770–1840* (Lexington, Kentucky, 1969); and Mack Walker, *German Home Towns: Community, State, and General Estate, 1648–1871* (Ithaca and London, 1971).

47 'Städte, Städteverfassung, Städtewesen' (anon.), in Wagener, ed., *Neues Conversations-Lexikon: Staats- und Gesellschafts-Lexikon*, XIX (1865), 626–7.

48 René Trautmann, *Die Stadt in der deutschen Erzählkunst des 19. Jahrhunderts, 1830-1880* (Winterthur, 1957), 93–101.

49 Reichardt, *Zur Begründung einer Allgemeinen Bauordnung in Sanitäts-, Sicherheits-, Verkehrs- und Aesthetischer Beziehung* (Hamburg, 1863), 3–4; Arminius (pseudonym for Adelheid Gräfin Poninska), *Die Grossstädte in ihrer Wohnungsnoth und die Grundlagen einer durchgreifenden Abhilfe* (Leipzig, 1874), 3, 44–134; H. Beta (pseudonym for Heinrich Bettzeich), *Wohl- und Uebelthäter in unseren Grossstädten* (1875), 3–10, 18–26, 38.

50 Goethe, quoted in Friedrich Bothe, *Geschichte der Stadt Frankfurt am Main* (3rd ed., Frankfurt a.M., 1929), viii; [Johann] Christern, *Geschichte der freien Stadt Hamburg und ihrer Verfassung* (2nd ed., Hamburg, 1846), iii-iv; Johann Hermann Duntze, *Geschichte der freien Stadt Bremen*, IV (Bremen, 1851), 872–3; Georg Wolfgang Karl Lochner, *Nürnbergs Vorzeit und Gegenwart* (Nuremberg, 1845), viii-ix.

51 Dronke, *Berlin* (first ed., 1846; rev. ed., 1953), 75–81, 84, 96–7, 233 ff., 12–16, 33–6.

52 J. J. Sheehan, 'Liberalism and the city in nineteenth-century Germany', *Past and Present*, no. 51 (1971), 118–22.

53 Welcker, 'Städte, städtische Verfassung, ihre Entstehung und Wirkung und ihre jetzige Aufgabe in Deutschland', in Carl von Rotteck and Carl Welcker, eds., *Das Staats-Lexikon: Encyklopädie der sämmtlichen Staatswissenschaften für alle Stände*, XII (Altona, 1843), 105–6.

54 Barthold, *Geschichte der deutschen Städte und des deutschen Bürgertums*, I (Leipzig, 1850), 5–6; Biedermann, *Frauen-Brevier: Kulturgeschichtliche Vorlesungen* (Leipzig, 1856), 264–5.

55 Faucher, *Vergleichende   Kulturbilder   aus   den   vier   Europäischen*

Millionenstädten: Berlin, Wien, Paris, London (Hannover, 1877), v-vi, 1–2; Springer, *Berlin: Die deutsche Kaiserstadt* (Darmstadt, 1878), 4–6.

Chapter 4

1   Tucker, *Progress of the United States in Population and Wealth in Fifty Years, as Exhibited by the Decennial Census* (New York, 1843), 127; Godkin (anon.), 'Our great cities', *The Nation*, IX (1869), 404.

2   C. Rosenberg and C. Smith-Rosenberg, 'Piety and social action: some origins of the American public health movement', in Charles Rosenberg, *No Other Gods: On Science and American Social Thought* (Baltimore and London, 1976), 109–22.

3   *Ibid.;* for further discussion of Hartley, focusing on his charitable activities, see Paul Boyer, *Urban Masses and Moral Order in America, 1820–1920* (Cambridge, Mass., and London, 1978), 86–94.

4   *Ibid.* 72–3.

5   On Mayo, *Symbols of the Capital: Or Civilization in New York* (New York, 1859), see Charles N. Glaab and A. Theodore Brown, *A History of Urban America* (2nd ed., New York and London, 1976), 54.

6   Michael H. Cowan, *City of the West: Emerson, America, and Urban Metaphor* (New Haven and London, 1967), 61–2.

7   *Ibid.*, 186.

8   *Ibid.*, 85; Morton and Lucia White, *The Intellectual versus the City: From Thomas Jefferson to Frank Lloyd Wright* (Cambridge, Mass., 1962), 29.

9   Janis P. Stout, *Sodoms in Eden: The City in American Fiction before 1860* (Westport, Conn., and London, 1976), 75–7, 61–3, 122–7; White, 44–6; for negative comments on Manchester by other, less well known Americans, see John F. Kasson, *Civilizing the Machine: Technology and Republican Values in America, 1776–1900* (New York, 1976), 58–61.

10   Stout, 73–5, 77–87; White, 61–2, 53; Stout, 129–34.

11   *The Writings of Herman Melville*, VII (Evanston and Chicago, 1971), 13, 230, 240; for anti-urban stereotypes in the works of more popular authors of the period, see Stout, 21–54, and Adrienne Siegel, *The Image of the American City in Popular Literature, 1820–1870* (Port Washington, N.Y., and London, 1981), 13–92.

12   White, 26–7; Cowan, 151–64, 249.

13   *Ibid.*, 253–61.

14   Thomas Bender, *Toward an Urban Vision: Ideas and Institutions in Nineteenth-Century America* (Lexington, Kentucky, 1975), 11; Stout, 106–12; Hawthorne, *The Blithedale Romance*, in *The Complete Novels and Selected Tales*, ed. N. H. Pearson (New York, 1937), 525; see also the general remarks on the theme of the city in American literature in Stout, 7, 9–10, 12, 15.

15   Glaab and Brown, 54–5.

16   Lathrop, *Metropolitan Influence: Cities in Their Relation to the World's Evangelization* (New York, 1851), quoted in Bender, 10.

17   Quotations from Chapin taken from Boyer, 74.

18   Tappan, *The Growth of Cities* (New York, 1855), 15, 24, 29.

19   Siegel, 7, 92–177.

20   B. J. L[ossing], 'Growth of cities in the United States', *Harper's New Monthly Magazine*, VII (1853), 171–5; Bayrd Still, *Urban America: A History with Documents* (Boston, 1974), 93.

21   Glaab and Brown, 59–65; Still, 93–4.

22   Fitzhugh and Goldfield quoted in B. A. Brownell, 'The idea of the city in the American South', in Derek Fraser and Anthony Sutcliffe, eds., *The Pursuit of Urban History* (1983), 144–5; Still, 109–11.

23   *The Works of Walt Whitman,* ed. M. Cowley (New York, 1948), I, 153.
24   *Ibid.,* 234–5, 410, and II, 215; see also David R. Weimer, *The City as Metaphor* (New York, 1966), 14–33.

Chapter 5

1   Briggs, *Victorian Cities* (New York and Evanston, 1965), 52.
2   For the social and economic as well as the intellectual background, see Gareth Stedman Jones, *Outcast London: A Study in the Relationship between Classes in Victorian Society* (Oxford, 1971), *passim*, esp. 280–314, and Bentley B. Gilbert, *The Evolution of National Insurance in Great Britain: The Origins of the Welfare State* (1966), 21–58. The most revealing account of the intellectual changes experienced during these years by a single individual is Beatrice Webb, *My Apprenticeship* (1926).
3   Anthony S. Wohl, *The Eternal Slum: Housing and Social Policy in Victorian London* (1977), 200 ff., and Wohl, 'Introduction', in Mearns, *The Bitter Cry of Outcast London* (Leicester and New York, 1970), 13 ff.; see also the text of *The Bitter Cry* on 55–75.
4   Wohl, *The Eternal Slum,* 211–12; Stead's editorials are reprinted in Wohl, ed., *The Bitter Cry,* 81–8.
5   For Salisbury's and Chamberlain's articles, see *ibid.,* 113–53; for lists of other writings from the period that dealt with housing and poverty, see Jones, 290, and Anthony S. Wohl, 'The bitter cry of outcast London', *International Review of Social History,* XIII (1968), 205–6; for Lambert's article, see *Contemporary Review,* XLIV (1883), 916–23; for Reaney's article, see *Fortnightly Review,* XLVI (1886), 687–95; see also Arnold White, *The Problems of a Great City* (1886), 14–15: 'From the cheap lodging-houses, from the railway arches, from the crowded streets, rises an ever-increasing volume of inarticulate and unquenchable misery. Compared with the nomadic tribes of tropic countries ... the nomads of London are but miserable savages.... Notwithstanding the combined efforts of all the churches and the machinery of all the societies, no real advance is being made in the process of killing out the prolific powers of evil'.
6   On Booth's life, see St. John Greer Ervine, *God's Soldier: General William Booth* (2 vols, New York, 1935); on the connection with Stead, see Wohl, ed., *The Bitter Cry,* 23.
7   Booth, *In Darkest England,* 11–12.
8   On this whole subject, see P. J. Keating, 'Fact and fiction in the East End', in H. J. Dyos and Michael Wolff, eds., *The Victorian City: Images and Realities* (London and Boston, 1973), II, 585–602.
9   For biographical background and analysis of the major works, see Adrian Poole, *Gissing in Context* (1975); see also the discussion in Raymond Williams, *The Country and the City* (New York, 1973), 222–5.
10   Gissing, *Demos* (2nd ed., 1892), 25–6.
11   Gissing, *The Nether World* (2nd ed., 1890), 10, 274, 392.
12   T. S. Simey and M. B. Simey, *Charles Booth: Social Scientist* (1960), 65–70; E. P. Hennock, 'Poverty and social theory in England: the experience of the eighteen-eighties', *Social History,* I (1976), 70–1; Booth, *Life and Labour ... First Series: Poverty,* I (rev. ed., 1902), 172.
13   Harold W. Pfautz, 'Introduction', in Booth, *On the City: Physical Pattern and Social Structure,* ed. Pfautz (Chicago and London, 1967), 18–19; Booth, *Poverty,* I, 6; Simey, 94; R. Glass, 'Urban sociology in Great Britain: a trend report', *Current Sociology,* IV, no. 4 (1955), 46.
14   For Booth's definitions of the eight classes, see *Poverty,* II (rev. ed., 1902), 20.

15   For tables that summarize the statistics on poverty, see *ibid.*, I, 36, and II, 21; for the longer quotations, see I, 173–4, 39.

16   *Ibid.*, 177, 146–9.

17   *Ibid.*, 6; Pfautz, 43.

18   Booth, I, 166–9; Pfautz, 33–4, 84.

19   'Mr. Charles Booth on the London poor', *The Spectator*, LXVI (1891), 854; 'Life and labour of the people in London', *The Spectator*, LXX (1893), 389.

20   *Ibid.*, 389; see also C. Black, 'Labour and life in London', *Contemporary Review*, LX (1891), 218, and Hennock, 79.

21   Gregory (anon.), 'The inhabitants of East London', *Quarterly Review*, CLXIX (1889), 456; Kidd, *Social Evolution* (London and New York, 1895), 79–80; see also, although it does not refer specifically to Booth, the comment by a leading Liberal politician, Charles Dilke: 'The London which perhaps most interests the foreign observer of the day is the London of Whitechapel, and thieves' suppers, and Salvation Army shelters – the London of the poor, the London of the misery which accompanies, at London, as at Liverpool, and Glasgow, and New York, enormous commercial wealth' (in his article 'London', in Nancy Bell and H. D. Traill, eds., *The Capitals of the World* [1892], II, 15–16).

22   Pfautz, 82; Asa Briggs, *Social Thought and Social Action: A Study of the Work of Seebohm Rowntree, 1871–1954* (1961), 8–18, 23–5; see also Philip Abrams, *The Origins of British Sociology, 1834–1914* (Chicago and London, 1968), 138–40.

23   For Rowntree's definitions of poverty, see Rowntree, *Poverty*, 86–7; for his percentages, see *ibid.*, 298; for the quoted sentences, see *ibid.*, 133–4.

24   *Ibid.*, 142, 144–5.

25   *Ibid.*, 298–301, 304–5.

26   R. G. Davis, 'Slum environment and social causation', *Westminster Review*, CLXVI (1906), 251, 255; F. Tillyard, 'English town development in the nineteenth century', *The Economic Journal*, XXIII (1913), 547–60. Two major works by social scientists were L. Chiozza Money, *Riches and Poverty* (ten editions between 1905 and 1911; not specifically about cities) and A. L. Bowley and A. R. Burnett-Hurst, *Livelihood and Poverty: A Study in the Economic Conditions of Working-class Households in Northampton, Warrington, Stanley, and Reading* (1915). On the story of legislative developments, see Gilbert, *The Evolution of National Insurance*, 102 ff.

27   Zola, *L'assomoir*, trans. L. W. Tancock (Penguin Books, 1970), 23–4, 21.

28   Zola, *Paris*, trans. E. A. Vizetelly (New York and London, 1898), I, 1–2, 14–15. For the most thorough treatment of Zola's depiction of Paris in all his novels, see Nathan Kranowski, *Paris dans les romans d'Emile Zola* (1968); see also Volker Klotz, *Die erzählte Stadt: Ein Sujet als Herausforderung des Romans von Lesage bis Döblin* (Munich, 1969), 230–53.

29   Haussonville, 'L'enfance à Paris', *Revue des deux mondes*, third series, XVII (1876), 481–511, XVIII (1876), 575–604, XX (1877), 36–79, XXVII (1878), 598–627, XXVII (1878), 891–927, XXX (1878), 241–71, XXXI (1879), 346–74, XXXII (1879), 818–53; for the quoted phrases, see XVII, 482.

30   Haussonville, 'La misère à Paris', *Revue des deux mondes*, third series, XLV (1881), 812–49, XLVII (1881), 611–51; also, 'La vie et les salaires à Paris', *Revue*, LVI (1883), 815–67; see esp. XLV, 812–13, 824–6, XLVII, 630–50, and LVI, 817.

31   On empirical social research in France during this period, see Terry Nichols Clark, *Prophets and Patrons: The French University and the Emergence of the Social Sciences* (Cambridge, Mass., 1973), 122–46. Clark suggests that the relative unimportance of poverty surveys both in France and in Germany compared with Britain and the United States stemmed from the low level of private charity on the continent.

32   For a major study in the Le Play tradition that focused on workers in Paris, see

Pierre Du Maroussem, *La question ouvrière* (4 vols, 1891–4).

33   One work among many in this genre, which paid more attention than most to problems specific to workers who lived in towns, was J. Borin-Fournet, *La société moderne et la question sociale* (1893); see esp. 357–450.

34   See, for instance, A. Anquetil, *L'abandon des campagnes: causes, conséquences, remèdes* (1909), 77–8; also, L. Ferrand, 'La hausse des loyers urbains: ses causes, ses répercussions sociales', *La réforme sociale*, LXVIII (1914), 127–38.

35   On the origins and activities of the Association, see Dieter Lindenlaub, *Richtungskämpfe im Verein für Sozialpolitik* (Wiesbaden, 1967), I, 1–43; see also Anthony Oberschall, *Empirical Social Research in Germany, 1848–1914* (Paris and The Hague, 1965), 21–2, and Fritz K. Ringer, *The Decline of the German Mandarins: The German Academic Community, 1890–1933* (Cambridge, Mass., 1969), 146–51.

36   *Die Wohnungsnoth der ärmeren Klassen in deutschen Grossstädten und Vorschläge zu deren Abhülfe* (*Schriften des Vereins für Sozialpolitik*, Vols. XXXI–XXXII; Leipzig, 1886). There is a vast body of highly detailed literature on housing written in Germany during the late nineteenth and early twentieth centuries. See Josef Stammhammer, *Bibliographie der Social-Politik* (2 vols, Jena, 1896-1912), I, 646, and II, 789–90, 791–805; also, Lutz Niethammer and Franz Brüggemeier, 'Wie wohnten Arbeiter im Kaiserreich?', *Archiv für Sozialgeschichte*, XVI (1976), 63–8.

37   *Verhandlungen der am 24. und 25. September 1886 in Frankfurt a.M. abgehaltenen Generalversammlung des Vereins für Sozialpolitik* (*Schriften*, Vol. XXXIII; Leipzig, 1887), 7, 10–11.

38   In *Schriften*, Vol. XLIV (Leipzig, 1901), 261–384. Lindemann was the leading Social Democratic expert on municipal affairs.

39   *Verhandlungen des Vereins für Sozialpolitik über die Wohnungsfrage und die Handelspolitik* (*Schriften*, Vol. XCVIII; Leipzig, 1902), 17–18. For later surveys of the economic and social life of industrial workers, see F. Schumann and R. Sorer, *Auslese und Anpassung der Arbeiterschaft in der Automobilindustrie und einer Wiener Maschinenfabrik;* R. Kempf, *Das Leben der jungen Fabrikmädchen in München*; and M. Morgenstern *et al.*, *Auslese und Anpassung der Arbeiterschaft in der Lederwaren–, Steinzeug- und Textilindustrie* (all in *Schriften*, Vol. CXXXV; Leipzig, 1911–12).

40   Woodruff D. Smith, 'The emergence of German urban sociology, 1900-1910', *Journal of the History of Sociology*, 1979, p. 13.

41   Ostwald, *Dunkle Winkel in Berlin* (Vol. I, 1905); Winter, *Im unterirdischen Wien* (Vol. XIII, 1905); Schuchardt, *Sechs monate Arbeitshaus* (Vol. XXXIII, 1907); Südekum, *Grossstädtisches Wohnungselend* (Vol. XLVI, 1908).

42   Oberschall, 28–9; Göhre, *Three Months in a Workshop: A Practical Study*, trans. A. B. Carr (London and New York, 1895), 19 ff., 36–40.

43   Oberschall, 81–2, 94–106. Levenstein's major work was *Die Arbeiterfrage* (Munich, 1912).

44   Weber, *Die Grossstadt und ihre sozialen Probleme* (Leipzig, 1908), 7–8, 28–9, 41–2, 87–8, 98–9; on Weber's views about urban culture and morality, see below, ch. 7; on his proposals for urban reform, see A. Lees, 'Critics of urban society in Germany', *Journal of the History of Ideas*, XL (1979), 80.

45   Kretzer began writing novels about workers in Berlin in the 1880s with *Die beiden Genossen* (1880) and *Meister Timpe* (1888) and churned out many more in the 1890s. Conrad began what was intended to be a German counterpart to Zola's Rougon-Macquart series with *Was die Isar rauscht* (3 vols, Leipzig, 1888-93).

46   On the whole subject of the relationship between cities and literary culture in Germany during this period, see Roy Pascal, *From Naturalism to Expressionism: German Literature and Society, 1880–1918* (1973), 124–60. On urban poetry, see Wolfgang Rothe, ed., *Deutsche Grossstadtlyrik vom Naturalismus bis zur Gegenwart* (Stuttgart, 1973), 5–21.

47   *Ibid.*, 43–4, 46.

48   *Ibid.*, 79. See also Oskar Hübner and Johannes Moegelin, *Im steinernen Meer: Grossstadtgedichte* (Berlin-Schöneberg, 1910), 89–128. In the verses of many of the poets who followed Rilke — especially Georg Trakl, Georg Heym, and Franz Werfel — images of coldness, hardness, stone walls, torment, and death sustained the impression of the *Grossstadt* as a cruel place in which to live, but there was little if any reference to identifiably lower-class experience. Their sense of malaise embraced the whole city, and the physical environment served as a source of symbols for a pervasive poverty of the spirit, not as something that concerned them in its own right.

49   Robert H. Bremner, *From the Depths: The Discovery of Poverty in the United States* (New York, 1956), 23–5. For much of the rest of what follows in this chapter, I have drawn heavily on this splendid work, esp. 67–107, 140–84.

50   Bellamy, *Looking Backward, 2000–1887* (New York, 1960), 206, 213–14.

51   James B. Lane, *Jacob A. Riis and the American City* (Port Washington, N.Y., and London, 1974), 5–11, 15–36, 39–44, 48–68.

52   Riis, *How the Other Half Lives: Studies among the Tenements of New York*, ed. D. N. Bigelow (New York, 1957), 2–3, 17, 34; see also his *The Children of the Poor* (New York, 1892) and *Out of Mulberry Street: Stories of Tenement Life in New York City* (New York, 1898).

53   These articles were collected in Robert A. Woods *et al.*, *The Poor in Great Cities: Their Problems and What Is Doing to Solve Them* (New York, 1895).

54   Charles Howard Hopkins, *The Rise of the Social Gospel in American Protestantism, 1865–1915* (New Haven, 1940), 121 ff.; Henry F. May, *Protestant Churches and Industrial America* (New York, 1949), 118; Gladden, 'Poverty', *The Century*, XLV (1892–3), 246.

55   R. H. Walker, 'The poet and the rise of the city', *Mississippi Valley Historical Review*, XLIX (1962), 90–1.

56   Howells: *A Hazard of New Fortunes* (New York, 1965), 56; *Impressions and Experiences* (New York, 1896), 252–3. For a fuller discussion of Howells' views of the city, see Morton and Lucia White, *The Intellectual versus the City* (Cambridge, Mass., 1962), 95–116.

57   *The Works of Stephen Crane*, I (Charlottesville, 1969), 11; see also David B. Weimer, *The City as Metaphor* (New York, 1966), 52–64.

58   For background and analysis, see Blanche H. Gelfant, *The American City Novel* (Norman, Oklahoma, 1954), 42–94; White, 124–38; Weimer, 65–77; and Bremner, 170–4.

59   Dreiser, *Sister Carrie*, ed. N. M. Westlake *et al.* (Philadelphia, 1981), 23, 489.

60   Dreiser, *The Color of a Great City* (1930), 34–43, 77–80, 85–99, 129–32, 173–83, 207–15. For discussion of other novelists who wrote about poverty during the early part of the twentieth century, see Bremner, 174–84.

61   Reynolds, *The Housing of the Poor in American Cities*, in *Publications of the American Economic Association*, VIII (Baltimore, 1893), 131–262; Gould, *The Housing of the Working People* (Eighth Special Report of the Commissioner of Labor; Washington, 1895), 436.

62   See Allen F. Davis, *Spearheads for Reform: The Social Settlements and the Progressive Movement, 1890–1914* (New York, 1967) and below, ch. 9.

63   Subtitled *A Presentation of Nationalities and Wages in a Congested District of Chicago* (New York and Boston, 1895).

64   *Ibid.*, vii–viii.

65   *Ibid.*, 11.

66   Robert A. Woods, ed., *The City Wilderness: A Settlement Study* (Boston, 1898), 288, 290; on other social research by men and women involved in settlement work, see Davis, 30, 85–6.

67   Hunter, *Tenement Conditions in Chicago* (Chicago, 1901), 11–12.
68   DeForest and Veiller, eds., *The Tenement House Problem*, I (New York and London, 1903), 10.
69   Bremner, 151.
70   Bremner, 154–6; Shelbey M. Harrison, *The Social Survey* (New York, 1931), 13–16; Clarke A. Chambers, *Paul U. Kellogg and the Survey: Voices for Social Welfare and Social Justice* (Minneapolis, 1971), 23–40. For discussion of Booth's survey as a model for the Pittsburgh survey, see Graham Taylor, 'The standard for a city's survey', *Charities and the Commons*, XXI (1908–9), 508. The Russell Sage Foundation carried out half a dozen of its own surveys along the lines of the Pittsburgh survey between 1912 and 1914. After changing the name of its journal from *Charities and the Commons* to *The Survey* in 1909, the Charities Publication Committee published a social study of Birmingham, Alabama, and a study of labor problems in all the major steel centers in the United States (Bremner, 156–7).

Chapter 6

1   Cantlie, *Degeneration amongst Londoners* (1885), 8–19, 24–5; for biography, see *Who's Who* (1906), 283.
2   Cantlie, *Physical Efficiency: A Review of the Deleterious Effects of Town Life upon the Population of Britain, with Suggestions for Their Arrest* (London and New York, 1907), 12.
3   Cantlie, *Degeneration*, 20–1, 23.
4   Fothergill: 'The effects of town life upon the human body', *National Review*, X (1887), 166–72; *The Town Dweller: His Needs and Wants* (1889), 16, 89, 96–7, 108–9
5   Williams-Freeman, *The Effect of Town Life on the General Health, with Especial Reference to London* (1890), 5, 19, 26, 34–5.
6   White, *The Problems of a Great City* (1886), 131; Brabazon, 'Decay of bodily strength in towns', *The Nineteenth Century*, XXI (1887), 673–6.
7   Blatchford, *Merrie England* (1908; first ed., 1894), 30, 58. For further discussion of contemporary views of this problem, see Gareth Stedman Jones, *Outcast London: A Study in the Relationship between Classes in Victorian Society* (Oxford, 1971), 127–51.
8   On this whole subject, see Bentley B. Gilbert, *The Evolution of National Insurance in Great Britain: The Origins of the Welfare State* (1966), 60–91; for Rowntree's views, see *Poverty: A Study of Town Life* (1901), 216–21.
9   Cantlie, *Physical Efficiency*, 50, 12, 18–19, 27; Masterman, *The Condition of England* (1909), 103.
10   Bordier, *La vie des sociétés* (1887), 121, 132–3, 136, 139 ff., 146–51.
11   Levasseur, *La population française*, II (1891), 397–8, 401–2.
12   Meuriot, *Des agglomérations urbaines dans l'Europe contemporaine: essai sur les causes, les conditions, les conséquences de leur développement* (1897), 369–73, 387; Lannes, 'L'influence de l'émigration des campagnes sur la natalité française', *Revue politique et parlementaire*, II (1895), 309–29; A. Anquetil, *L'abandon des campagnes: causes, conséquences, remèdes* (1909), 80.
13   Jean Guillou, *L'émigration des campagnes vers les villes et les conséquences économiques et sociales* (1905), 454–5. For full-scale treatments of depopulation, none of which have much to say about cities as such, see the following: Arsène Dumont, *Dépopulation et civilisation: etude démographique* (1890); Henry Clément, *La dépopulation en France* (1910); and Jacques Bertillon, *La dépopulation de la France* (1911). The only twentieth-century work I have found that focuses on the city as an especially culpable hindrance to population growth is the brief and not very incisive

article by E. Cacheux, 'Influence des grandes villes sur la dépopulation', *Revue philanthropique*, XXXVII (1916), 513–18.

14 Hansen, *Die drei Bevölkerungsstufen: Ein Versuch, die Ursachen für das Blühen und Altern der Völker nachzuweisen* (Munich, 1889), 39; for an extensive summary and critique of the book, see Elisabeth Pfeil, *Grossstadtforschung* (Bremen-Horn, 1950), 43–8; see also Klaus Bergmann, *Agrarromantik und Grossstadtfeindschaft* (Meisenheim am Glan, 1970), 50–6.

15 Ammon's most important works on this subject were *Die natürliche Auslese beim Menschen: Auf Grund der Ergebnisse der anthropologischen Untersuchungen der Wehrpflichtigen in Baden und anderer Materialien* (Jena, 1893) and *Die Gesellschaftsordnung und ihre natürlichen Grundlagen: Entwurf einer Sozial-Anthropologie zum Gebrauch für alle Gebildeten, die sich mit sozialen Fragen befassen* (Jena, 1895). His ideas are summarized in *ibid.*, 115–23, in Pfeil, 48–51, and in Bergmann, 56–63.

16 Bauer, *Der Zug nach der Stadt und die Stadterweiterung: Eine rassenhygienische Studie* (Stuttgart, 1904), 17–73, 163–4; C. Röse, 'Die Grossstadt als Grab der Bevölkerung', *Arztliche Rundschau*, XV (1905), 259–60; Hanauer, 'Die Sterblichkeit in der Stadt und auf dem Lande', *Kommunale Praxis*, IV (1904), 272–3.

17 Ballod: *Die Lebensfähigkeit der städtischen und ländlichen Bevölkerung* (Leipzig, 1897), 68; *Die mittlere Lebensdauer in Stadt und Land* (Leipzig, 1899), 60–90; and 'Sterblichkeit und Fortpflanzung der Stadtbevölkerung', *Jahrbücher für Nationalökonomie und Statistik*, XXXVIII (1909), 541.

18 Thurnwald, 'Stadt und Land im Lebensprozess der Rasse', *Archiv für Rassen- und Gesellschaftsbiologie*, I (1904), 730 ff., 875, 833.

19 Mayr, 'Die Bevölkerung der Grossstädte', in *Die Grossstadt: Vorträge und Aufsätze zur Städteausstellung* (Dresden, 1903), 104, 129–36; Weber, *Die Grossstadt und ihre sozialen Probleme* (Leipzig, 1908), 13–14.

20 Theilhaber, *Das sterile Berlin: Eine volkswirtschaftliche Studie* (1913), 43, 48, 74–5.

21 Sohnrey, *Der Zug vom Lande und die soziale Revolution* (Leipzig, 1894), iii, vii (for fuller discussion of his ideas, see Bergmann, 63–70, 89–102); Wulle, 'Die Gefahren der Grossstadtentwicklung für das deutsche Volk', *Konservative Monatsschrift*, LXX (1913), 898.

22 Rost, 'Die Lebenskraft deutscher Städte', *Soziale Revue: Zeitschrift fur die sozialen Fragen der Gegenwart*, 1910, pp. 49, 55; Matthias Salm 'Stadt und Land', *Soziale Kultur*, XXIII (1913), 279, 284.

23 Wulle, 904–5; Bergmann, 69; Kenneth Barkin, *The Controversy over German Industrialization, 1890–1902* (Chicago and London, 1970), 160–2; Rost, 57.

24 Ballod, 'Die Wechselbeziehungen zwischen Stadt und Land, Bevölkerungs- politik, Militärtauglichkeit', in Fr. Edler *et al.*, eds., *Arbeitsziele der deutschen Landwirtschaft nach dem Kriege* (1918), 38–9, 29–30, 36, 41.

25 Riis, *How the Other Half Lives*, ed. D. N. Bigelow (New York, 1957), 47, 81, 124–7; Hunter, *Tenement Conditions in Chicago* (Chicago, 1901), 152–60; Robert W. DeForest and Lawrence Veiller, eds., *The Tenement House Problem* (New York, 1903), I, 445–70.

26 Bryce, 'Effects upon public health and natural prosperity from rural depopulation and abnormal increase of cities', *American Journal of Public Health*, V (1915), 51; Henderson, 'Are modern industry and city life unfavorable to the family?', *American Journal of Sociology*, XIV (1909), 669–72; Thompson, 'Race suicide in the United States', *Scientific Monthly*, V (1917), 160–5, 267.

27 Weber, 'The significance of recent city growth: the era of small industrial centres', *Annals of the American Academy*, XXIII (1904), 223–4.

Chapter 7

1   Alan D. Gilbert, *Religion and Society in Industrial England: Church, Chapel and Social Change, 1740–1914* (London and New York, 1976), 23–48; Hugh McLeod, *Class and Religion in the Late Victorian City* (1974), 281–3.

2   Mearns, *The Bitter Cry*, ed. A. Wohl (Leicester, 1970), 61.

3   Bonar, *Does God Care for Our Great Cities? The Question and the Answer from the Book of Jonah* (1880), 83–4, 90–1.

4   Davidson, *The City Youth* (5th ed., 1898), v–vi, 5–6, 46.

5   Winnington-Ingram, *Work in Great Cities: Six Lectures on Pastoral Theology* (1895), 3–21, 34.

6   For biographical background, see Lucy Blanche Masterman, *G. F. C. Masterman* (1939) and the introduction by Bentley B. Gilbert to a new edition of *The Heart of the Empire* (1973). The other contributors to that volume were Frederick W. Lawrence, Reginald A. Bray, Noel Buxton, Walter Hoare, P. W. Wilson, A. C. Pigou, Frederick W. Head, G. P. Gooch, and George M. Trevelyan. Masterman's essay, 'Realities at home', served as a general introduction. See also his 'The social abyss', *Contemporary Review*, LXXXI (1902), 23–35 (a review of Rowntree); *From the Abyss: Of Its Inhabitants by One of Them* (anon., 1902); 'The English city', in L. Oldershaw, ed., *England: A Nation, Being the Papers of the Patriots' Club* (London and Edinburgh, 1904); and *The Condition of England* (1909), esp. 96–156.

7   Masterman, 'Realities at home', 7–8, 25–30.

8   *Ibid.*, 34; Masterman, *From the Abyss*, 33, 66–7.

9   For biography, see Gilbert, *Heart of the Empire*, xxx–xxxi.

10   Bray, 'The children of the town', in *The Heart of the Empire*, 119, 124–5, 126.

11   Bray, *The Town Child*, 45–50, 55–6.

12   Terry N. Clark, *Prophets and Patrons: The French University and the Emergence of the Social Sciences* (Cambridge, Mass., 1973), 105; Des Cilleuls, 'Les grandes agglomérations devant l'économie sociale', *La réforme sociale*, XXIX (1895), 641–8, 653–4.

13   Wuarin, 'La crise des campagnes et des villes', *Revue des deux mondes*, CLIX (1900), 1887.

14   Meuriot, *Des agglomérations urbaines dans l'Europe contemporaine: essai sur les causes, les conditions, les conséquences de leur développement* (1897), 344–54. The great sociologist Emile Durkheim published his famous work on suicide, *Le suicide: étude de sociologie*, in the same year that Meuriot's study appeared. He mentioned that the incidence of suicide was higher in cities than elsewhere, but only in a footnote, and he added that 'the proposition is only broadly true and has many exceptions'. See the English edition, *Suicide*, trans. J. A. Spaulding and G. Simpson (1952), 137.

15   There is no historical work of any substance that deals specifically with the relationships between churches and cities in modern Germany. For background on Protestant social thought in general during the period, see F. Karrenberg, 'Geschichte der sozialen Ideen im deutschen Protestantismus', in Wilfried Gottschalch *et al.*, *Geschichte der sozialen Ideen in Deutschland* (Munich, 1969), 571–623. There is an enormous body of both primary and secondary literature that illuminates the important topic of 'social Catholicism' in Germany (see Franz Josef Stegmann, 'Geschichte der sozialen Ideen im deutschen Katholizismus', in Gottschalch, 325–560), but relatively few Catholic clergymen dealt explicitly with the problem of the city. Two exceptions, both of which combined moderate criticisms with expressions of confidence that the *Grossstadt* could be redeemed, were Heinrich Swoboda, *Grossstadtseelsorge: Eine pastoraltheologische Studie* (2nd ed., Regensburg, 1911) and A[nton] Heinen, *Die Grossstadt und ihr Einfluss auf Welt- und Lebensauffassung* (M. Gladbach, 1913).

16   Heitmann, *Grossstadt und Religion*, Vol. I: *Die religiöse Situation in der Grossstadt* (Hamburg, 1913), 8, 39–46.

17 Dibelius, *Unsere Grossstadtgemeinden, ihre Not und deren Überwindung* (Giessen, 1910), 5–6; Naumann, 'Grossstadt oder Kleinstädte?', in *Patria: Jahrbuch der 'Hilfe' 1903*, ed. Naumann (Berlin-Schöneberg, 1902), 48; Classen, *Grossstadtheimat: Beobachtungen zur Naturgeschichte des Grossstadtvolkes* (Hamburg, 1906), 166–9.

18 Rogge, 'Die Bedeutung der Grossstädte für das Volksleben', *Die Reformation: Deutsche evang. Kirchenzeitung für die Gemeinde*, VIII (1909), 389–90, 375–6; Ernst, *Sommerfrische und Grossstadt: Betrachtungen und Bedenken* (Stuttgart, 1901; Vol. XXVI, no. 4, of *Zeitfragen des christlichen Volkslebens*), 38–42, 34–5; Schlegelmilch, *Grossstadtnot und -hilfe* (1909), 4–5.

19 Fritz Stern, *The Politics of Cultural Despair: A Study in the Rise of the Germanic Ideology* (Berkeley and Los Angeles, 1961), 130; George Mosse, *The Crisis of German Ideology: Intellectual Origins of the Third Reich* (New York, 1964), 22–3; Klaus Bergmann, *Agrarromantik und Grossstadtfeindschaft* (Meisenheim am Glan, 1970), 70–85; Gary D. Stark, *Entrepreneurs of Ideology: Neoconservative Publishers in Germany, 1890–1933* (Chapel Hill, 1981), 95–8.

20 Sohnrey, 'Der Zug der Landmädchen nach der Stadt', *Das Land*, XVIII (1910), 302–5; l'Houet, *Zur Psychologie der Kultur: Briefe an die Grossstadt* (Bremen, 1910), 3, 61–3.

21 Ostwald, *Zuhältertum in Berlin* and *Das Berliner Spielertum* (Vols. V, XXXV; 1905, 1908); Magnus Hirschfeld, *Berlins Drittes Geschlecht* and *Die Gurgel Berlins* (Vols. III, XLI; 1905, 1907); Emil Bader, *Wiener Verbrecher* (Vol. XVI, 1905); Wilhelm Hammer, *Die Tribadie Berlins* and *Zehn Lebensläufe Berliner Kontrollmädchen* (Vols. XX, XXIII; 1906, 1905); J. Werthauer, *Berliner Schwindel, Moabitrium: Szenen aus der Grossstadt-Strafrechtspflege*, and *Sittlichkeitsdelikte der Grossstadt* (Vols. XXI, XXXI, XL; 1905, 1907, 1907); Max Marcuse, *Uneheliche Mütter* (Vol. XXVII, 1906); Hans Hyan, *Schwere Jungen* (Vol. XXVIII, 1906); M. Baer, *Der internationale Mädchenhandel* (Vol. XXXVII, 1908); Leo Benario, *Die Wucherer und ihre Opfer* (Vol. XXXVIII, 1908); Georg Buschan, *Geschlecht und Verbrechen* (Vol. XLVIII, 1908); Alfred Lasson, *Gefährdete und verwahrloste Jugend* (Vol. XLIX, 1908).

22 Scheffler, 'Die Grossstadt', *Die Neue Rundschau*, XXI (1910), 884, 886.

23 Tönnies, *Community and Society: Gemeinschaft und Gesellschaft*, trans. and ed. C. P. Loomis (New York, 1963), 227, 33–5, 65, 76–7, 226, 229, 237–40; on Tönnies' social thought in general, see Arthur Mitzman, *Sociology and Estrangement: Three Sociologists of Imperial Germany* (New York, 1973), 39–131, and Fritz K. Ringer, *The Decline of the German Mandarins: The German Academic Community, 1890–1933* (Cambridge, Mass., 1969), 164–71. For an example of the use of Tönnies' concepts by a conservative clergyman to distinguish between peasants and urbanites, see Gustav Mahr, 'Stadt und Land', *Das Land*, XXVI (1918), 97.

24 Originally published in *Die Grossstadt: Vorträge und Aufsätze zur Städteausstellung* (Dresden, 1903) under the title 'Die Grossstädte und das Geistesleben', Simmel's essay has been translated and reprinted under the title 'The metropolis and mental life' in K. Wolff, ed., *The Sociology of Georg Simmel* (Glencoe, 1950), 409–24. For a much fuller discussion of Simmel's ideas about cities, see Michael P. Smith, *The City and Social Theory* (New York, 1979), 88–126. Simmel's sociology, with its soaring intuitiveness, displayed qualities that one might expect in a work of imaginative literature rather than in a work of social science. For views of urban life similar to his by other writers who made no effort to produce anything but imaginative works, see especially the poetry of many of the expressionists, with its pervasive emphasis on individual loneliness. On this point, see Wolfgang Rothe, ed., *Deutsche Grossstadtlyrik vom Naturalismus bis zur Gegenwart* (Stuttgart, 1973), 15 (also, for selected poems, 107–97).

25 Thurnwald, 'Stadt und Land im Lebensprozess der Rasse', *Archiv für Rassen- und Gesellschaftsbiologie*, I (1904), 728, 881, 723, 725; Weber, *Die Grossstadt und ihre*

sozialen Probleme (Leipzig, 1908), 11–15, 23–4.

26   Washburn (anon.), 'City life in the United States', *The Contemporary Review*, XL (1881), 721, 725. For another article that examines the morals of immigrants in somewhat more detail, see J. R. Commons, 'City life, crime and poverty', *Chautauquan*, XXXIX (1904), 115–23, esp. 118–19.

27   Dickerman, 'The drift to the cities', *Atlantic Monthly*, CXII (1913), 351–3.

28   Aaron I. Abell, *The Urban Impact on American Protestantism, 1865–1900* (Cambridge, Mass., 1943), 1–10; see also Paul Boyer, *Urban Masses and Moral Order in America, 1820–1920* (Cambridge, Mass., 1978), 132–42.

29   Strong, *Our Country*, ed. J. Herbst (Cambridge, Mass., 1963; a reprint of the 1891 edition with a biographical introduction), 171–6.

30   *Ibid.*, 177–9, and Strong, *The Twentieth Century City* (New York, 1898), 76.

31   Loomis, *Modern Cities and Their Religious Problems*, with an introduction by Strong (New York, 1887), 86, 91–2, 99.

32   *Ibid.*, 100–6. See the discussion of both Strong and Loomis in Henry F. May, *Protestant Churches and Industrial America* (New York, 1949), 112–17. For similar views expressed by Methodists, see G. P. Mains, 'The church and the city', *Methodist Review*, LIV (1894), 221–37, and P. H. Swift, 'The problem of religious life in the city', *Methodist Review*, LX (1900), 405–17.

33   Henderson, 'Are modern industry and city life unfavorable to the family?', *American Journal of Sociology*, XIV (1909), 668–79.

34   Addams, *The Spirit of Youth* (Urbana, 1972; a reprint of the 1909 edition, with an introduction by A. Davis), vii–viii.

35   *Ibid.*, 4–5, 27, 71.

36   Reaney, 'Outcast London', *Fortnightly Review*, XLVI (1886), 695.

37   Masterman: 'Realities at home', 11; *From the Abyss*, 2–3; 'The English city', 61; *The Condition of England*, 120.

38   Levasseur, 413; Meuriot, 407.

39   Choisy, 'L'émigration rurale dans les villes', *La réforme sociale*, XXIII (1892), 690; A. Anquetil, *L'abandon des campagnes: causes, conséquences, remèdes* (1909), 79–80; Wuarin, 888.

40   Le Bon, *The Crowd* (1896), 14–18, 24–5; for biography and for analysis of Le Bon's ideas, see Robert A. Nye, *The Origins of Crowd Psychology: Gustave Le Bon and the Crisis of Mass Democracy in the Third Republic* (London and Beverly Hills, 1975), esp. 59–121; see also Susanna Barrows, *Distorting Mirrors: Visions of the Crowd in Late Nineteenth-Century France* (New Haven, 1981), 162–88.

41   Tönnies, 227, 231.

42   J. Jaeger, 'Das Anwachsen der Grossstädte', *Die Grenzboten*, XLVIII (1889), 209; Sohnrey, *Der Zug vom Lande und die soziale Revolution* (Leipzig, 1894), viii–ix; Bergmann, 59–60.

43   Buhli, 'Grossstadt und Land in ihrer kulturellen und wirtschaftlichen Wechselbeziehung' (a lecture given in 1910), in *Reden und Aufsätze, 1900–1921* (Munich and Berlin, 1922), 10–11; l'Houet, 18–21; Wapler, 'Der Einfluss der Grossstadt auf dem Land', in Ernst Bunke, ed., *Arbeit für Grossstadt und Land* (1911), 74; Rogge, 376.

44   Schäfer, 'Die politische und militärische Bedeutung der Grossstädte', in *Die Grossstadt: Vorträge und Aufsätze zur Städteausstellung* (Dresden, 1903), 264–5; Schlegelmilch, *Landflucht und Stadtsucht* (1909), 5–6.

45   Beusch, *Wanderungen und Stadtkultur: Eine bevölkerungs-politische und sozial-ethische Studie* (Mönchen-Gladbach, 1916), 100–2; for complete statistics on elections for the Reichstag during the imperial period, see Koppel S. Pinson and Klaus Epstein, *Modern Germany: Its History and Civilization* (2nd ed., New York, 1966), 601–2.

46   'Das Schicksal der Grossstädte', *Hammer: Blätter für deutschen Sinn*, III

(1904), 245; Classen, *Das ltadtgeborene Geschlecht und seine Zukunft* (Leipzig, 1914), 35–6; l'Houet, 27.

47 Strong, *Our Country*, 176–7, 182, 186.

48 Loomis, 61–5, 66, 104–6. For a slightly later expression of the same general viewpoint in a leading periodical that specialized in the exposure of social ills, see H. J. Fletcher, 'The drift of population to cities: remedies', *Forum*, XIX (1895), 738; for the views of an important sociologist, see E. A. Ross, 'The mob mind', *Popular Science Monthly*, LI (1897), 390–8.

49 On this whole subject, see Charles N. Glaab and A. Theodore Brown, *A History of Urban America* (2nd ed., New York and London, 1976), 159–208; see also Martin J. Shiesl, *The Politics of Efficiency: Municipal Administration and Reform in America, 1880–1920* (Berkeley and Los Angeles, 1977); Richard Hofstadter, *The Age of Reform: From Bryan to F. D. R.* (New York, 1955), 173–212; and Robert H. Wiebe, *The Search for Order, 1877–1920* (New York, 1967), 167–76.

50 Strong, *Our Country*, 181; Loomis, 100; White, 'The government of American cities', *The Forum*, X (1890), 357; James B. Bryce, *The American Commonwealth* (3 vols, London and New York, 1888); for Kipling quotation, Bayrd Still, *Mirror for Gotham: New York as Seen by Contemporaries from Dutch Days to the Present* (New York, 1956), 250. More extensive and detailed criticisms, together with lengthy proposals for reform, appeared during the 1890s in Alfred R. Conkling, *City Government in the United States* (New York, 1894), in Frank J. Goodnow, *Municipal Problems* (New York, 1897), and in many other books and articles as well.

51 Justin Kaplan, *Lincoln Steffens: A Biography* (New York, 1974), 130–1.

52 Steffens, *The Shame of the Cities*, introduction by L. Joughin (New York, 1957), vi.

53 *Ibid.*, 2–5, 7–8.

54 For fictional accounts that supported Steffens' line of attack, see Theodore Dreiser's depiction of Frank Cowperwood's dealings with the politicians of Philadelphia and Chicago in *The Financier* (New York, 1912) and *The Titan* (New York, 1914).

55 E. P. Thompson, *William Morris: Romantic to Revolutionary* (1977), 125, 118; quotations from Morris' lectures in William Ashworth, *The Genesis of Modern British Town Planning* (1954), 171.

56 Besant, *All Sorts and Conditions of Men*, 31–2, 47, 74; Morrison, *Tales of Mean Streets* (1921), xxvii.

57 Unwin, *Town Planning in Practice: An Introduction to the Art of Designing Cities and Suburbs* (1909), 4, 10–14.

58 Ashbee, *Where the Great City Stands: A Study in the New Civics* (1917), 41–2, 66. On this whole tradition as it affected town planning, see Walter L. Creese, *The Search for Environment: The Garden City, Before and After* (New Haven, 1966).

59 Pearson, *National Life and Character: A Forecast* (1893), 156–9.

60 Masterman, *From the Abyss*, 35–7, and *The Condition of England*, 121; see also Masterman, 'The English city', 90–1.

61 See George R. Collins and Christiane C. Collins, *Camillo Sitte and the Birth of Modern City Planning* (New York, 1965).

62 *Ibid.*, 76–7; Henrici, *Von welchen Gedanken sollen wir uns beim Ausbau unsrer deutschen Städte leiten lassen?* (Trier, 1894), 9, 11, 16.

63 Fischer, *Stadterweiterungsfragen mit besonderer Rücksicht auf Stuttgart* (Stuttgart, 1903), 5, 10; Gurlitt, 'Der deutsche Städtebau', in Robert Wuttke, ed., *Die deutschen Städte: Geschildert nach den Ergebnissen der ersten deutschen Städteausstellung zu Dresden 1903*, I (Leipzig, 1904), 23–4, and 'Zur Theorie des Städtebaues', *Zeitschrift für Kommunalwirtschaft und Kommunalpolitik*, II (1912), 450. *Der Städtebau* first appeared in 1904; its subtitle was *Monatsschrift für die künstlerische Ausgestaltung der Städte nach*

ihren wirtschaftlichen, gesundheitlichen und sozialen Grundsätzen. The *Städtebauliche Vorträge aus dem Seminar für Städtebau an der königlichen technischen Hochschule zu Berlin,* ed. Joseph Brix and Felix Genzmer, began to appear in 1908. For a good general statement about the defects of modern city planning, see the first publication in this series, Felix Genzmer, *Kunst im Städtebau* (1908), 23.

64   Mangoldt, 'Warum sind unsre neuen Stadtteile so hässlich?', *Der Kunstwart,* XXIII, pt. 1 (1908), 153–5; Rost, 'Der Städtebau', *Soziale Kultur,* XXIX (1909), 65; Kalkschmidt, 'Die Grossstadt als Heimat', *Der Türmer: Monatsschrift für Gemüt und Geist,* XII (1910), 551, 553.

65   Scheffler, *Berlin: Ein Stadtschicksal* (1910), 178–80, 183, 227; Weber, 17.

66   Petermann, 'Die geistige Bedeutung der Grossstädte', in *Die Grossstadt,* 213–14, 221–3, 226–30.

67   Steinhausen, *Geschichte der deutschen Kultur* (Leipzig and Vienna, 1904), 712, 714; Breysig, 'Die Stadt und das Land', *Konservative Monatsschrift,* LXIX (1911), 264.

68   Langbehn, *Rembrandt als Erzieher* (anon., Leipzig, 1890), 110–13.

69   Lienhard, *Neue Ideale nebst Vorherrschaft Berlins* (4th ed., Stuttgart, 1920), 142–4, 149–55, 158–9, 171, 180, 185–6; on both Langbehn's and Lienhard's views of Berlin, see Bergmann, 104–6, 111–15.

70   Fulda, 'Berlin und das deutsche Geistesleben', *Der Greif,* I (1913), 185–99; see also Scheffler, *Berlin, passim,* and S. Lepsius, 'Uber Berliner Kultur', *März,* Jan. 1907, pp. 142–53.

71   See Morton and Lucia White, *The Intellectual versus the City* (Cambridge, Mass., 1962), 54–74, and *The Education of Henry Adams* (Boston, 1918), 499.

72   White, 75–94; James, *The American Scene* (New York, 1967), 83, 76–7, 112.

Chapter 8

1   Levasseur, *La population française,* II (1891), 338–41.

2   *Ibid.,* 355, 359, 412–14.

3   *Ibid.,* 414–15.

4   Meuriot, *Des agglomérations urbaines dans l'Europe contemporaine: essai sur les causes, les conditions, les conséquences de leur développement* (1897), 29, 409–12.

5   *Ibid.,* 451–2. For a slightly later work written in the same spirit by another Frenchman, see Jean Guillou, *L'émigration des campagnes vers les villes et ses conséquences économiques et sociales* (1905), esp. 421–81.

6   Weber, *The Growth of Cities* (reprinted, Ithaca, 1962), 20–154.

7   *Ibid.,* 157, 213, 411–13, 417–20.

8   *Ibid.,* 347–51, 355–7.

9   *Ibid.,* 370–88; see also 392 ff. for criticisms of the idea that the city produced 'dwarfed, stunted men and degenerates'.

10   Bücher: 'Die Grossstädte in Gegenwart und Vergangenheit', in *Die Grossstadt: Vorträge und Aufsätze zur Städteausstellung* (Dresden, 1903), 8–9, 29–31; 'Die inneren Wanderungen und das Städtewesen in ihrer entwicklungsgeschichtlichen Bedeutung', in Bücher, *Die Entstehung der Volkswirtschaft* (Tübingen, 1893), 303–4.

11   Rümelin, 'Die Bevölkerungslehre', in Gustav Schönberg, ed., *Handbuch der Politischen Oekonomie,* I, 3rd ed. (Tübingen, 1890), 736–7; Wirminghaus, 'Stadt und Land unter dem Einfluss der Binnenwanderungen: Ein Ueberblick über den gegenwärtigen Stand der Forschung', *Jahrbücher für Nationalökonomie und Statistik,* Third Series, IX (1895), 17–18, 19–20; Oppenheimer, 'Die Entstehung der Grossstädte', *Neue Deutsche Rundschau,* X, pt. 1 (1899), 563; Weber, *Die Grossstadt und ihre sozialen Probleme* (Leipzig, 1908), 2, 8.

12   Beloch, 'Antike und moderne Grossstädte', *Zeitschrift für Sozialwissenschaft,* I (1898), 413; Boos, *Geschichte der rheinischen Städtekultur von ihren Anfängen bis zur*

Gegenwart mit besonderer Berücksichtigung der Stadt Worms, IV (1901), 679–80.

13   Kalkschmidt, *Grossstadtgedanken: Studien u. Ratschläge aus der ästhetischen Praxis* (Munich, 1906), 12–13; Linke, 'Die Grossstädte und ihre Entwicklung', *Die Neue Welt*, 1905, p. 285; Lee, *Deutsche Städtebilder aus dem Anfänge des 20. Jahrhunderts* (1906), 103–4, 138–44.

14   Eyth, quoted in Emil Stutzer, *Die Deutschen Grossstädte, Einst und Jetzt* (1917), 152; Wermuth, 'Berlin arbeitet', *Der Kunstfreund*, II (1915), 97.

15   Moll, *Der Einfluss des grossstädtischen Lebens und des Verkehrs auf das Nervensystem* (1902), 6, 10, 31–2; Fehlinger, 'Der Einfluss der Stadtkultur in biologischer Beziehung', *Die Naturwissenschaften*, III (1915), 429–31.

16   Digby, 'The extinction of the Londoner', *Contemporary Review*, LXXXVI (1904), 123–4.

17   Hodder, ed., *Cities of the World*, IV (1889), 131, 255; 'Town and country', *The Spectator*, LXII (1889), 197.

18   Stein, 'Grosse Stadt und Grossstadt', *Nord und Süd*, LIII (1890), 70; Waentig, 'Die wirtschaftliche Bedeutung der Grossstädte', in *Die Grossstadt*, 181; Kalkschmidt, 26–7.

19   Howe, *The City: The Hope of Democracy* (New York, 1905), 25.

20   Harrison, 'Historic London', *Macmillan's Magazine*, XLIX (1884), 401; Morley quoted in Hodder, IV, 226.

21   Escott, *England: Its Peoples, Polity, and Pursuits* (2nd ed., 1890), 75–6, 89, 91.

22   Delon, *Notre capitale: Paris* (1888), 1–3, 5; Simond, *Paris de 1800 à 1900*, III (1901), 3, 619.

23   Oettingen, *Berlin* (Leipzig, 1907), 23–4; Adolf Streckfuss and Leo Fernbach, *500 Jahre Berliner Geschichte: Vom Fischerdorf zur Weltstadt* (1900), 783–94.

24   Goering, *Dreissig Jahre München: Kultur- und Kunstgeschichtliche Betrachtungen* (Munich, 1904), 21–2, 30; Haushofer, *Bayerns Hochland und München* (2nd ed., Munich, 1911), 65. For a more recent work on Berlin that focuses much of its attention on cultural developments during these years, see Gerhard Masur, *Imperial Berlin* (New York and London, 1970).

25   Wilson, *The Memorial History of the City of New York: From Its First Settlement to the Year 1892*, IV (New York, 1893), 54–187, 208–31, 344–70, 413–37, 456–97, 575–619; Lamb and Harrison, *History of the City of New York: Its Origin, Rise, and Progress*, III (New York, 1896), 834–8, 853–63; Roosevelt, *New York* (New York and London, 1895), 213.

26   Stern, 'Einige Worte über städtische Cultur', *Socialistische Monatshefte*, VII (1903), 612.

27   For example: R. Breuer, 'Das Licht und die Schönheit der Grossstadt', *Die Welt der Technik*, LXVIII (1906), 1–8; Kalkschmidt, 40–1; J. Corbin, 'The twentieth century city', *Scribner's Magazine*, XXXIII (1903), 259–60.

28   Platz, 'Um die Seele des Grossstadtmenschen', *Hochland*, IX (1912), 386; Sims, ed., *Living London: Its Work and Its Play, Its Humour and Its Pathos, Its Sights and Its Scenes*, I (1904), 3, 6.

29   Endell, *Die Schönheit der grossen Stadt* (Stuttgart, 1908), 23, 26, 29, 31, 49, 60, 67–8.

30   Hueffer, *The Soul of London: A Survey of a Modern City* (1905), 13, 114, 160, 170–1.

31   Dreiser, *The Color of a Great City* (1930), 79.

32   *Ibid.*, 1–3, 156.

33   Weber, *The Growth of Cities*, 405–6.

34   *Ibid.*, 403–4, 407–8.

35   Guillou, 456; Kalkschmidt, 39–40; see also L. W. Busbey (anon.), 'The

wicked town and the moral country', *The Unpopular Review*, X (1918), 376–92.
    36   Weber, *The Growth of Cities*, 439–40.
    37   Zola, *Paris*, trans. E. A. Vizetelly (New York and London, 1898), II, 574–5, 725, 743–4.
    38   Evan R. Jones, *The Life and Speeches of Joseph Cowen, M. P.* (1885), 430.
    39   Linton, 'Town or country?', *The New Review*, IX (1893), 379–83.
    40   Sombart, *Der moderne Kapitalismus*, II (Leipzig, 1902), 237–8; Waentig, 81–2.
    41   Tews, *Grossstadtpädagogik* (Leipzig, 1911), 15, 109. On Bray and Addams, see above, ch. 7.
    42   Whitlock, 'The city and civilization', *Scribner's Magazine*, LII (1912), 630–1.
    43   Harris, *City Life* (Birmingham, 1883), 4, 7.
    44   Barnett, *The Ideal City*, in Helen Meller, ed., *The Ideal City* (Leicester, 1979), 55.
    45   Seeberg, 'Zur Psychologie der Grossstadt', in Ernst Bunke, ed., *Arbeit für Grossstadt und Land* (1911), 31–2; Koch, *Stadt und Land* (Göttingen, 1917), 4–5; Tews, 13; Karstädt, 'Die sittliche Bedeutung der Grossstadt', *Das Freie Wort*, XI (1911–12), 549–50.
    46   Bröger, 'Unsere Heimat', in Wolfgang Rothe, ed., *Deutsche Grossstadtlyrik vom Naturalismus bis zur Gegenwart* (Stuttgart, 1973), 71.
    47   Weber, *The Growth of Cities*, 408–9, 435.
    48   Woolston, 'The urban habit of mind', *American Journal of Sociology*, XVI (1912), 614.

Chapter 9

    1   On Vaughan, see above, 45–7. For background on private charity, see David E. Owen, *English Philanthropy, 1660–1960* (Cambridge, Mass., 1964) and Robert H. Bremner, *American Philanthropy* (Chicago, 1960).
    2   Robert A. Woods, *English Social Movements* (3rd ed., New York, 1897), 175; Aaron I. Abell, *The Urban Impact on American Protestantism* (Cambridge, Mass., 1943), 118–35; Herbert A. Wisbey, Jr., *Soldiers without Swords: A History of the Salvation Army in the United States* (New York, 1955), 1–131. For Booth's view of the urban poor, see above, 110.
    3   Booth, 'Salvation Army work in the slums', *Scribner's Magazine*, XVII (1895), 102–14.
    4   Besant, *East London*, 350–8; Haggard, *Regeneration: Being an Account of the Social Work of the Salvation Army in Great Britain* (1910), 233.
    5   Stelzle, *Christianity's Storm Centre: A Study of the Modern City* (New York, 1907), 111; Sears, *The Redemption of the City* (Philadelphia, 1911), 71. Stelzle's and Sears' works also called attention to a wide range of other church-related efforts to reach out to the urban lower classes, ranging from the institutional churches themselves to various church missions and the Young Men's Christian Association.
    6   Allen F. Davis, *Spearheads for Reform: The Social Settlements and the Progressive Movement, 1890–1914* (New York, 1967), 3–8; Henrietta Barnett, *Canon Barnett: His Life, Work, and Friends* (New York, 1921), 302–14; A[gnes] F. Young and E. T. Ashton, *British Social Work in the Nineteenth Century* (1956), 223–34.
    7   Barnett, 'University settlements', in Barnett, *Practicable Socialism: Essays on Social Reform* (rev. ed., London and New York, 1895), 165–74.
    8   Barnett, 'A retrospect of Toynbee Hall', in Barnett, *Towards Social Reform* (New York, 1909), 255–70; see also Barnett, '"Settlements" or "Missions"' (first published in 1897), in *ibid.*, 271–88, and 'Twenty-one years of university settlements', in Barnett, *Practicable Socialism: New Series* (London and New York, 1915), 121–31.

For more detailed information concerning the courses that were offered and the various clubs and other organizations that were located at Toynbee Hall, see Mrs. Barnett's biography, 326–96. Other articles by Barnett, by some of his co-workers, and by settlement workers at Oxford House in Bethnal Green and elsewhere appeared in John M. Knapp, ed., *The Universities and the Social Problem: An Account of the University Settlements in East London* (1895).

9   Barnett, 'A retrospect of Toynbee Hall', 266–7.

10   Gorst, '"Settlements" in England and America', in Knapp, 6, 9, 28.

11   Besant, *East London* (1899), 344–8; Branford, *Interpretations and Forecasts: A Study of Survivals and Tendencies in Contemporary Society* (New York and London, 1914), 302, 304.

12   Davis, *Spearheads for Reform*, 8–14.

13   See Allen F. Davis, *American Heroine: The Life and Legend of Jane Addams* (New York, 1973).

14   See above, 167–8.

15   Addams, *Twenty Years at Hull-House, with Autobiographical Notes* (New York, 1910), 120–4; on the sense of uselessness, see also Davis, *Spearheads for Reform*, 37–8.

16   Addams, 112.

17   *Ibid.*, 125, 109, 167, 342–99, 427–52; for a similar work on one of the leading settlements in New York, see Lillian D. Wald, *The House on Henry Street* (New York, 1915).

18   Davis, *Spearheads for Reform*, 13; Woods, *English Social Movements* (3rd ed., New York, 1897), 79–118. For Tucker's assessment, see his essay on 'The work of Andover House in Boston', in Woods, ed., *The Poor in Great Cities: Their Problems and What Is Doing to Solve Them* (New York, 1895), 177–92.

19   See Eleanor H. Woods, *Robert A. Woods: Champion of Democracy* (Boston and New York, 1929).

20   Woods, ed., *The City Wilderness* (New York, 1898), 265, 270, 273–4.

21   See Woods, *The Neighborhood in Nation-Building: The Running Comment of Thirty Years at the South End House* (Boston and New York, 1923), *passim*, esp. 285, 293–5, 302, 327, and *The Settlement Horizon: A National Estimate* (written with Albert J. Kennedy; New York, 1922).

22   Stelzle, 135–8; Sears, 65–6.

23   Addams, 285–6, 320; Woods, *The Urban Wilderness*, 276, 304–6; Riis quoted in Bayrd Still, *Urban America: A History with Documents* (Boston, 1974), 296; Davis, *Spearheads for Reform*, 180, 194–217. Davis also points out (on p. 244) that many men and women who held positions of power during the New Deal — including Harry Hopkins, Frances Perkins, Henry Morgenthau, Jr., Herbert Lehman, and Adolph Berle — had been influenced in earlier years by their experiences in settlements.

24   Chamberlain, 'Municipal government — past, present, and future', *The New Review*, X (1894), 649, 651–2.

25   Dolman, *Municipalities at Work: The Municipal Policy of Six Great Towns and Its Influence on Their Social Welfare* (1895), 121–2, 123, 129. For a recent overview of these developments by a historian, see Derek Fraser, *Power and Authority in the Victorian City* (New York, 1979), which focuses on several of the same towns; see also H. E. Meller, *Leisure and the Changing City, 1870–1914* (London and Boston, 1976), which illuminates the growing emphasis on the provision of culture in the city of Bristol.

26   Escott, *England: Its Peoples, Polity, and Pursuits* (2nd ed., 1890), 69.

27   For example: William Arthur Shaw, *Manchester, Old and New* (3 vols, ca. 1894); Ramsay Muir, *A History of Liverpool* (Liverpool, 1907); Margaret C. D. Law, *The Story of Bradford* (1913); J. S. Fletcher, *Leeds* (1919).

28   Robert K. Dent, *The Making of Birmingham: Being a History of the Rise and Growth of the Midland Metropolis* (Birmingham, 1894); J. Ralph, 'The best-governed city in the world', *Harper's Monthly*, LXXXI (1890), 99–111; Hibbs, 'Birmingham', in Edwin Hodder, *Cities of the World*, IV (1889), 46; Dolman, 1–2; J. H. Muirhead, ed., *Birmingham Institutions* (Birmingham, 1911), 103, 138–9.

29   George MacGregor, *The History of Glasgow* (Glasgow and London, 1881), 511, 516; Andrew Wallace, *A Popular Sketch of the History of Glasgow* (Glasgow, 1882), 194–5; R. Wilson, 'Glasgow', in Hodder, IV, 146.

30   Fisher, 'Glasgow — a model municipality', *Fortnightly Review*, LXIII (1895), 607–22; Dolman, 64–84; see also James H. Muir, *Glasgow in 1901* (Glasgow, 1901), 44–71.

31   James Bell and James Paton, *Glasgow: Its Municipal Organization and Administration* (Glasgow, 1896), xix–xxiii, 52–3; D. M. Stevenson, 'Preface', in *Municipal Glasgow: Its Evolution and Enterprises* (Glasgow, 1914), 2.

32   Harrison, 'The transformation of London', in *The Meaning of History* (new ed., New York and London, 1902), 430, 433–4, 436.

33   Gomme, *London* (1914), 344–5, 350.

34   For biographical background, see Philip Boardman, *Patrick Geddes: Maker of the Future* (Chapel Hill, 1944); see also H. E. Meller, 'Patrick Geddes: an analysis of his theory of civics, 1888–1914', *Victorian Studies*, XVI (1973), 291–315.

35   See Geddes' lectures on 'Civics: as applied sociology', in The Sociological Society, *Sociological Papers*, I (1905), 101–18, and II (1906), 57–111; his 'A suggested plan for a civic museum (or civic exhibition) and its associated studies', in *ibid.*, III (1907), 197–236; and his 'Civic education and city development', *Contemporary Review*, LXXXVII (1905), 413–26.

36   Geddes, *City Development: A Study of Parks, Gardens and Culture-Institutes* (Edinburgh, 1904).

37   Geddes, *Cities in Evolution: An Introduction to the Town Planning Movement and to the Study of Civics* (1915), xxv–xxvi, 229, 243, 399–402; for a more detailed discussion of the legislation to which Geddes was referring, see William Ashworth, *The Genesis of Modern British Town Planning* (1954), 167–190; on town planning more generally, see Anthony Sutcliffe, *Towards the Planned City: Germany, Britain, the United States and France, 1780–1914* (Oxford, 1981), with specific attention to early twentieth-century Britain on 62–87.

38   Geddes, *Cities in Evolution*, 47–8, 174–221.

39   Horsfall, *The Improvement of the Dwellings and Surroundings of the People: The Example of Germany* (Manchester, 1904); Lunn, *Municipal Lessons from Southern Germany* (1908); Tawney, 'Municipal enterprise in Germany', *Economic Review*, XX (1910), 423–37; Dawson, *Municipal Life and Government in Germany* (1914), *passim*, esp. viii, 442–5; on Horsfall's and Dawson's admiration for Germany more generally, see Günter Hollenberg, *Englisches Interesse am Kaiserreich: Die Attraktivität Preussen-Deutschlands für konservative und liberale Kreise in Grossbritannien, 1860-1914* (Wiesbaden, 1974), 194–7, 230–42.

40   On administrative personnel, see Dawson, 86–116, and Wolfgang Hofmann, *Zwischen Rathaus und Reichskanzlei: Die Oberbürgermeister in der Kommunal- und Staatspolitik des Deutschen Reiches von 1890-1933* (Stuttgart, 1974), 32–56; for the best recent surveys of German municipal development during this period, see R. Krabbe, 'Munizipalsozialismus und Interventionsstaat: Die Ausbreitung der städtischen Leistungsverwaltung im Kaiserreich', *Geschichte in Wissenschaft und Unterricht*, XXX (1979), 265–83, and Sutcliffe, 9–46.

41   For information on the exhibition, see the following: Robert Wuttke, ed., *Die deutschen Städte: Geschildert nach den Ergebnissen der ersten deutschen Städteausstellung zu Dresden 1903* (Leipzig, 1904), I, xi–xlvi (with numerous articles by experts in the rest of

Vol. I and an impressive assortment of illustrations in Vol. II); *Katalog: Deutsche Städte-Ausstellung* (Dresden, 1903); Rudolf Lebius, ed., *Was lehrt die I. Deutsche Städte-Ausstellung?* (Dresden, 1903); and H. Woodhead, 'The first German municipal exposition (Dresden 1903)', *American Journal of Sociology*, IX (1904), 433–58, 612–30, 812–31, and X (1904), 47–63.

42 Wuttke, I, xxxvi, xx-xxi, and Kappelman, 'Die deutschen Städte am Anfang des zwanzigsten Jahrhunderts', *Preussisches Verwaltungs-Blatt*, XXVI (1904), 130.

43 *Schriften des Vereins für Sozialpolitik*, CXVII–CXXX (Leipzig, 1906–12), esp. Vol. CXXVIII: *Gemeindebetriebe: Neuere Versuche und Erfahrungen über die Ausdehnung der kommunalen Tätigkeit in Deutschland und im Ausland* (1908); Most, *Die deutsche Stadt und ihre Verwaltung: Eine Einführung in die Kommunalpolitik der Gegenwart* (Berlin and Leipzig, 1912), I, 14–17, 50; Ehrler, 'Städtewesen, modernes', in Julius Bachem and Hermann Sacher, eds., *Staatslexikon*, 3rd ed., V (Freiburg im Breisgau, 1912), 160; Fuss, 'Das kommunale Leben der modernen Grossstadt', *Jahrbuch für Gesetzgebung, Verwaltung und Volkswirtschaft im Deutschen Reich*, XXXV (1911), 49.

44 *Verhandlungen des ersten Kongresses für Städtewesen Düsseldorf 1912* (Düsseldorf, 1913), I, v-xi, xiv, xvii; see also O. Most, 'Die Städteausstellung Düsseldorf 1912', *Zeitschrift für Kommunalwirtschaft und Kommunalpolitik*, II (1912), 312–14.

45 Martin Wehrmann, *Geschichte der Stadt Stettin* (Stettin, 1911); *Chemnitz in Wort und Bild: Festschrift zur Einweihung des neuen Rathauses* (Chemnitz, 1911); Otto Richter, *Geschichte der Stadt Dresden in den Jahren 1871 bis 1902* (Dresden, 1903); *Leipzig: Ein Blick in das Wesen und Werden einer deutschen Stadt* (Leipzig, 1914); Wilhelm Leinung and Franz Mueller, *Magdeburg im Wandel der Zeit* (Magdeburg, 1910); Georg Ritter von Schuh, *Die Stadt Nürnberg im Jubiläumsjahre 1906* (Nuremberg, 1906); Otto Brandt, *Studien zur Wirtschafts- und Verwaltungsgeschichte der Stadt Düsseldorf im 19. Jahrhundert* (Düsseldorf, 1902); Eberhard Gothein, Georg Neuhaus, *et al.*, *Die Stadt Cöln im ersten Jahrhundert unter Preussischen Herrschaft, 1815 bis 1915* (2 vols, Cologne, 1915–16); Sigmund Schott, ed., *Mannheim seit der Gründung des Reiches, 1871-1907* (Mannheim, 1907); Friedrich Bothe, *Geschichte der Stadt Frankfurt am Main* (Frankfurt a. M., 1913).

46 Stein, ed., *Monographien deutscher Städte: Darstellung deutscher Städte und ihrer Arbeit in Wirtschaft, Finanzwesen, Hygiene, Sozialpolitik und Technik* (39 vols, Oldenburg, 1912-33). The volumes that appeared before the First World War treated Neukölln, Magdeburg, Darmstadt, Cassel, Berlin-Wilmersdorf, Danzig, Frankfurt a. M., Berlin, and Dessau.

47 Lindenberg, *Berlin in Wort und Bild* (1895), 4–8; Adolf Streckfuss and Leo Fernbach, *500 Jahre Berliner Geschichte: Vom Fischerdorf zur Weltstadt* (1900), 764–94; Goldschmidt, *Berlin in Geschichte und Gegenwart* (1910), 292–366.

48 Kaeber, 'Geschichtliche Entwicklung der Berliner Kommunalverwaltung', in Stein, ed., *Berlin* (*Monographien deutscher Städte*, VIII, 1914), 10–11.

49 Stutzer, *Die Deutschen Grosstädte, Einst und Jetzt* (1917), 89–90; Wilms, 'Deutschlands geistige und wirtschaftliche Weltstellung: Deutschlands Städte', *Die Woche*, 1917, p. 751; see also A. Wermuth, 'Berlin arbeitet', *Der Kunstfreund*, II (1915), 97–9, and Ernst Kaeber, *Berlin im Weltkriege: Fünf Jahre städtischer Kriegsarbeit* (1921).

50 On this whole subject, see J. Sheehan, 'Liberalism and the city in nineteenth-century Germany', *Past and Present*, no. 51 (1971), esp. 126–37; for the views of an influential *Oberbürgermeister*, see [Franz] Adickes and [Ernst] Beutler, *Die sozialen Aufgaben der deutschen Städte* (Leipzig, 1903), 59–69.

51 Lindemann, *Die Deutsche Städteverwaltung: Ihre Aufgaben auf den Gebieten der Volkshygiene, des Städtebaus und des Wohnungswesens* (2nd ed., Stuttgart, 1906), 428; 'Die deutsche Städteausstellung zu Dresden', *Kommunale Praxis*, III (1903), 309–10; E. Wurm, 'Der deutsche Städtetag und die deutsche Städteausstellung', *Die Neue Zeit*,

XXI (1903), pt. 2, p. 770.

52   'Eine moderne Industriestadt', *Kommunale Praxis*, XII (1912), 1660; 'Eine Ausstellung Alt- und Neu-Köln', *Kommunale Praxis*, XIII (1913), 618.

53   Hirsch, *25 Jahre sozialdemokratischer Arbeit in der Gemeinde: Die Tätigkeit der Sozialdemokratie in der Berliner Stadtverordnetenversammlung* (1908), viii; Fischer, *Das sozialistische Werden: Die Tendenzen der wirtschaftlichen und sozialen Entwicklung* (Leipzig, 1918), 251–83.

54   Shaw, *Municipal Government in Continental Europe* (New York, 1895), 289–90, 322; Howe, *The Modern City and Its Problems* (New York, 1915), 131; see also Howe, *European Cities at Work* (New York, 1913), 3–270, William B. Munro, *The Government of European Cities* (New York, 1909), 109–208, and J. R. Mullen, 'American perceptions of German city planning at the turn of the century', *Urbanism Past and Present*, II (1976-7), 5–15.

55   See above, pp. 175–8.

56   Wilcox, *Great Cities in America: Their Problems and Their Government* (New York, 1910), 6. There is a vast secondary literature on efforts to improve the governance of American cities during the progressive era. For general overviews, see Charles N. Glaab and A. Theodore Brown, *A History of Urban America* (2nd ed., New York and London, 1976), 159–208, and Martin J. Schiesl, *The Politics of Efficiency: Municipal Administration and Reform in America, 1880–1920* (Berkeley, Los Angeles, and London, 1977); see also Paul Boyer, *Urban Masses and Moral Order in America, 1820–1920* (Cambridge, Mass., and London, 1978), 233–276.

57   Ely, *The Coming City* (New York, 1902), 16, 27, 73.

58   A. H. Grant, 'The conning tower', *The American City*, I (1909), 20; Woodruff, 'American municipal tendencies', *National Municipal Review*, I (1912), 17–19.

59   Wilcox, *The American City: A Problem in Democracy* (New York, 1904) and *Great Cities in America* (New York, 1910); Beard, *American City Government* (New York, 1912); Zueblin, *American Municipal Progress* (New York and London, 1902; greatly expanded 2nd ed., 1916) and *A Decade of Civic Development* (Chicago, 1905); Pollock and Morgan, *Modern Cities: Progress of the Awakening for Their Betterment Here and in Europe* (New York and London, 1913); Cooke, *Our Cities Awake: Notes on Municipal Activities and Administration* (Garden City, 1918); Howe, *The City: The Hope of Democracy* (New York, 1905) and *The Modern City and Its Problems* (New York, 1915).

60   On Howe's life and thought, see his classic autobiography, *The Confessions of a Reformer* (New York, 1925); see esp. 85–145 on his political experience in Cleveland.

61   Howe, *The City*, 24, 26, 27–8.

62   Howe, *The Modern City and Its Problems*, 52–4, 165–75, 194–210.

63   Zueblin, *American Municipal Progress*, 2nd ed., xi-xii, 401.

64   Woods, *The City Wilderness*, 305–6; Quincy, 'Municipal progress in Boston', *The Independent*, LII (1900), pt. I, 424–6; see also F. Lowell, 'The municipal service of Boston', *Atlantic Monthly*, LXXXI (1898), 311–322.

65   Howe, *The City*, 52–5, and *The Modern City*, 173–4, 205–6; Tom L. Johnson, *My Story*, ed. E. Hauser (New York, 1911), xxxix; see also Hoyt L. Warner, *Progressivism in Ohio, 1897–1917* (Columbus, 1964).

66   E. C. Hopwood, 'Newton D. Baker's administration of Cleveland and its accomplishments', *National Municipal Review*, II (1913), 461–6; C. C. Arbuthnot, 'Mayor Baker's administration in Cleveland', *National Municipal Review*, V (1916), 226–41.

67   Weyl, 'The brand of the city', *Harper's Magazine*, CXXX (1915), 774–5; for another essay written for a popular audience that combines general praise for urban morals with specific approval for the wide range of responsibilities taken on by city

governments, see L. W. Busbey, 'The wicked town and the moral country' (anon.), *The Unpopular Review*, X (1918), 376–92, esp. 382. See also the comment by Woodrow Wilson in an address given in 1910 on 'The clergyman and the state': 'Every man I meet tells me the same thing; that the city he is in is suddenly acquiring a civic consciousness' (reprinted in Ronald G. White, Jr. and C. Howard Hopkins, eds., *The Social Gospel* [Philadelphia, 1976], 182–3).

68   See A. Sutcliffe, 'In search of the urban variable: Britain in the later nineteenth century', in Derek Fraser and Anthony Sutcliffe, eds., *The Pursuit of Urban History* (1983), 262–3.

69   For a convenient survey of these developments in the United States, see Glaab and Brown, 136–58.

Chapter 10

1   On this whole subject, see Anthony Sutcliffe, *Metropolis, 1890-1940* (1984), esp. the contribution by Peter Hall, 'Metropolis 1890-1940: challenges and responses'.

2   In this connection, see H. J. Dyos, 'Agenda for urban historians', in Dyos, ed., *The Study of Urban History* (1968), 17–18, 23.

3   Inge, *England* (1926), xi, 29, 86, 186, 218; see also Martin J. Wiener, *English Culture and the Decline of the Industrial Spirit, 1850–1980* (Cambridge, Eng., 1981), 111–13.

4   Crawford and Balcarres, *The City and the State* (Birmingham, 1928), 10, 19, 23–32.

5   Williams-Ellis, 'A civic sense in England? Our squalid towns', *The Spectator*, CXXXII (1924), 278–9, 663–4.

6   Glass, *The Town and a Changing Civilisation*, 90–1, 93, 97–8, 104, 109, 124, 130–1.

7   Priestley, *English Journey* (New York and London, 1934), 66–7, 147, 155, 227; see also Wiener, 123–5, for emphasis on Priestley's basically antimodernist social values.

8   Orwell, *The Road to Wigan Pier*, 19–20, 52, 66, 70–1, 75 ff.; see Bernard Crick, *George Orwell: A Life* (Boston, 1980), 180–206, on this chapter in Orwell's career and also 104–36, on his earlier explorations of working-class life in the English and French metropolises, which Orwell recorded in *Down and Out in Paris and London* (1933).

9   Cole, 'London — one-fifth of the nation', *Fortnightly Review*, CXLVII (1937), 57–66; Shanahan, 'Great cities and their economic problems', *Economica*, VIII (1928), 51–63.

10   Branford, 'A sociological view of Westminster', *The Sociological Review*, XXII (1930), 226.

11   Hamilton, *Modern England, as Seen by an Englishwoman* (1938), 173–4; Pearson, *London's Overgrowth and the Causes of Swollen Towns* (1939), 9, 149. Two other works that contained full-scale attacks on London formulated in terms that were readily accessible to a nonspecialist audience were Paul Banks, *Metropolis, or the Destiny of Cities* (1930) and Robert Sinclair, *Metropolitan Man: The Future of the English* (1937).

12   William Ashworth, *The Genesis of Modern British Town Planning: A Study in Economic and Social History of the Nineteenth and Twentieth Centuries* (1954), 201–2, 220–5; Robert Fishman, *Urban Utopias in the Twentieth Century: Ebenezer Howard, Frank Lloyd Wright, Le Corbusier* (New York, 1977), 83–5; Gordon Cherry, *The Evolution of British Town Planning* (New York and Toronto, 1974), 120–30; Hall, 26–8.

13   Cohen-Portheim, *The Spirit of London* (1935), 107, 112; see also Steen Eiler Rasmussen, *London: The Unique City* (1937).

14   Smith, ed., *The New Survey of London Life and Labour*, I (1934), 4, 7, 17, 22, 31, 35–6, 48, and IX (1935), 3 ff., 40; for background, see R. Glass, 'Urban sociology in

Great Britain: a trend report', *Current Sociology*, IV, pt. 4 (1955), 47–8.

15   Robson, 'The outlook', in Laski *et al.*, eds., *A Century of Municipal Progress: The Last Hundred Years* (1935), 463.

16   Redford, *The History of Local Government in Manchester* (3 vols, 1939–40), III, 380, 381, 384; see also Shena D. Simon, *A Century of City Government: Manchester, 1838-1938* (1938), George H. Poumphrey, *The Story of Liverpool's Public Services* (Liverpool and London, 1940), and 'Building the city', *The Listener*, 1938, pp. 276–8 (Birmingham), 331–3 (Manchester), 435–7 (Bristol), 546–8 (Edinburgh), 667–8 (Belfast), 721–2 (Cardiff).

17   Albin, *La vrai figure de la France* (1922), 176–8, 183–4; Rodrigues, *La France éternelle* (1919), 50, 59; Warnod, *Visages de Paris* (1930), 323; see also, more generally on cities and still from a favorable standpoint, P. Bourdeix, 'La concentration urbaine: métropolisme et régions urbaines', *Mercure de France*, CCXXXVII (1932), 324–51.

18   Maurel, *Paris: ses origines, sa croissance, son histoire* (1932), 360–5, 368–9.

19   I have relied heavily for my remarks on Le Corbusier on A. Sutcliffe, 'A vision of utopia: optimistic foundations of Le Corbusier's doctrine d'urbanisme', in Russell Walden, ed., *The Open Hand: Essays on Le Corbusier* (Cambridge, Mass., and London, 1977), 218–43; see also Fishman, 163–263.

20   For an admirable survey of this period, see Walter Laqueur, *Weimar: A Cultural History* (New York, 1974).

21   Sander, *Geschichte des deutschen Städtewesens* (Bonn, 1922), 5–6, 18.

22   Waldstein, 'Zur kulturellen Lage der Grossstadt', *Neuwerk: Ein Dienst am Werdenden*, XI (1929), 126–9.

23   Osborn *et al.*, *Berlins Aufstieg zur Weltstadt* (1929), 204–12, 224–6; see also Friedrich Bothe, *Geschichte der Stadt Frankfurt am Main* (3rd ed., Frankfurt a. M., 1929), 337–59.

24   See Otto Ziebill, *Geschichte des Deutschen Städtetages: Fünfzig Jahre deutscher Kommunalpolitik* (Stuttgart and Cologne, 1955).

25   Paul Mitzlaff and Erwin Stein, eds., *Die Zukunftsaufgaben der deutschen Städte* (2nd ed., 1925), 1; Mulert, 'Die deutschen Städte', in *Deutschland: Jahrbuch für das deutsche Volk 1928* (Leipzig, 1928), 134, 136, 138, 140; see also Fritz Elsas and Erwin Stein, eds., *Die deutschen Städte: Ihre Arbeit von 1918 bis 1928* (1928).

26   Kaeber, 'Die Weltstadt als Heimat', in Hans Brennert and Erwin Stein, eds., *Probleme der neuen Stadt Berlin: Darstellungen der Zukunftsaufgaben einer Viermillionenstadt* (*Monographien deutscher Städte*, ed. E. Stein, XVIII; 1926), 205–6; Böss, 'Sechs Jahre neues Berlin', in Brennert and Stein, 13, and *Berlin von Heute* (1929).

27   Cramer, 'Gegenwart: Das neue Köln', in *Köln: Werden, Wesen, Wollen einer deutschen Stadt* (Cologne, 1928), 37–8, 48, 51–2, 55–6, 66–7. On other cities, see the following: Hans Ströbel, ed., *Dortmund: Ein Blick in eine deutsche Industriestadt* (Dortmund, 1922); [Hans] Luther *et al.*, *Essen* (*Monographien deutscher Städte*, XI; 1923); Karl Weishaupt and Paul Boltze, eds., *Stettin* (1925); Heinrich Haacke, ed., *Aus Barmens Wirtschaft und Kultur* (Barmen, 1926); Nuremberg, Stadtrat, ed., *Nürnberg* (*Monographien deutscher Städte*, XXIII; 1927).

28   Wolfgang Rothe, ed., *Deutsche Grossstadtlyrik vom Naturalismus bis zur Gegenwart* (Stuttgart, 1973), 21–5, 215, 216, 217, 277; see also Robert Seitz and Heinz Zucker, eds., *Um uns die Stadt: Eine Anthologie neuer Grossstadtdichtung* (1931). The great urban novel to come out of Germany in this period was Alfred Döblin, *Berlin Alexanderplatz* (1929; trans. E. Jonas as *Alexanderplatz Berlin: The Story of Franz Biberkopf*, New York, 1931). Döblin, a psychiatrist and an active socialist as well as a novelist, used experimental techniques which he developed under the influence of James Joyce's *Ulysses* in order to explore the lives of Berlin workers and criminals.

29   Beth Irwin Lewis, *George Grosz: Art and Politics in the Weimar Republic*

(Madison, 1971), 46–7; Theda Shapiro, 'New York — Paris — Berlin: A tale of three cities in art, 1890–1945', in Anthony Sutcliffe, ed., *Metropolis, 1890-1940* (1984).

30   Scheffler, 'Die Zukunft der Grossstädte und die Grossstädte der Zukunft', *Die neue Rundschau*, XXXVII, pt. 2 (1926), 522–4, 529.

31   Mangoldt, *Das Grossstadtproblem und die Wege zu seiner Lösung* (1928), 3, 29, 35–52.

32   Oppenheimer, 'Stadt und Land in ihren gegenseitigen Beziehungen', in Max Adler *et al.*, *Festschrift für Carl Grünberg* (Leipzig, 1932), 390, 395. For similar views among practicing architects and planners, see the following titles, to which many more could be added: Erich Gloeden, *Die Inflation der Gross-Städte und ihre Heilungsmöglichkeit* (1923); Otto Blum, 'Das Grossstadt-Problem', *Neubau*, VI (1924), 9–11, 21–4, 46–9, 93–6, 129–32; Gustav Langen, *Stadtplan und Wohnungsplan* (Leipzig, 1927); and Th[eodor] Fischer, *Die Stadt* (Munich, 1928), 14–16. See also Barbara Miller Lane, *Architecture and Politics in Germany, 1918–1945* (Cambridge, Mass., 1968), 90–103, on decentralized planning in Frankfurt, and Werner Hegemann, *Das steinerne Berlin* (1930).

33   For general background, see Kurt Sontheimer, *Antidemokratisches Denken in der Weimarer Republik* (Munich, 1962); George L. Mosse, *The Crisis of German Ideology: Intellectual Origins of the Third Reich* (New York, 1964); and David Schoenbaum, *Hitler's Social Revolution: Class and Status in Nazi Germany, 1933-1939* (Garden City, 1966). More specifically on ideas about cities, see Elisabeth Pfeil, *Grossstadtforschung* (Bremen-Horn, 1950; more detailed on the history of pre-1945 thinking in Germany than the revised edition that appeared in 1972), 63–86, and above all, Klaus Bergmann, *Agrarromantik und Grossstadtfeindschaft* (Meisenheim am Glan, 1970), 174–360.

34   See H. Stuart Hughes, *Oswald Spengler: A Critical Estimate* (2nd ed., Boston, 1962) and Bergmann, 179–93.

35   Spengler, *The Decline of the West*, Vol. II: *Perspectives on World History*, trans. C. F. Atkinson (New York, 1928), 90, 91, 108, 98, 92, 97, 100, 94.

36   *Ibid.*, 102–7.

37   Weidel, 'Stadt und Land in kulturphilosophischer Beleuchtung', *Mitteilungen der Pädagogischen Akademien in Preussen*, II (1927), 28–35.

38   Grimm, *Der Kampf des Bauerntums mit der Grossstadt* (1927), 4, 40–94. 115–16.

39   Korherr, 'Berlin', *Süddeutsche Monatshefte*, XXVII (1930), 366–412 (quotation on 371). On Grimm and Korherr, see Bergmann, 193–205. For other strongly anti-urban writings from the years 1929–32 that display many of the attitudes evident among Spengler and his disciples, see the following: A. E. Günther, 'Die Grossstadt', *Jungnationale Stimmen*, IV (1929), 171–6; Franz Heindorf, *Von rechter Art in Deutscher Stadt: Gegen die Vorherrschaft des Minderwertigen, gegen Vergewaltigung Deutscher Art* (Halle-Saale, 1929); E. Niekisch, 'Verödung der Städte', *Blut und Boden*, II (1929), 268–70; Günther Thaer, *Stadtvolk und Landvolk: Ein problem des Tages* (1929); W. Schmied-Kowarzlik, 'Grossstadt und Weltanschauung' and A. Kiessling, 'Die Seele des Grossstadtkindes', *Philosophie und Leben*, VI (1930), 121–6, 132–7; G. Schreiber, 'Die Volkskunde der Grossstadt', *Der Heimatdienst*, X (1930), 156–7; K. Seesemann, 'Geist und Seele als Problem der Grossstadt', *Baltische Monatsschrift*, LXI (1930), 551–61; F. H. Schwank-Telfan, 'Grossstadt ist Seelennot', *Die Bergstadt*, XIX (1931), 331–4; Eugen Schmahl, *Menschen in der grossen Stadt* (Oldenburg, 1932). For evidence of comparable thinking in school textbooks, see H. L. Poor, 'City versus country: anti-urbanism in the Weimar Republic', *Societas — A Review of Social History*, VI (1976), 177–92. On academic historians, see Bernd Faulenbach, *Ideologie des deutschen Weges: Die deutsche Geschichte in der Historiographie zwischen Kaiserreich und Nationalsozialismus* (Munich, 1980), 97–8.

40 For much of the following, see Bergmann, 297–360; see also Pfeil, 76–86.

41 Rosenberg, *Der Mythus des 20. Jahrhunderts* (57th ed., Munich, 1935), 550–8.

42 Günther, *Die Verstädterung: Ihre Gefahren für Volk und Staat vom Standpunkte der Lebensforschung und der Gesellschaftswissenschaft* (2nd ed., 1936).

43 *Ibid.*, 10–12, 21–2, 23, 29, 31.

44 *Ibid.*, 8–9, 24.

45 Burgdörfer: 'Die Zukunft der Städte', *Archiv für Bevölkerungswissenschaft (Volkskunde) und Bevölkerungspolitik*, IV (1934), 231, and *Zurück zum Agrarstaat? Stadt und Land in volksbiologischer Betrachtung* (1933), 92–3. The change in demographic patterns had indeed been dramatic. In the years 1911–14, the rate of annual population increase for Germany as a whole had averaged 1.23 percent whereas in the years 1930–33 it had averaged only .49 percent; see Dietmar Petzina *et al.*, *Sozialgeschichtliches Arbeitsbuch III: Materialien zur Statistik des Deutschen Reiches 1914–1945* (Munich, 1978), 32. As Burgdörfer had pointed out during the late 1920s, at that point the annual birth rate in Berlin stood at only 9.9 per thousand, less than two-thirds the rate in London and Paris and barely one-third the rate in Moscow; see his *Vom Leben und Sterben unseres Volkes* (1929), 12. For parallel expressions of concern by a medical doctor who gave no indication whatsoever of political sympathy for the right, see W. Hagen, 'Die Groszstadt als biologisches Problem', *Das neue Frankfurt*, V (1931), 63–70.

46 Burgdörfer, 'Verstädterung im Lichte der Bevölkerungsstatistik und Bevölkerungspolitik', *Volk und Rasse*, XI (1936), 172. *Volk und Rasse*, a semi-scholarly journal, printed numerous articles by other authors during the 1930s who expressed views much like Burgdörfer's.

47 Lindner and Böckler, *Die Stadt: Ihre Pflege und Gestaltung* (Munich, 1939), 18; see also Robert R. Taylor, *The Word in Stone: The Role of Architecture in the National Socialist Ideology* (Berkeley, 1974), 252–5.

48 On Darré, see Bergmann, 297–314; see also Günther, 46–54, and Burgdörfer, *Zurück zum Agrarstaat?*, 95–109. More generally on Nazi agricultural policy, see David Schoenbaum, *Hitler's Social Revolution: Class and Status in Nazi Germany, 1933-1939* (Garden City, 1966), 152–77.

49 See, for instance, Ernst Hamm, *Die deutsche Stadt im Mittelalter* (Stuttgart, 1935), Fritz Mielert, *Romantik alter deutscher Städte* (Bad Rothenfelde, 1935), and Karl Gruber, *Die Gestalt der deutschen Stadt* (Leipzig, 1937); for a sympathetic view of small cities in the present, see 'Lob der kleinen Stadt', *Neues Volk*, VII (1939), Heft 6, pp. 12–17.

50 Rosenberg, 556–7, 554.

51 Lindner and Böckler, 49, 122; Feder, *Die neue Stadt: Versuch der Begründung einer neuen Stadtplanungskunst aus der sozialen Struktur der Bevölkerung* (1939), 26, 68; see also Gerd Albers, *Entwicklungslinien im Städtebau* (Düsseldorf, 1975), 95–6.

52 On this point, see Schoenbaum, 160–3, 174–6, and Lane, 205–6.

53 G. Theunissen, 'Erziehung zur Stadt', *Kunst der Nation*, II (1934), 1–2.

54 Hellpach, *Mensch und Volk der Grossstadt* (Stuttgart, 1939), vi; also in Hellpach, see 30–1, 75, 77, 112, 118, 120, 123 for additional comments that suggest urban advantages.

55 F. Linke, 'Schlusswort', in B. De Rudder and F. Linke, eds., *Biologie der Grossstadt* (Dresden and Leipzig, 1940), 199.

56 W. Wenzel, 'Wachsende Weltstädte', *Berliner Kommunale Mitteilungen*, X (1939), 69; H. Trappe, 'Kann die Grossstadt Heimat sein?', *Die nationalsozialistische Gemeinde: Zentralblatt der NSDAP für Gemeindepolitik*, VI (1938), 642–3; on the relations between state and local authority, see Horst Matzerath, *Nationalsozialismus und kommunale Selbstverwaltung* (Stuttgart, 1970).

57 Hellpach, 120; Wallenstein, 'Der Grossstadtmensch', *Technokratie*, 1935, pp.

45–7; A. Fischer, 'Kampf und Sieg der NSDAP', in Hans Spethmann, ed., *Die Stadt Essen: Das Werden und Wirken einer Grossstadt an der Ruhr* (1938), 34–40.

58   Taylor, 257–69; Joachim Petsch, *Baukunst und Stadtplanung im Dritten Reich* (Munich and Vienna, 1976), 102–13; J. Thies, 'Hitler's European building program', *Journal of Contemporary History*, XIII (1978), 413–31; Speer, 'Deutscher Städtebau', *Volk und Reich*, XV (1939), 260–3.

59   See Bergmann, 307–8, on Darré's recognition of the need to acquire land in the East in order to make possible a shift of population from the cities to the land.

60   Poor, 177.

61   Twelve Southerners, *I'll Take My Stand: The South and the Agrarian Tradition* (new ed., New York, 1962), xix.

62   *Ibid.*, 20.

63   *Ibid.*, 57–8.

64   See also L. Rubin's introduction to this edition, Richard H. King, *A Southern Renaissance: The Cultural Awakening of the American South, 1930–1955* (New York and Oxford, 1980), 52–6, and B. A. Brownell, 'The idea of the city in the American South', in Derek Fraser and Anthony Sutcliffe, eds., *The Pursuit of Urban History* (1983), 142–3; on more straightforward anti-urbanism among rural midwesterners, see Don S. Kirschner, *City and Country: Rural Responses to Urbanization in the 1920s* (Westport, Conn., 1970), 23–56.

65   Gruening, 'New York', *The Nation*, CXV (1922), 571–5.

66   Dos Passos, *Manhattan Transfer* (New York and London, 1925), 380–1, 402–4. For a fuller analysis, to which I am much indebted, see Blanche H. Gelfant, *The American City Novel* (Norman, Oklahoma, 1954), 138–66.

67   See Roy Lubove, *Community Planning in the 1920's: The Contribution of the Regional Planning Association of America* (Pittsburgh, 1963).

68   Stein, 'Dinosaur cities', *The Survey*, LIV (1925), 138.

69   Chase, 'The future of the great city', *Harper's Magazine*, CLX (1929), 84; see also the article by another member of the Association, the forester-conservationist Benton Mackaye, 'End or peak of civilization?', *The Survey*, LXVIII (1932), 441–4, an article that takes Spengler's theories as its point of departure. For another essay written in the same vein by one of the editors of *The New Republic* (not a member of the Association but obviously a sympathizer with its goals), see George Soule, 'Will the cities ever stop?', *The New Republic*, XLVII (1926), 105–7. On Chase and Soule, who played leading roles more generally on the intellectual left during the interwar years, see Richard H. Pells, *Radical Visions and American Dreams: Culture and Social Thought in the Depression Years* (New York, 1973), *passim*.

70   See Pells and Lubove, *passim*, for more on Mumford within the contexts of ideology and planning; see Morton and Lucia White, *The Intellectual versus the City: From Thomas Jefferson to Frank Lloyd Wright* (Cambridge, Mass., 1962), 204–8, for emphasis on Mumford's anti-urbanism. For a more balanced view, see Park Dixon Goist, *From Main Street to State Street: Town, City, and Community in America* (Port Washington, N. Y., and London, 1977), 143–57. The key texts by Mumford from the 1920s and 1930s are 'The city', in Harold E. Stearns, ed., *Civilization in the United States* (New York, 1922); 'The intolerable city: must it keep on growing?', *Harper's Magazine*, CLII (1926), 383–93; and *The Culture of Cities* (New York, 1938).

71   *Ibid.*, 252, 253, 234, 239, 250–1, 266.

72   Boyer, *Urban Masses and Moral Order in America, 1820–1920* (Cambridge, Mass., and London, 1978), 290–2.

73   Mumford, *The Culture of Cities*, 228–30, 255.

74   *Ibid.*, 232, 273, 278.

75   *Ibid.*, 300–401.

76   For a contemporary critique of Mumford, see H. M. Jones, 'Metropolis and

utopia', *North American Review*, CCXLVI (1938), 170–8.

77   Quoted in Boyer, 284.

78   Beard, 'New York, the metropolis of today', *The American Review of Reviews*, LXIX (1924), 609–24.

79   Mencken, 'Metropolis', in *Prejudices: Sixth Series* (New York, 1927), 209–16.

80   Bayrd Still, *Mirror for Gotham: New York as Seen by Contemporaries from Dutch Days to the Present* (New York, 1956), 300–1.

81   Bessie Louise Pierce, ed., *As Others See Chicago: Impressions of Visitors, 1673–1933* (Chicago, 1933), 496–7, 507, 511, 380.

82   Desmond, 'America's city civilization: the natural divisions of the United States', *Century*, CVIII (1924), 548–55; Tilden, 'Cities', *World's Work*, LV (1931), 46–50; see also Blaine A. Brownell, *The Urban Ethos in the South, 1920–1930* (Baton Rouge, 1975).

83   Beard, 'The city's place in civilization', *National Municipal Review*, XVII (1928), 727; 'Twenty-five years of *The American City* — and of American cities', *American City*, XLIX (1934), 53–6; see also C. A. Dykstra, 'The future of American cities', *American City*, XLIX (1934), 53–4.

84   See Fred H. Matthews, *Quest for an American Sociology: Robert E. Park and the Chicago School* (Montreal and London, 1977); Robert E. L. Faris, *Chicago Sociology, 1920–1932* (San Francisco, 1967); and James F. Short, 'Introduction', in Short, ed., *The Social Fabric of the Metropolis: Contributions of the Chicago School of Sociology* (Chicago and London, 1971).

85   In addition to their monographic works, several members of the Chicago school wrote texts in which they attempted to portray urban society more broadly for students and other nonspecialists. See the following: Nels Anderson and Eduard C. Lindeman, *Urban Sociology: An Introduction to the Study of Urban Communities* (New York, 1928); William F. Ogburn, *Social Characteristics of Cities: A Basis for New Interpretations of the Role of the City in American Life* (Chicago, 1937); and Stuart A. Queen and Lewis F. Thomas, *The City: A Study of Urbanism in the United States* (New York and London, 1939).

86   Faris, 124.

87   See the following synthetic studies, which belong to the same genre as the primary works cited above in n. 85: John Giffin Thompson (apparently an economist rather than a sociologist), *Urbanization: Its Effects on Government and Society* (New York, 1927); Pitirim Sorokin and Carle C. Zimmerman, *Principles of Urban-Rural Sociology* (New York, 1929); Niles Carpenter, *The Sociology of City Life* (New York, 1932); Maurice R. Davie, *Problems of City Life: A Study in Urban Sociology* (New York, 1932); Noel Pitts Gist and L. A. Halbert, *Urban Society* (New York, 1935); Earl E. Muntz, *Urban Sociology* (New York, 1938); and Howard Woolston, *Metropolis: A Study of Urban Communities* (New York, 1938).

88   Park, 'The city: suggestions for the investigation of human behavior in the urban environment' (1915), in Park *et al.*, *The City* (Chicago, 1925), 45–6; Smith, 'Social science research and the community', in T. V. Smith and Leonard D. White, eds., *Chicago: An Experiment in Social Science Research* (Chicago, 1929), 221, 242–3; see also Park, 'The city as a social laboratory', in Smith and White, 1–19.

89   Park, 'The city', 24–5; White, 163. (The Whites quote several other passages from Park's works in order to fit him as best they can into an anti-urban tradition.)

90   Bogardus, 'Social distance in the city', in Ernest W. Burgess, ed., *The Urban Community: Selected Papers from the Proceedings of the American Sociological Society, 1925* (Chicago, 1926), 48; Wirth, 'Urbanism as a way of life', *American Journal of Sociology*, XLIV (1938), 1–24.

91   Park, 'The urban community as a spacial pattern and a moral order', in Burgess, *The Urban Community*, 11; Burgess, 'The growth of the city', in Park *et al.*,

The City, 50–1; for Park's own assessment of some of the detailed studies of 'natural areas', see his 'The city as a social laboratory', 8.

92 Wirth, 2; Boyer, 369.
93 Park, 'The city', 25, 41.
94 *Ibid.*, 14, 24, 38–9 (also on Park, see Goist, 119–20); Anderson and Lindeman, 217–18, 354, 357–62; Woolston, 89, 305–6.
95 Merriam, 'Urbanism', *American Journal of Sociology*, XLV (1940), 729.

Chapter 11

1 Raymond Williams, *The Country and the City* (New York, 1973), 290–1.
2 Burton Pike, *The Image of the City in Modern Literature* (Princeton, 1981), 6–7.
3 For the classic expression of this view, see José Luis Sert, *Can Our Cities Survive?: An ABC of Urban Problems, Their Analysis, Their Solutions* (Cambridge, Mass., and London, 1942), a work based on proposals formulated between 1928 and 1937 by the Congrès Internationaux d'Architecture Moderne.
4 See Robert Fishman, *Urban Utopias in the Twentieth Century: Ebenezer Howard, Frank Lloyd Wright, Le Corbusier* (New York, 1977), 92–160, on Wright.

Bibliographical Essays

The selection of primary sources

A book of the sort I have written, in which the most important primary sources figure prominently within the main body of the narrative, does not require a full bibliography, and there is no need to list all the works cited in my notes and the many others written during my period that could have been cited. What does seem appropriate, in the first place, is to provide a more detailed account than is customary in works of intellectual and cultural history of how the writings that have been considered were selected. I have accumulated the titles of books and essays and read many of these works as systematically as possible with a view to answering the questions posed in the preface, and there is no reason why the reader should remain ignorant of how I set about my task.

My initial objective was to locate and at least to skim all the general books and pamphlets on cities written in Britain, France, Germany, and the United States and published in the nineteenth century or the first four decades of the twentieth. Omitting most works that focused narrowly on such topics as city government and city planning, I sought out those writings whose authors attempted to take stock at some length of the reasons for urban growth and the quality of urban life. The subject catalogues of several major libraries were indispensable for this purpose. The Library of Congress has sections on 'Cities and towns' and on 'City and town life', each of which comprises subdivisions for general works and for items on individual countries. The printed subject catalogues for books acquired by the British Museum since 1880 list numerous works under both topical and geographical subheadings beneath the general heading 'Towns'. In the Bayerische Staatsbibliothek in Munich and in the Deutsche Staatsbibliothek in East Berlin, numerous works are listed both under 'Stadt' and under 'Grossstadt'. In order to supplement the listings for these libraries, I consulted the relevant sections in Robert Alexander Peddie, *Subject Index of Books Published before 1880* (4 vols, 1933-48) and in standard guides to the book trade in Britain and Germany: the *English Catalogue of Books* (1801-; subject indexes for 1837 and years thereafter); Christian Gottlob Kayser, *Vollständiges Bücher-Lexikon* (36 vols, Leipzig, 1834-1911; covers the years 1750-1910; subject indexes for the years 1750-1832 and 1891-1910); and the *Deutsches Bücherverzeichniss* (Leipzig, 1920-42, 1953-69; for the period 1911-60; excellent subject indexes throughout). Unfortunately, the closest French equivalent to these sources, Otto Henri Lorenz, *Catalogue générale de la librairie française, 1840-1925* (34 vols, 1867-1945) does not contain subject indexes; instead it divides books into topical areas that were too broad for my purposes, and I have not used it.

I have gathered articles on cities from a wide range of periodicals, popular as well as scholarly, with the help of reference works that permit rough comparability for three of the four countries. For British and American magazines, I have used *Poole's Index to Periodical Literature* (6 vols, Boston and New York, 1882-1908; covers the period 1802-1906); the *Reader's Guide to Periodical Literature* (Minneapolis and New York, 1905-; covers the period 1890 to the present); the *International Index to Periodicals* (New York, 1916-; covers the period 1907 to the present); and the *Subject Index to Periodicals* (1919-25, 1928-62; covers the periods 1915-22 and 1926-61). The Germans began to index their periodicals relatively late, but they made up for their delay with extreme thoroughness in Felix Dietrich and Reinhard Dietrich, *Bibliographie der deutschen Zeitschriftenliteratur mit Einschluss von Sammelwerken* (Leipzig and Osnabrück, 1896-1944, 1949-62; indexes articles in several thousand periodicals for the years 1860-1944 and 1947-61). This source yielded, among others, the titles of dozens of articles published in journals so obscure they could not be obtained anywhere in the United States or in Berlin. They constitute the great majority of the items that have come to my attention at which I have not at least glanced, but so many other articles in German magazines were available that this limitation was of little consequence. The French again proved least cooperative. There is no index of French periodical literature for this period whatsoever. In order to compensate for the absence of such a source, I scanned the tables of contents for the years indicated in the following journals: *Annales des sciences politiques* (1886-1936); *Journal des économistes* (1841-1940); *Réforme sociale* (1881-1927); *Revue d'économie politique* (1887-1940); and *Revue internationale de sociologie* (1893-1939). The paucity of what I found compared with the numerous articles on cities published in Britain, Germany, and the United States only confirmed my sense of the relative unimportance of the urban question for most French writers.

Another body of literature I have attempted to plumb in some depth on the European side consists of books whose authors undertook either to describe and analyze the present condition of society in one country or to comprehend broad aspects of modern society in general. To compile lists of such books, I consulted the catalogues of the Library of Congress and the British Museum and Peddie, *Subject Index*, noting works about Great Britain, England, France, and Germany that appeared under such subheadings as 'Description and travel', 'Topography', 'Social conditions', 'Social life', and 'Population'. In the catalogues for the British Museum, I also noted most of the British, French, and German works listed under 'Social science: general works'. For other general works on social conditions published during the period, I used Judith Blow Williams, *A Guide to the Printed Materials for English Social and Economic History* (2 vols, New York, 1926); Joseph Stammhammer, *Bibliographie des Socialismus und Communismus* (3 vols, Jena, 1893-1912) and *Bibliographie der Social-Politik* (2 vols, Jena, 1896-1912); and the sections on 'Bevölkerung' and 'Gesellschaft' in the first volume of *Dahlmann-Waitz: Quellenkunde der deutschen Geschichte* (10th ed., Stuttgart, 1965). In examining over 400 of these books, I sought wherever possible to isolate the urban variable — to determine the importance of clearly urban phenomena in men's overall views of their countries and their times. A great many of these works yielded very little for my purposes, but others had much to say about city life, and their inclusion was essential.

As I have emphasized throughout this book, urban questions have been asked and answered with reference not only to cities in general but also to vast numbers of individual cities. Obviously, no one could hope even to glance at everything written in the period about all the cities in Europe and America. Nor would the effort to do so prove especially rewarding, inasmuch as the great bulk of it focused on topics and problems of quite ephemeral interest. Such writing, while it offers a rich lode of ore for local historians, did not belong within my purview. I therefore proceeded as follows. Relying primarily on B. R. Mitchell and Phyllis Deane, *Abstract of British Historical*

Statistics (Cambridge, Eng., 1962), B. R. Mitchell, *European Historical Statistics, 1750-1970* (New York and London, 1975), and the *Encyclopedia Britannica* (10th ed., 1902), I compiled lists of the twenty largest cities in Britain, twenty of their counterparts in Germany, and ten in France in 1900-1901 (thirty-six of which exceeded 200,000 inhabitants and all of which exceeded 100,000). For books on each of these cities, I consulted one or more of the following sources: subject catalogues in the libraries listed above; Peddie, *Subject Index;* Charles Gross, *Bibliography of British Municipal History* (New York, 1897); Erich Keyser, *Bibliographie zur Städtegeschichte Deutschlands* (Cologne, 1969); and Philippe Dollinger, *Bibliographie d'histoire des villes de France* (1967). In each case, I accumulated the titles of what appeared to be general histories and descriptions published between 1820 and 1940 and then looked at as many of these works (the great majority, well over 500) as it was feasible for me to obtain. I have made no effort to perform a comparable operation for American cities, but I have examined several dozen books about New York. Many of the books about these cities were mere chronicles or guidebooks, and some conveyed little beyond impressionistic glimpses of the urban scene, but others revealed important aspects of urban consciousness that would have remained far less accessible had I limited my reading to books and essays on city life in general. Writings about the four great metropolises were especially valuable, but life in many lesser cities also gave rise to comments and reflections that provided grist for my mill.

Beyond the sources accumulated according to the criteria outlined above, I have also included some more specialized materials that came to my attention along the way, on topics such as population growth, the settlement house movement, and municipal reform in particular American cities. These works acquired importance for my purposes inasmuch as they could be seen in relationship to themes and movements whose significance had already begun to emerge from the central core of writings that I had gathered systematically during the initial stages of my research.

Secondary Sources

The following paragraphs indicate the major works that bear directly on my topic and some other writings that have stimulated my thinking about it. Many of them offer extensive suggestions for further reading in secondary as well as primary sources.

For a panoramic tour of the urban past by one of the foremost writers treated in this book, see Lewis Mumford, *The City in History: Its Origins, Its Transformations, and Its Prospects* (New York, 1961). The most up-to-date overview of European urbanization is Lynn Hollen Lees and Paul Hohenberg, *The Making of Urban Europe* (Cambridge, Mass., 1985). American urban historians are well served by Charles N. Glaab and A. Theodore Brown, *A History of Urban America* (2nd ed., New York and London, 1976). Two recent collections of essays display the practice of urban historical research by scholars from many countries, underlining the importance of the international perspective that is becoming increasingly widespread in the field: Derek Fraser and Anthony Sutcliffe, eds., *The Pursuit of Urban History* (1983), and Anthony Sutcliffe, ed., *Metropolis, 1890-1940* (1984). The *Urban History Yearbook* (Leicester, 1974-) contains an excellent 'Current bibliography of urban history' as well as numerous reviews of books on many countries. For current American work, see also the *Journal of Urban History* (1974-). For Germany, see *Informationen zur modernen Stadtgeschichte* (1970-).

Among general studies of ideas about cities, one of the most stimulating is Carl E. Schorske, 'The idea of the city in European thought: Voltaire to Spengler', in Oscar Handlin and John Burchard, eds., *The Historian and the City* (Cambridge, Mass., 1963). See also D. Martindale, 'Prefatory remarks: the theory of the city', in Max Weber, *The City*, trans. and ed. D. Martindale and G. Neuwirth (New York and London, 1958). Elisabeth Pfeil, *Grossstadtforschung* (2nd ed., Hannover, 1972) contains a long introductory overview of work by her predecessors that is indispensable. On Simmel and Wirth, among more recent figures, see Michael P. Smith, *The City and Social Theory* (New York, 1979). A recent interpretive essay is James Dougherty, the *Fivesquare City: The City in the Religious Imagination* (Notre Dame and London, 1980).

On the city in literature, see the interesting essays by Burton Pike, *The Image of the City in Modern Literature* (Princeton, 1981) and Irving Howe, 'The city in literature', *Commentary*, LI (May 1971), 61–8. For more detailed studies of major authors, see Volker Klotz, *Die erzählte Stadt: Ein Sujet als Herausforderung des Romans von Lesage bis Döblin* (Munich, 1969) and Donald Fanger, *Dostoevsky and Romantic Realism* (Cambridge, Mass., 1965). See also Monroe K. Spears, *Dionysus and the City: Modernism in Twentieth-Century Poetry* (New Haven and London, 1970). On the visual arts, we have a penetrating essay by Theda Shapiro, 'New York — Paris — Berlin: a tale of three cities in art, 1890-1945', in Sutcliffe, *Metropolis*.

The best general study of the history of modern city planning is Anthony Sutcliffe, *Towards the Planned City: Germany, Britain, the United States and France, 1780-1914* (Oxford, 1981). It does not, however, entirely supersede Leonardo Benevolo, *The Origins of Modern Town Planning*, trans. J. Landry (Cambridge, Mass., 1971) or Françoise Choay, *The Modern City: Planning in the 19th Century*, trans. M. Hugo and G. R. Collins (New York, 1969). See also Anthony Sutcliffe, ed., *The Rise of Modern Urban Planning, 1800-1914* (1980); Gordon E. Cherry, ed., *Shaping an Urban World: Planning in the Twentieth Century* (1980); and Robert Fishman, *Urban Utopias in the Twentieth Century: Ebenezer Howard, Frank Lloyd Wright, Le Corbusier* (New York, 1977).

For Britain, two works deal both with cities and with ideas about cities. Asa Briggs, *Victorian Cities* (New York, 1963) is a stimulating synthesis. The late H. J. Dyos and Michael Wolff edited a magisterial collection of essays, *The Victorian City: Images and Realities* (2 vols, London and Boston, 1973), the second volume of which contains numerous items on the city in Victorian thought and culture. B. I. Coleman, ed., *The Idea of the City in Nineteenth-Century Britain* (London and Boston, 1973) is a well-edited and quite useful anthology of primary sources. Ruth Glass, 'Urban sociology in Great Britain: a trend report', *Current Sociology*, IV (1955), no. 4, pp. 5–76, offers a bibliographic survey that reaches back into the nineteenth century. More specific studies bearing on the early part of the period are G. Davison, 'The city as a natural system: theories of urban society in early nineteenth century Britain', in Fraser and Sutcliffe, *The Pursuit of Urban History*; S. E. Finer, *The Life and Times of Sir Edwin Chadwick* (1952); M. W. Flinn, 'Introduction' to Chadwick, *Report on the Sanitary Condition of the Labouring Population of Gt. Britain* (Edinburgh, 1965); M. J. Cullen, *The Statistical Movement in Early Victorian Britain* (New York, 1975); P. Richards, 'R. A. Slaney, the industrial town and early Victorian social policy', *Social History*, IV (1979), 85–102; R. A. Soloway, *Prelates and People: Ecclesiastical Social Thought in England, 1783-1852* (London and Toronto, 1969); and Steven Marcus, *Engels, Manchester, and the Working Class* (New York, 1974). For the late nineteenth and early twentieth centuries, see Gareth Stedman Jones, *Outcast London* (Oxford, 1971); Anthony S. Wohl, 'The bitter cry of outcast London', *International Review of Social History*, XIII (1968), 189–245, and *The Eternal Slum: Housing and Social Policy in Victorian London* (1977); E. P. Hennock, 'Poverty and social theory in England: the experience of the eighteen-eighties', *Social History*, I (1976), 67–91; T. S. Simey and M. B. Simey, *Charles Booth: Social Scientist* (Oxford, 1960); W. H. Pfautz, 'Introduction' to Charles Booth, *On the City: Physical Pattern and Social Structure*, ed. Pfautz (Chicago and London, 1967); Asa Briggs, *Social Thought and Social Action: A Study of the Work of Seebohm Rowntree, 1871-1954* (1961); and Bentley B. Gilbert, *The Evolution of National Insurance in Great Britain: The Origins of the Welfare State* (1966). On poets and novelists, in addition to several essays in Dyos and Wolff, *The Victorian City*, see Raymond Williams, *The Country and the City* (New York, 1973); on Dickens, see F. S

Schwarzbach, *Dickens and the City* (1979). The basic history of city planning is William Ashworth, *The Genesis of Modern British Town Planning: A Study in Economic and Social History of the Nineteenth and Twentieth Centuries* (1954). It may be supplemented with Walter L. Creese, *The Search for Environment: The Garden City, Before and After* (New Haven, 1966); Gordon Cherry, *The Evolution of British Town Planning* (1974); and the introduction in Helen E. Meller, ed., *The Ideal City* (Leicester, 1979; on the ideas of Barnett and Geddes). Three stimulating and important works that touch on attitudes toward cities throughout much of the period are E. R. Norman, *Church and Society in England, 1770-1970* (Oxford, 1976); Raymond Williams, *Culture and Society* (1958); and Martin J. Wiener, *English Culture and the Decline of the Industrial Spirit, 1850-1980* (Cambridge, Eng., 1981).

For France, there is much less. The most useful book by far is Louis Chevalier, *Laboring Classes and Dangerous Classes in Paris During the First Half of the Nineteenth Century*, trans. F. Jellinek (New York, 1973). An older work that covers a small part of the same ground in greater detail is Hilde Rigaudias-Weiss, *Les enquêtes ouvrières en France entre 1830 et 1848* (1936; reprint, New York, 1975). See also William Coleman, *Death Is a Social Disease: Public Health and Political Economy in Early Industrial France* (Madison, 1982). On novelists and poets, see Robert Minder, 'Paris in der französischen Literatur (1760-1960)', in *Dichter in der Gesellschaft: Erfahrungen mit deutscher und französischer Literatur* (Frankfurt am Main, 1966) for a useful overview. An exhaustive study is Pierre Citron, *La poésie de Paris dans la littérature française de Rousseau à Baudelaire* (2 vols, 1961). See also N. Kranowski, *Paris dans les romans d'Émile Zola* (1968). Marie-Claire Bancquart, *Images littéraires de Paris: fin de siècle* (1980) is less useful than it at first appears. Susanna Barrows, *Distorting Mirrors: Visions of the Crowd in Late Nineteenth-Centry France* (New Haven, 1981) is excellent.

For Germany, much of Pfeil, *Grossstadtforschung* is directly relevant. Klaus Bergmann, *Agrarromantik und Grossstadtfeindschaft* (Meisenheim am Glan, 1970) is basic and excellent. Hans Oswald, *Die überschätzte Stadt: Ein Beitrag der Gemeindesoziologie zum Städtebau* (Olten und Freiburg im Breisgau, 1966) has a stimulating chapter on critics of cities. See also H. Poor, 'City versus country: anti-urbanism in the Weimar Republic', *Societas*, VI (1976), 177–92. I have taken a different approach in 'Critics of urban society in Germany, 1854-1914', *Journal of the History of Ideas*, XL (1979), 61–83. So has James J. Sheehan in 'Liberalism and the city in nineteenth-century Germany', *Past and Present*, no. 51 (May 1971), 116–37. For a recent essay on scholarly developments, see W. D. Smith, 'The emergence of German urban sociology, 1900–1910', *Journal of the History of Sociology*, 1979, pp. 1–16. See also Anthony Oberschall, *Empirical Social Research in Germany, 1848-1914* (Paris and The Hague, 1965). An overview of literary responses to the city appears in Friedrich Sengle, 'Wunschbild Land und Schreckbild Stadt: Zu einem zentralen Thema der neueren deutschen Literatur', *Studium Generale*, XVI (1963), 619–31. René Trautmann, *Die Stadt in der deutschen Erzählkunst des 19. Jahrhunderts, 1830-1880* (Winterthur, 1957) is quite useful, as is Roy Pascal, *From Naturalism to Expressionism: German Literature and Society, 1880-1918* (1973). On poetry, see Wolfgang Rothe, ed., *Deutsche Grossstadtlyrik vom Naturalismus bis zur Gegenwart* (Stuttgart, 1973) and Karl Riha, 'Zwischen Jugenstil und neuer Sachlichkeit: Zu zwei Grossstadtlyrik-Anthologien', *Archiv für Kommunalwissenschaften*, XIX (1980), 200–16. The ideas of planners and architects figure prominently in several works. See Rudolf Hartog, *Stadterweiterungen im 19. Jahrhundert* (Stuttgart, 1962); Gerd Albers and Klaus Martin, eds., *Entwicklungslinien im Städtebau: Ideen, Thesen, Aussagen, 1875-1945* (Düsseldorf, 1975); George R. Collins and Christiane Craseman Collins, *Camillo Sitte and the Birth of Modern City Planning* (New York, 1965); Kristiana Hartmann, *Deutsche Gartenstadtbewegung: Kulturpolitik und Gesellschaftsreform* (Munich, 1976); and Barbara Miller Lane, *Architecture and Politics in Germany, 1918-1945* (Cambridge, Mass., 1968). Numerous works deal broadly with intellectual and cultural responses to modernization. For the early and middle decades of the nineteenth century, see John G. Gagliardo, *From Pariah to Patriot: The Changing Image of the German Peasant, 1770-1840* (Lexington, Kentucky, 1969); Mack Walker, *German Home Towns: Community, State, and General Estate, 1648-1871* (Ithaca and London, 1971); and Theodore S. Hamerow, *The Social Foundations of German Unification, 1858-1871*, Vol. I: *Ideas and Institutions* (Princeton, 1969). For the period after 1871, see George L. Mosse, *The Crisis of German Ideology: Intellectual Origins of the Third Reich* (New York, 1964); Fritz Stern, *The Politics of Cultural Despair: A Study in the Rise of the Germanic Ideology* (Berkeley and Los Angeles, 1961); Fritz K. Ringer, *The Decline of the German Mandarins: The German Academic Community, 1890-1933* (Cambridge, Mass., 1969); Gary D. Stark, *Entrepreneurs of Ideology: Neoconservative Publishers in Germany, 1890-1933* (Chapel Hill, 1981); Wolfgang R. Krabbe, *Gesellschaftsreform durch Lebensveränderung* (Göttingen, 1974); and David Schoenbaum, *Hitler's Social Revolution: Class and Status in Nazi Germany, 1933-1939* (Garden City, 1966).

For the United States, several chapters in Glaab and Brown, *A History of Urban America* are especially useful, as is Bayrd Still, *Urban America: A History with Documents* (Boston, 1974). Though too one-sided, Morton and Lucia White, *The Intellectual versus the City: From Thomas Jefferson to Frank Lloyd Wright* (Cambridge, Mass., 1962) is still basic. Paul Boyer, *Urban Masses and Moral Order in America, 1820-1920* (Cambridge, Mass., and London, 1978) is most illuminating. See also Park Dixon Goist, *From Main Street to State Street: Town, City and Community in America* (Port Washington, N. Y., and London, 1977). For a highly useful study of ideas about one aspect of urban experience, see Robert H. Bremner, *From the Depths: The Discovery of Poverty in the United States* (New York, 1956). Attitudes toward New York are treated in Bayrd Still, *Mirror for Gotham: New York as Seen by Contemporaries from Dutch Days to the Present* (New York, 1956). For the early and middle parts of the nineteenth century, see Thomas Bender, *Toward an Urban Vision: Ideas and Institutions in Nineteenth-Century America* (Lexington, Kentucky, 1975) and Michael H. Cowan, *City of the West: Emerson, America, and Urban Metaphor* (New Haven, 1967). About the late nineteenth and early twentieth centuries, see Aaron I. Abell, *The Urban Impact on American Protestantism, 1865-1900* (Cambridge, Mass., 1943); Henry F. May, *Protestant Churches and Industrial America* (New York, 1949); Richard Hofstadter, *The Age of Reform: From Bryan to F.D.R.* (New York, 1955); Allen Davis, *Spearheads for Reform: The Social Settlements and the Progressive Movement, 1890-1914* (New York, 1967); James B. Lane, *Jacob A. Riis and the American City* (Port Washington, N. Y., and London, 1974); Jon C. Teaford, *The Unheralded Triumph: City Government in America, 1870-1900* (Baltimore, 1984); and Martin J. Schiesl, *The Politics of Efficiency: Municipal Administration and Reform in America, 1880-1920* (Berkeley and Los Angeles, 1977). On urban sociology, see Fred Matthews, *Quest for an American Sociology: Robert E. Park and the Chicago School* (Montreal, 1971) and Robert E. L. Faris, *Chicago Sociology, 1920-1932* (rev. ed., Chicago, 1970). For the interwar years, see also Blaine A. Brownell, *The Urban Ethos in the South, 1920-1930* (Baton Rouge, 1975) and Richard H. Pells, *Radical Visions and American Dreams: Culture and Social Thought in the Depression Years* (New York, 1973). There are several studies of the city in American literature. George Dunlap, *The City in the American Novel, 1789-1900* (New York, 1965) is thorough and dull. Janis P. Stout, *Sodoms in Eden: The City in American Fiction before 1860* (Westport, Conn., 1976) covers some of the same ground more readably. Also on the nineteenth century, see Adrienne Siegel, *The Image of the American City in Popular Literature, 1820-1870* (Port Washington, N. Y., and London, 1981). Robert H. Walker, 'The poet and the rise of the city', *Mississippi Valley Historical Review*, XLIX (1962), 85-99, is based on a survey of 6,000 volumes of verse published during the period 1876-1905. Blanche H. Gelfant treats the twentieth century in *The American City Novel* (Norman, Oklahoma, 1954). David R. Weimer, *The City as Metaphor* (New York, 1966) treats a select number of major authors, from Whitman to Auden.

Index